BERMUDA
AN ECONOMY WHICH WORKS

80 answers to questions you may wish to ask
about the economy of Bermuda.

by

Robert Stewart

To John Duckie,

With best wishes

Bob Stewart

ISBN number 0-9681743-0-2.
First edition: 1997.

Printed in Bermuda
by

THE
ISLAND
PRESS
LIMITED

TABLE OF CONTENTS.

Introduction

7. What is insurance?

8. How does the insurance industry affect Bermuda?

9. What benefits do Bermudians get from the presence of exempt companies?

10. Did you know? - Some random and interesting facts about Bermuda.

11. What is the Bermuda Monetary Authority?

12. What is the Bermuda dollar and how strong is it?

13. What is meant by Bermuda being described as an international financial centre?

14. Why did Hong Kong companies wish to establish a domicile in Bermuda?

15. What is the Balance of Payments and how important to Bermuda is it?

16. Is Bermuda a commodity?

17. What is globalisation of the world economy and how will it affect Bermuda?

18. Should Bermuda be a global village or a fishing village?

19. How important to Bermuda is the confidence of the international financial community?

20. What is restructuring and reengineering and how it will it affect Bermuda?

Part III - The Economy and Government

1. What is meant by the term Bermuda Inc?

2. What role should the Bermuda Government play in the economy?

3. Would it make any economic difference if there was a PLP government?

4. Should McDonalds be allowed to operate in Bermuda?

5. Should Bermuda have a national lottery?

6. What is the budget and why is it important?

7. What did the budget say to Bermudians in respect of the fiscal year 1996/97?

8. Does Government do a good job?

9. How important is education to the job prospects for an individual and to the Bermuda economy?

10. Is economic theory of any assistance in dealing with crime in Bermuda?

11. How is income redistributed in Bermuda?

12. What happened to inflation?

13. What is the national debt?

14. Should Bermuda levy income tax?

15. Is the Bermuda tax system fair?

16. Should any Government functions be privatised?

17. Should the Department of Tourism be privatised?

INTRODUCTION

"Economists are like Bangkok taxi drivers ; put two of them together and you will have four opinions, any of which will take you careering in the wrong direction at great expense."

MIKE CARLTON

I began writing this book with the idea of making it read like any other economics text, chapters on the main industries, how the banking system works and so on. However, I soon realised there would be considerable redundant material as Bermuda is effectively absorbed into the world economy by, for example, having interest rates determined by outside forces. I therefore concluded it would be easier for the reader, as well as myself, to state a number of questions which the general public may like to be answered about the Bermuda economy and try and provide some of the answers.

In addition, many ideas are proposed by political parties and interest groups and I thought it would be helpful to express my views on how effective these ideas would be in the context of Bermuda. Another benefit would be that some readers would not care to read anything about Karl Marx or Adam Smith, (volumes of learned works are available about their ideas) and it would be easier for the reader to turn to issues which were of direct or immediate interest.

Why 80 questions, rather than 100? There is no real answer to that question other than I was running out of time and space and questions so I stopped at the point I thought was appropriate. I am sure there are many questions I have not been able to answer but I would be happy to try at some future date to express my views on issues which readers might wish to raise.

Books about finance and economics tend to be critical and it is fashionable, and perhaps, even right, to abuse economists and their ilk because we tend to pour cold water over many of society's inherited assumptions and prejudices. There are good reasons for economics being dubbed the dismal science. We also undermine many proposals for reform of society to the everlasting despair of reformers, dreamers, social engineers, do-gooders and politicians because we draw attention to such inconvenient things as facts, consequences, results, efficiency, competitive pressures and so on. Giving offence to many who work hard (like many civil servants) is not my objective but being critical often results in a degree of injustice because any writer tends to generalise. Economics is concerned not only with the immediate effects of a policy or its popularity with the community or with politicians. It is also concerned with long term impact and the consequences of that policy not only on some well-connected group but its general application and effects on the whole population.

That being said, there are several major themes running through the series of essays in this book which the reader should bear in mind when he comes to the more critical passages about the Bermudian economy.

Firstly, there is note of and admiration for, the phenomenal attainments of the

Bermudian economy. I can think of no other country which has enjoyed such economic prosperity during the past fifty years. Singapore and Hong Kong come close, but the quality of life in those countries is considerably lower than that enjoyed by the people who are fortunate enough to live in Bermuda. Bermuda has also enjoyed full employment for 50 years, an achievement particularly significant in the late 1980s and 1990s in which no other country has been as successful. Prosperity, full employment, a pleasant business environment, political stability and social harmony are no mean achievements these days and Bermuda's record is difficult to beat.

No one is successful without a reasonable amount of luck and the winning formula of Bermuda has been due, in part, to that. Many developments external to Bermuda have contributed much to its success. These would include, for example :

- The creation of the modern airline industry, mainly in the United States, which has enabled large numbers of passengers to travel inexpensively to resorts like Bermuda since 1945.

- The stupidity of foreign governments (particularly the UK and USA) who imposed high marginal income tax rates on their populations and high corporate taxes thus enabling offshore financial centres like Bermuda to flourish.

- The scandals, incompetence and huge monetary losses which took place in the 1980s in the insurance markets at Lloyds of London. These man-made misfortunes enabled the captive insurance business in Bermuda to expand into a broad-based insurance industry rivalling that of Lloyds.

Bermuda's success is also due to:

- A remarkable group of men like Sir Henry Tucker, Sir Howard Trott, Sir James Pearman, Sir Dudley Butterfield, Sir Bayard Dill and Sir Harry Butterfield, who were able to seize opportunities to make Bermuda a part of the modern world economy.

- Wise and restrained government.

- Its location.

- Its delightful climate.

- The hard work, political maturity and perspicacity of the talented, resourceful and adaptable people who live in Bermuda.

The second theme is largely a by-product of the first, and that is the risk of complacency which can arise after a long record of success. In 1996, there are many in authority who act and speak as if they believe that the impressive performance of the Bermudian economy is divinely ordained and that the rest of the world owes Bermuda a living. A generation of Bermudians have been led to believe that secure jobs, ever rising living standards, shorter working hours, satisfying work, high quality health care, racial harmony, a delightful environment, personal fulfillment, low taxation and a top ranking in economic standards are their natural birthright.

Such views are obvious nonsense that it is almost a waste of time to refute them. However, it is surprising how many people, in my experience, take the smooth functioning of the Bermuda economy for granted believing that it "just happens" and that the major issue for Bermuda is how the economic pie is distributed, not how it is created and preserved. Arguments about the "just distribution" of the economic pie invariably leads to contempt for the wealth creating process and, ironically, is led by many educated people who should know better.

Complacency is also accompanied by a failure by many to appreciate that a continuation of Bermuda's success requires an ability to implement constructive change. It also requires an understanding of the fact that the world, particularly the world of business and finance, is in a state of continuous flux and that Bermuda and Bermudians need to adapt to this new world in order to maintain the high standards of living to which they have become accustomed. Adaptation is not a matter of choice and it is not an option to be selected or rejected. Economic change can result in job losses and can have an adverse impact on those who lack marketable skills and advanced training.

Let me give three examples of where changes may have to take place in order to come to terms with the modern world:-

- Bermuda is a highly protective economy ; non-Bermudians may not own, for example, more than 40% of the shares of a company operating in Bermuda.

- Over the past 25 years or so a significant bureaucracy has been created which has negative power over new ideas or procedures. The best example is the power of the Ministry of Labour, Home Affairs & Safety to prevent organisations hiring whom they believe to be the best staff. To remain competitive it is necessary for top class people to be in charge.

- The new economic climate in which businesses reorganise, restructure or reengineer is slowly reaching Bermuda but its consequences are rarely discussed openly mainly because of the social difficulties which are likely to arise.

The third theme centres around the decline of tourism and its associated problem of poor, or non-existent profitability in the hotel industry. This is partly as a consequence of the second theme I mention, namely a failure to appreciate the strength of foreign competition and the pace of change in the world of business and of the tourism industry in particular. There is a refusal to face or recognise unpleasant facts such as that we live in a ferociously competitive world economy and that gradual time-consuming solutions are not going to resolve immediate and pressing difficulties. Governments tend to operate by consensus, and this often slows down the decision making process. In a competitive world market economy, it is the market, not governments, which create jobs, opportunities, generate spending power and create wealth. The tourist industry is the largest employer on the island, and is essential for the employment of the majority of the unskilled labour force who cannot acquire the necessary skills and training to enter the world of international business. One of the issues facing Bermuda is how to prevent a split in society between the affluent (and mainly white) who are employed in international business and the lowly paid employed in tourism and retailing - most of whom are black.

A fourth issue running through this book is what is known as commoditisation. A terrible word but an even worse concept. To be a commodity producer of anything means that success is wholly dependent on price because the product you are selling cannot be differentiated in any meaningful way from similar products being sold by competitors. The customer, or the client, is therefore mainly interested in price and if the price is high, or perceived not to be good value, sales wither and business goes into decline. In too many respects the hospitality industry in Bermuda is working itself into this unenviable position partly because of the complacency I have referred to, and partly because of the intense competition from others who have learned many of the lessons Bermuda has taught them, and partly because the brand "Bermuda" has been allowed to slip. "Bermuda's reputation or its 'brand' is its most critical asset".[1]

The fifth theme is that clouds on the economic horizon, unlike natural clouds of weather, can be dispelled by resolute action and sensible reforms. There is a tendency to ignore warning signs, to believe that the future will be the same as the past, or that those who urge reform and change are being hyper-critical of those in power. Too often remedial action and reforms can disturb the cosy relationships of powerful vested interests which have done well in the past. To create difficulties for others, even for good reasons, is not usually in the character of Bermudians and especially in Bermudian politicians many of whom are not natural decision makers and are not financially astute.

Each of the above five themes will be explored in much more detail, but let me turn to a possible bias of which the reader should be aware. I believe that the millions of independently made financial decisions of individuals (known by the shorthand of "the market") is superior to any other method of directing or running the economy. In addition, each individual is wholly responsible and accountable for his (or her) own life with exceptions being made for those who are elderly, too young or are physically or mentally incapable. This is not to say that I blindly accept all the consequences of leaving economic matters to the market. It is a powerful tool to be used but it needs to be understood. It is ironic that during the past 50 years when market forces were unpopular elsewhere in the world, Bermuda was able to thrive because of its widespread acceptance of the market system. Foreign governments, mainly the British and the American, now understand the wisdom and power of markets. Because of this, the economic advantages Bermuda enjoyed in the past are now diminished. There has been a tendency in Bermuda in the past few years increasingly to rely on the wisdom and skill of politicians and civil servants despite the fact that their record elsewhere has been so dismal. Innovative and consistent economic decision making does not usually arise from government action.

The reader should constantly keep in mind the above paragraph for economics is not always an objective science but a subject on which personal views constantly intrude.

---

[1] Commission on Competitiveness, page 22.

Finally, there is a tendency for many economists to be "politically incorrect" and I am no exception. However, I would like to ask readers to excuse any lack of political correctness in using the masculine "he" throughout the text instead of trying to use the "he/she" combination or clumsy gender-free pronouns. This is not due to a lack of sensitivity but is done in order to make the text a little more readable. I hope I have succeeded.

It would be wrong not to acknowledge the help I have received in putting this collection of essays together. Susan Fairhurst helped me to understand the complications of word processing and was of invaluable help on the many occasions I got stuck. Mrs Carol Martin and Mrs Pamela Paynter did heroic work in helping with my many re-writes, and in interpreting my handwriting. Without them I would never have been able to finish the job. George Rushe and Karen Diel read the manuscript and made many helpful comments which will make the text more understandable. For errors, ommissions and opinions I must be held accountable.

HOW ECONOMIES FUNCTION

1

1. PLEASE GIVE A BIRD'S EYE VIEW OF THE ECONOMY OF BERMUDA BY IDENTIFYING TEN OF ITS MAIN CHARACTERISTICS.

The ten most important characteristics of the Bermuda economy are :

1. Bermuda is small, its population is under 60,000 (58,460 to be exact) which is roughly equal to a small town in America or Britain. It is the same size as say Altoona, Pennsylvania or Wansbeck, Northumbria in England about whom few people have heard. About two-thirds of the population is black, and the remainder is white. In addition, of that population approximately 23 percent are non-Bermudians, or immigrants, most of whom are white and young and many (although by no means all) earn high incomes because they are highly skilled and work in international business.

2. Although Bermuda is small and insignificant in the world financial picture, it is remarkably successful and its per capita income of about $27,500[1] per annum is one of the highest in the world, higher than even that of the United States which is usually thought of, wrongly, as being the richest country in the world.

3. Bermuda's prosperity rests on two industries - tourism and international business. Ten years ago tourism was more important, producing about 60 percent of Bermuda's foreign earnings, international business about 35 percent and the balance being mainly income arising from servicing US, British and Canadian military bases. In 1996, the military has gone (the Cold War was won), tourism is depressed and accounts for just under 45 percent of foreign earnings, with international business flourishing (at least after the independence referendum) and accounting for about 55 percent of foreign earnings. The major hotels are not making profits and there is strong evidence that tourism is in very poor shape.

4. Race relations are important. The growth of international business and related activities, and the decline of tourism has left many in the black population as poor relations of the white population. This creates social, political and economic problems which I shall explore later.

5. Bermuda is very much a capitalist or free enterprise society with government playing a relatively minor role in the management of the economy compared with other countries. Many, including myself, believe this to be one of the main reasons for its historical success. Businessmen enjoy a higher social status in Bermuda than most other places I can think of, there is no welfare state and the main concern of people is to earn enough money to enjoy the good life which Bermuda offers. Government expenditure for the fiscal year 1995/1996 amounts to around BD$458 million, or BD$7,800 per capita.

6. Bermuda is also a place of low taxation, government taking in taxes approximately 25 percent of Gross National Product (GDP) compared with about 40 percent of GDP taken by the governments of the United

---

[1] Bermuda Government, "Facts and Figures 1996."

1

States and Canada. Low taxation, and in particularly the absence of corporate taxes and income tax, is one of the main reasons why international business seek to establish a presence in Bermuda.

7. At the same time Bermuda is an expensive place in which to live. Ordinary goods and services are expensive by comparison with prices in the United States and the cost of housing is particularly high as one would expect in a wealthy island of only 20 square miles. To buy a two bedroom cottage in a pleasant area would cost approximately BD$400,000 and to rent would cost around BD$2,000 to BD$2,500 per month.

8. Visitors to Bermuda are always pleasantly surprised when they fail to find any over evidence of poverty.[2] They are also surprised to find that Bermuda does not have any significant unemployment similar to that found elsewhere in the world. This is a major accomplishment although there is some evidence that the situation is changing for the worse. Crime is also low by comparison with other parts of the world although that situation too is deteriorating. In 1996, there have been several violent attacks on tourists and one particularly vicious murder of a young Canadian girl.

9. Union membership is very high by comparison with other countries in the world and labour relations are generally poor especially in the hotel industry.

10. Bermuda is still a British Colony which on the face of it is a demeaning and old fashioned status. In 1995, there was a referendum to determine whether Bermuda should become an independent nation and this was rejected decisively by a majority of two to one. The significance of this political aberration in the modern world will also be explored later.[3]

The foregoing is a highly simplified portrait for clearly the Bermuda economy is much more complex than the short list of its highlights given above but I trust it provides the reader with an introduction to the subject.

2. WHAT ARE THE THREE MAIN MISCONCEPTIONS WHICH THE PUBLIC HAS ABOUT THE BERMUDA ECONOMY?

"The placeless society is the awakening omnipresence that will allow everything - people, goods, resources, knowledge - to be available anywhere, often instantaneously, with little regard for distance or place. We already see it in many forms. CNN broadcasts bring an Ethiopian drought into lush living rooms. Multinational appliance companies subcontract manufacturing to wherever it is cheapest. Capital ebbs and flows freely around the girth of the globe defying government controls. Mass immigration into Western Europe and North America continues. Everywhere, people, money, goods and knowledge flow so effortlessly from point to point that place becomes an irrelevant concept."

WILLIAM KNOKE

---

[2] Evidence perhaps that income tax fails to redistribute wealth.
[3] See Part IV 18.

There is a widespread but mistaken belief by the public and some public figures, that the Bermuda government has the ability and the power, in the long term, to determine the future of the Bermudian economy and that the gut-wrenching changes now taking place in other parts of the world will leave Bermuda largely unaffected. The belief of government omnipotence and Bermuda's exemption from the rules of economics arises from a fundamental misunderstanding of how integrated modern economies now are in the modern world.

In November, 1995 in the space of one week I travelled to Guatemala and to India. On Lake Attilan in Guatemala I visited several Mayan Indian villages and saw at first hand people whose style of life had not changed significantly from what it was 1,000 years ago selling vegetables, woven cloth and cooking utensils in a simple market place with thousands of buyers. The following week in Bombay, India I saw similar markets when walking around that city.

The ordinary people of Guatemala and India were carrying out basically similar commercial activities which I have seen in places as diverse as Thailand, England, Japan , Peru, USA and France and all of which have been carried on for thousands of years in all parts of the world. The people were buying and selling goods and services in a market place without any necessity for or thought of government involvement. In other words most economic activity is a bottom-up activity, a spontaneous social process which is as old as man. Billions of transactions are freely carried out each day and government can no more control these activities than King Canute could control the waves.

The fact is that democratic governments, including the Bermuda government cannot control economies and they never have nor would they want to if economic efficiency is a desired objective. The collapse of communism in 1989 and the remarkable successes of the Asian Tigers, New Zealand and the economic resurgence in Latin America provide evidence that economic freedom for the public is much more effective in stimulating economic growth and development than governmental controls and regulations.

In the 1996 book "Economic Freedom of the World" it is demonstrated that GDP per capita growth is twice as great where economic freedoms are greatest. In Africa, for example, where economic freedom is at the lowest the rate of growth was the worst. This is usually attributed to colonial exploitation but the facts tend to show that post-independence governments imitated the socialist controlled states of Western Europe. Small countries (but large compared to Bermuda) with high economic freedom and high economic growth rates are Hong Kong and Singapore who are ranked one and three respectively. Many countries penalise themselves because governments intrude and exercise too much control over the commercial energy of their populations.

For governments to believe that they can acquire and be able to process and understand the billions of pieces of information needed to make effective decisions in an economy, even one as simple as Bermuda, is what Nobel prize winning economist Fredrich von Hayek called "the fatal conceit."[1] The communist governments of USSR and Eastern Europe have come the closest to trying to

---

[1] "The Fatal Conceit - The Errors of Socialism" by F.A. von Hayek 1986.

exert minute control over all economic matters but the whole enterprise eventually imploded in 1989 because of the astounding inefficiencies government interventions generated - not much of a testament or monument to the idea of government controlling economies.

What governments can and should do is provide a framework within which commercial activity can flourish and ordinary people can prosper. Bermuda has been very good at that in the past and still is. Bermudian prosperity arises not from government direction but from individuals being able to do business with minimal government intervention and having the right economic environment in which to grow wealthy.

The following are examples of what that environment should be but is far from exhaustive:-

- An absence of corruption.
- An impartial system of law and justice.
- A sound currency and in a small country like Bermuda having that currency tied to a reputable large currency like the US dollar.
- Low inflation and low or non-existent levels of government debt.
- An open economy with few protectionist measures.
- High levels of domestic saving .
- A well structured educational system with heavy investment in the development of people.
- An independent central bank.[2]
- Low levels of taxation.
- A good infrastructure of roads, harbours, electrial power and communications.
- An understanding that it is more important for wealth to be created than redistributed.

A quick scan of that list shows that Bermuda conforms with most of the conditions necessary for economic success - and the reader will have noted that there is a heavy emphasis on limited intervention by government in the economy.

The second misconception is that many of the protectionist measures in place protect Bermudians and improve their financial well being. This issue will be discussed in detail later but cutting off Bermuda from many of the competitive economic influences of the world does not preserve prosperity, it tends rather to destroy it. The most basic protectionist policy is that of Bermudianisation which has now become a sacred cow. Informed opinion suggests that each non-Bermudian employed on the island creates two jobs for Bermudians either directly or indirectly.

Non-Bermudians also tend to be highly skilled and there is a bonus by having a free gift of capital to Bermuda in having the services of say a highly skilled experienced engineer or investment manager as Bermuda does not have to pay the

---

2 Which Bermuda does not have.

high costs of training. Yet political discourse, frequently of a xenophobic nature, would suggest that the non-Bermudian labour force does little but create problems in the housing market, in education and in the number of private cars on the island

Those who favour heavy protectionist measures are the economic equivalent of the flat earth geographers and despite the strong, almost compelling, evidence from other parts of the world that protectionism reduces living standards many people in public life who should know better are apologists for a system which ultimately penalises the poor in favour of the wealthy and powerfully connected.

A third public misconception of how the eonomy works arises in connection with the serious problem of the lack of profitability in the hotel industry - the foundation of tourism in Bermuda and the industry which employs most people particularly those with fewest marketable skills. There is a naive belief that an industry which lost $41.472 million ($17.476 million in 1991 alone) between 1988 and 1995 will continue to invest in Bermuda and continue to employ Bermudians. All the evidence from other industries, and even common sense, would tell the reader that investors do not continue indefinitely to invest money in businesses which incur losses in the long term. This may happen for one or two years but it does not continue for very long. Yet the public , labour unions and to a lesser extent government, continues to stick their heads in the sand hoping that the bad news will go away and that we can avoid the necessary and painful changes needed to make that industry profitable once more.

Many of the issues mentioned above will be raised later in this book but the reader should bear them in mind for they are fundamental to an understanding of what in micro terms is one of the economic marvels of the western economic system.

3. WHY SHOULD ANYONE BE INTERESTED IS THE DISMAL SCIENCE OF ECONOMICS?

"Economics is the "dismal Science" because it reminds us at every turn that everything has a cost and therefore a price, that nothing can be consumed unless it has first been produced, that nothing can be produced without work and sacrifice and, above all, that we have to make choices between competing satisfactions, between today and tomorrow and between conflicting values and goals."

PETER DRUCKER

Economics was dubbed by Thomas Carlyle as the dismal science, and for a dismal subject it is the subject of endless news stories. One would have to be a rapid fire and enthusiastic channel surfer to avoid news stories about economics on T.V. although they are seldom given this title otherwise the viewer would switch to more stimulating programmes like Oprah Winfrey or Phil Donahue.

The rate of inflation, employment levels, layoffs at a hotel, financial frauds, banking scandals, stock market crashes, changes in interest rates, even robberies are all subjects which feature regularly on the news. In terms of politics, it is difficult to understand what is going on unless you have a little understanding of the dismal science of economics. Almost every day of one's life one will run up against the realities of the economy. Earning a living involves an understanding of the subject and so does the spending of the money earned. Without some knowledge of the basic truths of economics the dice will be loaded against you in life. Bermuda is not different to elsewhere in the world because financial events such as jobs, tourist arrivals, layoffs or inflation have as great an interest for Bermudians as they do on the residents of, say, New York.

The common denominator of news stories about the economy is money and the impact such stories have on the viewers' wallet, and it is money which provides the focus and interest for many people. It is a commonplace observation that people like to have money in their pocket, the more the better. There are a few exceptions to this rule - Trappist monks for example - but money and a high regular income tends to make people happier and more contented with their lot in life. If you the reader like to have money, to enjoy money, understand from where money comes, why so little of it sticks to you or how to use money then you should acquire an interest in the dismal science of economics. However, if your interests are confined to literature, poetry or music then the subject of economics will be boring.

Money provides people with the freedom to acquire that they need and desire. In its most basic form these needs are food, clothing, medical attention and shelter - needs which are not met for about 75 per cent of the world's population. When basic needs have been met individuals can enjoy the real pleasures of life - things like entertainment, travel, and luxury goods (for most of the world) such as TV, automobiles, telephones and so on. There has always been a close connection between prosperity and freedom, a theme to which I shall return later.

The enjoyment of money has often caused more trouble to the conscience of those who have it, when they remember the injunction of Jesus, that it is easier for a camel to go through the eye of a needle than for a rich man to enter the Kingdom of God. If anyone needs an excuse not to labour and earn money what better one can be found. One can at the same time feel both good in the religious sense and can avoid the inconvenience of having to get up early in the morning, or stay late at the office.

Unfortunately, not that many people show as great an interest in the other side of the money coin which is, that in order to enjoy the benefits of money, it is necessary to produce the goods and services which other people buy in return for the money they pay us. In order to have hard cash it is necessary first to engage in hard work.

Anyone with a passing interest in human affairs will recognise, without benefit of a public opinion poll, that many of those with a passionate interest in the spending of money have only a cursory interest in expending the energy required to earn it. This arises largely from the fact that creating wealth is a much more difficult process than spending income. However, it goes much further than this; the other issue which consumes the interest of politicians and the public is the distribution of income. Why do many people become obscenely wealthy under the capitalist system whilst many, many more live in poverty? Questions like this are answered by economics.

It is another commonplace observation that some people have more money than others; bankers tend to be richer than barbers, lawyers wealthier than librarians. Some countries are richer than others. Citizens of the United States, one of the world's richest countries, are much better off than the citizens of Haiti, one of the world's poorest countries.[1]

	GDP $ billion	GDP Per Capita
Bermuda	1.92	$28,293
USA	6,388.0	24,753
UK	1,043.0	17,965
Switzerland	254.0	36,399
Bangladesh	26.0	222
Haiti	2.2	200
Hong Kong	105.0	17,842
Singapore	55.0	19,293
Jamaica	3.7	1,500

For economists such matters are of continuing interest. Why should bankers be wealthier than barbers and why are Americans richer than Haitians? The question of why some countries, professions, social groups, races, individuals prosper whilst others languish, stagnate or fail to make any noticeable progress is one which has intrigued governments, economists and journalists for years. For Bermudians who live in one of the world's richest countries, the question should also of some interest as one of the major risks to which we are exposed is that from being one of the richest countries in the world it is but a short step to being one of the poorest.[2]

What then is economics? It is basically the study of how human beings choose to use scarce resources in order to satisfy economic needs like food and shelter. How to produce the goods and services needed, how to distribute them - now or in the future - amongst the differing groups in society like employees, shareholders, and owners of property. Economics also provides a means of analysis of the costs and benefits of using scarce resources like land, labour, capital and time. It is also involved with the need to describe, explain, analyse and correlate human behaviour with respect to employment, payment and share of income. All of this involves an understanding of finance and economic policy and is involved with such questions as how we can make ourselves more efficient and competitive[3], and how we can preserve the natural environment.[4]

Economics is also important in exposing the sloppy thinking which accompanies wishful thinking, good intentions and hoping for things to work out. Good intentions do not necessarily result in good policy or good outcomes as rational analysis is a more effective and powerful tool than emotion. These com-

---

[1] 'The Economist' "World in Figures 1996."

[2] See for example the problems associated with profitability of the hotel industry, in Part II 4.

[3] See Part III 18 concerning the issue of competitiveness.

[4] See Part I 11 for a discussion of the environment.

ments may sound boring and uninspiring but the insights gained into how society works is worth the time and effort.

Economics is also closely involved with other areas of interest such as history, psychology, politics, mathematics, statistics, the bible (oddly enough) and sociology. History is obviously very important and the combination of economics and history touches on such sensitive issues as slavery and racial discrimination, or on why Bermuda is wealthy today by comparison with countries like Jamaica.

Very little has been written by way of commentary on the modern Bermuda economy which is surprising given its long record of success. Many of the views I express will be challenged, many will no doubt be found to be wrong, many readers will disagree with what I write. That is the essence of the subject for there is no correct view, opinion or analysis. Everyone is touched in some way by the economy and how you are touched will affect the way in which you understand how it works. I have been one of the beneficiaries of the successful Bermudian economy and as a result I favour modest and not too radical change for the future. Others may disagree. It is this disagreement which makes the study of economics so stimulating and it is one reason why most people in Bermuda should take an interest in the "dismal science."

4. ARE THE MUSINGS OF DEAD ECONOMISTS LIKE ADAM SMITH, KARL MARX AND JOHN MAYNARD KEYNES OF ANY RELEVANCE TO MODERN BERMUDA?

"The ideas of economists and political philosophers, both when they are right and when they are wrong, are more powerful than is commonly understood. Indeed the world is ruled by little else. Practical men, who believe themselves to be quite exempt from any intellectual influences, are usually the slaves of some defunct economist. Madmen in authority, who hear voices in the air, are distilling their frenzy from some academic scribbler of a few years back ...soon or late, it is ideas, not vested interests, which are dangerous for good or evil."

JOHN MAYNARD KEYNES

In the course of casual conversation about business matters with educated people I have often used the names of Adam Smith, Karl Marx and Lord Keynes and their relevance to Bermuda but have often received stares of incomprehension as a result of mentioning their names. I have discovered over many years that many Bermudians have either never heard of these people or have only a hazy notion of their importance and relevance to the economy of Bermuda. When one also takes into consideration the fashionable educational theory of dismissing ideas of Dead White European Males (DWEMS) it is not surprising that their importance is diminished or even dismissed.

Politicians often state what they think are original economic theories but they are only parrotting ideas - some of which have been discredited - many of which originated from the pens of the three men whose works I will try and summarise later. Understanding of such matters as disputes between employers and employees, the level of government interference in the economy, the greed of merchants, the jobs people do, the economic uncertainty about the future are only examples of what the writings of Smith, Marx and Keynes still have to teach us about modern Bermuda. An understanding of how Bermuda works is difficult to achieve without having a passing knowledge of what writers of the past (and present) have said about how our economic system works. Let me start at the beginning by bringing up the name of Adam Smith whose writings have had a revival in recent years because of the economic policies of Margaret Thatcher in the UK and President Ronald Reagan in the United States some of whose advisers wore ties with the portrait of Adam Smith as a mark of respect to this remarkable man.

(1) __ADAM SMITH (1723 - 1790)__.

Adam Smith was a member of a distinguished and talented group of individuals who lived at the end of the eighteenth century, whose ideas revolutionised and improved the world and are still of major relevance to the world of the 20th century. Some of his contemporaries were George Washington, Thomas Jefferson, James Watt , Wolfgang Amadeus Mozart, and Napoleon each of whom transformed in many different ways the societies in which they lived. This was a distinguished group which lived and produced works at the end of the 18th century, an era known as the Age of Reason or the Enlightenment. This period produced remarkable advances in medicine, chemistry, physics, mathematics, philosophy, music as well as in the terrible twins of economics and politics. Many of the ideas put forward during this period contributed directly to the upheavals of the French and American Revolutions which in turn have shaped the 20th century world.

Smith's importance in changing the commercial world, how it is organised and how it thinks about economic problems of itself is probably more lasting and more fundamental, than most other economists as it still addresses directly many questions of major economic and social concern in the world today. He was born in Kirkcaldy, Scotland, and his father died a few months before his birth. He was not an imposing or dominating man - he had bulging eyes, a big nose, and a nervous twitch which was complemented by a speech impediment. However, he was humourously modest stating that he was, *"a beau in nothing but my books."* Adam Smith spent most of his working life teaching logic and moral philosophy at Glasgow University and was the classic absent minded professor who, at times, lost touch with the common day world around him. Like many men of genius he was something of an eccentric and he had little interest in women, the only woman to have any influence over his life was his mother to whom he was devoted until her death. Unlike many famous people he lived a happy and contented life, receiving the profound respect of his peers during his life time. Another of his famous quotations tends to sum up his personal life, *"What can be added to the happiness of a man who is in health, who is out of debt, and has a clear conscience."*

Smith's major ideas were expressed in the book entitled "An Inquiry into the Nature and Causes of the Wealth of Nations" (now known simply as The Wealth of Nations) published in 1776, the same year as Thomas Jefferson's masterpiece, the American Declaration of Independence, and the invention of the steam engine by James Watt - two of history's happy coincidences. As an aside Adam Smith supported the American colonists against the British and had he been alive in the 20th century he would undoubtedly have supported Bermuda's independence. His book provided a comprehensive and organised theory of economics in elegant 18th century prose which demonstrated the folly of many contemporary ideas such as arbitrary government restrictions (some of these restraints of trade are still part of contemporary Bermuda) and he stressed the importance of the contribution of labour in the productive process. Even today it is probably the best selling economics text book ever written.

Smith formulated several major ideas although according to the Austrian economist Joseph Schumpeter his book, "did not contain a single analytic idea, principle or method that was entirely new." What then were his ideas?

Firstly, he recognised that self interest (or greed) is the major driving force or the great motivator in day to day economic relationships and that major benefits would accrue to mankind if such natural drives could be harnessed . In a much quoted passage he stated;

"It is not from the benevolence of the butcher, the brewer, or the baker that we expect our dinner but from their regard to their own interest. We address ourselves, not to their humanity but to their self love, and never talk to them of our necessity but of their advantages. Nobody but a beggar chooses to depend chiefly upon the benevolence of his fellow citizens."

He then went on to say in a much more powerful insight that;

"Every individual endeavours to employ his capital so that its produce may be of greatest value. He generally neither intends to promote the public interest, nor knows how much he is promoting it. An individual who intends only his own gain is lead by an invisible hand to promote an end which was no part of his intention. Nor is it always the worse for the society that it was no part of it. By pursuing his own interest he frequently promotes that of the society, more effectually than when he really intends to promote it. I have never known much good done by those who affected to trade for the public good."

Having identified, in eloquent terms, the potential of this unflattering characteristic of mankind, Smith has been falsely accused for being the arch-priest of selfishness but rather than praising self-interest, he simply reported that it was the wellspring from which most, if not all, economic advancement takes place and he drew attention to the way in which this potentially destructive force works for the benefit of the social good. Nor was he an apologist for big business ; he believed that professional management would ever be successful - one of the few issues on which he was wrong - but he did note that

"People of the same trade seldom meet together, even for merriment and diversion, but the conversation ends in a conspiracy against the public, or in some contrivance to raise prices."

These sentiments are often overlooked when his name is reverently mentioned at meetings of such organisations as the Chamber of Commerce, Lions or Rotary. Apart from identifying the tendency of big business to try and "rip off" the public, he was one of the first to understand the importance of labour in the productive process and how important it was in raising productivity to improve the standard of life of everyone.

Secondly, Smith also understood that the countervailing power to self interest in the economic system was competition. If merchants raise their prices too high in order to make excessive profits or because they are inefficient, customers will move their business to competitors. Put into the local Bermudian context this is the main reason why Bermudians fly to such watering holes as Raleigh, North Carolina to take advantage of the lower prices and variety of choice. Self interest determines that an individual's money will spent wisely by that individual and he will go where prices are the best, and the competition which arises from reasonably cheap transportation means that the consumer can benefit . In addition, if high profits are earned this will attract new entrants to the industry and competition will take place. On the other hand, if profits are insufficient or inadequate, the businessman will fail. Failed businesses are not the same thing as a failed economy because failures make it possible for resources (land, Labour and capital) to be used more productively by those who believe they can be successful. The whole process will constantly renew and invigorate itself as circumstances and tastes change. This dynamic combination of self-interest and competition was a revelation in the revolutionary times of 1776 and in many ways it still is as the belated conversion of the former USSR and Eastern Europe in the early 1990s proved.

Thirdly, the heady mixture of self interest and competition, also known as the market, is able to process an amazing amount of information and as a consequence direct the flow of land, labour and capital to their most productive uses. Each working day literally billions of decisions are made by business people and consumers to sell, buy, manufacture, ship, investment, disinvest, enter business , expand and so on. Every one of such decisions has a connection with other business decisions and these are sorted by the invisible hand to which Smith referred. That hand, or magic wand, has presided over a staggering increase in economic wellbeing and has lifted countless millions out of the misery and grinding poverty which has been their fate since time began. The job of gathering this information, and in understanding it, is beyond the power of any politician or civil servant, or anyone else for that matter, but it is not beyond the power of the market which provides some semblance of order out of the apparent chaos of billions of decisions.

In an 1958 article entitled "I, Pencil"[1] Leonard E. Read, Founder of the "Foundation for Economic Education" wrote about the countless pieces of information, knowledge, raw materials and skill which have to be manipulated, processed and organised by the global market economy in order to manufacture a simple technologically unsophisticated product like an ordinary wooden pencil.

---

[1] Which is repeated each year in the periodical "Imprimis" published by Hillsdale College, Michigan.

So complex and intricate is this process that no one man, or even a small group of men, possesses the necessary knowledge and raw materials needed to make a pencil. Only the market place with its carrot of self-interest and its stick of competition can make this complex process work successfully. Governments, the Bermuda Government is a good example, constantly seek to prevent the discovery and processing of information by erecting trade barriers such as tariffs, quotas, exchange controls or limitations in corporate ownership all of which are incorrectly stated to be in the public interest. The result is that such interventions invariably impede the efficiency of the market system by undermining the flow of information needed to make rational economic decisions. This brings us to the fourth major insight of Smith, that of limited government.

The Wealth of Nations demonstrated in an eloquent way that the markets operating through the mixture of competition and self interest would provide most of the goods and services required by consumers. Governments should get out of the way and allow individuals maximum freedom to achieve their economic ends. He did recognise that the market could not provide everything required by the public and that only collective action through the activities of government would provide essential goods required by all citizens. Smith argued strongly that government should confine itself to three major tasks :-

- To provide military defence by "defending the people from the violence and invasion of other independent societies."
- To provide police and a judicial system.
- The provision of public works such as roads, bridges, harbours which *"can never be for the interest of any individual, or small number of individuals, to erect and maintain."*

There were several other important observations made by this remarkable man, such as the division of labour, that is to say job specialisation which could be mentioned but I have concentrated on the major points made by him in this most revolutionary of books. The word revolutionary is used deliberately because the market forces (or capitalism) he described are unruly, disconcerting, unpredictable, disquieting, and disruptive because the economic system Smith described led to changes in the world as revolutionary as anyone can think of. Adam Smith in his masterpiece of 1,097 pages combined the practices, ideas and philosophies of the 18th century applicable to economic organisation into an eloquent statement of revolutionary doctrine. It became a best seller all over the world and had a tremendous influence over the Founding Fathers of the United States becoming, in effect, a capitalist declaration of independence from the suffocating societies of Europe with their emphasis on birth and privilege. This helped launch an "economic revolution in thought" which when combined with the industrial revolution in Britain released in the words of Smith "universal opulence which extends itself to the lowest ranks of the people" whose state since the beginning of time had been one of tyranny and misery.

(2) KARL MARX. (1818 - 1883)

Karl Marx was born in Trier , in what is now Germany, was of Jewish background although he later converted to Christianity. The implementation of his economic philosophy (known as Marxism or communism) , particularly in China and the former USSR, has made him the most influential economic thinker since Adam Smith. He was an academic scribbler par excellence whose revolutionary tracts "The Communist Manifesto" (1848), and "Das Kapital" (1867) which have had so much malign influence, are probably the most widely known (but not necessarily read) economic publications in the world. Marx saw himself as the champion of the common man against the impersonal and harsh consequences of the market economy and argued that by following his philosophy workers would be led to the promised land. His lifetime and writing coincided with the tremendous and rapid expansion in industrial output in the West, which arose from new and changing technologies. The severe social distress which these changes wreaked on the new industrial and urban classes in the absence of any social programmes to relieve distress, or modern amenities in the new industrial slums such as Manchester in England made his tracts more appealing to the general public.

His main theory was breathtakingly simple. The owners of capital, the capitalists (or the bourgeois) in order to earn larger profits, had always exploited, the workers (or the proletariat), on whom all production depended. To increase profits even further it was necessary to increase investment, which led to increased exploitation, which in turn led to increased production and so on, but sooner or later capitalism must collapse because profits would ultimately have to decline as the increased production could no longer be sold at a profit. This would then create unemployment amongst the exploited workers and eventually they would unite and depose the capitalist employers , create a dictatorship of the proletariat, which would then lead to the abolition of private property and social classes, and eventually to a classless society. The implicit conclusion was then everyone would live happily ever after. Marx stated that when private property was eventually abolished, men would no longer be objects for exploitation but would be given dignity, status and power in the new classless society.

As we now know things did not work out that happy way in countries such as China, USSR , Cuba, Vietnam and Cambodia which embraced Communism. Five year economic plans disintegrated into chaos, the Utopian ideals turned into horrors of mass murder with the police state and the classless society was characterised by a privileged group of appartatchiks who lived off the fat of the land whilst the workers starved. Indeed contrary to his predictions the workers in Britain, Germany and the United States became increasingly prosperous, contented and even complacent whilst their counterparts in the Communist regimes grew increasingly impoverished. Because of its obvious failures of corruption, injustice, hypocrisy, lies and incompetence the whole system collapsed ignominiously in the USSR and Eastern Europe in 1991 and now shows increasing strain in China and elsewhere. Reality was completely different from the ideal of communism and instead of governments withering away as he forecast it threw up ruthless dictators like Stalin, Mao Tse Tung, Castro, Ho Chi Minh, Colonel Mengistu and Pol Pot who took sadistic delight in murdering millions of their countrymen.

Marx saw the life of the common man being dictated by blind social forces presided over by a conspiracy of the bourgeois and over which the worker had little or no control. Men (and women) were depicted as helpless victims who only required a prophet or visionary to lead them from their dark life under the capitalist system. What they got was Stalin, Mao Tse Tung and other thuggist communist dictators.

Interestingly, much liberal and multicultural theory today embodies the philosophies of the class struggle as depicted by Marx. People of colour, indigenous natives and women regardless of circumstances, talent or individuality are depicted as the new oppressed proletariat. Multinational companies and the wealthy middle class white male are viewed as representatives of the bourgeoisie. Anyone who catches the nuances of some political debates can see the shadowy forms drawn by Marx 140 years ago.

The basic fallacies of Marxism were that :

- individuals perform best when they are herded into vast collectives rather than being allowed to pursue what Adam Smith called their own self interest;
- bureaucrats and politicians can run an efficient egalitarian economy.

The personal life of Karl Marx was a total disaster. Like many intellectuals he was unable to handle money and was always in debt. If it was not for an industrialist called Engels, Marx would have had to work for a living like everyone else and his works would not have been published. He led a spectacularly unhealthy life, drank and smoked a lot, never exercised, was grossly overweight and he had boils or carbuncles all over his body, including his face. He was subject to uncontrolled fits of rage and in 1873 had a nervous collapse. He exploited a long suffering servant, Helen Demuth, who bore him an illegitimate child, and she was the only member of the working class he ever knew. His relationships with his wife Jenny , a tired disillusioned woman, his children and his sons in law were material for the Oprah Winfrey show. His Cuban son in law Paul Lafargue was part negro and Marx delighted in calling him a gorilla. Marx, in short, was a thoroughly objectionable character with no saving graces, whose personal life was a disaster. One of the world's great unsolved mysteries is how this hypocrite with such detestable qualities was able to appeal to the middle class intellectuals of the nineteenth and twentieth centuries.

He was also an expert in the sound-bite, long before that modern term of the television age was ever coined. Many of his aphorisms are classics as the following representative sample shows:-

- *the workers have nothing to lose but their chains.*
- *religion is the opium of the people.*
- *the ruling ideas of each age have been the ideas of its ruling class.*
- *a spectre is haunting Europe - the spectre of communism.*
- *the history of all hitherto existing societies is the history of the class struggle.*
- *workers of the world unite*
- *from each according to his abilities, to each according to his needs.*
- *the class struggle necessarily leads to the dictatorship of the proletariat.*

It was his ability to coin the short pithy memorable phrase which allowed his economic philosophy to be saved from the oblivion it deserved. However, many of his views found favour with disgruntled intellectuals and politicians and the conversion of Lenin and Mao Tse Tung made it possible for many of his theories to be implemented with horrendous consequences for three or four generations of Russians and Chinese who have led impoverished and stunted lives by comparison with their contemporaries in the West. Instead of losing their imaginary chains the workers and people of Russia, China and elsewhere acquired real chains and rulers who became mass murderers and as a result led sad miserable lives. In the 74 years, between 1917 and 1991, during which the Communist Party held power in the former USSR, it ruined the country and enslaved its people. The Russian people owe nothing but misery to Marx.

Why was communism (or Marxism) unsuccessful? Like Marx's theories, the three reasons for its staggering failure are also breathtakingly simple.

1. Most of the benefits of the tremendous increase in productivity in the Western democracies which occurred in the nineteenth and twentieth centuries has accrued largely to the working classes. The capitalist owners did not hog all of the increased wealth but shared it with their employees. The 1996 worker in the USA earns about 25 times the real income of the worker in 1900. The rise in social status and political power of the average worker is just as great. Many of the large employers like Cadbury, Rowntree, Carnegie, Rockerfeller and Ford left much of their great wealth for the benefit of society and the poor - whilst under Communism the people starved. Just as it is a mystery why Marx appealed to the intelligentsia, it is difficult to comprehend why it has taken people so long to realise that communism and its cousin socialism is a recipe for poverty, oppression and general misery.

2. A more profound reason for failure is that Marxists, communists and socialists deny themselves the information or economic data required to keep a modern economy functioning. The great delusion of Marxists is the belief that politicians and bureaucrats can obtain the right quality of economic intelligence from the civil service to manage an economy. This "fatal conceit" automatically guarantees failure because the modern economy is so complex that it is beyond the capability of any bureaucrat or organisation to acquire the necessary information to make sound decisions. That data can only be supplied by the market based on the billions of decisions made daily by customers making known their wishes through the price system.

3. The increased sophistication of the economy and the increasing wealth of the workers who changed from being unskilled, untutored oafs into highly skilled and educated employees allowed employees to own the organisations for whom they worked. Almost every worker in the world today is a part owner of the system which employs him and this ownership can arise directly by owning shares in the enterprise or , as is more frequently the case, arises indirectly through pension funds (who own about 50% of quoted shares), through insurance policies or by self employment. In the end

Marx was right - the workers would own the means of production but ownership arose not because of revolution arising from exploitation but through the democratic market system and from the freedom and dignity which improved productivity creates.

In conclusion, the death of communism arose because it simply did not work. For a doctrine whose greatest claim was that it had a unique understanding of economic relationships and motivations and their impact on everyday life, this was a death blow. Less than 75 years after Communism began in Russia the battle between capitalism and communism is finally over. Capitalism won.

For the descendents of the three or four generations of Russians and others whose lives were wasted on Marx's barren theories an immense challenge faces them and that is how to build capitalism again from the wreckage of the economy they have had the misfortune to inherit. This is proving to be an immensely difficult task, some would say impossible, for the skills necessary to be a successful capitalist may have been destroyed over the past 70 years. Communism was excellent at producing things which nobody wanted, failing to produce the essentials of the good life, and commiting scarce-capital to projects which were thought to create prestige but not wealth. As the old Russian joke had it "We pretend to work, and they (the party bosses) pretend to pay us." Marxism turned out to be a complete and utter disaster for those who had the misfortune to live under it.

(3) JOHN MAYNARD KEYNES. (1883 - 1946)

There could be no one as diametrically opposed to Adam Smith and Karl Marx as John Maynard Keynes. Whilst Smith was an absent-minded professor, Keynes was sophisticated, witty and worldly; Marx was an ill-tempered outsider and loner whilst Keynes was on a first name basis with the rich, famous and powerful and was at ease in the power circles of politics as he was with the artistic and literary. Yet of the three most important economists who ever lived, his is the name absent from the book which ranks the world's most influential persons in history.[2]

He was born in England in 1883, a gifted child in today's parlance, his mother being the first female graduate of Cambridge University and his father a learned economics scholar. His younger life was one of privilege - prep school, Eton, King's College, Cambridge and the upper reaches of the civil service at an early age. During the First World War he worked at the Treasury and was responsible for relations with Britain's allies and with conserving foreign currency reserves by that time in short supply. He attended the Peace Conferences at Versailles but was disgusted with the short-sighted nationalism and chicanery of the politicians and resigned to write a highly critical and acclaimed book about his experiences entitled "The Economic Consequences of Peace." This book predicted the effect of reparations on the German economy and contained entertaining but highly-offensive portraits of the leading figures - Lloyd George[3], Woodrow Wilson and Georges Clemenceau. Being forthright and witty as well as

---

[2] "The 100 - A Ranking of the Most Influential Persons in History" by Michael H. Hart.

[3] Lloyd George was described as "This goat-footed bard, this half-human visitor to our age from the hag-ridden magic and enchanted woods of Celtic antiquity."

being right fingered him as being untrustworthy in official circles and it was not until the Second World War that he was trusted by the politicians and the bureaucracy.

The worldwide depression of the 1930s baffled the profession of economics. Banks, businesses and whole industries like agriculture collapsed and buckled in every major nation and the politicians and bureaucrats floundered having no idea of how to solve the immense financial problems. The major exception was Adolph Hitler whose intensely nationalistic policies led Germany out of the depression but at great subsequent cost. In the United States Franklin Delano Roosevelt promised the poor and unemployed a "New Deal" but despite a whole battery of alphabet soup governmental agencies and resolute leadership he was unable to make much headway against the Depression which had lead to widespread poverty, misery and unemployment (which in the United States hovered around 25 percent). Most governments were paralysed as the electorate terrified of the economic consequences lost faith in capitalism and democracy and flirted with either National Socialism (Nazism) or Communism.

Keynes published his most influential work "The General Theory of Employment, Interest and Money" in 1936, a complex, difficult and badly organised book which owed most of its influence to a band of younger economists who conveyed its messages to the paralysed official world and to a larger public. There were two major points in his book which changed the whole subject of economics for several decades.

Firstly, the depression was not a temporary phenomenon as there was no self-correcting mechanism in capitalism to restore normality of employment, prices and business confidence. Entrepreneurs were not prepared to invest and because of general uncertainty about the future they simply kept their cash in banks. The technical term was a liquidity preference. Cutting wages - the conventional way of dealing with unemployment - was no longer appropriate as it would simply make the situation worse by reducing demand for goods and services which would mean fewer sales and more unemployment. Keynes identified the problem as one of being able to create sufficient purchasing power in the economy as a whole.

Secondly, this led ultimately to the acceptance of the theory that when there was a fall in general demand it was necessary to increase purchasing power throughout the economy and the only agency big enough and powerful enough to do this was the government acting through the monetary system and through the tax system. Increasing liquidity through the banking system was by itself insufficient because of the liquidity preference problem - coloquially described as pushing on a piece of string. The only certain way of increasing general, or aggregate demand in the economy quickly was through the fiscal system by reducing taxes to the public and by increasing government borrowing and spending. When aggregate demand was high prosperity ensued; when aggregate demand was low business activity decreased as sales fell and as a result jobs disappeared. During times of weak demand the trick was to increase demand by means of government spending through borrowing and private spending through tax reductions. When economic conditions boomed the trick was to reduce government spending and increase taxes.

There was almost a natural beauty to this theory of economic behaviour - the key to perpetual prosperity had apparently been found. This theory gave birth to the modern economy of the late 20th century with its politically popular objectives of full-employment and, for politicians, a significant increase in their power by being able to manipulate taxes and government borrowing. Government borrowing became something of a virtue and there were many politicians only too happy to push the process forward. The power of the state could be increased beyond any dictator's wildest dreams and the electorate were happy because it provided economic security.

This was a revolution in economic thinking. Government spending more than it raised in taxation whilst at the same time reducing taxes went against all the economic orthodoxies of the time. This was why Keynesian economics was never widely practised - except in Germany - until after the Second World War by which time Keynes's ideas had become mainstream. The Labour Government in Britain was easily convinced and practised Keynesian economics from 1945. It took longer in the United States and it was not until the Presidencies of Kennedy and Johnson that the idea of government taking responsibility for the health of the economy was generally accepted by the public. Government was ahead of public opinion for in 1946 the Full Employment Act was passed by the US Congress which assigned responsibility for maintaining full employment and hence prosperity to the President.

Without Keynes there would have been no International Monetary Fund, Marshall Plan (which restored prosperity to Europe), or European economic miracle after the Second World War. Indeed, many subscribe to the theory that had Keynes not written his book capitalism may well have disappeared from the face of the earth. Government spending generated prosperity in such areas as the airline business, home ownership, public highways, and public higher education. The modern 20th century world owes much to the original mind of Keynes with the result that his ideas have influenced everyone who has lived in the Western world. Bermuda has been a major beneficiary of the prosperity which has been generated in the United States without which there would not have been a tourist industry of the current size. In addition, the tax and spend policies of the American Government has led to many corporations taking appropriate action to minimise their tax bill and as a by product the offshore financial business has been created. It is not an exaggeration to say that without the economic ideas of Keynes Bermuda would still largely be a fishing village off the coast of North Carolina.

The postscript to Keynes ideas is that governments forgot a major part of Keynesian theories. He was a far better analyst for depressions than he was for prosperity although by the time prosperity arrived in the West Keynes had died from overwork in 1946. When economic conditions boomed, governments were supposed to reduce their expenditure and increase taxes to pay off past borrowings. Politicians were not prepared to court unpopularity with the electorate by increasing taxes - usually the kiss of death in modern politics or to reduce government spending because of its unpopularity with key interests groups like the educational establishment and civil service unions. When economic boom conditions exist, as they did in the late 1960s and early 1970s, governments were not prepared to increase taxes and reduce spending. The result was inflation and anyone who has lived through the past 30 years knows the havoc caused to the economy by that phenomenon. Keynes himself stated that "there is no subtler, no surer means of overturning the existing basis of society than to debauch the currency." This was one of his unintended legacies to the economic system although it is one from which we are recovering.[5]

The importance of Smith, Marx and Keynes to modern day Bermuda is probably not very obvious and so I will mention several important points arising from their writings to show their importance to the society in which we live.

Bermuda clearly sings with gusto to the music written by Adam Smith - the rewarding of individual initiative through the profit system, the acceptance of private property, limited government (non-intervention in the economy is critical for society's economic efficiency), free markets although there are vestitages of restrictions and the specialisation of jobs which arises from free trade within an international economy. Smith's ideas are the foundation or cornerstone on which our economic society is built and not coincidentally the basis of much of our political freedom. He demonstrated that by sticking to the music, capitalism through dramatically increased productivity would efficiently deliver ever increasing incomes to everyone, including the average worker, and Bermuda is quite clearly a beneficiary of this insight.

Keynes's influence is not quite so obvious, but the recent history of high rates of inflation are a reminder of his main idea that governments through their spending can influence the level of economic activity, both positively in that widespread general unemployment is a relic of the 1930s, but negatively in that if his policies are used in the wrong circumstances inflation can result. The fact is that he was instrumental in restoring faith in capitalism. Most important for today's world he give intellectual justification for the increased influence of government intervention in the economy.

At first sight the influence of Karl Marx would be thought of as minimal but that conclusion would not be wholly accurate. For example, the presence of NATO military bases in Bermuda arose from the fact that Russia and Eastern Europe subscribed to the theories of Marx and that such theories had a military dimension to them. When they were exposed as being unworkable by the collapse of Russia the military bases in Bermuda were closed.

Less obviously, Marx considered the individual to be simply a pawn of forces he could not influence, control or even understand and he would suffer from intermittent unemployment, social injustice and unremitting exploitation. Historical economic forces governed the life of the individual and Marx found it difficult to understand that individual talents and energy like those of the Rockerfellers,

---

[5] See Part III 12 for a discussion of the issue of inflation.

Fords or Carnegie could change the course of economic history. This led in part to the 'victim theory' of society in which it is believed that if an individual is poor, unemployed or facing other adverse circumstances he is not at fault, but can blame others for his misery. He is not accountable or responsible for his own actions. Life is just a conspiracy of the wealthy and powerful against the poor and working man.

Secondly, Marx always considered that employers would exploit their employees in order to make larger profits and the poor employer/employee relations which exist in Bermuda owe something to this mistaken belief. He also predicted and relished the idea of the class struggle - workers versus the middle class and this philosophy is a central feature of the philosophy of the PLP.[6] The corrosive victim psychology, lack of individual responsibility , absurd conspiracy theories, employer/employee battles and the class struggle are all ideas widely prevalent in Bermuda which originate largely from Marx.

5. WHY IS THERE A CLOSE CONNECTION BETWEEN THE ECONOMY AND POLITICS ?

"Political economy; two words that should be divorced - on the grounds of incompatability."

'WALL STREET JOURNAL'

James Carville, a political adviser to Prsident Clinton in the Presidential election of 1992, had a sign on the wall of the office of the campaign staff which stated, "It's the economy, STUPID." Whilst President Bush waffled on about foreign policy and the success of the US military in the Gulf War, Bill Clinton hammered away at his theme that the economy was in poor shape, unemployment was high and confidence low.

The important point is that the American electorate is passionately interested in their financial well being and only has limited interest in foreign affairs. Similarly in Bermuda, the electorate wants the good times to continue to roll and the governing UBP wishes to claim as much credit as possible for the success of the economy and wishes to paint the opposition PLP as incompetent, or worse, in financial matters. Hence politicians stressing their central role in a sound economy results in success at the polls, although in reality that claim is nonsense. Being associated with an economy which has gone wrong can result in electoral failure. To get their message over politicians use the language of economics which confuses, and somtimes influences the voter and gives the impression that politicians know what they are talking about.

Politicians are invariably attracted to things which are important to people usually because they can attract votes, or when the economy improves they can either take credit, or emphasise that improvements took place when they were in charge. It is therefore no surprise that there is a close connection between economics and politics, and in the early days of the subject it was known as political economy.

---

[6] This is not to suggest that the PLP is Communist or Marxist for it quite clearly is not. All I am suggesting is that some of their supporters borrow, probably unconsciously, from the ideas of Marx.

Money has two essential qualities which attract politicians like bears to honey. Money gives the owner power to influence people and freedom of choice. Politicans are interested in power, usually to increase it, and secondly they are interested in freedom usually to curtail it in order to increase their own power and influence.

It was not until the First World War (1914 - 1918) that politicians took it upon themselves to involve government in the day-to-day workings of the economy at which time politicians found out they could significantly increase taxation and also borrow for political purposes. This was achieved because of the pressing necessity to win the war, and when the war ended state intervention lapsed into its pre-war hands off the economy approach.

The breakdown of the world's economic system in the 1930s led politicians again to involve themselves more closely with the day to day workings of the economy, the precedent having been set by military necessity during the First World War. The most amibitious programme was President Roosevelt's New Deal (which allowed Roosevelt to win the Presidency four times) which led to the marriage between politics and economics becoming almost indissoluble.

Until the First World War and the New Deal, politicians had started from the assumption that revenues were fixed and as a consequence expenditures had to be shoehorned into what could be afforded. After the New Deal politicians under-stood quite clearly that taxes could be increased substantially to create revenues which could then be used to pay for programmes which could reshape society and coincidentally assure politicians of relection. Increasing state intervention in the 1930s and 1940s led logically to the unstated proposition that the income of tax-payers belonged to the government except for that which the government explic-itly allowed the taxpayer to keep.

At the same time, the acceptance of Keynesian theories, which falsely promised that governments could forever abolish unemployment and economic recessions, led governments in the United Kingdom and the United States to the awareness that they could win elections by adjusting monetary and fiscal policies in such a way that a boom could occur at the same time as an election. Political influence in the economy also increased the number of jobs available to be hand-ed out as political patronage to influential supporters. The match was immediate and irresistible, almost made in heaven, and economics and politics henceforth went together like Laurel and Hardy.

In the space of less than 30 years politicians had the power to reconstruct the state in a way which allowed them to win elections almost at will and to increase taxes at an undreamed of rate. Any politcian who tried to reduce the power of gov-ernment came against highly organised vested interests and even President Ronald Reagan and Prime Minister Margaret Thatcher were unable to halt the growth in state power. Bermuda came into this game some years later at a time when the old colonial regime gave way to new constitutional arrangments in 1968 and the growth of political parties, but fortunately is still very much a novice at it.

Economics was also useful to politicians for making rosy forecasts about the future. The electorate, wisely, rarely believes forecasts about the economy made by politicians but they believe, wrongly, credibility is enhanced if such forecasts are made by economists with an established reputation. In many cases politicians did not understand the limitations of the discipline of economics and overestimated its diagnostic and curative powers. Alas politicians and economists are just like other people - they cannot forecast the future any better than a gypsy reading tea leaves. This proposition can be proved by asking two simple questions:-

1. If economists can tell the financial future why are so few of them billionaires or even millionaires, and if they are so clever why don't they earn higher salaries?

2. Why is that investment houses and managers of mutual funds, who employ scores of economists, are unable to beat the stock market indices on a consistent basis? Despite the fact that there are well known economic names on the staffs of investment firms, these institutions cannot predict the imponderables of economic progress and the idiosyncracies of the capital markets.

Economics can help explain why things are as they are, or even as they have been, but it is limited at explaining how things will be. There is considerable evidence that the ups and downs of the economic cycle are beyond the control of politicians and that they can do little to change this fact of life. Politicians (and a few economists) believe they can control and shape events despite the overwhelming evidence to the contrary. For example in the USA billions of dollars have been spent since the mid 1960s for the purpose of eliminating poverty but poverty is worse in 1996 than it was thirty years ago. Oddly enough in the areas where there is almost universal consent by economists of foolish policies, rent control and protectionism are the best examples, politicians simply ignore the evidence because it is too difficult to explain to the voters.

Politics is about the exercise of power, and one of the most important levers of power is money. Economics theorises and explains about money and so arises a natural and compelling attraction between politics and economics because of the shared interest in the power of money.

In addition, politicians have to levy taxes in order to raise revenue for government. Much of the language used to persuade the public that taxes are a necessary and desirable thing, and the purposes to which the taxpayers money will be put, is couched in the language of economics. If a few high sounding phrases, combined with a rosy forecast about future well being can be assembled in a budget speech politicians can achieve what a former finance minister in France said about the taxes "it is the act of plucking the goose with the least amount of hissing."

The core of economy theory is useful and should be heeded by politicians, and not converted into false or unrealistic claims about the future. Bermuda has been very fortunate in that the unholy alliance between politics and economics has not made much headway. If the experience of elsewhere is anything to go by, Bermuda should keep it that way.

6. WHY DO ECONOMISTS DISAGREE AND WHY ARE ECONOMIC FORECASTS USUALLY WRONG?

"We've got a world economy now and it's just not possible for forecasters to understand and take into account all the resulting complexities and uncertainties."

LESTER THUROW

"The economics profession has sold people a bill of goods on which it can't possibly deliver - the notion that economists have the ability to make good long-range forecasts with any degree of consistency."

ROBERT CHANDROSS (*FORMER ECONOMIST AT LLOYDS BANK*)

Economists and economics have never been as highly visible, influential and received such widespread publicity as they do at present, and yet paradoxically never have economists and their writings been at such a low ebb. Yet despite repeated failures to predict what is going to happen next month, far less next year, their counsel is still eagerly sought. GDP calculations, Balance of Payments estimates and unemployment figures are usually drastically revised after they are published so that politicians, policy makers and the public are constantly baffled by what is reported.

Forecasting has become a boom industry which employs thousands of economists throughout the world in government or busily scribbling in financial magazines or on behalf of stock brokers. However, the record was so bad that it has led to one writer becoming so incensed[1] that in 1996 he devoted a whole book appropriately entitled "Lost Prophets" to the subject, reminding us of the biblical injunction to "*Beware of false prophets, which come to you in sheep's clothing, but inwardly they are ravening wolves*".[2] The famous investor Bernard Baruch once asked 'that if economists are so clever why are they unable to make a fortune on the stock market'. Disagreements, arguments and widely different forecasts are the norm with the result that the public is often baffled by any discussion of the subject of economics.

One major reason for public squabbles is that many economists are willing and able to testify on any side of any dispute. Is inflation caused by unions - yes say some, no say most. It is caused by big business seeking to take advantage of market shortages - yes say some, no say most. Is it caused by government's pressuring central banks to print more money - yes say most, no say some. Predictions on financial matters by economists are beginning to resemble the opposing arguments of counsel in the OJ Simpson trial. On the causes of inflation, the levels of unemployment, the impact of government spending programmes and many other key economic issues the opinions and forecasts of economists sound more and more like weather forecasts and all too frequently they have the same degree of accuracy. Economics is supposed to be scientific with practitioners schooled in assessing statistical facts, the evidence from research and providing impartial advice about policy issues. Why then do economists differ so greatly?

---

[1] Alfred Malabre, Jr , a columnist and editor for the Wall Street Journal.
[2] St Matthew 7:15

Firstly, many economists have ideological differences or different values in much the same as engineers have different values over the development of new weapon systems. Many are enthusiasts for free market solutions because they mistrust government intervention in the economic process. Others have a distaste for market solutions or a disbelief in their adequacy to resolve fundamental social problems such as health insurance or education.

Secondly, economists are reluctant to admit that they may not have the tools to provide solutions to difficult problems or that they simply do not know what to do. Economists are on fairly solid ground when it comes to micro-economic matters such as predicting the effects of legal minimum wages on employment, or the impact of rent control on residential accommodation. Knowledge is limited on macro-economic matters such as tax policy, the impact of governmental regulations and spending of levels of employment. How can labour productivity be increased in an economy which is heavily orientated towards services rather than manufacturing?[3] To what level can government tax the economy without creating disincentives? What role does education play in long term economic growth? These are questions to which no correct answers can be given because the state of knowledge concerning such matters is limited. Economists suffer from ignorance on many matters and they are understandly reluctant to admit it.

Thirdly, the time period to which their conclusions apply may differ. Lower tax rates tend to stimulate consumer spending in the short term but what is their impact on investment in the long term? Anyone who consults a doctor will be familiar with advice which may recommend immediate surgery and other advice from another practioner who will recommend rest. Economics is becoming akin to medicine as time constraints play an increasingly important role.

Forecasting any economy, no matter how straightforward is a hazardous undertaking. Unless economic forecasts are very short term or confined to some simple concept like the impact of a spate of bad weather on the price of wheat, they have repeatedly established a reputation of being wrong. As Professor Galbraith has said, *"There are two classes of forecasters. Those who don't know - and those who don't know they don't know."* The main reason they are wrong is that unlike physical sciences where the properties used to predict outcomes are well known, (for example, water always boils at 100 degrees centigrade, and always will), economics deals with the actions of millions, even billions, of people and people are notorious at times for being unpredictable, contrarian, fickle, stupid, irrational and responding to other pressures. If people were sheep or zombies, economic forecasting would be relatively easy. Fortunately they are not.

The objective for a small community like Bermuda is to be flexible and adaptable, two things at which we are very good, and to be alert to changes taking place around the world. These changes will have an impact on our business - the recession in the United States clearly affected our tourist business in the late 1980s - and we should be able to respond accordingly. There is no equivalent of the divine right of kings on markets and business.

---

[3] See Part I 18.

Economic forecasters are unable to predict changes in the economy with any degree of certainty or accuracy and it is abdication of responsibility for governments and business executives to use them as crutches to lean on in their decision making. Books like "Future Shock" and "Power Shift" by Alvin Toffler or "Megatrends" by John Naisbitt are stimulating and entertaining reading. They are good fun, make the reader think and are comparable to science fiction in that the imagination can take flight. However, they should not be taken too seriously.

P.T. Barnum probably made the most accurate forecast ever when he stated that *"There's a sucker born every minute"*. There are not many rich economists around and if by chance they happen to be wealthy the reader may rest assured that they did not earn their fortunes by following recommendations contained in their economic forecasts.[4]

7. WHY DO THE PUBLIC AND POLITICIANS APPEAR NOT TO UNDERSTAND THE ECONOMY AND ECONOMICS.

"The one thing clear now is that crowds 'think' very little, if at all, in the sense of impartial analysis or criticism. And this is notably true under the condition of a political campaign, and one of the results of modern technology is to give the governing process much of the character of a continuous campaign, the first principle of which is to create the crowd-mind. Anything that appeals to the crowd-mind must be simple and romantic. It cannot be expect to show anything but contempt for sound economic theory".

F.H. KNIGHT.(*FOUNDER OF CHICAGO SCHOOL OF ECONOMICS*)

The fact that the public or politicians have a limited grasp of economics is really what a reasonable person would expect. After all the subject appeals only to a few minds, and there are much better things to do with time than read about boring things like statistics, policy changes and making money. I have little interest in undertanding how the electrical system works in my house, working in the garden or tinkering with my car. Therefore, why should an electrician, gardener or mechanic be remotely interested in the financial system. Life is too short, time is limited and human intelligence is too limited to understand everything and besides it goes against the principle of the division of labour enunciated by Adam Smith.

Many of these reasons should not apply to politicians, who hold themselves up as fountains of knowledge on many matters and as much of their time is spent dealing with or debating economic issues. However as one sage remarked, "There is no rule of law which states that politicians have to be well-informed or intelligent." If there was half of Bermuda's politicians would be in jail.

Most of the public obtain their information (and entertainment) about public affairs from television. That medium is not the best forum to explain or analyse quite complex phenomena on which reasonable men can differ. For example, most economists are unanimous in their opinion that the imposition of rent control makes the problem of rented housing much worse for those who wish to rent.

---

[4] I also can't resist looking into the future as I do for example in Part II 17 and 18

TV is purely superficial. Impressions count and it has a high visual impact which makes it very difficult to explain why rent control is economic nonsense. It is much easier and makes for better viewing to show a teenage mother of two sick children living in bad conditions trying to explain how difficult it is to pay rent of $600 per month when she is only earning $1,000 per month. Most people would be outraged by these circumstances but what cannot come across on the TV is that the mother is probably having to pay high rent because rent controls reduced the supply of housing and pushed rents up.

About half of the impression created on TV arises from what someone looks like as an individual or what the backdrop is. A poor mother in a slum automatically gains sympathy at the expense of some well-dressed landlord sitting in an air-conditioned office. Only about 10 percent of the impact on the viewer arises from the content and what is actually said; this means TV is not good at communicating information about abstract ideas. It is therefore much easier for a TV producer (and for the ratings) to play on the human interest angle and create sympathy for the tenant rather than inform about complex economic issues.

Even print journalism deals awkwardly with the complications of economics. The public enjoys trials like OJ Simpson, scandals, action, wars, political scrapping and sports. In these things the conflicts are obvious and people have a position on them. The economy is not simple theatre. The productive process in which wealth and jobs are created is complex and unending and costs and benefits are difficult to disentangle. Conflicing evidence is hard to understand and it requires considerable effort. Some economic policies hurt - others benefit. There is no hero and no villain, no victim and no harasser, no simple morality play and the situation is not helped when experts give conflicting views. Complicated situations do not sell newspapers or advertising time on TV.

Viewers reactions to the evening news are determined not by rational interpretation of economic phenomena or the cold rational calculation of benefits and penalties but by their emotions. Keep It Simple, Stupid (KISS) is as much a part of TV news as it is of life-insurance salesmen.

A third reason why the public are slow to respond to economic issues is that many people often act irrationally and often against their own best interests. As a manager, I have lost count of the number of employees who fail to make maximum provision for their retirement when much of the cost is subsidised by the employer. The public is often fair game for advertisers who recognising this streak of irrationality, convince people who buy soap for example, that they are not buying something which keeps them clean but buying them eternal youth, beauty or attraction to the opposite sex.

Other examples of irrational beliefs and economic behaviour are not difficult to find:
- The public exaggerates the profits of public companies which are often small or non-existent.[1]
- Trade unions are seen to be selfless defenders of the worker rather than an organisation which sometimes takes advantage of the gullible.

---

[1] see Part II 4 and 5 for the discussion on the profitablity of the hotel industry and the retail industry

- People believe themselves to be worse off than they are.

Finally, in Bermuda many of the public are convinced that there are many conspiracies; for example, that Bermuda is governed by a close assocation of major Bermuda businesses. Simple prejudice also plays a part in that many Bermudians firmly believe that expatriate employees are illegally taking away jobs from Bermudian workers. Such beliefs are reinforced by some politicians who, often knowingly, inflame public opinion or support policies which are not for the common benefit but are self-serving responses to the irrational beliefs of their constituents. Too often economics assumes that people always act rationally and relentlessly pursue their own self-interest in the way Adam Smith describes when in reality many economic decisions are largely determined by irrational behaviour. This behaviour is often ignored by economists when describing the economy.

If the public often fails to understand economic issues, what about politicians? Unfortunately (or perhaps fortunately), few politicians anywhere - Bermuda is not an exception - really understand financial matters and for a very good reason. Business does not vote. The managers of the Bank of Bermuda and the Bank of N.T. Butterfield usually make critical remarks about government policies in their quarterly newsletter to shareholders which is usually ignored by the politcians or even more cleverly responded to by saying, (as a former Finance Minister did), "That Bermuda is not governed by the Bank of Bermuda's Board of Directors." Had critical statements been made by the 1,000 odd Bermudian staff who vote, the Finance Minister may have taken it more seriously. The last thing democratic politicians want to be seen doing is taking orders from bankers no matter how influential or no matter how right they are. Few votes are won by making speeches from the front door of a bank.

Broadly similar conclusions can be reached by looking at the behaviour of politicians elsewhere in the world. In no developed country in the world has there been organised resistance to high taxation, nationalisations or stupid economic policies. Because businesses do not vote, politicians can safely ignore them and continue about their business which can be, and often is, exercises in economic illiteracy.

Business proposals may have intellectual merit, be in the best interests of the country but they are usually politically irrelevant. Occasionally, political leaders emerge like Presidents Reagan and Bush, or Prime Minister Thatcher who are prepared to act in an economically rational manner but they are rare and usually unpopular - Mr Reagan was an exception to the rule. For example in 1996 the Indian electorate rejected the free-market reforms of Prime Minister Narasimha Rao and elected the nationalist Bharatiya Janata Party (BJP) which sees Western companies like Pepsi-Cola as an affront to Indian values. This will condemn India to repeat its past economic errors and remain a pauper country whilst its fellow Asian countries like Thailand and Malaysia continue to prosper.

Bermuda, like most other countries, has seen the increasing influence of government in the economic process as its share of GDP taken by taxation has grown but this has been matched by a decreasing respect for the economic wisdom of politcial leaders. The main reason for this is that unlike the past when Bermuda was run very much like a business organisation,[2] politicians can no longer pursue policies which they believe are in the best interests of their consituents or Bermuda, but only those policies which are easily understood by the electorate.

Much of the time voters do not really know what is in their best interests. The successful career of a politician and the governing party is very much dependent on a small group of largely uninformed voters. Therefore, instead of convincing voters of the validity of sound economic policies the Bermuda politician tries to find out what the voters believe - which is often nonsense - and they respond by having an economic policy in accordance with the wishes of the electorate. Short term political considerations become paramount and the long term implications are often ignored. Appearance is much more important than reality.

The electorate is consulted in this way not because the politicians believe that they are wise but because they fear them and fear of the electorate is not a sound basis on which to establish economic policy. Opinion polls therefore are a substitute for genuine economic policies and if the public is wrong the policies will be wrong.

For many years, the Bermuda electorate believed that government had a firmer grasp of financial matters than they had - and this was true as witnessed by the tremendous success which Bermuda has enjoyed - but the price for this success was not to continue to exercise this knowledge for the benefit of Bermuda but to succumb to the unenlightened prejudices of the voters.

There is not an easy way out of this dilemma and the last thing Bermuda wants is for financial considerations only to govern its policies. There is more to life than economics which is one reason why the public does not understand or even concern itself with the subject.

One way out of this dilemma is to follow the precedent set elsewhere. Intelligent politicans know that sound economic policies are difficult to understand, cannot be easily sold to the electorate on television and are often unpopular. They therefore join multi-national organisations like the World Trade Organisation, European Union, the North American Free Trade Association and OECD the rules of which compel them to follow sensible economic policies like free trade and limited protectionism. This I suspect is the major reason why Bermuda decided to join OECD whose main purpose is to end protectionist policies.

---

[2] see Part III 1 for comments about Bermuda Inc.

8. WHAT IS CAPITALISM?

"Every individual endeavours to employ his capital so that its produce may be of greatest value. He generally neither intends to promote the public interest, nor knows how much he is promoting it. An individual who intends only his own gain is led by an invisible hand to promote an end which was no part of his intention. Nor is it always the worse for the society that it was no part of it. By pursuing his own interest he frequently promotes that of the society, more effectually than when he really intends to promote it. I have never known much good done by those who affected to trade for the public good."

ADAM SMITH

Capitalism is usually defined as an economic system which stresses the accumulation and use of capital, the profit motive and is based on private and individual enterprise and ownership as it is practised in UK and USA and other Anglo-Saxon financial cultures like Bermuda. Its definition can be made more complicated by speaking about many of its variations in other countries such as industrial capitalism, merchant capitalism, democratic capitalism, monopoly capitalism, popular capitalism, Japanese capitalism, Scandanavian capitalism and a host of other variants.

Capitalism has received a bad press over the years being associated with greed, envy, conspicuous consumption, sometimes corruption, and other base human impulses but it is always associated with the burning desire of the participants to make money, often at the expense of other people. It is frequently regarded as something disreputable, oddly enough mainly in England where it is commonly believed to have originated. Capitalism works much better in practice than in theory (just as socialism works much better in theory than in practice) and I hope to show that this economic system has provided greater happiness and wealth than any other competing system.

Capitalism appeals to logic, to facts and to results - other systems depend on symbols, images, emotions, passions, ideologies, fantasies and conspiracy theories. Capitalism makes the individual accountable; its opposite, Marxism has the advantage of placing the blame for an individual's misfortune entirely on others. Nevertheless, its essential philosophical thrust is the accummulation of more and more money, an ideology which has unfortunately, no sense of value or inspiration around which individuals can rally. Preaching a sermon of consumption does not provide inspiration to the masses, and they need something closer to reality than an invisible hand. To avoid this prejorative label of being something not quite acceptable to polite society, as something which appeals to the basic instincts of people the term capitalism is often avoided and the more euphemistic term the free-enterprise system is used. But they mean the same thing.

Capitalism stresses the importance of private economic decisions, individual initiative and it operates without significant direction from government or by reference to a centralised economic plan. No one determines what should be produced, what the price charged should be or how much of any product should be supplied. Individuals or firms make such decisions for themselves and if they gauge the market accurately, they prosper like Bill Gates and if they get it wrong they pay the penalty like the shareholders of Pan-American Airlines who lost their value of their investment in the company.

Individual consumers are also free to spend their incomes in any way they wish without reference to any central authority hence the snobbish critisism that ordinary people prefer the TV show "The Young and the Restless" to Shakespeare. Consumers seek to maximise the benefit of their income by buying in the cheapest place. Producers seek to maximise their profits by selling at the highest price the market will bear. It is the tension between these two fundamental objectives which drives the dynamo of capitalism.

There are two important consequences which flow from these arrangements:-

1. Freedom is strongly associated with the capitalist system, many economists asserting that there can be no (or only limited) freedom without capitalism and vice versa. The individual is free to pursue what he perceives to be in his best self-interest and in the most quoted statement ever made in economics, repeated above, shows that individuals pursuing their own self-interest also end up by enriching the whole community as well as doing well for themselves. Steps to repress this acqustive instinct leads to coercion by government and produces economically counterproductive policies. This drive to improve economic status leads to the production of goods services required by the community at the lowest cost. This potentially destructive trait of human nature is harnessed for the benefit of all society, an example of private profits producing social gains. In addition, as society becomes more wealthy it becomes more independent of government making its membership more free.

2. Personal responsbility and accountability is attached firmly to the individual or commercial organisation so that mistakes are punished by financial loss and sound decisions are rewarded by high incomes. The market system makes it possible for consumers to instruct producers on what they are prepared to buy, encouraging innovation and imposing a discipline on the incompetent. The net result is that capitalism encourages the development of new products and processes so that the quantity and variety of goods produced exceeds that of any other economic system.

> *"The inherent vice of capitalism is the unequal sharing of blessings; the inherent virtue of socialism is the equal sharing of miseries."*
> WINSTON CHURCHILL

Any economic system is faced with the central dilemma of mankind - making choices. No country or people is rich or productive enough to satisfy all the wants of its population. If more of product X is wanted then less of product Y will be produced unless there is an increase in productivity. Societies can be organised in a way which determines that a central authority will make such important economic decisions or that a political party (like the Communist Party) will determine what and how much is produced and who will get what.

In the capitalist system it is individuals and firms who make such decisions using the price system as a mechanism for determining what is produced, and who will get what. Consumers are free to spend their incomes any way which pleases them, and business competes fiercely for their dollars. As a result capital and labour flows naturally into productive processes which best satisfy the customer.

Price is used as the mechanism for rationing the supply of goods and services. If you have sufficient money you can acquire what you wish; if you have no money you go hungry. This stark choice stimulates the individual to go out and earn an income so that he can provide for his economic needs and those of his dependents. People are on their own and are responsible for their own success or failure without any overall guidance or assistance from any central planner. Competition disposes of the incompetent rewarding those who are efficient at producing goods at the best prices, and utilising savings to invest for the future.

Production rises as a result, pulling up wages with it and everyone prospers. Contrary to what most people believe, capitalism puts the consumer or the public at the centre of process by making him king, and the businessman (or the capitalist) is the servant who is compelled to conform to the wishes of the customer. Capitalism is not a zero sum game in which one group benefits at the expense of another but a productive system which provides benefits to all.

The economic system as described was not always like that. Free enterprise reached its highest level of development in England in the years between 1500 and 1750 as a reaction against the arbitrary and capricious government control of economic life which existed at that time. When people began to increase trade, acquire property, compete, set prices and build businesses they resented and opposed government taxation, regulation and confiscation of their property.[1] This challenge to established authority was a fundamental revolution (although it sounds pretty tame in 1996) in the European world where the average person was thought of as a subject or prisoner of class, caste, religion or state. *"A man who is a merchant can seldom, if ever, please God"* wrote the early church philosopher St. Jerome. A man's position was established not by talent or industry but by his guild, his parents, or his place of birth. Changing, far less challenging, the established social order was as dangerous as it was unthinkable.

If capitalism and revolution against the established order has a birthday most people would declare it to be in the year 1776 when Adam Smith[2] an absent minded Scottish professor of moral theology published "The Wealth of Nations," and Thomas Jefferson wrote the American Declaration of Independence. Smith criticised the existing economic arrangements, called mercantilism a system in which the interests of the public was sacrificed to that of the state and the producer, and defended what came to be called capitalism (he never used the word) on the grounds that it was the most effective system for satisfying the needs of the population.

The Americans and their kindred spirits in Britain and Holland put it into practice. Smith's central ideas of individual freedom to determine prices, con-

---

[1]This trait of human nature has never changed

[2] see Part I, 4

sumers buying where they want at the lowest prices, limited government interference in the economy and personal responsbility are still at the heart of the economic systems of United States, Canada, United Kingdom and Bermuda.

Profits or losses play a pivotal role in the capitalist system as they signal what should or, just as important, should not be produced. If the capitalists judges the market accurately consumers will buy his products and he will be able to make high profits. If he gets it wrong he loses out and runs the risk of being declared bankrupt. The essential and compelling justification for the capitalist system is that the possibility of profit will result in private individuals producing products for which the public are willing to pay, and producing them at the lowest possible cost. However, the profit system will only work if it is clearly identified as a profit and loss system so that when businesses make errors, as they inevitably will, they directly bear the consequences. Should a government bail out an enterprise after losses have been incurred the fundamental justification of the free enterprise system is demolished.

It is the social dynamics between profit and loss, wealth and poverty, competition and self-interest, personal responsiblity and freedom, success and failure which allows capitalism to be superior to other economic systems. No other system has been so successful at delivering a high standard of living to so many people. It has produced more wealth in the 200 or so years since the industrial revolution than man has amassed since time began.

The basic fallacy of alternative economic systems like socialism is the belief that individuals do their best and are at their most productive in collective type arrangements rather than being allowed freely to pursue what they believe to be their own self-interest, and that governments and bureaucrats can run an efficient egalitarian economy. No other system has been attacked so frequently for its failures although capitalism has survived socialist governments, depressions, communist rivalry, OPEC oil shocks, world wars, periods of inflation and radical changes to world economies. It is thought of as being remote, abstract, heartless and impersonal - a system designed for the Rockerfellers which fails to provide for the poor and outcasts of society.

At various times capitalism has been accused of:

- Causing mass unemployment and prolonged depressions.
- Creating inflation.
- Generating stressful change.
- Having an unhealthy emphasis on money and wealth.
- Producing socially undesirable goods such as firearms.
- Failing to produce enough of socially desirable goods and services such as health care, education or assistance to the poor.
- Defending elitism in an egalitarian age.
- Creating large powerful corporations which are beyond the control of government.
- Worshipping commercial success at the expense of cultural activities.

- Rewarding the talented at the expense of those with limitations.
- Alienating the workforce and creating wage slavery.
- Creating an impoverished and disadvantaged under-class.
- Exploiting and dehumanising the workers.
- Creating great inequalities of wealth and influence.
- Causing social divisions between classes and races.
- Failing to take account of external costs like the environment

> *"Capitalism is a social order favourable to alertness, inventiveness, discovery and creativity. This means a social order based upon education, research, the freedom to create, and the right to enjoy the fruit's of one's own creativity."*
>
> MICHAEL NOVAK 1956.

These are substantial criticisms but capitalism, unlike socialism or communism, has never pretended that it would create utopia in this world but the many severe criticisms listed above has often put the system on the defensive.

Many foreign economies are converting to capitalism or reforming their economic philodophy but are experiencing difficult times. Mexico went into a tail-spin in 1995 when the Peso was devalued following a liberalisation of the economy. Many voters in the former USSR favour a return of the Communists. The status quo of poverty is ofter preferable to the distant prospect of wealth.

The capitalist system described above would be remarkable enough but there are three additional characteristics which make it even more remarkable.

Firstly, the links between freedom and capitalism are well established and this is evidenced from the practices of many countries across the globe. Many writers[3] have gone further and argued there is a moral dimension to capitalism. The argument is that the economic world does not fall neatly into two categories, the planned (with its implications of order, purpose and direction) or unplanned (with its implications of disorder, irrationality and greed) but that market economies belong to a third group - that of spontaneous creation and order which was brought into being unintentionally by individuals who implicitly understand the rules because it brings benefits to all members.

The market economy because of the benefits its confers has, like law and language, the implicit trust and support of individuals in much the same as when people speak they follow the rules of grammar. They may not know why they support the system, or how it works or even be able to explain it, but they recognise that freely exchanging products in the market is to their benefit.

This spontaneous creation by people results in a society which has a higher morality than one in which everyone has to fend for himself. Within small groups of humans economic co-operation is the natural method of human interaction. As

---

[3] Robert Novak, Friedrich Hayek, and Milton Friedman for example.

economies and societies develop and become more complex and bigger small group charactertistics such as loyalty, trust and charity do not work to the same extent and the advantages of the market system become dependent on the signals received through the price mechanism.

Secondly, the market system is able to coordinate the billions and billions of economic decisions made daily by people in their everyday life. It signals to the market that effort should be made to produce more of certain goods, and at the same time where supplies of a product exceed demand, it signals that less should be produced. It is the most efficient way of transmitting information to the producers of goods and services from those who wish to buy. These signals provide informtion about how to use resources in the most productive way. No central planning authority is required, indeed no central planning authority would be able to understand and interpret the signals from the market place, and no computer no matter how large or sophisticated could perform this function. The market is a form of discovery, a process which is extremely complicated in a modern economy as immense quantities of information about essential market intelligence concerning consumer incomes, costs of production, innovations, the creation of new products, new knowledge, original ideas, methods of production and the relationship between these variables needs to be processed and understood. This task is simply beyond any human intelligence.

Hence it follows that the market system is the most efficient mechanisim available for determining how an economy should work, because it originated within society without direct human design and it cannot be replaced by human design except at the risk of individuals losing their freedom to the central planning mechanism like the state. A planned economy is limited in scope to what the minds of the planners can understand and no human organisation can remotely understand the billions and billions of decisions which are made every day in an economy which is now international in scope. The unbelievable complexity of the market is a warning signal to those who would attempt to redesign it believing that human intervention would yield a superior result. It is nonsense to believe that the human mind is able to interpret and understand all the information flowing from market.

Thirdly, capitalism is unpredictable, disquieting and unruly, a system which is in constant flux rather than one which settles into a comfortable equilibrium. Those whose memories go back 30 years can remember a time when there were no video recorders, surround-sound stereos and airconditioning in cars. History books tell us that at the turn of the century there was no television, aircraft and antibiotics. In 30 years time our children and grandchildren will regard 1996 as the "olden days" in much the same way as we regard 1966 or 1906.

The adaptation to change is a major contributory factor in the successful longevity of capitalism although at the time change first makes itself known it can be disquieting to many and painful to those who are adversely affected. It is a major task of government to protect those directly affected without attempting to bring the change process to a halt. Progess and change have been described by Joseph Schumpeter as a process of "creative destruction."

34

Most people are ambivalent about the wrenching consequences which occur during a period of rapid economic change such as the one we are living through. Newspapers contain stories about firms reorganising or being forced out of business because they are no longer competitive. Blame is attached to investors such as pension funds, management or owners but rarely to consumers whose changes in buying habits have altered over the years. Managers (and capitalists) are the agent of change, the real changes are being forced on business because customers have altered their behaviour. It does not help when agents of change are not particularly attractive or senstive people as they become easy targets for the wrath of those adversely affected by business reorganisation.

Since 1979 about a third of jobs in the United States have been affected by corporate downsizing[4] and this drives a wedge between business and the public and employees. Who are the bad guys; the managers? The landlords? The board of directors? Or is it the customer who no longer is prepared to pay the price, or perhaps does not want the product? But the ultimate issue is not that of job losses arising from changes in demand but that of job growth. This brings us back again to Schumpeter's process of "creative destruction." It is only when businesses decline that other firms are able to grow and expand so that the economy can transform itself and thrive.

The fact is that there is no real alternative economic system to capitalism which works or which has any degree of credibility with the public that it will deliver both prosperity and freedom. Winston Churchill used to say of democracy that it was the worst form of government except for all the others. The same is true of capitalism; despite its many flaws it beats all the other economic systems many of which have been attempted and all of which have failed the acid test of producing what the consumer wants. The reality is that there is no real alternative to capitalism which can credibly deliver prosperity and freedom.

9. IS BERMUDA A CAPITALIST SOCIETY?

"The forces of a capitalist society, if left unchecked, tend to make the rich richer and the poor poorer."

JAWAHARLAL NEHRU, FIRST PRIME MINISTER OF INDIA

Asking whether Bermuda is a capitalist society is like asking if Karl Marx was a socialist or if the Pope is a Catholic. The answer is an unequivocal yes. However, capitalism is not a system with a check list to determine its pedigree or measure its ideological purity but one which is flexible and adapts itself to the social environment in which it operates in order to meet local sensibilities and philosophies. For example, in Japan private enterprise is characterised by cartels (groups of producers who set prices and levels of production) and is subject to government administrative guidance so that it is often difficult to say where private enterprise ends and big government begins. Capitalism in Scandinavia differs from capitalism in other West European countries which in turns differs from

---

4 See Part II 20 for a duscussion of this point

the capitalism practised in the United States which in turn differs from what is done in Bermuda. How then does Bermuda deviate from capitalism as practised elsewhere?

Firstly, it may be useful to summarise the salient features of capitalism :

- Talent and hard work are rewarded;
- There is limited central economic planning;
- The opportunity to make profits and the fear of making losses are its two main engines;
- Individualism;
- Freedom of the consumer to buy where he wants;
- Competition between producers and suppliers;
- Personal responsibility;
- Self-interest;
- Innovation and the introduction of new products;
- Savings and investment;
- Limited government intervention in the economy;
- Prices are a co-ordinating and discovery process;
- Morally superior to other economic systems;
- Ability to constantly change and adapt;
- Its record speaks for itself.

The reader should be able to tick the factors which apply to Bermuda and those which do not. Let me mention three of the most important capitalistic features which apply to Bermuda.

1. The absence of income tax enhances the process whereby talent and hard work are rewarded. Income earned by the individual can be retained without government, or anyone else, taking a large percentage of it.

2. The opportunity to earn profits is what drives firms and individuals to succeed although they are not always successful[1], and it is a measure of their success.

3. Personal responsibility is underscored by the fact that there is no formal welfare system in place similar to that which is found in Europe and North America.

However, let me mention three areas where Bermuda is considered to be not acting in conformity with capitalist principles.

1. Bermuda businesses are frequently criticised by its failure to provide equal opportunities to the majority black population and to females as the present system is alleged to favour white males. Those who make such allegations imply that firms do not maximise profits as they employ white males who are less efficient than black males or females. In short, their behaviour is irrational because they are acting against their own best finan-

---

[1] See Part II on the lack of profitability of the hotel industry and the retail industry.

cial interests. Opponents of this view argue that this is unlikely behaviour as banks and other commercial institutions wish to employ only those individuals who are the most productive, namely those who would create greater incomes or minimise local costs. Oddly enough it is those on the political left - the major critics of capitalism - who argue that government intervention is necessary to resolve the problem rather than insisting that private organisations conform more to capitalist principles. For if business organisations single-mindedly pursue profits - a major objective of capitalism - they would not wish to employ those who are less productive. Those who believe that commercial institutions do not provide equality of opportunity should, as a matter of logic, support measures which enhance competition and promote capitalism. It is one of the mysteries of economics that the opposite tends to be the case.

2. Bermuda still retains many elements of mercantilism, that economic system which gives monopolistic or favoured status to a small clique which depends on the government and the bureaucracy, or on which the government itself is dependent. This is a throwback to the era in which the Crown gave a charter to a group of entrepreneurs whereby they could exploit a commercial opportunity. Bermuda itself was established by means of such a Royal Charter. The McDonald's issue[2] (in which a former Premier of Bermuda sought to exploit a loophole in the government policy of no fast food franchises in Bermuda by cashing in political favours granted in the past) is a case in point. Should government be in a position in which it can reward its supporters with commercial privileges at the expense of the taxpayer. Success for the favoured few in such circumstances is not dependent on resourcefulness, innovation and hard work but is dependent on exercising influence with members of government and the bureaucracy.

3. Bermudians do not have free access to the broad range of commercial products and organisations common to other countries such as large department stores unless they are able to travel abroad. Nor can Bermudian employers employ foreigners without permission from the Department of Immigration. Such 'protections' tend to favour the politically influential and are not determined as they would be in a capitalism system by such things as price, quality or service. It is often argued, with some merit, that such protections are beneficial to the country at large but the point is that their existence deviates from the capitalist model which has served other parts of the world so well.

These are merely quibbles. Capitalism is alive and well in Bermuda. If it was not, the standard of living of every Bermudian would rapidly fall.

---

[2] See Part III 4.

10. WHAT IS THE IMPORTANCE OF PROFITS TO THE EFFICIENT WORKING OF THE ECONOMIC SYSTEM?

"You're in business for one thing - to make money. If you have another agenda join Rotary International."

ALBERT DUNLAP

"The worst crime against working people is a company which fails to operate at a profit."

SAMUEL GOMPERS

Bermuda is not unlike many other places in the world with regard to the way in which the general public views the subject of business profits. A typical view by the public of Bermudian companies is that whilst they may deliver goods and services with reasonable competence they are a major source of social injustice. Women and blacks are excluded from their boards of directors, from executive management and rarely feature in the register of shareholders. Profits are the fruits of exploitation of the labour force and are too high. Driven by a narrow consideration of extracting as much money as possible from the public (ripping them off is the most common term of abuse), companies despoil the environment, sell hazardous products like cigarettes, fail to install sound safety practices and when times are bad lay off workers who have given years of loyal and faithfull service.

In order to correct the situation there are any number of proposals just waiting to be dusted off to make sure that business organisations become "socially responsible" an elastic term which means all things to all men.

The objections to profits arises from the proposition, loved by socialists, that "production should be for people not for profit at the expense of others." But it is this desire for profit which makes it possible in the first place for production to take place. Producers and businessmen are not concerned with the needs of known people - the person who produces the wood used in Bermuda houses has no idea it will be used in Bermuda and if he did he would probably have no idea of where Bermuda was - but with the ability to balance costs and revenues in order to make an income or profit. Critics of the profit system may have never learned the lesson of generating income and profits which businessmen have to learn every day, or they may never have understood it (a common criticism of civil servants) or, more charitably they have forgotten it.

The high minded socialist slogan mentioned above has been used by intellectuals ranging from Aristotle, to Albert Einstein to Ottiwell Simmons. F.A. Hayek dismisses this fundamental misunderstanding in a delightful passage which I quote in full *"It is hence hard to believe that anyone accurately informed about the market can honestly condemn the search for profit. The disdain of profits is due to ignorance, and to an attitude that we may if we wish admire in the ascetic who has chosen to be content with a small share of the riches of this world, but which, when actualised in the form of restrictions on profits of others, is selfish to the extent that it imposes asceticism, and indeed deprivations of all sorts, on others."*[1]

---

[1] "The Fatal Conceit," page 105.

Probably the most effective debater of those who support the view given above is Professor Milton Friedman who in uncompromising terms argues that *"There is only one social responsibility of business - to use its resources and engage in activities designed to increase its profits provided it is open and free competition without deception and fraud."*

It is the business of business to make as much profit as possible and to divert attention from that objective puts at risk the most important function of business which is to put people and resources to work at maximum efficiency. If a company is responsive to shareholders it will tend to have the best management and the best products. Anyone with a connection to the company will do well - employees, suppliers and the community at large. It is as simple as that.

In the capitalist societies of which Bermuda is a part, profits are central to the whole system without them companies would go out of business and society would atrophy. In many ways we are seeing the consequences of firms which fail to make adequate profits. The Bermudiana Hotel closed some years ago and is an eyesore in Hamilton. Archie Brown, a long established retailer went into liquidation in 1996 with the loss of several jobs. The most certain way of earning high profits is to produce the goods and services consumers want and are willing to pay for. Profits are the main evidence of performance and are the foundation for a business organisation's reputation and it sends out a strong signal of corporate efficiency and value.

Ironically, those who are good at satisfying the consumer are often intensely disliked mainly because they make money or profits. The owners of businesses, or entrepreneurs, provide three key inputs to make their profits:

1. They are prepared to delay their own consumption. Instead of spending all their money on goods and services, they delay their own personal gratification and save and invest in activities which will produce future profits.

2. Profits contain a premium or return to those who are prepared to take a risk. Investments are not guaranteed and many make losses which means that the entrepreneur loses his investment - a common occurrence in Bermuda and during the past five years a more common occurrence than it once was. Those who are prepared to accept greater risks will, all other things being equal, earn higher profits than those who invest conservatively.

3. People who own and run businesses tend to be energetic, enterprising and have the ability to organise. As a result their talents are rewarded because they are able to bring to the market a "better mousetrap" than their competitors.

Profits may also arise from monopoly power or limited competition. However, they tend to be only a very small part of total profits because there is always a substitute for any product on the market. Market imperfections - usually lack of knowledge or sophistication on the part of the customer - can also generate additional profits but again these are only a small proportion of total profits.

Profits are paid out to the owners of businesses in the form of dividends.[2] Everyone who is a member of a pension fund or who owns a life insurance policy is as much an investor as someone who owns a business directly or who is an owner of shares in a quoted company. These dividends form part of the income of the individuals, especially to those who are retired on pension, and form part of the spending process which generates jobs and wealth. Those who dislike profits are often those who spend enormous amounts of time and energy arguing over how the income of society should be distributed or redistributed. Politics and the legal system are immense arenas for playing games about the distribution of income. The arguments become so heated and intemperate that at the end of the day there is contempt for the wealth creating parts of society.[3] Those who are engaged in the arguing do not add to the common wealth and do not create jobs and opportunities.

There has been no recent example of societies being able to organise themselves in an economically efficient way without harnessing or using the profit motive as an essential component of the financial system. The disastrous communist experiment of the last 80 years is probably the best example of an attempt to ignore the profit motive but that ended in spectacular collapse. Without that incentive the economic system just does not work efficiently.

Business organisations in Bermuda, as well as elsewhere, are increasingly under attack because they allegedly lack responsibility to society in general. On the one hand, they are criticised because they do not "donate" sufficient profits to charity, do not support the arts, they are unwilling to disclose more information to the public about their activities, are involved with the arms industry, or as was the case some years ago traded directly or indirectly with South Africa (Iraq is now the country favoured by international boycott). Because of the deficiencies in the Department of Education businesses are often asked to provide remedial education, or day-care centres for children or to adopt a school. Corporate charity and support of the arts amounts to corporate executives giving away other people's (shareholders) money and investors are not invited to social parties but have to pick up the tab.

In a sense such criticisms or additional tasks are a fundamental misunderstanding of how the economy works. The opposite view to that given in the previous paragraph is that the proper social role of the corporation is produce the best product it can, be that peanut butter, mousetraps or shoes, at the lowest price leaving it to individuals and governments to determine how much we spend on charities and the arts. Business organisations should stick to business and not attempt to become all-embracing social service agencies for which they are not particularly well qualified or well suited.

The role of profits is not quite as simple as I make it out to be. The fact is that each individual is a bundle of competing interests. We want high profits as shareholders because that results in high dividends, but we also want good schools, arts festivals, sporting events like the XL tennis classic and a just society. Maximising value for shareholders can be consistent with these things and is in fact a good

---

[2] Small businessmen are often unable to distinguish between their wages and profits for it is difficult to disentangle these two streams of income. Corporations are another matter.

[3] Some argue that Bermuda has reached that stage when a disproportionate amount of the tax burden is levied on the retail and hotel industries whose profits are minimal at best.

example of enlightened self-interest. Most of us do not try to squeeze the last penny out of life in our daily transactions and we try to bring balance to our economic lives just as we try to bring balance to other aspects of our lives.

Organisations while still highly focussed on making profits - which is the main reason for their existence - recognise that the longer term interests of business require a vision which goes some way beyond short term competitive or economic advantage. Examples abound of corporate social responsibility which are not necessarily motivated by the objective of making profits are large as possible. Employees prefer working for socially responsible companies like Levis, Starbucks and IBM. They are successful companies and they are socially responsible.

Finally, in organisations which enjoy steady and rising profits over the long term the benefits do not wholly accrue to the owners or shareholders. The employees and their families benefit from salaries and benefits paid, governments receive taxation to support public services, and suppliers are able to sell their goods and employ people. But most of all society and the community benefits for consumers and customers get an increasingly wide range of products and services which their parents and grandparents could never have imagined. Saran wrap, frozen food, airconditioning, on-line banking, home computers, compact-disc players and a host of products too numerous to mention.

Only critics living in countries which enjoy high incomes and those who are highly educated see the outcome of consumer choice, and new and improved products as being socially irresponsible.

11. IS THE MODERN ECONOMY INCOMPATIBLE WITH CONCERN FOR THE ENVIRONMENT?

"The penultimate Western man, stalled in the ultimate traffic jam and slowly succumbing to carbon monoxide, will not be cheered to hear from the last survivor that the gross national product went up by a record amount."

JOHN KENNETH GALBRAITH

"Further growth (in Bermuda) can only be achieved at the expense of the environment and the quality of life, and the costs of economic growth must be weighed carefully against the benefits. Bermudians in their quest to better themselves need to be careful not to kill the goose that laid the golden egg."

NICHOLAS WEINREB, FORMER GOVERNMENT ECONOMIC ADVISER

Do you, the reader, like clear blue seas, clean fresh air, cuddly animals like seals or Koala bears, trees and green fields? Do you also like many of the modern marvels of the twentieth-century economy such as airconditioning, colour television, antibiotics when you are ill, motor vehicles, foreign vacations, and a host of other modern products and services too numerous to mention? In addition, would you like the rest of the world, about 70 to 80 percent of the population, to enjoy these things and, additionally, for this large majority to avoid hunger, disease and a short life span? Asking these questions is a lot like asking if you are in favour of world peace, the end to terrorist bombs and to beautiful things. I would be surprised if 99 percent do not answer yes to all three questions. The relevant policy question is how to go about achieving all of these things which means being able to have a productive economy and at the same time being able to protect our environment. The challenge is to advance environmental reform whilst continuing to enjoy the fruits of a productive economy.

Concern for the environment by the public in Bermuda is widespread, almost an obsession with some, and rightly so because the main product Bermuda sells to the rest of the world is its beauty, unique style of life and its natural setting in the Mid-Atlantic Ocean. For example, motor vehicles were prohibited until 1947 mainly because of the fear, well-founded as it turned out, that they would destroy the character and appeal of Bermuda's environment. Even when motor vehicles were permitted, a speed limit of 20 miles per hour was imposed. Indeed, Bermuda has always had an enlightened approach to the environment long before the word became fashionable and before conservationist policies were chic.

The term "environment" is used to include a series of widely different issues. For the public it is a feeling or belief of a threat from risks which are outside their immediate control and experience, or where previously unsuspected, and where the degree of exposure to risk and danger is insidious or relatively unknown. The general public believes that much pollution could be avoided if businesses gave the issue more attention, greater priority and spent more money on it. Society is looking for a risk free world, where some whipping boy can be blamed for its problems.

The issue of preservation of the environment only became an issue after the publication in 1962 of the book "The Silent Spring" by Rachael Carson. Until then only exceptional and enlightened societies like Bermuda pursued policies which placed the environment high on the agenda of economic and social policy. Most people now understand the close connection between caring for the environment and Bermuda's continuing prosperity, although a significant minority treat Bermuda's public places with little or no concern for the damage done or for the economic consequences of their actions. Examples of environmentally damaging behaviour in Bermuda would include:

- throwing bottles and cans out of motor vehicles into the sea.
- speeding, reckless and dangerous driving making it difficult for the public to walk safely on roads.
- littering in public places.
- using stereos and other amplifying equipment without regard to others.
- failing to dispose of used engine oil after servicing motor vehicles.
- dumping garbage by the side of the road.

Many of the above examples are minor breaches of law but such laws often go unobserved. Government itself often fails to observe environmental good sense by :

- failing to maintain diesel burning government buses.

- taxing aviation fuel so that airlines ferry fuel from the United States mainland and elsewhere thus adding to overall atmospheric pollution.
- failing to enforce environmental rules and regulations.

The concern of Bermudians for the environment is a part of the much larger global question, namely that the future of the entire international economic system is highly dependent on advanced and developing countries balancing their use of natural resources such as energy, use of the seas and quality of the air in a way which continues to allow for economic growth. Failure to secure a proper balance between development and growth on the one hand and proper use of the environment on the other is one of the central economic dilemmas facing mankind at present.

For example, if population growth continues at its present rate in the developing world, or if the developing world had a level of consumption equal to that of Europe or North America, the physical environment would be overwhelmed. In some scenarios, this could lead to famine, war, chronic shortages of key resources and destruction of the physical environment. The one-fifth of the world's population which lives in the rich world (which includes Bermuda) are estimated to cause about 80 percent of global pollution and useage of natural resources.

The environment and the economy are integrated parts of our future world and are dependent on each other. Abusing the environment does not make good economic sense. At the same time, the creation of wealth makes it possible to protect the environment whilst allowing human beings an existence above that of subsistence.

MAJOR ENVIRONMENTAL ACCIDENTS

Year	Location	Type	Damage	Deaths
1978	English Channel	Oil Spill	223,000 tons of oil	-
1981	Tennessee	Nuclear Accident	100,000 gallons of radioactive fuel leaked	-
1984	Mexico City	Gas Plant Explosion	-	334
1984	Bhopal, India	Chemical Plant Explosion	-	3,849
1986	Cherynobyl, Ukraine	Nuclear Power	135,000 people evacuated	31
1989	Alaska	Oil Spill	Widespread Coastal Damage	-

Facing up to the challenges of the environment is one which the capitalist system has not been particularly good at, although many of the manufacturing processes have reduced the inputs of raw materials and energy per unit of output whilst at the same time minimising the poisons emitted into the atmosphere. Whilst the record of the West has not been particularly good until recently it is infinitely better than that of the old Communist regimes whose record is aptly summed up by the witticism that there are no conservatives in Poland because there is nothing worth conserving there. The evidence suggests that centralised planning, inefficiency, poverty and pollution run together. The command economics of communism which collapsed in 1989 were remarkable for their lack of concern for the customer and by their contempt for the environment.

In addition, the central planning by socialist regimes led not only to inefficiencies and poverty but to environmental degradation. In the odd way such societies operate, they fail to benefit from the fruits of an industrial society but multiply the environmental problems arising from an industrial economy. For example:

- The Amur tiger which once lived all over the former USSR is now confined to Premorski province near the Pacific Chinese border.
- The Yenisey River near the Arctic is polluted by plutonium from three upstream nuclear reactors whose wastes have been dumped indiscriminately since the 1950s.
- A group of smelters in Nonlsk, in Siberia, pump 2 million tons of sulfur into the atmosphere.

The main reason for such catastrophes is that no one in government cared. Provided bureaucratic targets were achieved, there were no organised groups to protest and customers were unable to bring any sanctions to bear on the polluters. As the former President Reagan has pointed out on several occasions, government is the problem, not the solution.

Increasing populations, particularly in Africa and Asia, coupled with economic development in Asia is putting our natural environment under great stress. The population of developing countries is five times that of the developed world, and is growing at a rate four times faster. There is a huge desire on the part of the people of the developing world to improve their living standards as they can see through TV and other media the huge gap between the West and themselves. It is simply not possible for those of us in the West to say that because of potential environmental damage they cannot have a life like that of ours. The drawbridge cannot be drawn up now that we in the Western world are safely across the moat.

In pursuing economic self-interest, people, consumers and business does not have much incentive to maintain the quality of the environment because they do not directly benefit from its preservation. Misuse of water resources does not cost the person who misuses them anything hence the tendency for some people to throw old bottles and cans into the sea to get rid of them. If a commercial organisation discharges its wastes into the sea - say a hotel discharging its sewage - there is no cost to the hotel but potential damage to the fish which live in the ocean and danger to the health of those whom swim in the area. By spending money to prevent this pollution the hotel would incur a penalty by increasing its costs (or reducing its profits) but the public advantage is that it would save the fish and not pollute the ocean.

In this simple example is demonstrated the distinction between private costs and what are known as spillover costs or externalities. Our fictitious hotel can treat the ocean as a free dumping-ground but the public pay the cost because they may have to pay a higher price for their fish and they suffer from pollution of the ocean. The modern market economy as presently constituted in Bermuda and the rest of the world is a weak mechanism for the prevention of pollution because costs and benefits are not shared by the same person. The hotel is only concerned with the costs of disposal, not with the spillover effects that arise to the community. The community is concerned with the state of the ocean and is indifferent to the profitability of the hotel industry. The full costs to Bermuda are not reflected in the costs incurred by the hotel.

Preservation of the environment can be a huge cost as Bermudians are about to find out. In 1996, the Bermuda Government proposed to dump several containers of asbestos at sea, a process which was initially considered to be environmentally harmless. Protests from environmental groups, including the world-famous Greenpeace, has resulted in a decision to ship the containers to UK at a cost of around $5 million (about $100 per resident), plus the potential liability of claimants who may be harmed by the disposal.

Failure of Bermudians to care adequately for the environment could easily result in a large diminution in our tourist business which could spell economic trouble. This is one reason why any proposal to change the physical environment is quickly and rightly scrutinised by any number of interest groups such as the National Trust one of whose main objectives is to preserve the physical, cultural and architectural heritage of Bermuda. To many dedicated environmentalists the rapid growth of the economy results in increasing pollution, noise and general disturbance to the established order and way of doing things. Economic growth in the opinion of many is simply not desirable because of the adverse impact on our environment and quality of life. For many environmentalists the best way to preserve our heritage is to oppose what businessmen regard as economic progress because such growth results in additional cars, construction, destruction of old buildings, more people, more garbage, more noise and so on. Full costs are not always taken into consideration when growth arises in tourism and international business.

The modern economic system has five major ways of attempting to control the adverse consequences of the pollution :

1. Redefining property rights.
2. Imposing direct regulations.
3. Imposing fees on those who pollute.
4. Selling pollution rights.
5. Subsidising through the tax system those who spend money to reduce pollution.

It is difficult to determine what is the most effective way to control pollution although Bermuda has mainly opted for solutions 1 and 2. Direct regulation has the disadvantage of being relatively inflexible and the challenge of finding the best combination of the above five policies is one with which the Bermuda government continues to grapple.

To tackle today's daunting environmental challenges three steps must be taken :

1. An effective dialogue is essential between government and business so that measures are enacted from a shared understanding of the costs and benefits.

2. Government has to create a legislative framework which liberates, rather than curtails, commercial drive and innovation.

3. Business has to accept a responsibility to tackle environmental challenges with vigour - seeing them as opportunities to improve the community rather than threats to their profitability.

In addition, it should be noted that Bermuda may have only limited control over its environment. For example, if there was a major oil spill miles out at sea it would be impossible for the Bermuda authorities to contain the spill and the tourist economy could be wrecked. Bermuda has had many brushes with environmental disaster as the following chart demonstrates:

SOME RECENT BERMUDA MARINE INCIDENTS			
Year	**Name of Vessel**	**Size in Tons**	**Cargo**
1978	MARIE BOEING	15,000	General
1983	TIFOSO	132,000	Ballast
1986	AGUILA AZTECA	230,000	196,000 tons of Mexican Crude oil
1986	SEALUCK	42,000	Grain
1991	4 near misses (2 of which were large oil tankers)		
1992	NORDIC PRINCE	38,000	Cruise Ship 500 gallons oil spill

For example, had the "Aguila Azteca" broken up in 1986 Bermuda could have had to deal with an oil spill of 230,000 tons (almost the same size as the Amoco Cadez disaster in Britanny, France which closed the beaches there for more than a year and ruined its tourist trade) which would have been, for Bermuda, an environmental and economic disaster of unparalleled proportions.

Two or three hundred years ago Bermuda was a very different place to what it is now - this statement would also be true of almost every other country in the world. Pollution in its existing form hardly existed, there were no motor vehicles requiring modern roads and other support systems, the sea and the land were in pristine condition. Unfortunately, the population of Bermuda lived by comparison with that of today a miserable existence. Medical science was in its infancy, there was no electricity, no airconditioning, travel for the poor was mainly by boat or by foot, for the rich by horse and carriage - horses creating their own pollution, working conditions were dangerous, and life expectancy was short.

As Bermuda modernised, particularly during the twentieth century the physical environment could no longer be regarded as something people took for granted. Open spaces disappeared as improved housing needs were met, the Pembroke Dump became a ghastly eyesore, smoke from spontaneous combustion at the Dump made life a misery for those who lived around it, noise from motor vehicles and radios changed peaceful areas into places of stress. Internationally, rivers were turned into running sewers, ocean pollution from oil and other noxious products became commonplace, the increasing use of fossil fuels (coal and oil) for energy led to air pollution, and the ground water was contaminated. As scientific knowledge increased the public became aware of the climatic effects of using fossil fuels in an indiscriminate way, the impact of agricultural and other chemicals on causing cancer, the destruction of the ozone layer and a host of other environmental problems. Such problems became matters of intense political and public debate particularly when public communications were revolutionised by television, telecommunications and now the Internet. In the global society there are few environmental secrets and public debates rage on a huge variety of environmental issues. There is usually one major culprit - the growth of the economy and the way it has transformed our physical environment. So great has this villain become that many public figures such as Barry Commoner, and many public interest groups support the idea of stopping economic change.

Modern communications have resulted in serious and highly complex issues being reduced to emotional sound bytes accompanied by dramatic television pictures of such things as sea birds being covered in oil or children suffering the effects of some new chemical product. Reasoned argument is often replaced by violent protests covered by the media, confrontation with governments and the police and often misinformation by extremist organisations who would like the world to revert to what it was a hundred or more years ago and to end the constant economic progress which has characterised the Western world since 1945. Single-minded environmentalists tend to portray decisions about the environment as issues of good versus evil, not as trade-offs between competing economic values, the major one of which is continued economic growth. Too often they part company with realism in the name of idealism. They would also prevent many poorer people in Asia, South America and Africa from being able to enjoy the standard of living which the Bermuda population now takes for granted. Science and technology is moving far too quickly for many people. The fear of the unknown is leading to many mistrusting businesses and governments and ignoring the huge progress which has been made during the past century and which many others in the world would like to share.

Capitalism and industrialisation which has caused much pollution and spoiling of the environment has also produced unprecedented wealth and improved living standards to much of the world and has improved the quality of the lives of millions of ordinary people beyond recognition of what it was and made them much more enriching, healthier and longer. The prosperity we all enjoy in the Western World has removed the greatest and most lethal form of pollution known to man, that of poverty. The virtual ending of poverty in the West, and in Bermuda, has been made possible because of the economic growth which results from business being able to participate in the free market system and operating within democratic government policies and legislation. As business and industry has improved living standards it has also improved methods of reducing environmental impact.

A thriving economy uses the environment as a resource which must be renewed like knowledge and will protect it because its ability to create the level of wealth which permits that protection to take place. Societies need to strike the right balance between economic growth and environmental protection which is not an easy job as it involves several hard choices. Just as knowledge is at the centre of economic power and influence, and the wealth creating process so it is at the centre of environmental improvements. A small example of this is that the California South Coast Air Quality Management District Agency has shown that a single motorised lawn mower used for 20 hours a year creates as much air pollution as a new car driven 20,000 miles.

Despite much evidence to show that the economic system is capable of reducing environmental pollution and in many cases is doing so very effectively - the pollution of the environment in North America and Western Europe is considerably less than what is found in the underdeveloped parts of the world such as India - many environmentally conscious people find themselves alienated from the economic process and from improvements in science and technology. They jump to the conclusion that technology, business, governments, consumerism and the high standard of living enjoyed in the West has failed and they frequently turn to quack remedies in their search for a simple answer to complex questions.

The consumer who is empowered to make his wishes known through the market has proved to be the best guarantor against pollution. Poor societies with low regard for the customer do most environmental damage as a stroll through many third world cities will attest. Many enthusiastic environmentalists continue to depict decisions about the environment as questions of good versus evil, not as economic trade-offs involving competing values, one of which is economic development and increased efficiency. Dogmatic environmentalists, like fascism, appeal to the frustrations of the so-called intellectual middle-class who love to tell lesser mortals how to conduct their lives. Enthusiasts are never more dangerous than when they are self-righteous. It is this alienation which is the driving force behind many fringe environmental groups. Such groups are frequently not interested in complicated solutions to difficult problems but in quick fixes such as ending the quest for improved living standards and an improved quality of life for the underprivileged. They no longer trust those in authority be it governments, the police, or business. Emotions, skepticism, feelings, passions, fears, irrational beliefs, quick fixes, knee-jerk reactions, misinformation, a point blank refusal to face facts, are only some of the factors which govern the environmental debate today.

Economics which is highly or wholly dependent on rational analysis, facts and evidence is often at a disadvantage when dealing with people's feelings on matters about which they feel strongly. As the world becomes the global village financial and business organisations are being confronted with people whose idea of reality is very different. The human tendency is to seek magical solutions, a silver bullet or a superman when confronted with economic dilemmas. It then becomes even more essential for rational discussion based on facts and a sense of proportion to take place.

Bermuda has handled its physical environment very well and over many years. As far as I know, Bermuda is the only country in the world to prohibit ownership of more than one private car per household, banned fishpots, has put a prohibition on such environmentally hostile things as neon signs, billboards and fast food[1] and has an ethos which continues to preserve the natural beauty of the Island. These are major achievements all of which have been applied within the modern free-enterprise system proving that the existence of a modern economy is compatible with concern for the environment.

12. IS BERMUDA WEALTHIER THAN MOST OTHER COUNTRIES?

"In every well-governed state wealth is a sacred thing ; in democracies it is the ONLY sacred thing."

ANATOLE FRANCE

"Wealth may be an excellent thing, for it means power, it means leisure, it means liberty."

JAMES RUSSELL LOWELL

The following table compares the GDP per capita income[1*] and other quality of life measures of several disparate countries and shows that Bermuda is very much ahead of the pack. The Human Development Index is a particular interesting index as it combines two other key measures of human welfare, literacy and life expectancy, with the crude per capita GDP in order to give a better picture of human development.

As the table shows Bermuda ranks just ahead of the both the United States and France both of which rank very highly by comparison with other countries, and is clearly ahead of countries like Ghana and Indonesia which is not surprising given the miserable living conditions experienced by the average person in these two nations.

---

[1] Except perhaps for McDonalds

[1*] See Part I 15 for a fuller discussion of this term.

COUNTRY	GDP PER CAPITA US$	PPP (USA=100)	LIFE EXPECTANCY		LITERACY %	HUMAN DEVELOPMENT INDEX
BERMUDA	26,600	not applicable	Men	70	99	93
			Women	78		
USA	24,753	100	Men	73	99	92.5
			Women	80		
FRANCE	22,363	83	Men	74	99	92.7
			Women	81		
TURKEY	2,125	22	Men	66	81.9	73.9
			Women	71		
JAMAICA	1,500	N/A	Men	72	98	74.9
			Women	77		
INDONESIA	732	12	Men	63	84.4	under
			Women	67		66.6
BRAZIL	3,018	24	Men	66	82.1	76
			Women	70		
INDIA	292	5	Men	63	49.8	under
			Women	63		66.6
GHANA	410	N/A	Men	54	60	66.6
			Women	58		
KENYA	266	6	Men	53	70.5	under
			Women	55		66.6

Purchasing power parity (PPP) takes into consideration the cost of living and what money can buy in different countries with the United States being the base of 100. The PPP statistic adjusts for living costs and other financial differences between countries by replacing market foreign exchange rates with a rate equal to the cost of a widely purchased common basket of goods and services. After adjusting for cost of living and exchange rates Turks on average have only 22 percent of the purchasing power of Americans. There are no comparable statistics for Bermuda but my guess (and it is no more than that) is that the average Bermudian because the cost of living is so much higher here has about 95 percent of the purchasing power of his friends in the United States. As an aside I doubt the accuracy of the life expectancy figures for Bermuda.

How much wealthier Bermuda is compared with others depends on what country you are comparing Bermuda with. The table above gives a wide range of the per capita incomes in countries as diverse as USA, France, Turkey, Jamaica, Indonesia, Brazil, India, Ghana and Kenya. [2]

According to the World Development Report for 1994, the real income of someone living in India was about one-twentieth that of someone living in the United States (or Bermuda) . Put another way, the poorest 20 percent of the world's population had an income of only 1.4 percent of global income, down

---
[2] Derived from "The Economist" World in Figures , 1996 edition.

from 2.3 percent in the past 30 years, whilst the share of the world's richest 20 percent (which clearly includes Bermuda) rose from 70 percent to an astonishing 85 percent. Rich countries clearly provide the citizens a much higher standard of living and quality of life than poor countries.

Another less scientific[3] test for determining how wealthy a country is simply by looking around. I have visited all of the above countries with the exceptions of Ghana and Kenya and one is immediately struck by the economic differences, some of them quite striking, with Bermuda. Dirty dishevelled people, environmental degradation, low life expectancy, begging, sharp contrasts between the rich and the poor, run down public buildings and a general lack of self respect are common characteristics. Anyone who has doubts about economic justice in Bermuda should pay a visit to Brazil and India. Even USA and France, the two rich countries in the table do not exude the prosperity of Bermuda, and just as important do not enjoy the quality of life we have in Bermuda.

However, when we come to compare the difference in the standard of living with countries which are classified as poor - which is countries in which about 80 percent of the world's population live - the dollar figures and what they represent becomes quite striking. Consider the following passage from "Workers in an Integrating World", published in the World Development Report of 1995:-

"An underemployed agricultural labourer living near Tamale in Ghana's savannah region works on average less than four days a week. When employed, he gets paid around $0.80 a day. During the cotton harvest there is enough work, but in winter jobs are scarce. He, his wife, and their five children live in a mud hut. His wife and ten-year-old daughter help care for their small vegetable garden, which supplies food for the family dinner table even when the father is not working. The parents worry about their children's future. They would like to move to an area with more job opportunities but cannot afford to lose the family's only assets, their one small plot of land."

The passage given above should be compared to the following fictitious character who lives in Bermuda in order to gauge the difference in the style of life between Bermuda and Ghana.

"Wendell is a building construction worker, or a skilled labourer, living in Parsons Road, one of Bermuda's poorer areas, located close to the capital Hamilton. He regularly works five days per week and, depending on the state of the construction industry, is often able during the summer to work an additional eight hours per week overtime. His regular pay is $16.00 per hour, and his overtime pays about $25 per hour. He can work all year round but during the winter in Bermuda it rains a lot and when this happens Wendell prefers to say at home and work on his new Toyota car which cost him around $20,000. He, his wife Sharon and two children aged 7 and 9 live in a modest two bedroom cottage with one and a half bathrooms which

---

[3] Known disparagingly as "anecdotal evidence".

although modestly furnished has two colour television sets, a stereo system with CD and cassette player, and one of his bedrooms is air-conditioned. Sharon also works as a receptionist at a well known international company and is paid around $2,500 month. Their combined incomes allow the family to have at least one foreign vacation per year which in 1995 was at Disneyworld in Orlando, Florida. On the spur of the moment Wendell and his wife left the children with his mother in mid- October, had a long weekend in New York, staying at the Marriott Marquis on Times Square, and took in two Broadway shows as well as some shopping at Macys and Saks Fifth Avenue. The weekend cost around $2,000, including the airfare, but as they had a good time it was money well spent. Their major concern is the future of their children, a boy and a girl. Sharon would like their son to be lawyer and their daughter a teacher or accountant. Wendell is less ambitious but would like his children to earn at least $50,000 per annum by the time they are 30 although he is not sure what jobs pay that sort of money. They intend to save regularly in order for their children to go to a good university in the States so that on their return to Bermuda they can enjoy a well paid and high status job."

The fictitious passage above is not an unusual scenario for a young couple who are hardworking and ambitious for their children. The key differences between Bermuda and Ghana (it could be any of the above countries except USA and France) are:-

- The regular work week.
- The high wage ($16 per hour versus 80 cents per day).
- The quality of housing.
- Ownership of a new car, 2 tv sets, and airconditioning.
- The opportunity for Sharon to work in a white-collar job.
- The number of children (2 in Bermuda, 5 in Ghana).
- The life style - holidays in New York versus maintaining a vegetable garden)
- The ambitions for their children.

I could continue mentioning such things as life expectancy, medical care, or political freedom (Ghana is a military dictatorship) but the point I wish to make is that life in Bermuda is significantly better than in most countries of the world, including the rich nations of the USA, Canada, Germany or France.

The really interesting and puzzling question for many people is this. Why have so many countries failed to improve the standard of living over the past 50 years or so? And why is it that many countries are much worse off today than they were 30 years ago? In sub-Saharan Africa most countries have deteriorated economically in the past 30 years whilst other countries such as Korea, Thailand and Singapore have bounded ahead.

Equally puzzling is the question of why do immigrants to the United States from countries with low incomes such as Haitians and Jamaicans earn much higher incomes than those born and raised in the United States within a short period of arrival. In Bermuda, the question to be asked is why do so many immigrants from low income countries like Portugal (from the Azores) and the West Indies out-perform local Bermudians? After all Haitians, Jamaicans and Portuguese do not become different people the moment they step onto the shores of Bermuda and the United States.

The question of why some countries are richer than others is answered in a recent study[4] which indicated that in poor countries the institutions and incentives in place are such that it is virtually impossible to raise their living standards and income. In rich countries like Bermuda and the United States one tends to find such things as an efficient, impartial and non-corrupt civil administration which provides good essential services like public health and education, the government does not steal from the people and legal contracts are enforced impartially. The worker is able to keep most of his income, taxation is not penal and there is a high degree of upward mobility. From rags to riches is not regarded as a fairy tale. Immigrants instinctively understand the meaning of opportunity and seize it with both hands.

> "I have no complex about wealth. I have worked hard for my money, producing things which people need. I believe that the able industrial leader, who creates wealth and employment is more worthy of historical notice than politicians or soldiers."
>
> J. PAUL GETTY

In order to sustain economic success it is essential to have in place a competitive market economy (or capitalism) - if that does not exist poverty will tend to be the rule. Competition is the spur to keep on improving the performance of the economy and when improvements take place everyone grows wealthier. When there is no competition or competition is prevented by laws, administrative rules and corruption the economy stagnates.[5] This is the major reason why protectionism does not at the end of the day protect the standard of living.

The wealth of a country is not determined by impersonal economic forces but by political failure to put in place appropriate incentives and sound administration. In a nutshell this is the essential difference between the standard of living of the United States and Mexico, or between Bermuda and Jamaica (or Ghana).

Are Bermudians better off than Turks, Peruvians or the people from Ghana? Absolutely.

---

[4] "The Political Economy of Poverty, Equity and Growth." by Deepak Lal and H. Myint.
[5] Is there a lesson here for 1996 Bermuda?

13. WHAT IS MONEY?

"There is nothing so degrading as the constant anxiety about one's means of liveliehood. I have nothing but contempt for the people who despise money. They are hypocrites or fools. Money is like a sixth sense without which you cannot make a complete use of the other five. Without an adequate income half the possiblities of life are shut off. It is not wealth one asks for, but just enough to preserve one's dignity, to work unhampered, to be generous, frank and independent."

"OF HUMAN BONDAGE" BY SOMERSET MAUGHAM

"There are few acts in which a man can be more innocently employed than in getting money."

DR. SAMUEL JOHNSON

"It is better that a man should tyrannize over his bank balance than over his fellow citizens.".

JOHN MAYNARD KEYNES

Most people, even those who are bad at figures or unworldly, have a very good practical idea of what money is, after all they have to buy the necessities of life, earn a living and save for the future. Even children know that money can be notes, coins, or deposits in the bank and only misers like money for money's sake and enjoy the thrill of counting it and touching it. Money is a subject which interests, even obsesses, many people and next to sex is probably the subject people think most about. The subject of money features heavily in the Bible with, as one might expect, contradictory message being given to different congregations. The one which gives me most concern is the injunction *"Lay not up for yourselves treasures upon earth ...But lay up for yourselves treasures in heaven."* This tends to restrict one's enthusiasm for overtime, especially on Sunday, but on the other hand I am comforted by the fact that the parable of the talents banishes profligates to the *"outer darkness where there shall be wailing and gnashing of teeth."*

Money changers were not the favourite people of Jesus and as a result money has had something of a bad press over the centuries. However, the German sociologist Max Weber believed the genesis for modern capitalism came from Calvinists who paid no attention to camel and needle parables but espoused the virtue of just rewards for hard work and dedication.

The purpose of money is to spend it on those goods and services such as vacations, music, clothing, and so on - the list is endless which we believe will make our life more enjoyable and satisfying. The paradox of money is, that it is only useful when we get rid of it by spending it and many people in Bermuda have a remarkable talent for doing just that. In an advanced economic system however, knowing what money is , becomes a much more complicated issue as I hope to explain later.

In primitive societies money can be and has been at different times things like cattle, stones, shells or women. In even more primitive societies money can be dispensed with altogether and a system of barter, or direct swap, arises by, for example, one man exchanging with another food for clothing. But barter is a clumsy way of conducting business. Consider this fictional advertisement "I am prepared to exchange two pairs of size 9 shoes, one colour Sony television set, and one Suzuki motor cycle for a three year old Toyota station wagon which must be blue in colour". Any person who placed that ad would spend hours and hours trying to locate someone who wanted shoes, a TV set, and a motor cycle in exchange for a car and there would be a high chance that he would fail. However, there would only a slight chance of failure if he put of price of $10 on the shoes, $200 on the TV set, and $500 for the motor cycle. The seller could then use the proceeds of around $710 to put towards the cost of the kind of car he wished to buy. Money in other words lubricates the system of exchanging goods and services, and acts as a common denominator to establish the relative value of various goods.

Without money the specialised economic system as we know it would simply not exist. If an economy is disrupted for a long period money can be items like cigarettes which were used as money in Germany after the Second World War. Or if an economy collapses as it did in the former USSR in 1991 the local currency can be replaced for major financial transactions by another, in this case the United States dollar. The Russian central bank estimates interestingly that approximately US$15 billion is in circulation mostly in $100 bills because there is no confidence by the Russian people in the value of the rouble. As an aside the United States Treasury estimates[1] that of the $400 billion officially in circulation in the USA about two-thirds, mainly in $100 bills, is used by other countries because of lack of confidence in the local currency, or is used by money launderers or simply because of commercial convenience. The convenience reason accounts for the approximately US$50 million in circulation in Bermuda which is about half of the $63 million[2] Bermuda dollar notes in circulation at the end of 1995.

Money is usually thought of as performing four main functions :-
1. It is a medium of exchange which permits the machinery of buying and selling to operate efficiently.
2. It is a measure of value and by extension a unit of account, which makes it possible to determine prices for all commodities. It is also the basis for such important functions as determining costs, maintaining accounts, and establishing wages and profits.
3. It is the standard for deferred payments such as loans or the provision of credit.
4. It provides for wealth to be stored in a convenient and efficient way which in turn allows savings immediately and without cost to be used later in buying goods and services.

Money is therefore desirable because it gives us the freedom to buy whatever we wish (provided we have sufficient of it) and it is accepted by the seller because he can then use that money to buy what he wants. The circular process of buying and selling is endless for our needs are almost without limit and it is one of the basic freedoms which people enjoy under the market (or capitalist) system.

---

[1] Reported in 'Time Magazine' February 12, 1996, page 50.
[2] The BMA Annual Report, 1995.

In addition, to the four functions of money there are three basic reasons why people wish to hold money, other than the thrill of knowing that they can spend it in the future.

1. Individuals and businesses hold money to carry out day to day transactions.

2. Apart from day to day expenditures, money is required for "just in case" circumstances such as illness, a car breaking down, or some essential repairs to a residence. Prudent people tend to keep some money aside for "rainy day" events.

3. The final reason is for speculative motives, such as taking advantage of an unexpected sale at your favourite store. Such money is also used to take advantage of changes in the prices of securities such as shares in public companies (known as equities) or in bonds which are debt instruments of governments and companies. It is this expectation of the future which is the most volatile of the three reasons for holding money.

I have been around money most of my life, either as a student or practitioner, and I would be hard put to give a clear definition of what money is. If you asked an economist, a banker, or a foreign central banker, what money is the answer would be totally confusing and in truth it is very difficult, even impossible, to give a clear and simple answer. However, understanding money in the context of the Bermuda economy is much easier than in major countries largely because Bermuda is so small that it has little impact on the international economy but also partly because in Bermuda the United States dollar circulates as freely as the Bermuda dollar and one Bermuda dollar equals one US dollar.

The question of what the US dollar (or the British Pound or the French Franc) is worth can be answered in much the same way as what is the value of the Bermuda dollar? The strength of a currency is highly or wholly dependent on the ability of a country to earn its way in the world and if it fails to do that the value of currency will fall (or in extreme circumstances cease to exist) relative to other currencies. There are many examples of this. In 1948 the British pound was worth U.S.$4.80 in 1996 it is worth around US$1.55, a fall of over two thirds. In 1962 the Jamaican dollar was worth two US dollars. In 1996 it is worth about two cents and it is now so unimportant that the rate is rarely mentioned in the financial press and is impossible to buy other than at exchange bureaus at airports.

On the other hand, the importance of the US dollar arises not only from the importance of the United States in the world economy, but also on the credibility of the United States government and the integrity of the Federal Reserve System. The US dollar is universally accepted because people trust the government of the United States and believe that it will follow sensible economic policies. The same arguments apply to many other large governments like Britain, France, Germany, Japan, Italy, Canada and so on all of whom cooperate and coordinate policies with the United States and are members of the international financial organisations like OECD, the IMF and the World Bank. When confidence, integrity and credibility are threatened or lost during periods of international monetary crisis there is a flight to the most stable and secure of currencies which is usually the United States dollar or the Japanese Yen.

In large countries there are many definitions of money. Ml, M being the short-hand used, means currency, coins, and demand bank deposits which reflects money's use as a medium of exchange. M2 is a broader measure and is M1 plus savings accounts, small certificates of deposit (CDs), and demand deposits reflecting its use as a store of value. M3 is an even wider measure and is M2 plus large CDs. Many economists believe that money cannot now be defined with any precision because of such innovations as credit cards, direct debit cards, and the way in which billions of dollars can be electronically shunted around the world by the click of a computer mouse. Indeed, there are some who argue that money in the form of notes, coins and deposits in bank accounts will dimish in impor-tance and may for all practical purposes cease to be a matter of any financial importance.

Many commentators believe that the description of money given above is accurate in the context of the agricultural and industrial ages which we are now leaving. The meaning of money in the global economy and new information age will be very different and cash will be used less and less for such routine matters as commerical transactions (paying for groceries) or as a store value (saving for the future) but increasingly money's major role will be to serve as a measure of value - something at which money has not been very good at because of past inflations. Money will be the tape-measure, the slide-rule which allows the pub-lic to compare the prices of different commodities.

Paper money was a great convenience when it replaced barter and gold coins as the public did not have to carry around heavy precious metals in their pockets and notes could be backed up by holding only small amounts of gold in the cen-tral bank to instill confidence in the system. A dollar was accepted as a dollar because the issuing government said it was worth a dollar. This is very much the system in Bermuda today as each Bermuda dollar note contains the statement "This note is legal tender issued under the Bermuda Monetary Authority Act 1969" and it is signed by two directors of the BMA. It is a dollar because the Bermuda Government authorises the BMA to tell the public it is worth a dollar.

In this modern age paper money is no longer an important means of storing value (particularly when there is fear of inflation) as we shrewdly prefer to invest our spare cash in stocks and bonds either directly or indirectly through mutual funds, insurance policies or pension funds. Cash stored in a mutual fund is backed up by the underlying value of publicly traded stocks like IBM not by statements of the full faith and credit of governments.

Moreover cash in the form of bank notes is dirty and unhealthy - some toll booth collectors in the United States wear latex gloves to protect themselves from germs. Cash is also expensive to maintain as costs are incurred in printing, safe-keeping, collecting, counting and it is unsafe as criminals have a strong attraction to it. Credit card companies, for example, have long understood that their cards are not really about credit but about convenience and safety. They are also about stimulating consumer spending as studies have shown the consumers spend about

25 percent more with a credit card than they do when they have to pay cash. Cash is reality, a credit card is a wish-list. In addition, it is now impossible to rent a car, buy an airline ticket or stay in a hotel without a credit card. Cash is too suspicious and it no longer the tool of the law-abiding citizen but the weapon of the criminal, the drug dealer and the money-launderer. Cash is on its way out. A British company, Mondex, is experimenting in the city of Swindon - close to London - with a card which will replace cash entirely. The close relative of cash, the cheque, is also a document which is headed for the knacker's yard. These cheques are expensive to process (it is estimated that one cheque in Bermuda costs $27.50 to process) and they are vulnerable to fraud. These are costs and responsibilities which banks would like to get rid of.

A simple definition of money is that it is the current liabilities of a bank. It is not gold, silver or even bank notes. This is the major reason why governments become decidely nervous when there is a threat to the banking system as there was with the collapse of the British bank Barings in 1995. Fortunately, that bank was too small to do much damage to the international banking system but the failure of a huge bank like Citibank would be another story entirely.

Think of the financial and personal chaos which would ensue in Bermuda if the Bank of Butterfield or the Bank of Bermuda failed and depositors were unable to get their money. Ultimately your money is backed by nothing but the confidence you repose in your banker - it is a trust even a form of faith which is as essential to commercial life as any religious belief in personal life. This is why I have made several references to the bible at the beginning of this essay. The next time the collection plate comes round at church, pray for your banker.

In this new global environment it is impossible to be sure what comprises money. It has now become little more than trillions of electronic and computer signals moving along communications networks (in fact travelling to satellites in outer space) of interlinked terminals in search of the best return and the most favoured market. These conditions create an unforgiving economic environment which punishes economic mismangement and rewards favoured countries and governments with capital (and jobs). Money can no longer be bottled up in substandard and inefficient economies. It has been converted from something real, something solid and substantial, something you could almost love into something which you can't touch, fondle or even see. Money has been robbed of its personality - it weighs nothing, moves faster than the speed of light, has no allegiance and no personality. It is pure raw information - the stuff of the future. The dollar bills in your pocket are now as outmoded as semaphore flags in the modern navy. It is an ephemeral concept eons away from the bags of gold which used to be stolen from banks by bandits in old cowboy movies. Governments may have to give up monetary policies in the future and have to be content with trying to regulate these new markets. This will be a vexing issue as we are likely to see the emergence of a volatile global economy very much beyond the control and even understanding of current government institutions.

14. HOW IS MONEY CREATED?

"Banking establishments are more dangerous than standing armies."

THOMAS JEFFERSON

Determining the amount of money needed for an economy to function efficiently is a difficult task and requires not only great skill but the necessary tools to do the job. In Bermuda, the skill is available through the Bermuda Monetary Authority and the three commercial banks but the tools to determine the quantity of money are very limited.

Money in Bermuda is largely determined exogeneously, that is to say by insitutions and authorities outside Bermuda. To understand this position it is necessary, briefly, to explain what happens in the larger countries and by way of example I have used the United States which is by far the largest and most important economy in the world but is also close to and its assumptions are fairly easily understood by the Bermudian public.

The central bank of the United States is the Federal Reserve System (the Fed) which was established in 1913 to regulate, supervise and strengthen the banking system by making it independent from political control. Because of the size of the United States the Fed divides the nation into twelve districts, each with a Federal Reserve Bank owned by the member banks of the district. The twelve districts are co-ordinated by the Federal Reserve Board in Washington, five members of which are appointed by the President for fourteen years and like judges cannot be removed except by impeachment.

Two other members (making the total seven)the Chairman and the Vice-chairman are appointed by the President for four years. The Chairman, at present Mr Alan Greenspan, is one of the most powerful figures in the American economic establishment partly because of his political independence, partly because of his reputation, but also because his decisions can profoundly affect the American economic system through the Fed's monetary policy.

The Fed is able to create money in three major ways.

Firstly, when a depositor puts money, say $1,000 into a commercial bank account, the bank acquires an asset of the cash, and the credit for the customer in the books of the bank is a liabilitiy. A proportion of the $1,000 deposit can be lent to customers of the bank but it has to keep available some cash to meet the demands of its depositor. Experience and prudence, plus the requirements of the Fed determine what that proportion should be. If it is determined by the Fed that the reserve ratio should be 20% , this means that the bank can lend 80 percent of each deposit it takes in. In our example, the bank can lend $800 to its customers. If that $800 is then deposited with the bank, the bank can lend out $640 (being 80% of $800; if that $640 is also deposited the bank can then lend out $512 (being 80% of $640). The process continues until the bank is able to lend out a total of $4,000 from the original deposit of $1,000.

The assets of the bank are, at the end of the process, $1,000 in cash, $4,000 in promises of borrowers to repay loans, and its liabities are $5,000 in deposits.

It can be seen that if the Fed changes the reserve ration downwards the money multiplier becomes bigger, and if it increases it to say 30%, the amount able to be loaned by the bank falls. By using its power to change reserve ratios the Fed exercises great power over the commercial banking system. Even the threat to change the reserve ratio results in immediate action by the banks. The essence of prudent banking is to maintain sufficient cash in the vaults of the bank to meet the demands of the depositors whilst at the same time lending out deposits in order to make a profit.

In the United States in 1992, deposits in the United States amounted to US$600 billion, whilst cash in the form of notes and coins amounted to only US$30 billion or five per cent of deposits. On the face of it this seems a risky business as depositors could theoretically claim $600 billion but find there is only $30 billion to meet their claims. Every bank in the world, including Bermuda, is in this position and provided depositors are confident that their cash requirements will be met when required no problem arises.

If confidence in the banking system disappears there is a major problem and a run on the bank can occur. A run on the bank means when depositors believe the bank will be unable to repay their deposits on time, and they will all try to withdraw their funds before the cash runs out. This is where the Fed exercises one of its most important functions, namely the establishment of appropriate reserve ratios for the commercial banks.

If the Fed determines that the reserve ratio of the banks is 20 per cent (historically it has fluctuated between 13 and 26 percent) this means that commerical banks must maintain cash or deposits with the Fed equal to 20 percent of their deposits. This means that banks can lend out 80 percent of the their deposits at a rate of interest greater than they are paying their depositors which is one of the main ways banks earn income for their shareholders.

In the event that depositors wish to withdraw more than 20 percent the Fed is willing and able to guarantee loans to the commercial banking system to meet its obligations. However, as a practical matter this guarantee is rarely required because public confidence in the banking system is never questioned - except in most unusual circumstances like the interwar depression (when 40 percent of American banks failed between 1929 and 1933).

The importance of the reserve requirement is that if the Fed believes commercial banks are lending too freely or are acting imprudently they can raise the reserve. On the other hand, if they believe the banks are acting too cautiously by not lending enough to the general public, they can lower the reserve requirements and banks can make more funds available to the public and business in order to stimulate economic activity.

By raising or lowering the reserve ratio the Fed is able to exert considerable influence over economic activity, which is why the delphic type pronouncements by the Chairman of the Fed is analysed exhaustively by financial journalists. The Chairman is believed by many to be the most powerful man in the country next to the President. The objective of the Fed is therefore to keep the economy supplied with the right amount of money. Too little creates problems in that economic activity would be lower than optimal. Too much creates problems in that spending would soon bump up against capacity. For example, increased economic activity would lead to increased hiring of labour, and if business continued to improve the only way firms could expand would be to tempt staff away from existing employment by offering higher wages and benefits. This in turn would push up production costs and inflation would be result. The trick therefore for the Fed is to make sure the economy is supplied with the "right" amount of money. Not an easy task.

Changing the reserve ratio is therefore a highly effective way of controlling the amount of money in the economy but it tends to be something of a meat cleaver, affecting the whole banking system in an undiscriminating way. For example, it may be necessary to restrict credit in the Northeast, keep it the same in the Midwest but expand it in the Southeast ; changes in the reserve ratio affects all banks in every area of the country.

A second way is to change the Fed discount rate, the interest rate which the Fed lends overnight money to commercial banks and which directly affects all commercial interest rates. By raising, or lowering, this rate the Fed can make it profitable or unprofitable for member banks to borrow. When rates are high borrowers may think twice about expanding their business or buying a new car and banks need to be much more cautious before lending to borrowers whose credit rating is not of the highest standard.

Tight money, as this is called , can then be applied to the Northeast but leaving other areas unaffected. This serves as a signal from the Fed about how it would like member banks to behave. Commercial banks tend to treat signals from the Fed in the same way you and I used to treat a warning from our fathers when we were children. They know if they fail to act in the appropriate way, more stringent and painful methods can be applied.

Thirdly, the Fed can use what is known as open market operations, which allows it to influence the supply and cost of money by buying or selling US government securities on the open market. The Fed may, for example, decide to expand the supply of money in order to stimulate economic activity, and it does this by buying government securities from dealers and paying for them by cheques drawn, not on the commerical banks, but on the Fed. When these cheques are deposited with the commercial banking system their deposits with the Fed increases which means they can lend out more to businesses and individuals. If the Fed decides that there should be a contraction in economic activity it will sell government securities to the public through the securities market who will then pay by cheques drawn on the commercial banks. The deposits which the banks retain at the Fed will fall and the banks in turn will have to call in, or reduce the number of, loans made to the public.

The globalisation of the world economy has made this simple model of control less easy to implement as large US corporations can now go to international banks, or foreign markets, and borrow foreign currency for expansion. That being said, central bankers are a small group of influential individuals who keep each other informed, formally and informally, and concerted action can be, and is, taken by the world's major central banks to influence economic activity.

Determining what the right supply of money should be is not a routine calculation as neither the Fed, nor other central banks, has at its disposal sufficient accurate information as to the real state of the economy at any point in time. It takes months, even years, to collect the data , analyse and interpret it and even then genuinely different views between central bankers may not lead to universal agreement.

The German Central Bank, the Bundesbank , has as one of its major objectives the elimination of inflation because of the distress caused in Germany in the 1920s because of hyper inflation. As the United States and Britain avoided that traumatic experience, they tend to be biased towards expansionary monetary policies. The economics profession has hewed to the Milton Friedman thesis that the money supply should be expanded only in line with the long term growth in a nation's output.

The arguments between the different schools of thought are intriguing but they do not affect Bermuda directly. Bermuda's monetary policies are determined by the actions of the two large commercial banks, and by the Bermuda Monetary Authority.[1*]

15. WHAT IS THE GROSS DOMESTIC PRODUCT (GDP) AND WHAT IS MEANT BY PER CAPITA INCOME?

"Though he may not always recognize his bondage, modern man lives under a tyranny of numbers."

NICHOLAS EBERSTADT[1]

The modern state, and Bermuda is no exception, is built on numbers. It is to statistics, usually official because the public believes in them, that politicians appeal when they claim they can do great things, or when they wish to brag of their wisdom. It is also to official statistics that bureaucrats appeal when they state they are acting for the common good and not on behalf of their own self interest.

The reader should beware: official statistics are not as impartial as their supplicants say they are. Thanks to the gullibility of the public, and to a certain extent because of their innumeracy, we can easily be duped into the myth of the all-wise state thus allowing politicians and bureaucrats to interfere in our lives even more frequently than they do now. When you contemplate buying a new car the motto should always be "let the buyer beware". When anyone analyses official statistics such as GDP they must be guided by the same motto.

Gross Domestic Product, or GDP, measures the output (or production) of goods and services of all labour and capital within a country without reference to the residence of that labour or the ownership of the capital. GDP can be measured in three different ways all of which, conceptually, should come up with the

---

[1*] This is dealt with in Part II 11.

[1] "The Tyranny of Numbers." by Nicholas Eberstadt 1996.

same result[2]. They are (1) calculating output, (2) calcuating income, and (3) calculating expenditure. Bermuda's GDP is calculated using the expenditure method ; the other two methods are not utilised because in a service economy calculating output is extremely difficult, and calculating income in a country with no direct taxes is impossible because there is no data base.

GDP should be distinguished from Gross National Product, or GNP, which is GDP plus the income of the residents of Bermuda which arises in other parts of the world[3]. GDP therefore deals with production of goods and services in Bermuda no matter who owns the assets or labour. GNP deals with income arising to Bermudians whether that income arises in Bermuda or overseas. A simple example may make this clearer. If I own shares in IBM, an American corporation, and receive income of $10,000 per annum that $10,000 does not form part of the Bermuda GDP, but does form part of the Bermuda GNP. Similarly, the $10,000 forms a part of the calculation to determine US GDP but is not part of the US GNP.

GDP is now the universally recognised system of measuring output, although many commentators wrongly use the terms GDP and GNP interchangeably. Compiling GDP figures is a huge exercise in large countries and as a consequence there are many amendments and revisions to the figures as additional data becomes available.

Per capita GDP is simply the total product of goods and services in Bermuda divided by the resident population. Thus in the fiscal year (April-March) 1993/1994 GDP at market (or current) prices was $1,840.2 million; divide that by the resident population of 59,000 gives a GDP per capita of $31,190. However, confusingly the "Fact & Figures" booklet published in 1996 by the Statistics Department of the Bermuda Government shows that the GNP per capita is $27,500 - which incidentally is about 70 times the average annual income of 50 percent of the world's population (Bermudians earn more in a week than most people in the world earn in a year)[4]. There are two points to note here:

1. There is a difference between GDP and GNP as noted above. GDP is now considered to be the better way of calculating per capita incomes and this is used more widely than GNP.

2. GNP for a wealthy country like Bermuda would normally be higher than GDP but the Government figures show it to be lower. The reason for this is that GDP on the government calculation is given at market prices, whilst the international useage stresses calculating GDP at factor prices - which means eliminating such items as indirect taxes.

There is a third complication on the use of GDP per capita in that "The Economist"[5] publishes Bermuda's GDP per head as $28,293 (the per capita income of the United States is reported at $24,753 making Bermuda 14.3% bet-

---

[2] They never do even in countries such as Canada which has an excellent statistical service

[3] Interestingly enough in the Statistical Department's "Facts and Figures 1996" it is GNP per capita which is used, not the more common GDP per capita.

[4] One reason why it is difficult to understand the admiration by several Bermudians and the PLP for the political arrangements in other parts of the world and for economic policies which have left most of the world's population in degrading poverty.

[5] "The Economist - Pocket World in Figures," 1996 Edition page 24.

ter than USA) whilst Bermuda calculates in GNP per head at $26,600. I have not found an explanation for this but the point I wish to make is that GDP calculations should be treated with considerable caution - as should all official statistics.[6] The official GDP of most countries misses about one-third of economic activity mainly because it fails to record the "black economy" such as home decorating or the drug trade. In the late 1980s Italy overtook the per capita income of France by making a calculation about its "black economy."

The per capita income is used to compare how well Bermuda is doing compared to other countries. For example, using "The Economist" figures stated previously Bermudians appear to be 14% better off than Americans. However, things are not that simple as the purchasing power of the dollar in the respective countries has to be taken into consideration.

Bermudians know that the cost of goods in the United States is much less than it is at home - the main reason why Bermudians tend to have excess baggage when they return from a trip to America - so the respective purchasing powers have to be factored in using a method known at purchasing power parity (PPP). PPP replaces market exchange rates with rates which are constructed for the purpose of equalising, as far as possible, the prices of a standard 'basket' of goods and services. Estimates are based on the United States which is given an index of 100.

Any country which has a figure less than 100 - say India[7] - indicates that the standard basket of goods and services can be purchased in that country for less than it would cost in the United States. The magazine "The Economist" prepares an annual survey of costs in different countries by using a tongue in cheek Big Mac version of PPP. It compares the prices of a Big Mac in many countries and correlates that to the comparative cost of living. It shows a remarkably close correlation with the PPP method.

There is no official PPP figures for Bermuda to determine the difference in purchasing power between Bermuda and the United States although my back of the envelope calcuation would put it at at about 120%, meaning that the same basket of goods in Bermuda would cost $120 but only $100 in the USA. When that is done we find that individual Bermudians are not 14% better off than Americans, but about 6% worse off because a dollar spent in Bermuda buys approximately 20% less than if it was spent in the United States. If the reader is confused , let me confuse you even further by showing limitations in GDP calculations.

In calculating GDP (which by now should be understood to be Grossly Deceptive Product) what does not get counted does not count. The market place and the use of money is the measure of anything and everything that goes into GDP.

---

6 See for example "The Tyranny of Numbers - Mismeasurement & Misrule" by Nicholas Eberstadt who goes into considerable detail about inaccuracies of government statistics.

7 See the chart contained in Part I 12 for more details

The concept of GDP is relatively recent arising during the Second World War when the British Government needed to know how much money it could get from taxation from the public.[8] Before that time there were only rough approximations of the income of a country. Since then statistical methods have developed and so has the subject of economics. No self-respecting country would be without its national income figures of GDP, GNP and consumer price indexes. But statistics measure only money transfers in the economy.

Here is a partial list of things missing from GDP calculations:

- Unpaid work in the house is not included. Because I cannot wield a hammer I increase the GDP of Bermuda by calling in a handyman everytime something goes wrong in my house. Others are adept at repairing things. My uselessness increases GDP, my neighbour's skill does not count.

- Putting your parents in a home for the elderly increases GDP because you pay and the country is richer. Look after them yourself and the country is poorer.

- Driving cars pollutes the atmosphere and causes accidents from time to time but increases GDP because of the money spent on running the vehicle and the payment of medical fees. The damage to the atmosphere as well as the damage to peace and quiet is not counted and is not therefore deducted from GDP[9].

- In many countries (Bermuda is something of an exception) there is a black economy where monetary transactions do not get recorded largely in order to avoid taxes or because the activity is criminal. The drug trade[10], for example, is part of the informal or black economy and although money changes hands there are no records. Adjustments are made from time to time in calculating this figure but it is only an inspired guess. Italy vaulted over other European countries in 1987 when it made an 18 percent adjustment to its GDP in order to account for transactions not reported to the tax authorities. Thus could GDP be increased by the stroke of a pen.

- Leisure time gets counted only if you spend money on it. Enjoying a walk or a view of the ocean does not add to GDP but paying to listen to loud music and drinking in a bar does.

- Cooking a meal at home does not enter GDP but having the same meal at a restaurant adds to income and hence GDP.

It can be seen that by adding up all the market transactions and coming up with a GDP does not really tell us a great deal about how comfortable, contented or happy an individual or country is. Living in Bermuda with its beautiful sea, clean environment and multiplicity of sporting facilities is surely much better (for some) than living in London or New York with possibly more money but with more dirt, crime, buildings and hassle.

Perhaps a more helpful measure of the well-being of mankind is the United Nations Human Development Index (HDI) which was introduced in 1990. This index compares the quality of life in different countries by measuring such things

---

[8] Wars play a very important role in stimulating economic thought.

[9] See Part I 11 for a discussion of the economy and the environment

10 Probably a major unrecorded industry in many economies, including Bermuda

as life expectancy, education, standards of health care, access to clean water and literacy as well as purchasing power as measured by GDP. Countries such as USA, Canada, Japan and UK have a high HDI - about 0.9 - whilst others such as Nigeria, Rwanda and Somalia range between 0.2 and under 0.1. Bermuda would clearly feature as one of the highest scores in this index.

GDP has its uses but it also has its limitations. Students of Latin know that the words "figure" and "fictitious" come from the same Latin root. Hence the statement that there "are lies, damned lies and statistics."

The way you see the world depends very much on the way in which you count things.

16. WHAT IS MEANT BY PROTECTIONISM AND IS IT A GOOD THING OR A BAD THING?

"Protectionist measures have fallen on us (Bermuda) over time like leaves. They have settled slowly until they have become a blanket. They stick to our shoes when we try to move about. Bermuda, because of its small size, will always need some restrictions or else we'd be swamped. But many (of the policies) no longer seem to serve their original purpose. It's time to review all of them and select those that enhance our competitiveness and prosperity and to discard the rest. What are the protections we really need and why? Where are those policies going to lead?"
RICHARD BUTTERFIELD (*QUOTED IN THE COMMISSION ON COMPETITIVENESS*)

Bermuda is one of the few rich countries in the world which produces very few tangible products for itself. Construction, some agriculture, gardening, and security services are examples of goods and services which are produced and consumed by Bermudians. Yet even those are significantly impacted by the necessity to import ; buildings could not be constructed without foreign cement or electrical fittings, grass could not be cut without importation of lawn mowers, crops could not grow without foreign seeds and fertilisers, and security would be ineffective without modern communications, foreign uniforms and equipment.

The products which are on sale in Bermuda stores almost without exception are imported from foreign countries, the television set which entrances most people is imported, probably from Japan or Korea whose citizens rarely visit Bermuda, food comes from the United States and Canada, clothing and footwear from the United Kingdom. The list is endless because of the simple fact that Bermuda cannot economically produce the goods, and increasingly the services, which are required to sustain acceptable living standards in the modern world.

A remote Island of 24 square miles is severely constrained from being able to produce its daily needs and this is impossible when these daily needs are composed of motor vehicles, international communications, medical supplies, oil products, gasoline, and sporting equipment. There is no need to go on. The point is that Bermuda would not exist in its present form without international trade.

The other side of the coin is that Bermuda attracts visitors to come to Bermuda for a vacation to enjoy one of the most delightful climates in the world, a beautiful island and the wonderful ocean. To American visitors Bermuda is a more attractive vacation resort than say Boston or New York. Similarly, businessmen find Bermuda a good place from which to conduct international business because of the absence of penal taxation and unnecessary regulation.

If the reader thinks for a moment about international trade, the living standards of large countries like France, United States and Japan would also be considerably reduced if there was no international trade. The position of almost every country in the world is fundamentally the same as that of Bermuda - freedom to trade and do business is essential to prosperity and the good life. Take away that freedom, and life would be less attractive, less enjoyable and immeasurably duller. No French wine, Italian opera, American movies, Japanese electronic gadgets and so on. The great puzzle is why do so many governments seek through protectionism measures to prevent their citizens from pursuing and engaging in such a harmless, beneficial and profitable activity as international trade?

Amidst the nonsensical policies of economic nationalism one important fact is often forgotten. The phenomenal improvement in the standard of living for almost everyone in the world over the past two hundred years has arisen because Bermudians, Americans and every other nationality have traded, cooperated and worked with people from many other countries. This has resulted in greater specialisation and more efficiency in the production of the goods and services required by people to enjoy the good life.

If countries had avoided and shunned foreigners on the grounds that foreigners took away business, their hard earned money or jobs the world (and hence Bermuda) would be a much poorer and less interesting place. Prosperity therefore depends entirely on trading and competing with foreigners and not retreating behind a wall of tariffs, quotas and other trade restrictions like exchange controls. National borders are doors and windows leading to opportunities, not moats and drawbridges to retreat behind.

In almost every year since the modern world began, say 1700, the degree of economic interdependence has grown bringing prosperity with it and thousands of new products from PVC piping to video recorders. And yet for reasons which few people can understand, politicians seek to impose legal restraints on the voluntary and harmless activities of their citizens, citing as justification for their actions that restrictions are necessary to maintain and improve living standards. Freedom to enter into a voluntary international contract or trading arrangement is one of the few acts between consenting adults of legal age on which governments impose restraints and yet these very acts are responsible for the progressive increase in living standards which have occurred in the past 50 years.

Perhaps the most foolish example from modern economic history of governments restricting their citizens from trading and improving their style of life was the Smoot -Hawley Tariff Act of 1930 in the United States. This act imposed tariffs on foreign goods by up to 60 percent and brought about and prolonged the interwar depression which blighted so many lives and which was one of the major factors in bringing about the Second World War. This is perhaps the best example of the Thomas Jefferson dictum that governments which govern least govern best. Or the President Ronald Reagan thesis that government is the problem not the solution to economic (and other) difficulties. As a footnote, the Smoot-Hawley Tariff Act also put paid to export of Bermudian agricultural products like onions and Easter lilies to the United States.

For a country which is wholly dependent on and benefits from international trade, Bermuda is markedly protectionist. The following list provides examples of existing protections and is far from exhaustive:-

- Exchange controls.
- Restrictions on foreign ownership of land and property.
- Tough immigration laws.
- Local companies must have at least a 60% Bermudian ownership.
- Foreign franchises like McDonalds and Burger King are prohibited.
- Prohibition of foreign banks.
- Restrictions on the hours stores may open.
- Residents are allowed to own only one private car.

Protectionism is usually defined as protecting domestic firms, labour and producers of goods and services from foreign competition, or from some adverse social or economic consequences not provided for in the market system. In the context of Bermuda many restrictions and protections make eminently good sense. Take for example, the prohibition against McDonalds and Burger King, which could be construed as protection for local restaurants. The more important reason is that fast food chains would detract from the attractiveness of Bermuda as a vacation resort for many of our visitors who live in the United States.[1] Bermuda wishes to position itself as being different from the United States (but not too different) but it was judged (correctly in my opinion) that allowing fast food franchises would make Bermuda a less attractive place for visitors.

The restrictions of the ownership of private cars often strike foreigners as being unduly restrictive. This is done to prevent Bermuda from being overwhelmed by motor vehicles - indeed motor vehicles were only allowed into Bermuda in 1947 after prolonged debate.[2] This is another example of a commercial restraint which was imposed for the common good and is supported by the public.

In many countries economic protection is accomplished by tariffs, exchange controls, voluntary restraints, harsh immigration controls and quotas with the result that consumers have to pay higher prices as domestic firms are able to charge higher prices because there is reduced foreign competition. It is a form of economic nationalism, which although usually highly popular with voters, invariably works against the best financial interest of the general public.

---

1 The issue of McDonalds is discussed in Part III 4.

2 When it was expected that no more than 400 cars would be on the road. Today it is 22,000.

The overwhelming body of evidence is that protectionism creates inefficiencies in the market place, is a tax on economic activity and as a result consumers are generally worse off. The only group in favour of retaining restraints of trade are those who directly benefit from them. Since the Second World War international organisations like the General Agreement on Tariffs and Trade (GATT)[3] and OECD have worked diligently to reduce or eliminate such barriers to international trade because they work against consumer interests and economic efficiency. This has been a major reason for the unparalleled prosperity which has been enjoyed in the West since 1945.

In many respects Bermuda is representative of the old fashioned mercantilist philosophy in vogue in the 16th, 17th and 18th centuries which put forward the mistaken view that nations are enriched if foreign competition is restricted. Most of the mercantilist policies arise from the close relationship between the government and the merchants classes and in Bermuda until around 1960, government and the merchant group[4] were very much the same people. In Europe and elsewhere, the support of the government was given to the merchants classes in return for the payment of taxes to maintain the military. Governments then pursued policies which protected the merchants from the so called evils of foreigners. The general population often supported these ideas, largely through ignorance, as merchants often claimed that their protection benefited the country as a whole. The mercantilist ideas were refuted by Adam Smith and others who showed that free trade benefited everyone, that specialisation in production led to improved efficiency and growth in trade, and that the close relationship, or the collusion, between the moneyed classes and government worked against the best interests of the general population. In other words, protectionism harmed the economy by imposing on it significant costs.

During the Nineteenth century the laisser-faire ideas of Smith prevailed in England which was a major reason why that country so dominated world trade during the nineteenth and early twentieth century. Nowadays, there are few economists or politicians outside Bermuda (Ross Perot and Pat Buchanan in the United States are notable exceptions) who support protectionism and the argument in favour of free and uninterrupted trade has been won. Bermuda, as in many other ways still remains another world.

If the case for abolishing many of the restrictions which Bermudians face is so compelling , why do we tolerate so many restraints on our economic freedom. Here are several of the major reasons:-

- A lack of understanding of economic matters by government.
- Inertia - some of our restrictions were imposed during very different economic circumstances to those which apply today. For example, exchange control was imposed during the Second World War in order to preserve foreign currency reserves. That war has been over for 50 years yet exchange control still exist[5]. Government programmes tend to take on a life of their own once they are created, and a cursory examination of the budget figures will show expenditure on programmes which have long outlived their use-

---

[3] Now the World Trade Organisation (WTO)

[4] Known as the 40 Thieves.

[5] although it has been relaxed considerably in recent years.

fulness (if there ever was any real justification in the first place). Rent control is a good example of this.

- Politicians and civil servants do not really trust individuals to make rational economic decisions, even although the basic assumption of the private enterprise system under which we live is that individuals should make their own financial decisions and reap the rewards if they make the right ones, and suffer penalties if they make the wrong ones. The Western experience is that people benefit most when they are allowed to make decisions in their own interest. Governments always tend to believe that they know better than the average man, hence the temptation to interfere with day to day decisions of ordinary people, and hence the cynics say the tendency of governments to always get it wrong. To the greatest extent possible, governments should keep their hands off day to day decision making within the economy because of the adverse consequences to the public.

- Organised interest groups tend to persuade governments that it is in the national interest to provide protection to national companies. The arguments always are hedged around with the necessity of preserving jobs, maintaining local ownership, unfairness because foreigners have some major advantage over domestic organisations, or that valuable income will be lost to Bermuda (meaning the firms or groups who are doing the lobbying). What really happens is that consumers pay higher prices than is necessary for the product in question and the benefit flows ultimately to the protected organisation. What is ironical is that many of the people who are penalised by the higher prices, are the most ardent supporters of the restrictions.

The battle between those who favour free trade and those special interests which support protection is a never ending one and many of the headlines in the financial press are directly related to this issue.

If the reader sees a headline entitled " fair trade" or a "level playing field", the chances are the argument is the old chestnut free trade versus protectionism. Such arguments are concerned about the influence and power which foreign organisations can wield in small communities like Bermuda. They are concerned about jobs, giving opportunities to Bermudians, and being able to determine their own destiny. Politicians are concerned about the loss of control as large foreign, or multinational, companies with vast financial resources cannot be pushed around. There is also a blow to national pride, local identity or the self esteem of locals which often originates from a sense of economic vulnerability and from a fear of the unknown. Many small communities always run the risk of closing people's minds to new opportunities and ideas which originate from the outside, particularly if, as in Bermuda's case, it has been very successful in the past. This tendency to look inwards encourages protectionism at the expense of the improvements which can arise from stressing change and accepting new ideas. Economic nationalism encourages everyone to build walls around the economy, divide the population from the rest of the world rather than building doors to give access to the forces of globalisation[6]. The new and the untried is always a threat to the comfortable.

A major factor affecting Bermuda trade is the process of globalisation which is sweeping the world in the 1990's affecting countries, communities, existing firms and most of all individuals. Governments can fall (like the former USSR), communities can find themselves devastated like the shipbuilding industries of the Northeast of England, companies go out of business (Pan American) and individuals lose their jobs. Indeed so powerful is the force of globalisation that the whole concept of a stable career and a secure job has been revolutionised in the past ten years. It is now conventional wisdom that an individual is unlikely to be able to join a firm or company at the age of 25 or so and remain there until retirement. Even the concept of getting an education or learning a trade or profession for life is now gone as most people joining the labour force today may have to engage in several occupations in different companies before they retire.

There are several processes involved with the concept of globalisation. Firstly, what are known as the factors of production are highly mobile. Capital moves through the world in an instant by means of pressing a few bars on a computer key board and labour can be recruited from anywhere in the world. Banks in the United States when faced with a shortage of computer staff simply advertised in Indian newspapers and received thousands of applications. Bermudians are familiar with the concept of British or Canadian accountants dominating the international company business sector. Ideas and knowledge, now the most important factor of production, are also highly mobile. CNN is viewed by millions in over a hundred countries, satellite TV is commonplace in such out of the way places like Ecuador, specialised professional magazines proliferate on newstands, the Internet allows individuals instantly to communicate with people they have never seen and never will see. Ideas and information make location almost irrelevant. The Fire department in Malmo, Sweden for example uses a computer in Cleveland , Ohio to search through its street data base. American Airlines uses staff in Jamaica to make travel reservations. Such examples can be repeated almost endlessly.

Secondly, consumers have multiple choices to make when they spend their money. Bermudians go to New York for a weekend of shopping much to the consternation of local merchants. Consumers can buy shirts, compact discs and computers from catalogues. Ten years ago that process would have been impossible and its impact locally is that Bermuda retailers now no longer compete only amongst themselves but are now competing with the world. Protectionism policies can no longer protect them from globalisation or from modern technology.

Thirdly, almost everything produced is available anywhere simultaneously and new products are produced with the world market in mind, not just one country. This means that competition for products and services comes from everywhere in the world and to be successful every producer needs to be a something of a world beater. Simply being in business for a long time or in a protected location is no longer an advantage. The days of saying to the customer "take it or

---

[6] See Part II 17 for a discussion of this issue.

leave it" are gone because if the customer is not satisfied he can buy immediately a better product elsewhere.

Fourthly, pure monopolies (or oligopolies) no longer exist, as activities once concentrated in one place or in one firm have moved to other places. New York as a financial centre is competing with London, Tokyo, Hong Kong, Singapore, Bermuda and a host of other places. Silicon Valley in California has competition from silicon bogs in Ireland, silicon glens in Scotland, or silicon harems in India. Economic isolation has ended.

Competition for international companies in offshore financial centres is also intensifying. Bermuda is no longer in the position of being a quasi monopoly supplier. Cayman, Vermont, Barbados, Singapore, Mauritius and a host of other jurisdictions are now openly in competition and if Bermuda fails to provide what the consumer wants quickly and efficiently he will go elsewhere. Corporate headquarters where decisions are made are now where the brains are and that can be literally anywhere, on a plane , in a hotel or visiting an affiliate overseas. Large offices with thousands of people toiling at desks passing information up and down are as obsolete as platoons of soldiers attacking machine gun nests, or exclusive dealerships in protected market places like Bermuda.

Collectively the forces that make for globalisation are revolutionising business, putting more and greater choices in the hands of the consumer who is now a dictator, and making the old world of protectionism as irrelevant as pigeons, semaphore flags or smoke signals in sending messages. If Bermuda wishes to continue its long enjoyed prosperity, globalisation will force it to join the rest of the world in providing world class standards of service and this means dismantling its protective barriers for no one can avoid, at least in the short term, the consequences of the irresistible forces of globalisation. Doing nothing or asking government for more protection simply means that competitors will intrude on your market as for example, Lands End has done to clothing retailers. Customers now want the best in the world, they want it now, and at the best price and failure to provide what the customer wants means they go elsewhere.

Protectionist policies are increasingly irrelevant to Bermudians because not allowing individuals complete freedom to make their own economic decisions will result in loss of business and loss of jobs in Bermuda. The free enterprise system when allied with modern technology and communications has made consumers free from the constraints of protectionist governments by making world markets available to everyone and at competitive prices. The market does not always work perfectly, nothing does, but allowing individuals to exercise their freedoms is surely better than allowing the alternative which is a civil servant determining what can and cannot be done. The presumption should favour the freedom, provided by the market because the alternative (if there is one) of bureaucratic command, is usually worse and invariably more inefficient.

Protectionism tries to prevent and interferes with the ordinary day to day workings of the market by making it difficult for willing buyers and sellers to reach an acceptable agreement. As a result, because the market is simply the sum of millions of independent decisions between willing buyers and sellers, the market distortions which arise invariably leads to everyone being worse off in the long run, not better off as supporters of protectionism would lead us to believe. Let me explain further.

If a manufacturer of a product or a provider of a service is prevented from hiring the best and brightest of staff, the invariable result is that what is produced will not be of the highest standard and, as a consequence, customers will be deprived of the best. If the customer is not satisfied the chances are that he will go elsewhere the next time he purchases the same or a similar product or service. The organisation is then penalised, as are other employees and the net effect is that everyone including customers are worse off (because the customer has had to go elsewhere) than if the organisation had unfettered discretion to make its own decisions.

Protectionism therefore does not always result in benefits to those it is designed to protect; the irony is that protectionism frequently fails to protect but instead it destroys. Initially, it gives the appearance of assisting those it was designed to help, but in the long run it is highly destructive and instead of improving things it makes them worse. Let me give a practical example of what I mean.

Let us assume that a Bermudian hotelier is compelled by the Department of Immigration to employ a poorly trained Bermudian bartender whom he believes is not up to the job; because of this government decision the hotelier cannot therefore employ a foreign bartender whom, in his honest judgment, will provide excellent service to the customers of the business. Please note that a government bureaucracy which has little or no direct experience of the industry has the power to override the decisions of a manager who understands the needs of his customers and who is intimately aware of day to day business problems. Only in the most unusual circumstances would the government department be more knowledgeable than the manager.

Let us assume further that a tourist customer goes into a bar and orders a drink from the Bermudian bartender who provides surly, incompetent and unpleasant service. The chances are that that customer will not have another drink or willingly return on future occasions. The net result is that the hotel has lost a customer and the revenue that goes with it, the rest of the staff have lost the gratuities that go along with a happy customer, and Bermuda may have lost forever a discontented tourist who on future trips may go elsewhere. The protection ostensibly provided by law to benefit Bermudians has exactly the opposite result in this example. Further the majority of competent Bermuda employees quickly come to understand that incompetence is not directly penalised and that it is protected by government policies. The incentive to provide top class service is therefore blunted, and customers are not kept happy. Bermuda runs the risk of being less competitive and everyone ends up being worse off.

The reason why the public believes that the protections provided by law have the effect the politicians say it will is because of the well documented fact that only rarely does the public appreciate the ACTUAL long term results of any protectionist policy. In understanding the effects of a protectionist policy, it is crucial to understand not only the intentions of the policy but its practical consequences, and not only the immediate results but the long term results, not merely the primary consequences of its effects but the secondary consequences, but especially not merely the effects on the protected group, firm or individual but the effects on everyone including the customer and the producer.

We have come to our present predicament through pursuing the reasonable objective of improving the living standards of Bermudians. We have implemented policies which have had temporary beneficial effects resulting from the slow speed at which people respond to changing circumstances and we have elevated them to eternal truths of Bermudian financial management.

Politicians and special interest groups are able to get away with the equivalent of economic murder because the public has a lazy habit of thinking only of some specific group, economic policy or process in isolation. As a result, major fallacies arise. No one is against hiring Bermudian bartenders because Bermudians deserve to be employed at jobs in their country. This is the policy in isolation and few people would argue against it. The secondary consequence of this policy is that the potential for substandard service is enormous, employees can become complacent because they believe they cannot be removed or disciplined or they just don't care. In such extreme circumstances, customers and the associated foreign exchange earnings are lost to competitors like Jamaica or Bahamas. Bermuda becomes less competitive and the general public suffers because the Bermudian economy is not as efficient as it could and should be.

Broadly similar arguments can be used about the other economic protectionist policies in Bermuda and the reader should try the same logic stated above to determine whether the following are in the best long term interests of Bermuda:-

- rent controls on housing.
- the restraints on non Bermudians owning more than 40% of the shares of a company which does business within Bermuda.
- shopping on Sundays.
- the restraints on non-Bermudians owning land and property in Bermuda.

There is a tendency for the public, egged on by politicians and special interest groups, to see only the immediate impact of any economic policy on special groups or individuals, and to ignore what the long term effects on all Bermudians will be. It is this tendency to neglect the secondary or long term consequences which explains the difference between good economic policies and bad, and which explains why politicians and interest groups often support policies which are not in the long term interest of Bermudians. Many of our public figures propose economic nonsense from the hustings because they are presenting, in the main, only half-truths.

To present the whole truth is difficult, requires long and sustained logical argument, and is bound to offend some powerful groups able to sway a bloc of votes. The audiences for a difficult subject can easily be inattentive and lose their concentration and complex economic arguments are impossible to encapsulate in a sound byte or a 60 second TV commercial. Henry Hazlitt who died in 1995 stated in his book, first published in 1946, that "the whole of economics can be reduced to a single lesson, and that lesson can be reduced to a single sentence. The art of economics consists in looking not merely at the immediate but at the longer effects of any act or policy; it consists in tracing the consequences of that policy not merely for one group but for all groups."[7]

Protectionism is an insidious process whose malignant effects are only understood by a few people who are able to discern the long term consequences. For most of the public, and for politicians, the short term impact and the underlying motives (which are usually good), are the test of whether a protectionist measure is a good thing or a bad thing. The long term consequences are lost to the illusion of the short term gains. But it is the long term impact on the economy and society which is important. Will the protectionist measure give Bermuda a substantial advantage in the economic jungle or will it, like a drink for an alcoholic, give an immediate good feeling but in the end be destructive? That is the test but one which is rarely applied by our financial decision makers.

It is difficult to maintain olympic standards if the day to day training sessions are conducted with a bunch of flabby team mates. To be competitive and maintain the competitive edge an athlete constantly has to compete in training with the best and continually work to improve his performance. So it is in the economic game. A country cannot be a world leader in income if it does not daily maintain its competitive edge and be responsive to changes elsewhere in the world. Sooner or later the competition will overtake it and steal its customers. For Bermuda, this has already occurred in the tourist business.

Bermuda, like the rest of the world, is divided into two kinds of people, those who want to prosper by competing and those who want to prosper by getting government to prevent their competitors entering the local market. Unfortunately, the facts from elsewhere and the results of recent years in Bermuda show that interventionist, regulating, and subsidising government is generally a servant of the established powers and the entrenched against the unorganised public. The lesson learned by most countries is that protectionism is generally harmful to the long term interest of the country and its citizens.

The inescapable conclusion is that protectionism creates inefficiency. As a result Bermuda becomes uncompetitive and in the process jobs and profits are destroyed as we have seen since about 1990 in the tourism and retailing businesses. Just as important, protectionism creates barriers to implementing change which is so essential to being successful in the new global economy. Protectionist policies destroy by stealth - they do not protect Bermudian businesses or Bermudian jobs. They are an illusion and by definition a bad thing for Bermuda.

---

[7] "Economics in One Lesson" by Henry Hazlitt.

17. WHY DOES BERMUDA NOT SUFFER FROM UNEMPLOYMENT LIKE OTHER COUNTRIES?

"An unemployed existence is a worse negation of life than death itself. Because to live means to have something definite to do - a mission to fulfill - and it the measure in which we avoid setting our life to something, we make it empty. Human life, by its very nature, has to be be dedicated to something."

JOSE ORTEGA Y GASSET

Bermuda has had quite a remarkable record of being able to provide full-employment for its labour force. This is a major achievement when comparing it with the record of other countries, including the United States which has a good record of job creation. About one-third of males in Britain without educational qualifications were unemployed in 1995. In the United States it was the same for white males, whilst for black Americans it was nearly 40 percent. Full employment is a characteristic of the Bermudian economy which marks off Bermuda as a wonderful economic success story.

As with most things this has not happened purely by accident - although there is an element of luck - but has occurred because the Bermuda government has pursued policies which have constantly allowed jobs to be created not destroyed. Let me go back to an article published more than thirty years ago in the English press by a British newspaper reporter named Margaret Fishley. She worked in Bermuda for 'The Bermuda Sun' at a time when Bermuda was in the throes of changing its form of government from being governed by an Executive Council largely appointed by the Governor (who in those days had real executive power) to one in which a Bermudian Cabinet was accountable to the House of Assembly.

"There are no old age pensions, no low cost-cost housing schemes, no unemployment insurance. Negroes feel at a disadvantage in getting jobs, and claim that the Board of Immigration admits unskilled foreigners too easily...and most of the wealth is still firmly in the grip of the white minority.[1] There is no economic planning and no serious attempt to develop secondary industries. There is no income tax, no estate duties, no profits tax and no laws against monopolies. A land tax is to be introduced soon, but is regarded as revolutionary. Customs duties are the main source of Government revenue."[2]

Had the Bermuda government at the time been foolish enough to follow the implied recommendations of Miss Fishley, Bermudians would almost certainly have suffered the same sort of unemployment levels as elsewhere. Income taxes, profit taxes and economic planning would have prevented the growth of the Exempted Company business and would have made Bermuda very different from the place it is now. All of the criticisms expressed by Miss Fishley and widely supported at the time by the PLP were reasons why Bermuda was able to thrive in the 1970s and 1980s when many economies like the United Kingdom regressed. Ignorance is truly bliss.

Let me bring the story forward to the 1990s for a look at a rich area of the world which suffers most from unemployment - and that is Europe.

---

[1] A feeling of deja-vu

[2] Beyond the Crossroads, Barbara Harries Hunter, pages 173-174.

Unemployment levels in Germany and France, the two largest economies in Europe, is about 12 percent of the general labour force up from around five percent in the 1970s. In Spain it is about 20 percent. For those under 25 years old and those over 50 it is about 20 percent in France and Germany.

In the United States by contrast the unemployment rate is about 5 percent of the labour force and about 12 percent for those under 25. In Bermuda unemployment is practically non-existent (in December 1994 65 jobs out of 34,143 or 0.2 percent)[3].

It is the rapid growth in non-pecuniary labour costs which is the main reason for the difference in unemployment rates between Europe and North America. Almost half of the costs of an employee in France and Germany are accounted for by costs for social security, health, unemployment compensation and other such taxes. A subsidiary reason is regulations which prohibit or restrict layoffs or which provide for sick leave, vacations or maternity leave.

Few people are against things like paid vacations, restraints on firing workers or sick leave but the fact of the matter is that such policies result in companies being reluctant to hire workers or expand the labour force when business improves. Laws and regulations which give employees permanent job protection make employing companies very reluctant to increase their labour force. Except for governments, of course. The laws of economics are rarely applied there.

Hence if you are a young job-seeker or a mother returning to work after maternity leave being able to secure a good job takes a long time - if you are lucky enough to find one. The only organisation where jobs have increased over the past 20 years is in government which is in contrast to what has happened in the United States.

In Europe, teenagers, other young people and those with limited skills can only find jobs in fast-food outlets and similar low paid occupations, or they are taken on the payroll on a part-time capacity. Many others enter what is known as the black economy where they are not officially recorded as being employed and where they are paid low wages.

High unemployment benefits (the dole) make it possible for many people never to hold a serious job during their lifetime. Apart from the loss of income that arises it means a stunted and limited life. Several studies in the U.K., Continental Europe and the U.S.A. have shown that people who have protracted periods on welfare or social security have their work skills eroded, lose important social skills like punctuality, and entrench the habits of depending on government for money. At the end of the day, this destroys potential earning power, character, initiative and self-confidence. European governments continue to do what, on the face of it, is electorally popular things like increasing welfare benefits and the minimum wage. This results in increased unemployment as employers cannot afford to hire employees whose productivity is low. A leading Labour Party MP in Britain, Mr Frank Field, has stated that "the benefit culture is increasingly destructive of honesty, effort, savings and self-improvement."[4]

---

[3] Bermuda Digest of Statistics 1995, page 51.

[4] 'The London Times', November 18, 1996.

Countries which have sought to legislate full-employment have ended up providing a guarantee of universal stagnation. By comparison, flexible labour markets have produced either low unemployment as in the United States or effectively nil unemployment as is the case in Bermuda. Job losses are difficult to handle in organisations struggling with changing customers and technology or having to meet brutal competition. The benefit of constant change is that economies ultimately become much more productive.

The European policies desribed above are broadly similar to what Miss Fishley was recommending for Bermuda thirty years ago. The result is that unemployment levels stay stubbornly high, a large number of potential employees never really enjoy a good job, and those over 50 have to take early retirement. This is hardly a scenario which reflects the current employment situation in Bermuda. Nevertheless there is evidence that some of the job destruction policies which have created so much havoc in Europe are now being applied in Bermuda. Examples are:

- Payroll tax now at a level of 12 percent.[5]

- New Pension proposals which in the absence of a corresponding payroll deduction from employees will push up the cost of employing staff.[6]

- Increasing regulations and mandatory provision for things like maternity leave and sick leave.

- Having a Bermudian under-study for key jobs.

By themselves such policies are not likely to result in Bermuda being like Europe but a continuation and intensification of them could mean that in 10 or 20 years Bermuda will have caught the European disease of unemployment.

That being said Bermuda is still a long way from the disastrous European (or even American) experiences and provided we avoid the calls for increased social wages we should continue in unemployment matters to be the envy of the rest of the world.

18. WHAT IS PRODUCTIVITY AND HOW IMPORTANT IS IT?

"Productivity is the prime determinant in the long run of a nation's standard of living, for it is the root cause of national per capita income. The productivity of human resources determines their wages, while the productivity with which capital is employed determines the return it earns for its holders. High productivity not only supports high levels of income but allows citizens the option of choosing more leisure instead of long working hours. It also creates the national income that is taxed to pay for public services which again boosts the standard of living. The capacity to be highly productive also allows a nation's firms to meet stringent social standards which improve the standard of living, such as in health and safety, equal opportunity, and environmental impact."

"THE COMPETITIVE ADVANTAGE OF NATIONS" - MICHAEL PORTER, PAGE 6.

---

[5] See the 1996/97 budget.

[6] See the Green Paper on 'A National Pensions Scheme for Bermuda' issued in June, 1995.

Simply defined productivity is the output per employee per man hour. How many customers can be served in an hour : if previously 10, and the number goes up to 11 productivity has increased by 10 percent. It is often thought of as working harder or working longer hours, and there is an element of this although it is better to think of productivity as working smarter, being more competent or thinking about how things could be done better. In essence it means working more productively without necessarily working longer and harder. Increases in productivity tend to come incrementally (or in small doses) almost imperceptively and rarely occur with much fanfare yet in the long run there is nothing more important to the health of an economy. A gain in productivity of three percent per annum translates into a doubling of everyone's income every 23 years. The miraculous effect of compound interest shows its full powers only over long periods.

There has, in historical terms, been an explosion in productivity over the past 200 years. Since the industrial revolution - the period approximately between 1750 and 1850 when new technology, education and the application of capital to the production process resulted in Britain becoming the workshop of the world for just under a 100 years and which led to change in the economic life of the rest of the world. Productivity has risen largely because labour was replaced by machines (or capital), scientific management was created in the late nineteenth century by Frederick Taylor in the Unites States, and energy (coal, gas and oil) replaced muscle in the manufacturing process.

Productivity, or output, has increased at about 2% to 3% per annum, and this has resulted in incomes rising dramatically. Instead of living a subsistence existence as was the norm for the average person 200 years ago, we in the developed world now enjoy a standard of living and have a disposable income which would have been the envy of kings 500 years ago. Not only are our incomes much greater, we live longer, enjoy better health, have greater leisure and have greater variety of life styles. Without that rising productivity we would die at before 40, be subjected to constant illnesses and infectious diseases, be dirty, probably have no or limited education, never travel, have a 12 hour working day, be constantly hungry and generally have a miserable existence by comparison with what we have today. An additional benefit created by rising productivity was that the class war predicted by Karl Marx never materialised. The working class who lived lives of unbelievable hardship in the early 19th century had by the early 20th century become enthusiastic members of the middle-class. The proletariat through the miracle of productivity had transformed themselves into the bourgeois.

Debates about productivity is something which is unique to capitalism. In many societies tradition plays a key role or the economy is controlled by a political dictator as it is in such countries as China or Burma and as a result proposing improvements to anything is frowned upon as it tends to upset or create difficulties for the established order. Capitalism on the other hand, despite what its critics say, is a form of questioning the old order, a form of revolution if you like, which constantly undermines the traditional way of doing things until it eventually destabilises existing procedures and institutions by making them financially irrelevant.

Capitalism is therefore central to the economic system we live under. It is unruly and disconcerting, a system of constant change and upheaval rather than one of stability and equilibrium. It was the reason why a small country like Singapore, population 3 million and 250 square miles[1], like Bermuda lacking in natural resources has been transformed into one of the most affluent areas in the world.

The purpose of jobs is not to keep people occupied between 9 and 5 but to create output, goods and services which the public and the world wishes to buy. If an organisation becomes more efficient and is able to produce the same output with fewer people it means that an increase in productivity has occurred. That is good news for the economy in general - although obviously not for the people directly affected. News reports do not spend much time spreading the real good news which is that productivity has increased but the press tends to lament that jobs have been lost as it did, for example, in early 1996 when the Bermuda Telephone Company restructured in order to become more efficient.[2]

Literally millions of jobs have been changed beyond recognition because of computers and related advances in technology. Bank tellers, secretaries, typists and telephone operators are only a few of the jobs which have changed or disappeared in the past 20 years. New jobs which enhance productivity like software design are created which generate higher incomes to the holders because their productivity is higher. People in possession of today's skills are handsomely rewarded for their increased productivity while those with yesterday's skills meaning low productivity suffer from lagging incomes. Technical change can be a cruel process as it tends to make skills redundant at a time when individuals are at their most vulnerable. Although technological advance makes everyone better off in the long-run, there are many individuals who are hurt in the process.

> *"Productivity is the key to affluence, yet horribly elusive. It is a term that can be applied to any factor of production - land, labour or capital - to measure the output of each unit. Statisticians labour long hours to produce half-decent figures, and then economists spend their careers pondering exactly what (if anything) the figures mean."*
> The Pocket Economist, 2nd edition, page 183

To maintain our constantly rising standard of living will not be as easy as it was. This mainly arises because most of the increases in productivity which have occurred in the developed world have taken place in industries which grow, make and move products like wheat and automobiles. The percentage of the population engaged in such activities has fallen dramatically over the past fifty years or so. Now only about 20 percent of the working population in advanced economies are involved with the manufacturing process and only about three percent are employed in agriculture significantly down from about 60 percent only a hundred years ago.[3]

---

[1] Although big by Bermuda standards.

[2] See Part II on the issue of restructuring.

[3] "The End of Work," Jeremy Rifkin, page 109.

The rest of the world has developed to the point that it increasingly resembles Bermuda in that a majority of the working population is engaged in personal services (such as tourism), financial services (such as insurance or banking) or other services such as software development. In New York City 90 percent of jobs are in service industries. With a predominately service economy, statistics find it extremely difficult to measure productivity with the degree of accuracy applicable to an economy which mainly produces tangible objects like tons of steel or thousands of TV sets. Services like medical care, financial advice or silver waiter service are hard to count and are more evident to customers than statisticians. Bean counters count beans, not the flavour of the coffee and the skill of the waiter. Service and knowledge workers are a heterogeneous group. They range from brain surgeons to short-order cooks, portfolio managers to porters, artists and writers to security guards although there are major differences in education, skill, knowledge, salary, social status, life-style and social beliefs.

To continue to increase productivity in services at the historical rate achieved by manufacturing in the modern economy is going to be a major challenge for developed economies - and was at the heart of the Commission on Competitiveness established by the Premier in 1992.[4] If the operator of a machine in a factory was out of shape and overweight it made no difference to his productivity because the machine did the heavy lifting. If a service worker like an accountant or surgeon lets his mind get out of shape by failing to keep up to date with his profession his productivity will fall quickly. During the period 1950 to 1980 which coincided with a long period of inflation, service industry economies like Bermuda were able to increase prices. The Bermuda economy benefited partly because it was an innovator in both tourism and international business and was able to charge premium prices, and partly because increases in service costs were easier to pass on to customers.

This fortuitous combination of circumstances is no longer the case. The world has changed dramatically over the past ten years with the result that rising productivity is the only true source of competitive advantage in the modern world and is, as it was the past, the main source of social stability. That productivity however is largely dependent on employees skill base and keeping it up to date. Despite talk about worker training and improved educational standards the public education system has waged war on objective standards, benchmarking and educational rigour.[5] Increasingly, governments are concerned about hiring and promotions based on race, gender, nationality, age and other factors unrelated to ability and productivity.

One of the indisputable laws of economics is that for any prolonged period of time incomes cannot increase faster than productivity. If productivity is stagnant then incomes will be similarly stagnant and when this is the case social tensions heighten. High producing knowledge workers - such as those who work in the Exempt Companies in Bermuda - are seeing their incomes move continuously higher. Low productivity and generally low skilled service workers in industries like the hotel, retail and restaurant business are finding that their relative wages are falling - and when the tourism industry is in a period of decline as it has been

[4] See Part III 18 for a discussion on the Commission.
[5] See Charles J. Sykes "Dunsbury Down Our Kids" much of which is relevant to Bermuda.

for some years - their absolute wages also fall with the inevitable result that they see themselves as a class apart. Society can become torn apart if one sector does spectacularly well whilst the other becomes financially worse-off. In 1996 Bermuda increasingly resembles the society of 30 years ago but instead of differences in wealth arising from race, they now arise from differences in productivity based on educational skills. To avoid this split in society and to increase the incomes of the poorly paid it is crucially important to raise every employee's productivity and this is not an easy task.[6]

One of the principal reasons for the existence of society and government is to provide their people with a rising standard of living and Bermuda has been very successful at that - at least until recently. Some organisations have traditionally expressed hostility towards improved productivity - trade unions for instance are renowned for resisting new and better methods of working. Politicians are hostile to change when it adversely affects their constituents. Some economic environments stimulate the upgrading process, the United States is probably the best international example - others do not. The major role for government is to provide an environment which leads to improved productivity for in the long run our continuing prosperity and social stability depends on it.

19. IS BERMUDA OVER POPULATED?

"It has been estimated that the human population (of the world) of 6,000 BC was about five million people, taking perhaps one million years to get there from two and a half million. The population did not reach 500 million until almost 8,000 years later - about 1650 AD. This means it doubled roughly once every thousand years or so. It reached a billion people around 1850, doubling in some 200 years. It took only 80 years or so for the next doubling, as the population reached two billion around 1930. The doubling time at present seems to be about 37 years."
Dr Paul R. Ehrlich, "The Population Bomb". 1968.

This is a difficult question to answer with an unequivocal yes or no. As Table 1 below shows the population of Bermuda has increased from just under 20,000 in 1911 to just under 60,000 in 1991. It has therefore increased threefold in a period of 80 years.[1] By comparison with the distant past (well not all that distant as there are many people still alive today who were born before 1911) Bermuda is overpopulated. There was also a significant increase of about 50% between 1960 and 1991.

---

[6] Especially when there is opposition from unions.

Table 1   **Bermuda's Civilian Population**

Year	Total	Male	Female
Census Figures[1]			
1911	18,994	9,070	9,924
1921	20,127	9,629	10,498
1931	27,789	14,174	13,615
1939	30,516	15,034	15,482
1950	37,403	18,148	19,255
1960	42,640	21,233	21,407
1970	52,976	26,671	26,305
1980	54,670	26,715	27,955
1991	59,324	28,911	30,413

Source: Census Office and Registrar General

However, if we ask the question from the point of view is Bermuda over-populated by comparison with other countries in the world, then the answer is an unequivocal "yes". The second table shows that by comparison with the USA, Canada and UK we are very densely populated with 3,160 per square mile, compared with 7 in Canada, but 14,180 in Hong Kong and surprisingly only 322 per square mile in China.

Table 2

Country	Population	Density Per Square Mile
Bermuda	58,460	3,160
U.S.A.	257.8 million	68
Canada	28.8 million	7
U.K.	57.9 million	616
Hong Kong	5.8 million	14,180
China	1,190.4 million	322
Barbados	256,000	1,542
Jamaica	2.55 million	602

Source: 1996 World Almanac

---

[1] This is about the same rate of increase in world population which grew from about 2 billion to 6 billion in the same period.

A third way of looking at the question is what population is needed to sustain our enviable quality of life. This requires a subjective answer but in my opinion Bermuda does not feel overcrowded, mainly because of the ocean, there is negligible unemployment, and a certain critical mass is needed to provide all the advanced skills necessary for a sophisticated economy.

Table 3

Population by Nativity, 1950 - 1991

YEAR	TOTAL	BERMUDA BORN	FOREIGN BORN	
1950	37,403	28,749	8,654	23%
1970	52,330	37,834	14,496	28%
1990	58,460[a]	42,634	15,823	27%

(a) Includes 3 persons who did not state their place of birth

Source: Bermuda Statistical Department.

A final comment on the number of people not born in Bermuda. This has stood at roughly one-quarter of the population as Table 3 above shows. There are few countries in the world which could absorb such a high proportion of foreign born without putting undue strain on the tolerance of the locally born. For the foreign reader, just imagine the social upheaval which would arise if one-quarter of the population of the United States (which prides itself as a nation of immigrants) or the United Kingdom was not native. It is a remarkable testimony to the open mindedness of Bermudians that anti-immigrant feelings are negligible.

Clearly there are limits to the number of people which Bermuda can accommodate otherwise life would be unbearable. The level of population also has a critical bearing on Bermuda's physical environment, an issue which is examined in an earlier essay. For many life is uncomfortable because of the shortage of housing, crowded roads or crowded schools. On the other hand there is a shortage of labour for many organisations. The population of Bermuda is at about the right level to support the standard and quality of life which most Bermudians seek. We are a long way from the apocalyptic vision contained in the introductory quotation. Nevertheless, the issue of the size of the world's population is one of the most serious problems faced by mankind. It is a question beyond the scope of this short essay.

20. WHERE IS BERMUDA ON THE SIGMOID CURVE?

"If it ain't broke, don't fix it."
RALLYING CALL FOR THE ANTI-INDEPENDENCE MOVEMENT IN BERMUDA.

"Life will never be easy, or perfectible, or completely predictable. It will be best understood backward, but we have to live forward."
CHARLES HANDY - AUTHOR OF "THE AGE OF PARADOX".

The sigmoid curve is like an S lying on its side ; it signifies and gives meaning to many of life's ups and downs and has been a source of fascination for centuries. It sums up in its curve the stories of people, countries, empires, companies and if you are imaginative enough love and relationships - subjects which are rarely explored in books about economics.

The Sigmoid curve is also a means of telling the story about constant growth and change, and a new curve can begin before the old one disappears or becomes obsolete. The curve at first moves downwards illustrating that as in life we start slowly and experimentally, taking time to learn how to do things. After a period we move up the curve as we become more competent, confident and stronger. When we become older or complacement and then we begin the slow agonising decline which evidences our inability to face new challenges or meet new conditions. Whilst the ageing process cannot prevent individuals from declining after a certain point, it is nevertheless possible throughout life to renew oneself. It is even clearer that countries and organisations who do not face human limitations also have the power to start to move upwards along a new curve and remain vigilant, creative and energetic for years, even centuries.

The secret of the Sigmoid curve is to start on a new curve before the old one declines to a point of no return. But where on the curve does one make the move? The trick is to find the right place to begin the renaissance and that is at point A on the curve shown below, when there is time, resources and opportunity to begin again.

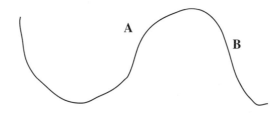

To wait until point B is reached is to flirt with disaster as events may have gone too far to allow for recovery. When point B is reached there may be insufficient resources to do anything but witness the downfall of the established order.

The trouble with starting to change at point A is that that is the time when all the evidence points to the fact that things are going well and that there is therefore no need to change. As the old saying goes "never change a winning team" or in the words of a more popular idiomatic Bermuda saying " if it ain't broke, don't fix it." It takes great effort and great leadership to convince people that when everything is going well it is time to change and lead the organisation or country onto the new curve.

This difficulty is compounded when the message is given to those further down the line as it discredits the current leadership of the organisation. However, to wait until point B on the curve may be too late as many organisations like Pan-American Airlines and Apple Computers have found to their cost. For many of the best companies in the 1990s the message which is being sent out by management is:-

1   We are successful and continue to be successful, and

2   If we wish to continue to be successful we must change our winning ways.

Capitalism is very good at reinventing itself because it receives constant intelligence from the market place advising how good or how bad it is. Countries are a different matter because whilst change for the better is desired voters may want the leadership to do absolutely nothing to disturb their comfortable life-style.

Many lessons can be learned from understanding how the Sigmoid curve applies to Bermuda when we consider the debate which is taking place about such subjects as:

* independence
* productivity
* educational change
* taxation
* pensions
* allowing fast food franchises.

But most of all there are lessons to be learned when we examine the current debate about the future of the tourist industry. Bermuda was a pioneer in tourism, it was spectacularly successful at it and became wealthy and happy as a result. However, there was and is mounting evidence that the condition of the business today is not as healthy as it was in previous years - guest numbers and their spending continue to decline. In my opinion, we have passed point A on the Sigmoid curve and are probably somewhere very close to point B. Many people who are close to the business see the difficulties ahead and want to start on a new curve - as evidenced by the implementation by the Minister of Tourism of a revised advertising campaign. Others continue to cling to the belief that the tourist customer has not changed and want things to remain as they were in the 1960s.[1]

---

[1] See the discussion on reengineering and restructuring.

It is always tempting and psychologically reassuring to believe that the world has always been the way it is at present and to fool ourselves that the rest of the world owes us a living and we will never have to change. It is very difficult for Bermuda and Bermudians to let go of a past which has been full of achievements just as it is much easier for countries to change after major policy mistakes - witness the renaissance of Japan and Germany after the disasters of the Second World War.

The story of economics and business is that there are many companies and organisations who believed they had found the philospher's stone and that their way of doing things was the only way. One of America's most admired companies, IBM learned the hard way when it came into contact with the upstart Microsoft, similarly in the retailing business when Sears had to compete with Walmart. The business world tends to favour those who are discontented and the future winners are people like Rupert Murdoch, Richard Branson and Ted Turner who challenge established orthodoxies. Complacency and success tends to be the enemy of innovation and change and the past is probably not the best guide for the future.

The paradox of success is that the factors which have enabled Bermuda to get to where it is may not, in a fast changing world, be the same to keep us where we want to be. We are being forced by the market place to challenge our previous assumptions underlying the first curve and to think about producing other options. Increasingly the motto in the world of the 1990s is to say "if it ain't broke, fix it." The question for Bermuda is to determine at what point we are on the Sigmoid curve and determine as a community if we are nearer to point A than point B. Unfortunately, we have to proceed by gut-instinct and judgement as there is no science to be employed.

BERMUDA AND THE
INTERNATIONAL ECONOMY

2

1. WHY IS THE UNITED STATES SO IMORTANT TO THE BERMUDA ECONOMY?

"We talk about the American Dream, and want to tell the world about the American Dream, but what is that Dream, in most cases, but the dream of mate-rial things? I sometimes think that the United States for this reason is the great-est failure the world has ever seen."

EUGENE O'NEILL (A FREQUENT VISITOR TO BERMUDA IN THE 1920s)

The same negative refrain can be gleaned from what a Mexican President was reputed to have said about the United States *"So far from God but so close to the United States."* For Bermuda the close proximity of America has been a major reason for its prosperity as I hope to demonstrate. If being prosperous and wealthy is failure, Bermuda has been one of the biggest failures the world has ever seen.

In the 1970s the then Prime Minister of Canada, Pierre Trudeau, said that the Canadian economy was so closely intertwined with that of the United States that it was like a mouse being in bed with an elephant. If Canada is a mouse, Bermuda is a pimple on a flea on a mouse. The United States economy not only dominates Canada and Bermuda, it dominates the whole of the Western hemisphere. Only the large countries of Europe and Asia come close to rivalling the economic, tech-nical and political leadership of the United States in the world.

It would not be much of an exaggeration to state that every country in the Western hemisphere is an economic subsidiary of the United States so sweeping is the size and scope of the American economy. Bermuda with a 60,000 popula-tion is so small and insignificant that its economy, for all practical purposes is as much a part of the United States as that of the state of Rhode Island.

The reader should pause to consider the following economic facts :-

- 90% of our visitors come from the United States.
- 60% of our imports come from the United States.
- Apart from British Airways, all scheduled airlines which fly to Bermuda are U.S. based.
- The Bermuda dollar is tied to the US dollar.
- Bermuda dollar interest rates move in sympathy with those in the United States.
- Most of the international companies in Bermuda are American owned.
- Most of our young people go to the United States for their university edu-cation.
- Most of our television programmes and movies originate in the United States.

On top of these facts, the following global considerations about the USA should also be borne in mind :

- Its record of international business success.

- Military leadership.
- Political dominance.
- Cultural dominance in areas like movies, TV and music.
- Technical leadership in areas like pharmaceuticals, telecommunictions and information technology (including computer software).
- Its university system attracts top students from around the world.

Some of this economic and cultural dominance does not benefit Bermuda. For example, Bermuda has acquired and imported some of the negative characteristics of the United States many of which have an adverse impact on economic and social life :

- The drug culture.
- Increasing crime and violence (although only a fraction of what exists in USA).
- High illegitimacy rates.
- Poor public education especially for those in the critical age group 12 to 16 years.
- Inequality of incomes.
- Perceived inequality of opportunity.
- Worsening race relations.

Although there are advantages of being an economic colony of the United States, when America goes into recession Bermuda suffers as a result. Most of our tourists originate from the mid-Atlantic and North Eastern states and when economic difficulties are experienced there it is immediately translated into financial trouble for Bermuda. If the United States tax laws or regulations change this could have an effect on many of the international companies incorporated in Bermuda. When the cold war ended in the late 1980s decisions made by the US military to close overseas bases had an impact on Bermuda. The Bermuda government exercised almost no influence over decisions by the American government to close its Naval Air Station in 1995. They were more influenced by adverse publicity than anything else.[1] With a stroke of the pen in Washington, the subsidy from Uncle Sam of US$8.35 million[2] ended, Bermuda's land area inceased by 10%, 710 jobs disappeared[3] and its airport had to be paid for and operated by the Bermuda government.

The good news about being dominated by the United States is that the North East and mid-Atlantic area is one of the wealthiest areas in the world, and that prosperity for many years migrated to Bermuda. The reader should try and imagine what the standard of living of Bermuda would be if it was located off the coast of Africa rather than the United States.

As I will repeatedly state, Bermuda's economy is built on two major industries. As a consequence, we are not unlike a company town in the United States which is wholly dependent on two key industries like automobile manufacture or

---

[1] In particular a television programme on ABC presented by Sam Donaldson.

[2] 'The Archer Report,' page 55.

[3] Ibid, page 52.

steel. When these two industries experienced chronic difficulties in the mid 1980s large cities like Gary, Indiana and Bethlehem, Pennsylvania found that their economies almost collapsed. If conditions changed for the worse in the United States, or what is more likely we fail to understand what makes tourism and international business work so effectively, our well-being could be drastically affected.

It may be uncomfortable being a mouse in bed with an elephant, but that pimple on the flea on the mouse can be extremely painful if the elephant scratches itself in the wrong place.

2. WHAT IS THE ARCHER REPORT?

"The objective of (The Report) was to measure the following values :
  * *the amount of employment in Bermuda attributable to each of the sectors (international companies, military bases, international tourism, other export activities like the banks and BIBA).*
  * *the amount of income created in Bermuda by these sectors.*
  * *the revenue received directly and indirectly by the public sector as a result of these activities".*

THE BERMUDIAN ECONOMY - THE IMPACT OF EXPORT EARNINGS IN 1992
(*THE ARCHER REPORT*)

The Archer Report is a regular study prepared for the Bermuda Government by Professor Brian Archer at the University of Surrey, England on the subject of the Bermuda Economy and its export earnings. It is carried out for the Ministry of Finance, the last occasion being February 1994 with an update on international companies being published in November, 1996.

The main document can be as intimidating and as dry as dust but it is full of facts, figures and conclusions about the sources of Bermuda's foreign exchange earnings. If the reader does not wish to go to the source document let me try to explain its importance in a more informal way.

What conclusions would be reached by a Bermuda resident of average intelligence - say, an MP, a plumber or even an international company manager - who took a casual stroll down Front Street on a Monday morning around 11:45 a.m. in July or August? He (or she) would see many tourists, mainly American, some shapely, some not, disembarking from cruise ships or coming into the city from a $200-a-night hotel room somewhere on the South Shore.

If our resident leisurely progressed the whole length of Front Street, by around noontime at Heyl's Corner he would see many well-groomed Bermudians and a few pale non-Bermudians, looking incongruous in three-piece suits, emerging from the two banks and several office blocks nearby. These employees escaping their TV monitors, telephones and office supervisors would be seeking the fresh air or, more likely, joining the tourists in the many bars and restaurants along Front Street.

If our resident himself enjoyed a noonday drink against the background of cash registers happily ringing away and reflected on the benefits to Bermuda of this scene, he would conclude, as did the 1996 update of the Archer Report, that the bedrock of our economy continues to be tourism and international business. For most Bermudians, a casual midday walk along Front Street plus a cool beer beats the hell out of ploughing through "The Bermuda Economy - The Impact of Exempt Company Earnings", published by the Ministry of Finance in 1994 and updated in 1996 by the "International Companies 1995"- Their Impact on the Economy of Bermuda" also published by the Ministry of Finance. They are not daunting documents but are full of figures which, unfortunately, can be offputting - except for eccentrics like myself who read figures with the same pleasure as my wife reads poetry.

What pearls of wisdom can be found in its almost 200 pages? Quite a number in my opinion, but no real surprises. The Bermudian economy is one of the most internationally dependent and vulnerable economies in the world, the principal sources of its income and prosperity being international business (including banking), tourism and until recently the three foreign military bases.

In 1995 there were 6,500 jobs dependent on international business, and a further 6,300 were affected by the industry. Of the 8,720 international businesses registered in Bermuda in 1995, about 275 have their own offices. Those who maintain a physical presence tend to be the well-known names. Sedgwick James, Marsh & McLennan, Johnson and Higgins, American International in insurance; Schroders, Fidelity and GT in financial services; Shell, Exxon, Jardine Matheson - all big names in finance, trading and manufacturing. Of the others who do not have a physical presence, our banks, lawyers, accountants and management companies are happy, for a fee, to look after them.

International companies directly employ 1,349 Bermudians (the number of non-Bermudians is 922). The employees received almost $225 million in salaries and a further $144 million was paid as fees to lawyers, accountants and banks. The Bermuda Government didn't do too badly either, collecting more than $46 million in taxes and other fees. All of this reinforces what most readers already know, namely that international business, particularly the insurance sector is a major prop of the economy. If this business vanished in a puff of smoke, more than 6,000 jobs would disappear entirely and another 6,000 would be adversely affected.

How are Bermudians making out in international business? Not bad, but not all that good. Based on a survey of ICD member companies between 1977 and 1995 the ratio of Bermudian to non-Bermudian has remained fairly static at around two-thirds. The low point was May, 1983 when the percentage of Bermudians was 63.2% and the high point was August, 1990 when it was 68.7%. Not much of a change in 18 years despite all the training courses, scholarships and other incentives to attract Bermudians into the field. In my experience, this is not because international companies fail to encourage or promote Bermudianisation (although this does happen) but because there are just not sufficient Bermudians available[1]. I would expect the situation to get worse in the future because of our falling birthrate.

In August, 1994 of the 1,349 Bermudians employed 1,036 were female and 313 male, confirming again what the informed observer already knows - namely, that there are many more female Bermudians employed by Exempt Companies and that many of the jobs Bermudians do in international business are the traditional female jobs of secretaries, typists (or keyboard operators) and book-keepers. Only 26% of management jobs were held by Bermudians. Still a long way to go for those who are ambitious. Nevertheless, more and more Bermudians are entering the international business field for the attractions of having a nine-to-five job in a pleasant office, with no heavy lifting and no seasonal disruption to salary.

Ambitious Bermudians have long been attracted to banking, an industry whose fortunes are very closely linked with international business. Bermuda's two big banks, the Bank of Bermuda Ltd, and the Bank of N.T. Butterfield & Son. Ltd., are Bermuda's equivalent of US and European multinationals having subsidiaries in such diverse jurisdictions as Hong Kong, Grand Cayman, London, Singapore, Mauritius, Isle of Man, Jersey and Luxembourg . The widespread geographical representation is not all that surprising given the vision of some of our early financial and banking leaders such as Sir Harry Butterfield and Sir Henry Tucker.

It has long been the inside view case that the two banks make little or no profit from local business although independent verification of this is hard to obtain. Increasingly, therefore, they need to earn more income from foreign subsidiaries and fees from Bermuda-based international clients. With its foreign branches Bermuda's role in international banking is out of all proportion to its importance in world commercial activity. The Bank of Bermuda earned $22 million overseas in the financial year ended June, 1996[2] - just under 50 percent of the Bank's net income for the year. The Bank of Butterfield earned $7.5 million out of a total net income of $29.1[3] million for the same period.

It is a remarkable testimony to the flexibility and adaptability of our banking institutions that they exceed international capital adequacy standards and they were smart enough not to become involved in Third World debt when it was fashionable in the 1980s. The two major banks employ about 3,600 staff. In the financial year ending June 1996, their total net income exceeded $76 million. Their combined assets came to $8.5 billion - try dividing that figure by 58,000, the size of Bermuda's population, and you will have an understanding of Bermuda's disproportionate impact in international banking.

Turning briefly to tourism, Dr. Archer reports that in each minute of 1994, tourists spent $861[4] and that more than 40 percent of public sector revenue came from this business. Accommodation, meals and gratuities account for about two-thirds of the expenditure of our tourists. The net gain to the balance of payments was $24.3 million and a further 5,728 jobs in addition to the 9,550 direct jobs were affected by tourism. More employment is created by tourism than by any other economic activity. Put simply, if the tourist doesn't come, most people don't

---

[1] See Part IV
[2] Bank of Bermuda annual report 1996.
[3] Bank of Butterfield annual report, 1996
4 I calculate that figure to be $840.

work. By itself this should be a great incentive to be polite, to be attentive to the needs of the tourist, and to preserve Bermuda as an attractive destination.

The mass of statistics in the report do not provide any shocks. Total arrivals for the past 12 years or so fluctuate around 500,000 most of whom come from the northeast of the United States, one of the highest disposable discretionary income areas in the world. Like so many things about Bermuda's economy, our fortuitous location speaks volumes about our success, and we are indeed fortunate to be located only two hours away from this market. Imagine how poor we would be if we were located in the Pacific Ocean two hours away from the coast of Chile.

Of our visitors, 25 percent earned incomes above $50,000 per annum and of the business visitors about 50 percent had incomes in excess of this amount. Now I know why the Fourways Inn, Tom Moore's and the Waterlot are always so busy.

However, when we look at the pattern of employment in hotels we find that the number of Bermudian males has fallen from 2,130 in 1979 to 1,400 in 1992; the number of females had also fallen from just under 2,000 in 1979 to 1,820 in 1992. Total Bermudian employment in hotels has fallen in 1979 from 4,129 to 3,220 and non-Bermudian employment is at about the same level. Clearly, the tourist industry is no longer as attractive for young Bermudians as it was some years ago.

I'll conclude by saying that Bermuda's per capita income (how much you have in your pocket to spend) of around $27,500[5] makes us one of the most affluent countries in the world. The annual per capita income for Haiti is $150, for Jamaica $ 1,500 , for the UK $17,965, for the Bahamas $11,330, for Canada $20,664, for Japan $31,451, and for the USA $24,753.[6] Our prosperity depends largely on our ability to earn overseas currency in our main industries of tourism and international business. We cannot for long spend more than we earn. If we do that, we would soon be rattling the begging bowl in much the same way as they do in India.

By comparison with the rest of the world, we do pretty well for a dot in the middle of the Atlantic. We have our economic troubles but they are trifles compared to other countries. Dr. Archer has shown the respective contributions of our main sectors of the economy and although international business is in reasonably good shape there are concerns about the performance of the tourism industry.

I mentioned at the beginning of this essay that we are economically vulnerable. How well we do economically is decided by our customers overseas. We are dependent on the fads and fashions of the tourist business, board room decisions and tax laws in foreign countries and, to a lesser extent, military strategy. We succeed or fail, given these uncertainties, on how well we keep our customers happy - not unlike a commercial enterprise or Bermuda Inc. if you like. If the tourist goes away with a smile on his face, if internationally we are seen to be politically stable and honest and provide top class banking, accounting, legal and management services we will continue to succeed. We have been good at all of this for many years. It is up to all Bermudians to keep it that way.

---

[5] Fact and Figures 1996 (The Economist reports per capita GDP at $28,293).

[6] All figures from "The World in Figures" 1996 edition published by 'The Economist.'

3. HOW IMPORTANT IS TOURISM TO THE BERMUDIAN ECONOMY?

"Bermuda has established a phenomenal record in tourism. It has built an economy based on tourism that has become a model for many other islands and countries. Bermuda's economy is dependent upon tourism. The island has one of the world's highest standards of living, and the majority of its propserity results from its tourism industry."

THE COMMISSION ON COMPETITIVENESS

A few indicators of the financial contribution which tourism makes to Bermuda will quickly and easily give the reader the quick answer that tourism is absolutely fundamental to the long-term health of the Bermudian economy. If the reader understands this essential fact he knows more about the economy of Bermuda than one who fails to understand the crucial importance of the tourism industry.

In 1994 tourism[1]:

- Generated 589,855 visitors to Bermuda of which 416,990 were staying visitors, the balance of 172,865 being cruise ship passengers.
- Created BD$525.3 million in direct incomes for Bermuda and Bermudians who work in hotels and other tourist related activities such as tour operators, taxi drivers and restaurants.
- These direct incomes are then spent within Bermuda creating a secondary stream of income.
- Contributed to the revenue of BD$170.5 million to the Bermuda Government - this relieves Bermudians of part of the unpleasant task of paying taxes.
- Directly and indirectly, created more employment (about 5,900 jobs) more than any other sector of the economy.

There are two essentials for small island economies like Bermuda ; (1) the creation of jobs, and (2) the earning of foreign exchange. Tourism has been very good at achieving both. It is able to absorb a relatively unskilled and uneducated labour and transform it into a force which creates value and income for Bermudians.

The cash spent by tourists cascades through the general economy creating incomes and jobs in restaurants, nightclubs, bars, taxis, tour operators and so on. The people in the direct line of tourist expenditure then spend money at supermarkets, to repair their homes, to refuel their vehicles, pay taxes and so on. This is known as the multiplier effect[2] which generates the prosperity which is a hallmark of Bermuda.

The success of tourism is a major accomplishment but, just as important, tourist related activities also buttress and complement Bermuda's international company business by providing, for example :-

---

[1] The data comes from the 1994 Archer Report.
[2] Any introductory textbook on economics will explain the importance of this term.

- sufficient airlift into Bermuda.
- quality accommodation.
- other personal services for the business visitor like transportation, leisure and restaurant facilities.

The Bermuda tourist industry saw significant growth following the end of the Second World War. The number of visitors for 1949 was 54,899; 142,330 in 1959; 370,000 in 1969 and in 1994 the corresponding figure was just under 590,000 the majority of whom (90%) came from the United States. This compares with about 3.5 million visitors to Bahamas and 1.3 million to Jamaica. 95% of visitors to Bermuda are white and 56% are female. Just over one-quarter earn incomes above $50,000 (although 1995 visitors were less affluent than they were in the past) and about 13 percent come for business related activity. About 40 percent are repeat visitors and surprisingly only about 15 percent said they would not return. In 1995 virtually all (98%) had favourable comments about Bermuda emphasising on the friendly people and physical beauty. European visitors were less complimentary than North American.

The highest number of arrivals was in 1987 when it was just over 637,314 but numbers have averaged around 550,000 for the past 20 years. Bermuda is very much a seasonal resort destination most of the visitors arriving between May and September. As a result, hotel occupancy is an anemic 60 percent or so. Delta Airlines brings the most visitors. Clearly, there are limits to the number of visitors which Bermuda can comfortably accommodate at any one time particularly during the summer months when visitor arrivals peak.

For many years Bermuda enjoyed enormous economic benefits from being a pioneer in the travel business. However, as competition has increased since the 1970s being a pioneer has many disadvantages as Bermudians who work in the business are finding out. There are a number of disturbing trends in the tourist industry which cause concern:[3]

- The number of visitors has plateaued.
- Cruise ship visitors, who spend less, have almost doubled in 20 years as airline arrivals have declined.
- Major hotels are not making profits.
- No new major hotels have been built for almost 30 years.
- Existing hotels require significant upgrading.
- Two major hotels have closed during the past seven years.
- Future growth is limited.
- Labour relations within the industry remain stubbornly poor.
- Bermuda is seen by its customers as being expensive.
- Crime against visitors has increased.[4]

Competitive pressures are intense as countries previously not involved in the travel industry enter the market offering competitive prices.

---

[3] This is explored thoroughly in the 1994 Commission on Competiveness Report.
[4] There was a particularly brutal murder of a young female Canadian tourist in 1996 for example.

The text of the following letter to The Editor of the Royal Gazette encapsulates what many visitors think of the Bermuda tourist product:

VISITOR'S VIEW

Less Than Bargained For
September 23, 1996

Dear Sir:

My wife Jamie and I have been coming to Bermuda for the last ten years. Year after year we've enjoyed this beautiful Island, its colourful landscape and blue green waters. In fact my wife, a published author, has just finished a romantic mystery novel which takes place, in large part, in Bermuda.

The reason I am writing to you is to express my concern about growing problems which, I believe, are beginning to hurt this Island.

First: The prices of everything from hotels to restaurants keep going up while the services, in my opinion, keep going down. (No taxis at the Airport for late arriving flights). They offer a hotel room for, say, $400 a night but the truth is, after all the taxes and surcharges, etc. its over $500. Surprise!

Restaurants are charging prices like nowhere else I've been and then include the tips in the bill whether you want to or not. There's no way to reward service, good or bad.

Even a 50 cents newspapaer (USA Today) cost $1.75 at the Sonesta Gift Shop. There's just no reason for these kind of mark-ups except to take advantage of people. Your own Mr. Trimingham described this situation on the local news the other night.

If you nickel and dime people to death, its no wonder they don't come back or tell their friends they recommend it here. I believe your visitors need to find a bargain now and then. There are no bargains here.

Second: The reckless driving of some of the locals is scaring even me. Visitors who are not used to driving mopeds are being tailgated and intimidated at every turn. No fun.

Third: Visitors should feel welcome guests here, but more and more it seems like they are not. Attitudes are changing.

As an entertainer and a recording artist for RCA records in the USA, I travel quite a bit and I know what can happen if you don't cherish your audience. They don't come back. You can't bite the hand that feeds you, and then charge them a fee to leave.

I love this Island. I hope my letter sheds some light on what I believe are important issues.

EDDIE ROBBIT, Los Angeles, California

The tourism industry is clearly facing difficult times and is desperately trying to find ways in which can become more competitive by improving the product, by reducing prices and and by increasing productivity - although the latter is difficult so long as labour relations are poor. Many proposals to improve the situation have been made and are easy to make but difficult, even impossible, under present circumstances to implement. Reinvestment in the quality of hotels is unlikely to take place when major hotels are losing money and when labour relations are bad.

A much greater problem faces the industry, in that places as diverse and geographically widespread like the Czech Republic, Costa Rica and Thailand are increasingly becoming competitors of Bermuda. As the shortage of foreign exchange and the switch to knowledge based economies imposes limits on a country's ability to raise its standard of living, more and more countries see tourism as a short term mechanism by which to earn foreign currency. Hence there are more and more new entrants to the industry and, as a result, it is extremely difficult to balance world-wide consumer demand with supply. Price stability cannot be established for long as competive forces drive down prices, resulting in sub-optimum returns to investors - something which the foreign owners of Bermuda hotels have known for a number of years.

Tourism is becoming what is called an empty-core business the characteristics of which are:

- Capital costs are high and often fixed when compared to the variable costs such as the costs of maintenance. In the context of Bermuda which has tough immigration laws and a shortage of manpower, labour becomes a fixed cost because of the inflexibility of the labour market and because hotels can only be operated if there is an abundant supply of willing staff to cater to the needs of guests. Such staff cannot be easily replaced by machinery.

- International capacity can be increased without reference to demand, and customers can move easily and quickly from one country to another as tastes change. For instance, a jaded office worker in the cold Northeastern United States can meet his vacation objectives just as easily by going to Jamaica as going to Bermuda. Sun and sand are now commodities which can be supplied by many destinations at low prices.

- Demand can be difficult to predict. Unlike the demand for staple commodities like motor gasoline, shoes and housing the demand for vacations vary with the state of the economy (as Bermuda found out during the recession of the late 1980s), consumer whims or airline schedules.

- Demand in a commodity business like tourism is highly dependent on price. An unforseen increase in price can lead to a disproportionate fall in demand by the customer. In circumstances when there is high elasticity of demand[5], costs need to be carefully controlled but this may be difficult because of high fixed costs or inflexibility in the labour market.

---

5 The meaning of the term elasticity of demand can be found in any elementary text book on economics.

Solutions to the difficulties of the tourism market are difficult. In other parts of the world employees in the hospitality industry are generally lowly paid. Bermuda's high wage economy is an economic boulder which is hard to push up the competitive hill. However, failure to come to grips with the problem could result in difficult financial consequences. It is difficult to understand why the penetrating analysis made by the Commission on Competitiveness in 1994 has not been followed up. Bermuda is a wonderful place to live in, it is a beautiful place (I have travelled all over the world and never seen anywhere as beautiful) , visitor comments are complimentary, it is close to the most prosperous part of the United States and it has many other attractive features. For the sake of Bermuda's future a solution needs to be found to the problems of tourism.[6]

4. WHAT ARE THE CONSEQUENCES TO BERMUDA OF AN UNPROFITABLE HOTEL INDUSTRY?

"Mr Simmons[1] basic flaw is his inability or unwillingness to understand that profit is the lifeblood of industry. Without it the industry dies. A dead industry pays no wages. He is a man blindly and stubbornly dedicated to killing the goose that lays the golden eggs."

MID-OCEAN NEWS - JANUARY 17, 1992

"Economic performance is the first responsibility of a business. A business that does not show a profit at least equal to its cost of capital is socially irresponsible. It wastes society's resources. Economic performance is the basis ; without it, a business cannot discharge any other responsibilities, cannot be a good employer, a good citizen, a good neighbour."

PETER DRUCKER

"Nothing contributes so much to the prosperity and happiness of a country as high profits."

DAVID RICARDO

It is commonly thought that having funds for investment purposes is a happy position to be in, but like anything else in life it is fraught with difficulties. The investor could take his money, say $1 million, put it under his mattress and in five years time he would still have his $1 million. Or again he could put it in a savings account and earn about 3.5 percent and after five years he would have about $1.2 million. The investor being a cautious man but wanting a higher return could invest in American government bonds paying around 6 percent which means that after five years his assets would be worth $1.284 million. He could be more adventuresome and invest it in the stock market, which over a prolonged period of time has paid on average just over 10 percent per annum. Assuming a return of 10 percent his $1 million would be worth about $1.645 million which is pretty good. He could really be foolish and invest directly in a company which owns hotels in Bermuda in which case his investment, if he was lucky, after five years could be worth as little as $300,000 or less than one-fifth of the value if he had invested in the U.S. stock market

---

[6] See for example, the proposal to privatise the Department of Tourism in section III 16.

[1] Former President of the BIU who retired in 1996.

The objective of making of profits for shareholders and investors in commercial enterprises is one of the driving forces and main tenets of capitalism. Profits enable a business to thrive, grow and generate opportunities for staff and government as well as shareholders. The absence of profits results in a business shrinking, or going out of business to the detriment of staff and investors. Profits are good news, losses bad news. Profits indicate success, losses underline failure, profits mean opportunity, losses impose severe limitations in the future. Profits are a source of the dynamism of capitalism but also a source of much criticism from opponents such as Karl Marx.

The opportunity to make profits is always related to the future although investment opportunities are usually predicted by reference to investment decisions made in the past. If the past record is good, investors are prepared to increase or renew their investments; if the record is bad they do the opposite. Profits therefore are not only a reward to the entrepreneur for having committed investment funds, they are the seed corn for the future.

One of the axioms of capitalism is that investors do not for long invest in projects which lose money. All other things being equal they invest their funds in assets which produce the best return depending on the risk they are willing to run. There is little or no risk taken by investing in U.S. Government securities but there is a relatively low return; there is some additional risk by investing in the stock market but there are higher returns if the risk and uncertainty can be tolerated. However, there is high risk and negative returns if you invest in the Bermuda hotel industry as the following table shows.

Profit and Losses 8 Major Hotels
For years 1987 - 1995

	U.S. $ 000s	Occupancy % Rate	Payroll Cost as a % of Sales
1987	7,429	68.8	31.8
1988	(3,891)	60.8	34.9
1989	(2,277)	65.0	36.2
1990	(5,502)	66.0	36.8
1991	(17,476)	59.1	39.0
1992	(12,446)	55.9	38.6
1993	(5,370)	64.8	36.6
1994	5,799	62.6	35.9
1995	(309)	61.9	38.1
Accumulated Losses	$34,043		

The above table, which makes depressing reading, particularly if you are the fictitious investor portrayed above, combines the results of eight hotels in Bermuda who account for over 60 percent of the capacity of the hotel industry and is prepared by an independent firm of Chartered Accountants.[2] The eight hotels are the largest operators in Bermuda and contain names like Elbow Beach Hotel, Marriott's Castle Harbour Resort and Sonesta Beach Resort. The total losses sustained in the hotel industry in the nine years between 1987 and 1995 amounts to a staggering $34.043 million with 1987 and 1994 yielding the only positive results. Occupancy rates average a meagre 60 odd percent showing that there is surplus capacity, even during the peak summer months. It is also very depressing news for Bermuda and Bermudians for if the main employers of Bermudian workers are not making money it means that the jobs and long-term prospects for many Bermudians are in jeopardy as well as the many employees whose prosperity is indirectly tied to the fortunes of the hotel industry. For employees there is only one thing worse than working for an employer which makes money from their business, and that is working for an employer who is not making profits. If there are no profits there are, in the long run, no jobs - just ask former employees of companies which have become insolvent.

As mentioned above investing deals with projected or anticipated profits in the future and is a judgement made by an organisation's management which is based largely, although not entirely, on the record of past performance. An investment in a hotel takes several years to pay for itself with the result that investors need to be reasonably well-assured that the prospects for profits are good. In addition, a hotel does not have many alternative uses - it cannot be converted into a warehouse or a manufacturing plant. Moreover unlike stocks and bonds, a hotel cannot be packed in a suitcase and shipped off to a more congenial home. Once the investment is made it becomes illiquid as the only way to get the investment back is to continue in business until the cash flow dries up. The investor is therefore taking a major risk with his money ; if he forecasts the future accurately he can earn acceptable profits but if he fails to predict future hazards he runs the risk of losing the funds invested in the project. The old adage "once bitten, twice shy" is a maxim which investors have followed for decades.

If an organisation continuously fails to make profits from its past investments it is not likely to repeat its previous mistake and invest or re-invest in the same enterprise unless there is clear evidence that the situation is likely to turn itself around. The view about profitability is always forward but the evidence on which to base a decision is almost always in the past.

Turning to the issue of the lack of profitability in the hotel industry in Bermuda, it can be quickly seen that given the dismal record of profitability, investors are likely to seek opportunities elsewhere. Bermuda has to raise its investment capital on international markets and these markets are highly competitive. In local Bermuda businesses relationships result in long-term ties between labour, managers, shareholders and the community. In international business, personal ties are not valued as highly and investors are more concerned with the objective measures of published accounts, returns on investment and clear economic goals. There has been no major new investment in a hotel in Bermuda since

---

[2] Cooper & Lines, which is associated with the international accounting firm Coopers & Lybrand International.

the Southampton Princess Hotel was built is 1972. If losses cannot be absorbed they will close operations down as has been done in two major hotels - the Bermudiana and the Club Med. The message is unmistakably clear. If profits cannot be made investors will not commit funds for the future development of Bermuda and unprofitable operations will be closed. A signal is being sent from the international market place to Bermuda that investment funds can be more profitably employed somewhere else in the world.

The other signal being sent by the market is that our potential customers and former guests no longer regard a vacation in Bermuda as providing good value. Bermuda is currently producing a product for which consumers are unwilling to pay. Or to use the current jargon Bermuda is not adding value to the business process which provides vacations for foreigners. Investors believe better returns can be obtained by buying for example, an eco-tourist vacation in Costa Rica and the competition from new and fashionable destinations is formidable. It means that the producer is not satisfying the customer who at the end of the day generates profits and pays salaries and wages. Profits are a signal of customer satisfaction; losses are an indication of customer disillusionment. If the customer won't pay there is no reason for international investors to invest in Bermuda because of the many profitable opportunities elsewhere in the world. Increasingly, new countries are entering the tourist market and providing an environment in which the investor can profitably invest for the future. The business environment in Bermuda is such that the long-term future of hotel industry is in jeopardy.

What are the consequences for Bermuda and Bermudians if these dire consequences arise?

- foreign exchange earnings from tourism will fall.
- jobs will be lost and the future employment for young Bermudians made more difficult.
- some hotels will be forced out of business.
- airline services will be reduced.
- the quality of hotels relative to our competitors will fall.
- tax revenues will decline.
- there will be an air of disrepair and neglect - as evidenced by the condition of the Bermudiana Hotel.
- investment for the future will not take place to the extent necessary to maintain Bermuda as a first-class resort.
- social tensions will increase because of the threat of unemployment.

International companies such as Aetna Insurance which owns Sonesta Beach Hotel require each operating unit to be financially sound. If an operating unit fails to meet standard performance criteria such as an adequate return on capital employed, generation of cash and dividends of an acceptable level or conforming to other benchmarks of efficiency requests for renewed investment will be rejected by shareholders at corporate headquarters. The result is that business goes into a decline, is closed or is sold. International investors have yet to establish a reputation for investing shareholder funds in assets which consistently fail to produce an adequate return on investment, or giving priority to investment in Bermuda simply because Bermudians are nice people.

Resolving the problems of continued losses in the hotel industry is not easy - if it were, the solution would have long ago been found. It requires a combination of:-

- reducing hotel costs, especially labour costs.
- improving labor productivity and labour relations.
- increasing occupancy rates from the low industry average of about 60%.
- making Bermuda a more attractive resort to visit.
- improved marketing and advertising.
- making sure Bermudians understand the importance of a healthy hotel industry to Bermuda.

The inability of the major hotel operators in Bermuda to make a healthy return poses a grave threat to Bermuda's prosperity. Resolving this unhappy situation is a major challenge to all Bermudians.

5. WHY IS RETAILING UNPROFITABLE AND IS THAT IMPORTANT FOR THE REST OF BERMUDA?

"Keep your shop and your shop will keep you."

THOMAS FULLER

"The monopoly of the retail store is rapidly collapsing. While twentieth century shoppers still clamber into their cars and fight for a place in noisy checkout lines, a new breed of shoppers is seeking greater convenience by turning to catalogues, toll-free ordering numbers, mail, television shopping, consumer product guides, computers and fax machines. Without ever leaving home, the new consumer has the products delivered to the door - and usually at a lower price."

WILLIAM KNOKE.[1]

The retail trade is the final link in a complex economic chain which stretches all the way back to the planner and dreamer, encompasses the manufacturer or farmer, the transportation system, the financial system and the distribution system until it finally reaches the most important person in the economic system - the customer or buyer. Retail outlets may be based on inventory located at the point of final sale such as a large department store like Triminghams or simply be a stall by the side of the road selling lemonade or snowballs. Increasingly, it may centralise stocks like a mail-order house or allow for orders to be placed through toll-free numbers. Whatever form the retail process takes it is the point where the might of the economic system meets the final consumer. For Bermuda it is important as retailing employs 4,231 people[2] with a further 1,561 employed in transportation and storage.

---

[1] "Bold New World," 1996 page 122.
[2] Employment Survey, 1995 page 9.

In the 1960s and before Bermuda was a shopper's paradise, a tourist attraction of some distinction and of world renown, with competitively priced products many of which were unavailable in parts of the United States.[3] In the 1990s, paradise has changed to financial hell, almost a collection of T shirt outlets and bazaars selling cheap knick-knacks. A handful of quality stores keep a stiff upper-lip and bravely, almost vainly, soldier on hoping for an economic revival. There are many stories of retailing woes and the prosperous world of the period prior to the 1970s is very very different from the reality of the 1990s. There is no longer much which is worthwhile for the tourist to buy and long gone are the days when Front Street was known as "the shop-window of the world" with a competitive price advantage and the profitable volume of trade that went with it. Today there is little price advantage over the United States - in fact quite the reverse given the low volume of turnover.[4] What has changed?

Much of what is happening in Bermuda's retail market is a replay of what has been taking place in the wider world outside Bermuda. In industry after industry there has occurred what is called "the collape of the middle". Many organisations had perfected the one size fits all solution but over the past decade customers like sheep have flocked to two extremes. On the one hand there are many discount stores - Walmart is the best known example in stores but the same trend is evident in computers (Dell) or in stock broking (Charles Schwab) - who compete solely on price with service being thrown in, almost as an afterthought. On the other hand, many businesses have gone after the customer who wants personal service, and individually tailored solutions to problems. Hence the growth in specialised foods, clothes (Calvin Klein) and top notch stores like Nordstrom. Because of these strategic trends the middle - occupied by many Bermudian stores - has become a no man's land and like many big names abroad have stagnated. As I will repeat time and time again the customer now understands his power and exerts it to the full. If business does not understand its customer it will face financial problems, sooner rather than later.

Retailing is regarded as an easy commercial option by many people ; you buy wholesale what people need, put on a huge markup, sell to naive and willing customers, sit back and count the contents of the cash register. The fact is that retailing is one of the most competitive, most technologically advanced and sophisticated industries in the Western world. When giants like Sears, K Mart and Woolworths experience hard times it should not be surprising that the Bermuda equivalents also face trouble.

The main reasons for this state of affairs are:

- Intense competition both domestically and abroad - outlet malls, mail order and discount stores abound in the United States, and increasingly so in Western Europe.

- Retailers are faced with high costs for labour and property as stores are in competition for labour and property with high-paying international companies.

- Retailing requires large amounts of costly capital to finance inventory.

---

[3] Due largely to shortages created by tariff barriers - most of which have now been removed.

[4] This comment applies to tourist related business generally in Bermuda.

- Import duties of up to one-third must be paid to the Bermuda government before the goods are sold. A sales tax added to the price at the point of sale would help the beleaguered retailers - an idea which is not endorsed by government.

- Information technology has revolutionised the retail business so that stores like Walmart in the United States can "pile them high, and sell them low".[5] From being a low-tech industry of the 1960s, computer inventory control, complex management information systems and high speed deliveries have transformed the industry and now make it one of most high-tech industries in the world. For example, Wal-Mart gathers information from its point of sale scanners and immediately transmits it to its major suppliers. They then make decisions on what items to ship, when and in what quantities. This process drives down costs by eliminating much of the clerical labour needed at each stage of the supply chain and the computer is more accurate than people.

- Customers are now much more cost conscious than they were twenty years ago - one reason is the virtual elimination of inflation.[6] In many households the adults are usually full-time employees who are unable to shop between the hours of 9 to 5 (although stores now open for much longer now than they did 10 years ago).

- Declining tourist figures reduce the number of customers and visitor spending continues to fall - the first nine months of 1995 saw expenditure fall to BD$398 million from $425 million in the same period in 1994.

- Bermudians travel more frequently and can buy at cheaper prices abroad.

- Customers are more interested in school fees, saving for retirement or medical costs than they are about stocking up on shirts, sweaters and furniture. In addition, they are not as clothes conscious as they were 30 years ago. A tee shirt and jeans can go a long way.

- Distance is no longer the friend of the retailer and Bermuda customers can buy from a mail order catalogue, often at a cheaper price, and have the goods delivered in two or three days. Internet shopping is providing another choice to consumers or, what is the same thing, additional competition to retailers.

- Market research techniques have revolutionised the industry and customers are much more fickle and unpredictable than in the past and constant changes in tastes, in store layout and sales techniques make the business very different.

What does all of this mean for Bermuda? Like the tourism industry, retailing is going through change pains and the future is difficult to predict - as it always is. Staff in many retail stores have not had an increase in salary for about 6 years. Many retailers do not have the answer to the industry's problems but one thing is clear and that is business as usual is not going to resolve anything.

---

[5] The alleged motto of Sam Walton the legendary founder of Walmart.

[6] As issue which is explained in Part III 12.

The present policy of prohibiting the entry of major stores from abroad like Sears, Walmart and Marks and Spencers no longer gives protection to local businesses from foreign competition. Many large foreign stores like Body Shop, Marks and Spencers and Tru-value have entered the local market through the back door by forming alliances with local entrepreneurs. Others can penetrate the Bermuda market by mail order and others simply wait until Bermudian shoppers go away for a shopping weekend.

> About two years ago when my son was at university in Florida, he convinced me that I required a Sony CD player costing about $1,000 which played up to 100 Cds and which was on special sale by a mail order company called Crutchfields based in Minnesota. The supplier guaranteed delivery anywhere in the United States within 24 hours. I was going to be in a restaurant in Georgia the next day and I was informed that delivery would take place within the guaranteed period. When I went to the restaurant I told the waiter I was expecting a package and sure enough after being there for about 2 hours I was informed of its delivery. A product made in Japan, ordered from Florida, distributed by a company in Minnesota, was delivered to a Bermudian in a restaurant in Georgia all within 24 hours. This is the face of modern retailing.

Some retail businesses continue to flourish, grocery and hardware stores for example, but the 60/40 ownership and control rule (at least as far as retailing is concerned) has outlived its usefulness for the simple reason that it is no longer effective in the 1990s for reasons mentioned above.

The changing nature of business has led to the ground collapsing under the feet of Bermudian retailers. Detecting changed patterns of consumer behaviour is difficult but all over the world customers are demanding better products at keener prices and it is therefore essential to maintain a careful watch over customer behaviour. The customer has changed but in many ways local retailers have not been able to change with the customer.

If local merchants are unable to cut the mustard whilst living under protectionist policies (or what is more likely is that because of protectionist measures local merchants failed to make the essential changes to their style of doing business until it became too late to do so) then it will be necessary to allow foreign retailers to provide the service to visitors and locals as it is necessary to have a flourishing retail sector for the benefit of tourists and for the quality of life of Bermuda residents.

If this is done, Bermuda can still retain its distinctive flavour of no neon signs, sky signs or other ostentatious methods of advertising. Those local firms which are able to adapt to the modern world will continue to prosper ; those who can't or won't will be part of the process of "creative destruction" which has been described elsewhere. The damage of this process is that Bermuda runs the risk of being a society divided into those who do well - mainly in international business - and those who are marginalised. The lack of profitability in the retail business has the same socially devisive consequences as the lack of profitability in tourism.

6. WHAT IS AN EXEMPT COMPANY?

"One of the strengths of Bermuda's business environment is the relevance of the regulatory structure to specific businesses without the costly bureaucracy that arises from a wide all encompassing regulatory structure. Because the banking industry is essentially locally-owned there is a strong vested interest in the banks ensuring that Bermuda's reputation as a quality jurisdiction is not tarnished."

BARRY SHAILER, EXECUTIVE VICE-PRESIDENT, BANK OF BERMUDA LIMITED.[1]

Since 1990, the most resilient sector of the Bermuda economy has been international company business. An Exempt Company is generally understood to mean non-Bermudian owned and controlled limited liability corporations which are incorporated in Bermuda and carry on from Bermuda (but not from within Bermuda) commercial, trading and other business transactions with the rest of the world. There are now about 9,000 such companies.

Corporations can also be formed for the purposes of holding assets outside their shareholders' jurisdictions or for ownership of shares in other Bermuda based international corporations. Exempt Companies may conduct their operations in any currency they wish and also maintain their accounting records, including audited financial statements in any currency. Most of the companies with a physical presence (about 275) are located in Hamilton although a few have an office outside the City and operate without any disadvantage. Examples are Nautilus Shipping in Warwick, Transworld Oil in Flatts Village and Shell and Esso in St George's.

Incorporation is achieved by registration of various documents with the Registrar of Companies and the Bermuda Monetary Authority (BMA), or can be accomplished as it was prior to 1970 by Private Act of Parliament. Control over the acceptability of organisations and individuals who wish to establish a presence in Bermuda is the responsibility of the Minister of Finance, who as a practical matter, delegates this function to the BMA. Applications for incorporation require, amongst other things, the proposed Memorandum of Association which sets out the powers of the company, bank references of the applicant if it is not a public quoted company, and if specialist services are to be provided, such as management consultancy, evidence of professional expertise. When the vetting

---

[1] Quoted in 'Offshore Outlook,' November 1994, page 2.

process is completed the Registrar of Companies issues a Certificate of Incorporation and the Memorandum of Association (which identifies the shareholders of the company) becomes a public document.

When the incorporation formalities are concluded the international companies formed in Bermuda are generally known as "Exempt Companies", exempt sometimes being understood by the general public, non-residents of Bermuda, and indeed by some of the companies themselves, as being exempt from corporate or income taxes. This is incorrect as exempt means being exempt from the laws which require that limited liability companies in Bermuda must have at least a 60 percent Bermudian share ownership and be controlled by Bermudians. In addition, Exempt Companies are not subject to the remaining exchange control regulations which apply to Bermudians, nor are they liable for stamp duties on documents they execute. The main advantages to operating from Bermuda are well known and shown in the captioned table below.

ADVANTAGES OF INCORPORATING IN BERMUDA.
• No taxation of income, dividends and capital gains.
• English Common Law traditions allow appeals from Bermuda courts to the Judicial British Committee of the Privy Council.
• Political and Economic stability.
• Ability to re-domicile without business interruption.
• Light and effective regulatory system - especially important for insurance companies.
• Economic infrastructure of telecommunications, roads, ports, airport, power supply etc
• Professional infrastructure of accountants (all of the big 6 accounting firms have a presence), lawyers, bankers, investment managers, insurance professionals, etc.
• Absence of corruption.
• Scandal free history (in financial matters)[2] and investor protection.
• Per capita GNP of $27,500.
• English is the official (and for most part the only) language.
• U.S.-Bermuda tax convention provides certain advantages to U.S. corporations.
• No exchange controls
• Major insurance market[3]

---

2 Although there is a difficult case involving a local insurance company before the courts at present.

3 See the next two sections for an elaboration of this point.

Exempt companies are usually subsidiaries of large international groups of companies whose head offices are located in major commercial centres in the USA, Canada, UK, Hong Kong, Germany and so on although an increasing number are established by wealthy individuals or smaller foreign corporations. They can also be formed by Exempt Companies or trusts already established in Bermuda or by individuals who are not Bermuda residents. The proposed shareholder in an Exempt Company requires approval of the BMA and any transfer of beneficial interest in the shares also requires authorisation by the BMA.

Exempt companies should be distinguished from local limited liability companies which Bermudians can create and control for the specific purposes of carrying on business in Bermuda. Examples of these would be The Bermuda Telephone Company Limited and a host of other local business like Holmes, Williams and Purvey Limited. Banks in Bermuda (of which there are three) are also local limited liability companies but shareholders in these institutions have a double liability for their shares.

Exempt companies are not allowed to compete with local Bermuda businesses or own Bermuda real estate but are limited to using Bermuda as a base for their business overseas. Banks are not allowed to be owned by a majority of non-Bermudian shareholders[4] but foreign trust companies have been permitted since 1991.

Exempt companies are managed and controlled by a Board of Directors elected by shareholders at the Annual General Meeting of the shareholders and a quorum (usually two directors) of that Board is usually resident in Bermuda although this is no longer essential. Exempt Companies pay an annual fee to the Bermuda Government the level of which depends on their activity and the amount of the share capital; a trading company would pay a minimum of BD$1,680 per annum (depending on its capital) whilst an insurance company could pay about BD$8,000 per annum plus an annual business fee. In addition, Exempt Companies pay other government taxes such as the employer's share of the payroll tax.

An added complication is that the term Exempted Companies is often used to refer to commercial entities such as partnerships, companies limited by guarantee, unlimited liability companies and other variations which legally and practically are not limited liability companies. To complicate things even further many branches of foreign companies are given consent by government (or are permitted) to trade from Bermuda and are known as Permit Companies. As can be shown from Table 1 this group makes up about ten percent of the international businesses which trade from Bermuda. However, for ease of reference the terms International Business and Exempt Companies will be used interchangeably and Exempt Companies will also refer to such bodies as partnerships and Permit Companies.

---

[4] First Curacao International Bank NV, Curacao owns one-third of the shares of the Bermuda Commercial Bank.

Table 1[5] International Company Businesses Registered in Bermuda 1994

	New Registrations			Number on Register at end of Quarter			
	Exempted	Exempted Partnership	Non-Resident	Exempted	Exempted Partnership	Non-Resident	Total
End of 1993	-	-	-	6,954	183	441	7,578
1st Qtr 1994	289	21	17	7,194	203	432	7,829
2nd Qtr 1994	243	14	11	7,175	217	439	7,831
3rd Qtr 1994	256	13	20	7,417	229	456	8,102
4th Qtr 1994	240	13	15	7,517	242	465	8,224

The earnings of Exempt Companies are not subjected to any Bermudian income or corporate taxes (for there are none) and most will possess a certificate from the Bermuda Government entitled, "The Exempted Undertakings Tax Protection Act, 1966 - Assurance" which, as the name implies, gives an assurance that, in the event of there being enacted any legislation imposing tax computed on profits or income, or computed on any capital assets, gain or appreciation or any tax in the nature of estate duty or inheritance, that any such tax will not be applicable to the company named until the year 2016 or such date in the future as is determined from amending the Act. This is issued to provide comfort to the owners of Exempt Companies who are, rightly, suspicious that future governments may seek to tax their profits.

The uncomfortable fact is that the Tax Protection Act can be repealed by the Bermuda Government at any time, (because of the sovereignty of Parliament principle) and the undertaking in their possession would be legally unenforceable. However, as a practical matter if the Bermuda Government was foolish enough to renege on its assurances, international business would lose confidence in Bermuda and many could vanish overnight. It is the mutual benefits derived from the presence of international companies in Bermuda which makes the assurance given by the Bermuda Government worth something.

The commercial activities undertaken by Exempt Companies are quite varied as Table 2 (reproduced from a report entitled "International Companies 1994 - Their Impact on the Economy of Bermuda," published by the Ministry of Finance) shows:-

---

5 Registrar of Companies data.

Table 2.[6]

Type of Business	Number of Businesses							
	1987	1988	1989	1990	1991	1992	1993	1994
Exempted Companies								
Insurance	1,232	1,321	1,310	1,302	1,310	1,307	1,315	1,343
Mutual Funds	130	166	98	211	213	23	298	321
Public Finance	49	61	55	47	48	46	60	54
Investment Holding	1,938	2,244	2,464	2,603	2,635	2,779	3,121	3,226
Commercial Trading	467	506	515	493	477	437	470	410
Insurance Broker/Manager	246	268	257	254	244	229	235	224
Other								
Managers/Consultants	341	378	388	411	435	461	527	555
Shipping	411	491	508	550	561	569	671	548
Natural Resources	167	183	217	229	241	257	243	248
Other, n.e.c.	965	544	575	602	648	707	329	973
1. Exempted Companies	5,946	6,162	6,487	6,702	6,810	7,022	7,269	7,902
2. Exempted Partnerships	82	92	99	126	135	155	183	242
3. Permit Companies	525	488	504	487	444	418	441	465
TOTAL	**6,553**	**6,742**	**7,909**	**7,315**	**7,389**	**7,595**	**7,893**	**8,609**

Government policies impose some restrictions on the activities of international companies. For example, they are not authorised to carry on banking, take deposits or engage in activities which the Bermuda Government considers repugnant such as arms dealing or any activity which would be contrary to the best interests of Bermuda or Bermudians.

International companies are regulated by various Acts of the Bermuda legislature the most important of which is The Companies Act, 1981. The Act deals with such issues as the responsibilities of the Board of Directors, financial statements, audit requirements, winding up provisions and other matters of corporate governance. Insurance companies, however, are subjected to much greater regulation than companies involved in other business activities. The main governing provisions applying to insurance activity being The Insurance Act 1978 and The Insurance Returns and Solvency Regulations 1980. Each insurance company has to submit annually to the Registrar of Companies:-

* A cover sheet stating the main classes of business and the premiums related to that business.
* A report by its auditors confirming that various financial statements and information are in accordance with the Act and Regulations.
* A statutory balance sheet and statement of income.
* A General Business Solvency Certificate signed by the insurance company's principal representative and two directors of the company.

---

[6] Ibid.

The critical importance of Exempt Companies to the economic health of Bermuda is explained when the questions of how Bermudians benefit from their presence and the significance of the Archer Report[7] are discussed.

7. WHAT IS INSURANCE?

"The serious study of risk began during the Renaissance, when people broke loose from the constraints of the past and subjected long-held beliefs to open challenge. This was a time when much of the world was to be discovered and its resources exploited. It was a time of religious turmoil, nascent capitalism, and a vigorous approach to science and the future."

PETER BERNSTEIN - "AGAINST THE GODS," 1996 PAGE 3.

"Insurance is an ingenious modern game of chance in which the player is permitted to enjoy the comfortable conviction that he is beating the man who keeps the table."

AMBROSE PIERCE, - THE DEVIL'S DICTIONARY.

The most important and the greatest number of Exempt Companies in Bermuda are engaged in insurance but the reader may wonder exactly what is insurance. One of the indisputable facts of life is that the future is full of hazards and it is unpredictable despite our complacent expectation that tomorrow will be very much like today. The prudent individual knows that he must be prepared for the unexpected and when that prudence is extended to business life we can see very clearly why a huge financial service industry like insurance is essential.

Stripped to its essentials, insurance is a means of sharing risks. It was originally established in connection with shipping which was considered the riskiest of business ventures in the past. However, as business progressed the concept was extended to cover all sorts of risks such as damage to property, damage to innocent third parties, injury from accidents, personal injury and unexpected (meaning premature) death. Insurance plays a central and pivotal role in the financial planning of individuals and in modern business because the unexpected and the hazards of day to day life can have a significant impact on the activities of large business organisations.

An understanding of insurance requires an equal understanding of risk or the potential outcomes of actions taken:-

- A may have an accident in his car, the result of which is that the vehicle worth $30,000 is totally wrecked.
- B may contact a debilitating illness which prevents him from working and earning a salary to support his family.
- C company may ship products to the other side of the world and they may get stolen or destroyed.

---

[7] See Part II 2.

114

- D may go on vacation to Africa and lose his suitcases and cash.
- E may die unexpectedly leaving a large mortgage on his house which his wife cannot afford to finance.
- F organisation may be sued for damage caused to the surrounding community from chemicals which have inadvertently leaked into nearby water.

The above are examples of the risks to which individuals and business organisations are exposed on a day to day basis. Everyone hopes that the events mentioned above will not occur but a glance at any newspaper reveals that such things frequently happen. To manage the risks mentioned an individual or a company can hope for the best and assume the risk themselves (or in some cases let their survivors or family pay the cost).

If an individual who is 70 years old is worth $5 million dollars it may not make a great deal of sense to pay a high insurance premium to insure his life for $250,000. Someone who does not travel does not need to buy travel insurance. However, if the risks to which people and organisations are exposed are to be managed effectively, the main way in which this can be done is to pay a premium to an insurance company who will assume all or most of the risk and pay the insured an amount on the occurrence of an event against which he is insured

If A has a car accident the insurance company will reimburse him $30,000 so he can purchase a new car. Just as important as being reimbursed by the insurance company are steps taken by A to lessen the risk of his being involved in an accident - by taking an advanced driving course for example or refusing to consume alcohol. Taking such steps can result in the insurance company recognising that A is a good risk and that his premium should be reduced accordingly. Alternatively, A can assume part of the risk himself by absorbing the first $1,000 cost of any accident which means the insurance company is not bothered by small claims (this reduces their administrative costs) and it also evidences a degree of responsibility by A.

The insurance company is able to provide cover against various risks because it pools or spreads the risk from a sufficiently large group of individuals who also wish to purchase insurance cover. The large pool is important because the workings of what is known as the law of large numbers which states that when a sufficiently large group of people face a similar low probability risk , for example, dying in a air crash, the number who die will be close to the estimated probability. The higher the large number the greater the accuracy of the estimated probability - such probabilities are determined by specialists called actuaries[1]. Insurance companies also diversify their risks by spreading it across good years and bad years, building up reserves in good years, or by spreading it geographically covering insureds in Europe as well as the United States because such societies are broadly similar.

Another key concept to understand is the crucial importance of the identity of the person wishing to buy insurance. Insurance companies, not surprisingly, wish to provide coverage to those individuals who are a low risk. In health insurance

---

[1] An actuary is someone who moved out of accountancy because he couldn't stand the excitement.

non-smokers are preferred to smokers, and the young are preferred to the old. High risk individuals (or companies) are more likely to take out insurance cover but may wish to conceal the fact that they are high risk. Hence the identity and the relevant history of individuals clearly affects the premium. Anyone taking out a large life insurance cover may have to submit to a medical examination, motor vehicle insurance cover may depend on whether the vehicle is kept locked in a garage, or fire insurance on a house may be dependent on having fire alarms in place.

Until the 1980s the cost of insurance was only a small part of the cost of doing business. Fire, loss and accidents were the main risks covered. Much of this changed when the concept of liability was changed - mainly by the United States courts. Liability was traditionally based on negligence which required a plaintiff to show that the business had failed to follow appropriate processes or standards. The adoption by the courts of strict liability required businesses to pay damages for accidents in a much broader set of circumstances, often retroactively, the rationale for which was that producers could absorb greater liability by charging more for their product. In addition, in several States juries tended to award punitive damages to plaintiffs who had been injured by the alleged negligence of big business.

Asbestos companies were penalised for failing to advise workers of potential cancer risks from breathing asbestos dust; cigarette manufacturers for failing to warn smokers that cancer might arise from smoking their product and so on. The large number and the amounts awarded led to a significant increase in the number of lawsuits brought against manufacturers of products considered to place the public at risk many of which were frivolous and inspired by tort lawyers who were paid on a contingency basis.[2] The strict accountability rules led to many companies going out of business entirely ; Cessna discontinued the production of light aircraft and resource companies like Manville were bankrupted. It is estimated that about 25 percent of the cost of a ladder arises from the insurance cover which has to be purchased by the manufacturer to meet potential liability claims. In addition, the concept of the "deep pocket" evolved as litigious lawyers sought to take actions against large wealthy companies who were more likely and able to settle than the small store who sold their product.

During the mid and late 1980s there emerged a growing crisis in the insurance industry for several reasons:

- There were a number of natural and man-made disasters such as the Lockerbie bombing of a Pan American World Airways flight, an oil spill from the 'Exxon Valdez' in Alaska, Hurricane Hugo in the Caribbean, Hurricane Andrew in Florida and the San Francisco earthquake. As a result of these occurrences major property losses were reported and paid. The financial impact was such that several insurance companies either withdrew from the business, went into receivership or reduced coverage to the market.

- Insurance companies had allegedly underpriced their product in the early 1980s as they competed for business. The premiums collected were then

---

[2] If the plaintiff was successful the lawyer was paid a portion of the award, usually one-third. If he was unsuccessful the lawyer received no fees. This arrangement is forbidden under English law which governs Bermuda.

used to earn high investment returns with the result that many companies failed to earn profits on their insurance business but were compensated by investment income.

- The underpricing of insurance premiums and the disasters referred to earlier led to large insurance losses and, as a consequence, premiums were subsequently raised to unrealistic levels.
- The insurance industry suffered from a shortage of capital which led to them reducing the amount of business they were prepared to write.
- The rise in potential liability claims because of the surge in litigation in the United Sates led insurance companies to increase their premiums.
- Lloyds of London which was (and still is) the world's principal re-insurance market was exposed in the 1980s and early 1990s to a huge loss of confidence as investors (or names) lost money or withdrew from the market. In addition, there was strong evidence of gross management incompetence, fraud, conflicts of interest, poor underwriting standards, and an unrealistically high cost structure.

In short, by the mid-1980s what was once a cosy predictable almost pedestrian industry with a history of 200 years of stability, run mainly in or through London by several who were incompetent, unethical and dishonest had changed into one where financial uncertainty and potentially high losses were the norm, where huge claims for pollution and asbestosis were swamping the market and where increasing government regulation was taking place. Losses at Lloyds for the years 1988 to 1992 were more than US$12 billion and because of the nature of business are still mounting and are relatively unknown even in 1996.

In London, a major part of an industry which had depended on trust, confidence and reputation had attracted too many sharks and crooks who covered the spectrum from being negligent to being fraudulent. The mirror image of the crooks were the naive names (or investors) suckered in by the cachet of being a part of Lloyds of London and unaware of what unlimited liability meant in practice. In 1871 there were 675 names and by 1990 there were over 31,000 all eager to make a quick buck but most of whom lacked the skill or sophistication to know what was going on. Unlimited liability was the obligation they did not understand and which they should have never assumed. There was also, at one stage, a real risk that Lloyds would be unable to pay some of its claims - a situation which had never occurred before in its 200 year history.

Business does not like messy situations and uncertainty and many fertile minds were able to devise corporate structures which enabled insurance to continue unabated but in a location which was not encumbered by a legacy of past claims, questionable business practices and incompetence.

As a consequence of the unacceptable practices in London and the changed nature of the risks to which international businesses were exposed, many large international industrial corporations began to form in the early and mid 1980s captive insurance subsidiaries in offshore locations like Bermuda which had a clean reputation, a relatively low cost structure, minimal but effective regulation and no direct taxation. Most important of all the location was outside the legal system of the United States.

Bermuda has been active in the insurance industry for many years and is acknowledged as the birthplace of the captive insurance concept. This was developed (although not originated) by Fred Reiss who established Bermuda's first captive management company, International Risk Management, in 1962.

Before that American International (AIG) had established a presence in Bermuda shortly after the end of the Second World War when many of its international activities in China were nationalised by the Communists. Major corporations like Shell and Esso had established captive insurance operations in the 1950s. However, it was still a relatively small business activity until the convulsions in international insurance occurred in the 1980s.

Bermuda suddenly became a very attractive place in which to do business. The Exempt Company business was long established, as was captive insurance operations, Bermuda was close to New York and London, it had good airline connections and communications, and most of all no taxation and minimal regulation but a high reputation for honesty and no corruption.

Most important of all was the right of appeal to the English legal system all the way through to the Judicial Committee of the Privy Council. Insurance is a business which is long-term. Claims may take years to emerge and there can arise complicated disputes about coverage which may need resolution in commercially respected courts of law. The right of appeal to England also meant that entrapment in the American legal system could be avoided.

First a word about captive insurance - the rock upon which the Bermuda insurance industry is built. A captive insurance company is typically a subsidiary of a large international manufacturing or trading corporation (usually American or British) which has many operating units in different parts of the world each unit requiring insurance cover for such risks as fire, explosion, third party liability or marine. Each affiliate could buy its insurance cover in the insurance market of the country in which it operates. Or the parent could obtain such insurance on a global basis which meant lower premiums and better and more consistent insurance coverage. A further benefit could be obtained for the group of companies if some of the risk, usually a small part, were retained in an insurance company wholly owned by the parent. The captive insurance structure therefore allowed major corporations to retain some of the risk and the premium but the captive was still able to obtain reinsurance protection at a lower rate for all its operating units throughout the world.

Apart from retaining the premium and securing better and cheaper reinsurance protection the captive structure had other advantages :

- Cash could be retained with the parent by means of current account transactions through the books. Alternatively, investment income could be earned by the captive from premiums received from affiliates.

- Tax deduction for insurance costs could be claimed on premiums paid by affiliates to the Bermudian insurer.
- Some risks such as exposure to nuclear accident are not easily insurable, or cover simply may not be available.
- Companies could ultimately benefit by managing and controlling their overseas operations in a safer manner.
- Manufacturing companies could provide extended warranties on their products.
- Costly claims handling could be avoided as subsidiaries could be trusted to make only valid claims hence reducing the need for investigations and the hiring of professional claims adjusters.
- Risks of non-payment by affiliated clients were considerably reduced.

In short, captive insurance became a profit centre for international companies.

It is estimated that there are about 2,500 captive insurance companies in the world of which about half are incorporated in Bermuda.[3] Captives also account for about 10 percent of the worldwide commercial insurance market.[4] The list of companies which own and operate captives in Bermuda reads like a 'Who's Who' of business or a list of the Fortune 500 and FTSE 100 quoted stock exchange companies. So successful was the captive concept that other locations such as Grand Cayman and Barbados sought to emulate Bermuda by creating an environment to attract international business.

There were however potential hazards. In the early 1980s it became fashionable (for tax reasons) for many captives to provide insurance coverage to non-affiliated organisations. This turned out to be an unhappy experience as many companies were unable to provide competent underwriting resources and, frankly, did not understand the hazards of the insurance business. The most prominent victim of this error of judgement was Mentor Insurance, owned by Murphy Oil[5] which eventually went into liquidation. The captive insurers of several other oil companies, Esso, Atlantic Richfield and Gulf Oil, also lost money on such ventures and it was an expensive introduction to the insurance industry.

The activities of captives was also be taken a step further by companies in the same industry banding together and forming a mutual. One of the best known examples of this is Oil Insurance Limited which was formed in Bermuda in the early 1970s to provide insurance cover for companies in the oil industry - often those too small to establish their own captive.

The next major step in conceptual thinking about insurance in Bermuda was to establish insurance operations which would be able to provide insurance cover to international businesses. When the man-made flaws in the insurance market became apparent in the mid-1980s Bermuda had already installed the regulatory and financial infrastructure to allow and encourage for substantial expansion. The result is that 10 years later Bermuda now provides about 9 percent of the world's

---

[3] 'Offshore Outlook,' March 1994, pages 7 and 8.

[4] 'Post Magazine,' August 5, 1994.

[5] A classic example of Murphy's law.

global reinsurance market.[6] This is a remarkable achievement.

Much of the story commences with ACE Limited which was established in Bermuda in 1985 during a period of crisis for the insurance industry. It was created specifically for the purpose of providing to major corporations excess liability cover which had shrunk in the United States because of huge losses incurred by the insurance industry and further potential losses from such hazards as pollution and asbestosis, and the poisonous litigation atmosphere in the U.S. ACE initially provided U.S.$100 million of excess cover to major corporations such as IBM, Shell and USX all of whom were shareholders in the new venture as well as being insureds. The main business was to provide cover for catastrophes - random events like explosions which can have a significant impact on the profit statement (and even on the balance sheet) of major corporations. This high risk market had dwindled because of the dreadful experiences and underwriting mistakes of the 1970s and early 1980s.

Bermuda was a natural location. First of all it was not the United States with its litigation problems and it did not have 50 individual state insurance commissioners each making their own decisions. In addition, apart from its pioneering work with captives, Bermuda had a sensible and effective regulatory system in place which was largely self regulated through the Insurance Advisory Council,[7] the members of which were appointed by the Minister of Finance.

John R. Cox, the first Chairman of ACE, stated that, "Bermuda was chosen as offshore headquarters back in 1985 for more than just economic reasons. Very simple - enlightened regulation. Everybody in the world said taxes - that we came here because there were no taxes. But taxes had no bearing on it. The reasons were regulatory."[8] Regulation elsewhere in the world is oriented towards the consumer - in Bermuda it is oriented towards business and the reputation and solvency of those who provide the insurance cover. When the benign regulatory process was combined with low taxes, the ability to hire the best people in the world, sound products and no history of corruption or fraud it was not difficult to understand why Bermuda was found to be an attractive place to do business.

Through a remarkable combination of shrewd commercial skill, enlightened legislation and regulation, commercial ineptitude overseas, an impossible American legal system and an attractive commercial infrastructure the Bermuda insurance industry has gone from strength to strength. It showed what could be done when astute financial brains met with government flexibility and understanding. It was a unique partnership which has been of immense benefit to Bermudians and business alike. It was a business coup of major proportions.

The regulatory process was amended substantially in 1995 (in consultation with the insurance industry) to take into account the monumental changes which had occurred in the Bermuda marketplace during the 1990s because of the highly capitalised (half the capital now supports commercial type insurance) property and casualty insurers and reinsurers. There are now four classes of insurance licence:

---

[6] See the Bermuda Government Economic Review 1995, page 12.

[7] I was a member of this organisation in the early 1980s.

[8] 'The Bermudian Magazine,' January 1996.

1. **Class 1** licences apply to single parent captives which insures only risks of the parent and affiliates. The minimum share capital and surplus is BD$12,000.

2. **Class 2** licences apply to captive organisations which write up to 20 percent non-related business. Capital required will be BD$250,000 and actuarial certification will be required every three years.

3. **Class 3** licences apply to captive organisations writing third party business of more than 20 percent non-related business. Capital required will be BD$1 million and actuarial and solvency requirements will be stricter.

4. **Class 4** licences is a new category embracing highly capitalised companies which write significant amounts of direct excess liability and property risks. BD$ 100 million of capital is required and solvency and actuarial certification is strict. There are also dividend restraints if solvency is impaired.

Most of the 1,300 insurance companies would be either Class 1 or Class 2 licences. There was little opposition to enhanced regulation as in the words of the then Finance Minister, "This is an industry that has matured, and it is necessary that our legislation keep pace with its growth and complexity in order to protect those involved in the industry as well as Bermuda's enviable reputation in the world of global insurance."

The creation of ACE in 1985 was followed by a raft of big international insurers such as Exel Limited, Mid Ocean Limited, Partner Re and a host of others eager to benefit from the welcome business climate. Insurance from being a relatively sleepy and predictable, necessary but boring industry has transformed the business climate of Bermuda. And Bermuda because of its sound policies has in its way transformed the insurance business. It is to the question of how insurance affects Bermuda that I turn to next.

8. HOW DOES THE INSURANCE INDUSTRY AFFECT BERMUDA?

"Our successful international growth is a natural extension of ACE's philosophy to support the needs of the insurance marketplace We offer quality products, attract world-class underwriting talent and reward innovative thinking."

WILLIAM LOSCHERT, EXECUTIVE VICE PRESIDENT, ACE LIMITED.[1]

As a major component of the Exempt Company industry, insurance activities have a major impact on the Bermudian economy. The size of the insurance sector, its importance and its growth were commented on in the previous section but it is now appropriate to look in greater detail at how the industry affects the Island.

---

[1] 1995 Annual Report, page 4.

First, there are always three basic considerations which feature prominently in any discussion about the Bermudian economy. These have been mentioned many times but they are so important that it does no harm to repeat them again. They are :

- Jobs which pay well and have potential for advancement and growth.

- The earning of foreign exchange to provide the means to pay for the international goods and services Bermudians need.

- Social stability which is so essential for the future prosperity of Bermuda's two main industries international business and tourism.

There is no doubt that the insurance industry provides Bermudians with well paid jobs with future prospects - this point is so obvious that it does not require me to labour it. The same is true about the foreign exchange earnings generated by the industry. Social stability can be more tricky. Insurance is an industry which hires brains, sophistication and middle class attributes like conservative dress, punctuality and respect and understanding of established authority. Qualities not controversial in themselves when looked at in isolation. However, as has been mentioned elsewhere is this series of essays [2] not all Bermudians are persuaded that such middle class attributes are important or believe that they participate in the financial benefits which insurance organisations assuredly bring to Bermuda and Bermudians. BIBA and other organisations are aware of this potential problem and are seeking to find solutions to it but the possibility of alienation of a large sector of the local population, mainly young black males, can be a cause for concern.

Secondly, the insurance industry has brought to Bermuda a dynamism which has been lacking in the older industries like retailing and tourism whose misfortunes are also commented on elsewhere in this book.[3] They have developed new products for the international insurance market like satellite insurance, they are vibrant prosperous companies but most of all they have the ability to compete internationally without protectionist measures and provide a stimulus to Bermudian economic culture which, is lacking in areas like retailing. This culture of going head to head with the rest of the world utilising the advantages Bermuda has in such areas as sensible regulation and low taxation is what the economic game is all about and a major benefit is the pride which accompanies the accomplishment of being part of a winning combination.

> Insurance companies continue to provide the most important single contribution to international business earnings, generating around $228.4 million in 1994.[4]

The dynamism brought to the international market place is also accompanied by a degree of dynamism brought to Hamilton by the numbers of young prosperous Bermudians dining out, buying clothes and enjoying their high standard of

---

[2] See the discussion of the Swain Report in Part IV 13.

[3] See the discussions on these issues in Part II 4 and 5.

[4] 1995 Economic Review, page 11.

living. This atmosphere should be compared with the mournful atmosphere which can be found in areas which prosperity has not touched.

Thirdly, insurance is dependent on two forms of capital. One is clearly financial and large organisations carelessly speak of billions of dollars as if figures that size were loose change.

More important for Bermuda is the intellectual capital. In the words of Brian Duperrault, CEO of ACE Insurance, "We have very few employees, and the ones we have in our key areas of business - underwriting and claims administration - are world class."[5] In order for Bermuda to enjoy a world-class standard of living it has to be able to meet world-class standards of performance and productivity and the insurance industry does exactly that. That is a tall order for any community let alone one which has a population of less than 60,000. It underlines the importance of one of the issues I have tried to stress in this book namely, that in the modern world highly-skilled labour cannot be driven or led by authoritarian structures or by restrictive work policies like inflexible immigration rules.[6]

The sort of labour force Bermuda needs for its future can only be attracted - not driven - by congenial work conditions such as low taxation, a high quality of life and a welcoming local populace. Bermuda has been fortunate and shrewd enough to welcome intellectual capital in the past and it is vital that it continue to do so.

Fourthly, 'a job is a job is a job' philosophy is no longer acceptable, and rightly so, to large numbers of young people. They want a job which provides upward mobility, high salaries and social prestige. The insurance industry provides such opportunities provided Bermudians are able to show they are top class.

The high salaries of Bermuda insurance executives disclosed by Business Insurance and published in the 'Royal Gazette'[7] could stimulate the vice of envy in Bermudians not in the industry or it could stimulate the virtue of trying to reach what seems a very attractive goal of earning in the region of a million dollars per annum. It certainly beats lifting bags of cement in 90 degrees of heat on a building site for $400 per week. Traditionally and fortunately, envy has not been a characteristic of Bermudians and I imagine many thirty something employees are licking their lips in anticipation of following in the footsteps of senior executives in the insurance sector. If they are, this is excellent news for Bermuda and the insurance industry should be welcomed for making it possible for young Bermudians to have such ambitious goals.

Fifthly, the development of the insurance business is an example of how the Bermuda economy benefits from errors of judgement made elsewhere in the world but particularly in the United States. Let me mention two examples of what I mean:

1. As mentioned in the previous essay John Cox of ACE mentioned that his organisation located in Bermuda because of poor regulation in the United

---

[5] See 'Risk Management' magazine, October 1995.

[6] Fortunately for Bermuda, The Ministry of Labour, Home Affairs & Safety understands this vital point although the opposition PLP still has to demonstrate their understanding of it.

[7] On September 6, 1996.

States. Had that regulation NOT been enlightened or sympathetic to business I doubt if ACE and other major insurance corporations would have established themselves in Bermuda.[8]

2. Most countries suffer from high income and corporate taxes. Bermuda fortunately does not have direct taxes, and although not many companies will admit to it, low taxation in Bermuda is a significant benefit to locating here and provides a big competitive advantage. A big threat to Bermuda's economy would be the introduction of a flat tax as advocated by Malcolm Forbes but, fortunately for us, that is unlikely to materialise in the near future.

Finally, the insurance industry is providing a small Island with credibility in a major industry. In 1994 net premiums written were $14.9 billion - giving Bermuda about 9% of the word's reinsurance capacity, and total assets were $76.1 billion. The number of insurance companies at the end of 1994 were 1,401.[9] Bermuda was a pioneer in tourism and acquired an importance in that industry out of all proportion to its size. Insurance is doing something similar for international financial business and thereby makes it possible for Bermudians to consolidate their position as one of the most fortunate and affluent countries in the world.

From a platform of welcoming captive insurance companies owned by major corporations to progressing to being a leader in a highly competitive business is no mean achievement. It shows what can be done when the conditions are right for business to expand. The Bermuda Government showed great foresight when it established its light and understanding regulation of the industry, kept taxation low, and provided an honest and efficient administration. The smart thing to do is keep it that way so that Bermuda and Bermudians can continue to benefit from the present arrangement.

9. WHAT BENEFITS DO BERMUDIANS GET FROM THE PRESENCE OF EXEMPT COMPANIES?

"The $431 million spent in Bermuda by the international companies during 1994 formed revenue to Bermudian companies and the public sector, and income to households. Most of this revenue and income was re-spent in Bermuda and thereby set in motion secondary flows of money within the economy, which in turn generated additional revenue, income and employments. The process continues throughout several rounds of transactions, but the volume diminishes as money leaks abroad to purchase imports and into savings."
INTERNATIONAL COMPANIES, 1994 - THEIR IMPACT ON THE ECONOMY OF BERMUDA.[1]

As the quotation stated above indicates, the benefits Bermudians obtain from the presence of Exempted Companies are enormous and the disadvantages insignificant. If there were no (or few) international companies incorporated in

---

[8] Or more accurately in some cases incorporated in Cayman and its operations in Bermuda. This means that if things go wrong in Bermuda companies like ACE can move quickly and operate elsewhere. This tends to concentrate the minds of politicians.

[9] 1995 'Economic Review,' page 12.

[1] Published by the Ministry of Finance in 1995 - all figures quoted in the text are taken from this publication.

Bermuda, Bermudians generally would be less sophisticated and very much poorer as our foreign exchange earnings would fall significantly, job opportunities would be greatly limited, and even with regard to such minor matters as sporting and cultural events Bermudians would suffer as Exempt Companies are major sponsors.

In much the same way as when the activities of Exempt Companies were discussed, it is important to remember that these companies are not a undifferentiated corporate mass but differ quite markedly in their contribution to the economy of Bermuda. As of 1994 of the 8,224 companies registered in Bermuda, only 3 percent or up to 277 had a physical presence in the sense that they employed their own staff, occupied an office building, and paid the payroll tax. Those companies with an establishment in Bermuda accounted for about three-quarters of international company expenditure and many of them are well-known international business names - American International Insurance Company, Exxon International and Oil Insurance Limited to name only three organisations. The other 7,947 (8,224 - 277) companies were either associated with the 277 which had a physical presence or were administered by Bermuda management companies.

The various management companies are involved with the provision of such services as banking, corporate secretarial services, provision of directors and officers, financial, acounting and legal services. The three banks in Bermuda, acounting firms and most law firms supply directly or indirectly such sevices as many Exempt Companies are too small or do not have sufficient transactions to justify their own employee presence in Bermuda. The organisations providing these services tend (though not always) to be members of Bermuda International Business Assocation (BIBA) an organisation, unlike the ICD, which is directly involved in promoting international business. It is worth noting that there is some mystery attached as to whether there is 277 companies or some lesser number because of the discrepancy between data compiled by the Tax Commissioner and the International Companies Division of the Chamber of Commerce (ICD). Shell, for example, is a physical presence Exempted Company but there are four employing companies (involved in different businesses like insurance and trading) which would be included in the 277 but not in the ICD figures.

Since 1992 the earnings from international companies has been greater than that from tourism although tourism is the biggest employer. During 1994 Exempted Companies spent $431 million in Bermuda on such things as utilities, office rentals and professional fees. The biggest single category of expenditure was $168.9 million spent on salaries and associated benefits like health insurance. Put another way if there were no Exempted Companies the salaries earned by Bermudians from employment would be dramatically less. In addition there is what is known as a multiplier[2] effect as those who receive salaries or professional fees spend them on such things as entertainment, hiring of ancillary staff like maids or gardeners, or otherwise spend their income in local stores and for local services. However, that is not the end of it as Exempt Companies pay local taxes. In 1994 these amounted to $40.5 million (of which $27.6 million was for annual

[2] this is a technical economics term which is explained further in the text.

taxes), purchase goods and services from local suppliers and provide direct benefits to Bermudians like scholarships which in 1994 amounted to $4.4 million. Such spending creates jobs and incomes although the multiplier's impact diminishes as incomes received are either spent on imports or saved so that it leaks out of the circular flow of income.

What is not recorded are the benefits of an indirect nature such as donations to charities and the provision of cultural events like the Bermuda Festival, or sporting events like the XL Tennis Classic or the Merrill Lynch golf shootout both of which are televised providing Bermuda with free advertising.

The term multiplier used above is a term used to describe the change which occurs in income and employment as a result of a change in spending. International companies incur expenditure in Bermuda because of their operation on such things as salaries, rent and professional services. This is income to the recipients of this expenditure, and they in turn spend their incomes on goods and services from other parts of the Bermudian economy.

If for example, Exempt Companies spend $100 million on salaries (the actual figure is $169.8 million) this becomes income to the employees who then spend their income. If they save some of their income, say 10%, they would then spend $90 million on goods and services which then generates incomes elsewhere in the Bermuda economy but some of that expenditure "leaks" out in the form of imports, say 60% of the income. The balance which is spent and remains in Bermuda, $30 million (being 100 - 10 - 60) is then spent by Bermudians except that they too save and spend income on imports. If the same proportion (70%) leaks out of the economy the remaining $9 million (30 - 21) is spent in Bermuda and if there is the same leakage of 70% the income left to circulate in Bermuda falls to $2.7 million. The process continues with each new round of spending which is equal to 30% of the prior round. Eventually the process comes to an end.

The spending of Exempt Companies therefore percolates through the whole economy so that almost every Bermudian benefits directly - as employees do, or indirectly as restaurants or gardeners do. At the end of the day Professor Archer calculates that in 1994 international companies and their visitors[3] created $661.3 million of income in Bermuda which is about $11,000 for each Bermudian. It can be seen, therefore that Exempted Companies generate a huge amount of income and everyone benefits from their presence. It is therefore something of a mystery as to why, occasionally, some Bermudians criticise the presence of non-Bermudian employees of Exempt Companies. One way of looking at these employees is to regard them as full-time tourists who continually pour money and jobs into the Bermudian economy for the benefit of Bermudians. This brings me to the number of jobs created by the presence of Exempt Companies.

The number of jobs provided by Exempt Companies is well documented, the number being 2,214 which is 6.48 percent of the labour force, of whom 1,348 are Bermudians although only 326 were Bermudian males. One of the great employment mysteries is why Exempt Company employment does not atttract the

---

[3] see comments further in the text with regard to visitors.

Bermudian male, and in particular the black Bermudian male. Is there a reverse glass-ceiling in place? Or is it because many female Bermudians are employed in quasi clerical positions at input data clerks, secretaries or bookkeepers? Non-Bermudian males exceed non-Bermudian females by a ratio of more than 2 to 1. As the following table shows [4] more than 11,000 jobs (and incomes) directly or indirectly are affected by the activities of international companies in Bermuda. Their loss to the community would be catastrophic.

The Amount of Employment Created in Bermuda by the Trading Activities of International Companies in 1994			
			Number of Workers
	Type of Company		
Item	Insurance Related	Non-Insurance Related	All
Direct (1)	1,480	734	2,214
Secondary	1,420	1,916	3,336
Total	2,900	2,650	5,550
Additional Jobs affected (2)	3,200	2,600	5,800

Notes:

(1)   The number of non-Bermudians employed by the International Businesses in August 1994 was 866.

(2)   The number of additional jobs affected are those where income levels and hours of work are influenced by the tertiary effects of international company business activities. These jobs are likely to continue in the absence of international company activities, but at a reduced rate of remuneration.

Not only do Exempt Companies add to the income and number of jobs in Bermuda, but they generate many visitors who in many ways are indistinguisable from tourists. These visitors use taxis, occupy hotel rooms, visit places of tourist interest, play golf and tennis and spend money in restaurants. It is estimated that approximately 15,000 business travellers, accompanied by 12,600 wives and friends, came to Bermuda in 1994. Various other estimates have been made from time to time and it would not surprise me if the combined figure was close to 100,000.[5]

The Exempt Company business and tourism fit nicely together and complement each other's activities. Business visitors require airline connections, good hotels and fine restaurants as well as a pleasant place to visit. Moreover, they tend to visit all year round and do not concentrate their visits during the high season.

---

[4] Page 14, 'International Companies 1994 - Their Impact of the Economy of Bermuda.'
[5] A figure which the ICD believes to be the more accurate

As will be discussed in the profitability of the hotel industry, anything which detracts from making Bermuda an attractive place to visit also detracts from making Bermuda an attractive place to do international business. The contribution of Exempted Companies to the quality of life, the raising of the standard of living, providing high quality knowledge based jobs, contributing to the social and artistic life of Bermuda, providing revenue for the Bermuda Government and contributing to our earnings of foreign exchange is really quite remarkable for an isolated island in the middle of the Atlantic. It is no surprise that many other island communities and countries - Barbados, Mauritius and the Cook Islands - seek to copy the initiatives and innovations of Bermuda.

Just as Bermuda faces competition in toursim from many countries, so too is the competitive pressures from other jurisdictions. In the advertising section of "The Economist" magazine of September 28th, 1996 incorporation in the following countries were advertised by a London promoter of companies:

- Bahamas, Belize, British Virgin Islands, Delaware USA, Gibraltar, Hong Kong, Hungary, Ireland, Isle of Man, Jersey, Madeira, Mauritius, Nevis, and Seychelles.

When international companies can be incorporated in Hungary it is reasonable to say that competition for international business in future years may well rival that of tourism. If so, we are in for a bumpy ride.

10. DID YOU KNOW? - SOME RANDOM AND INTERESTING FACTS ABOUT THE BERMUDA ECONOMY.

1. The estimated revenue expenditure for the Department of Education (including the Ministry headquarters) for 1996/97 is $51.8 million.[1] The number of pupils in school at 31 December, 1995 was 6,322 (4,143 primary 2,179 secondary) making the cost for each about BD$7,170 per annum. The comparable cost at private school is around BD$6,000 (in most cases under that figure).

2. Private schools in Bermuda have an enrolment of just over 3,100 pupils - about one-third of the school population.

3. Between 1980 and 1994 the Caribbean overnight tourist arrivals increased by 104.9%. In the same period, the comparable percentage for Bermuda was a decline of 15.4%,

4. The costs of Bermuda going independent (there were 4 options) were estimated in the Green Paper[2] at between BD$798, 557 and BD$2,239,505.

5. Between 1982 and 1993 wages and benefits increased by around 102% ; the cost of living increased in the same period by 62%.

6. The GDP of Bermuda has not changed significantly in 8 years. Other countries like USA and UK have increased at the rate of around 2.5% per annum.

7. Tourists in Bermuda in 1994 spent $861 per minute.

---

[1] Budget Statement for 1996/97, page 24.

[2] Green Paper, pages 16 and 17.

8.   It is estimated that government will employ 4,594 people in 1996/97.

9.   Prison budget for 1996/97 is $12.193 million. The total number of prisoners at 31st December, 1995 was 288, making the annual cost per prisoner $42,337.

10. The percentage of school children at private school is as follows : UK 7.2%, USA 11.5%, Bermuda 34%.

11. Bermuda has 3,160 people per square mile. Canada has 7 ; USA 68 and UK 616.

12. There are 552 chartered accountants in Bermuda in 1996 of which 160 are Bermudian.

13. In the fiscal years 1996/97 customs duties raised 30.5% of revenue. In 1986/87 the comparable figure was 42.2%.

14. In the fiscal year 1996/97 government expenditure was estimated to be 25% of GDP ; in 1986/87 the comparable figure was 18.8%. The percentage spent by the United States governments (federal, state and local) in 1928 was under 10%.

15. The unfunded liability of the government Contributory Pension Fund was BD$1,087 million as at July 31, 1990.

16. Government borrowing in the fiscal year 1996/97 will be at the rate of BD$100 per minute.

17. It will cost BD$58,000 per hour to run the Bermuda Government in fiscal year 1996/97.

18. The deficit on the Public Service Superannuation Fund at 31st March, 1992 amounted to BD$89.1 million or 44 percent of liabilities.

19. The value of Bermuda dollars and coins circulating in the Bermuda economy on December 31, 1995 was BD$62.5 million an increase of 11 percent over the previous year.

20. In 1995, estimated earning from Bermuda's capital investments were BD$117 million.[3]

21. The accumulated losses for eight major Bermuda hotels for the years 1987-1995 amounted to BD$34.043 million.

22. In 1995 the total assets (mainly the assets of depositors and shareholders equity) of Bermuda banks amounted to BD$8.475 billion.

23. Chase Manhattan Bank has estimated that $2.1 trillion in personal wealth is kept offshore in international financial centres like Bermuda.

24. Bermuda allowed private cars in 1946 on the assumption that there would not be more than 400. There are now around 22,000.

25. In 1995, there were 48,236 motorised vehicles - roughly 2,000 per square mile.

26. Under the provisions of the Exempted Undertakings Tax Protection Act, 1996 most Exempt Companies in Bermuda are exempted from the payment

---

[3] From the Bermuda Monetary Authority.

of income, corporate, capital gains and other direct taxes until the 28th March, 2016.

27. There are just over 2,000 local companies but over 8,500 Exempt Companies.

28. As at 31st December, 1995 Bermuda's 15 Class 4 excess liability and property catastrophe reinsurance companies had a capital and surplus of US$8 billion ; gross insurance premiums were $3.1 billion ; and total assets were $14.8 billion.

29. The Bermuda insurance industry's share of the world reinsurance market is 9%. This is fourth after Germany (37%), U.S. (23%), and Switzerland (10%).

30. In the field of catastrophe reinsurance the Bermuda was the market leader with about one-third of the global market.

31. Crime costs each individual living in Bermuda an estimated BD$1,300 per annum.[4]

32. There are 412 private security guards in Bermuda and 489 police officers.

33. It costs about $80 to bring each tourist to Bermuda.

34. About 10 percent of Bermuda visitors by air come to Bermuda for international company business purposes.

35. It is estimated by the BMA that there could be between $25 million and $50 million U.S. dollars in circulation in Bermuda. This is an interest-free loan to the United States government.

36. It is estimated that in the year 2010, there will be 7,467 people in Bermuda over the age 65 which will be just over 12 percent of the population.

37. In 1995 there were 34,133 jobs in Bermuda of which 26,612 (78%) were held by Bermudians ; in 1994 there were 34,143 jobs of which 79% were held by Bermudians.

38. Whites are twice as likely as blacks and others to be employed in decision making positions.[5]

39. In terms of population Bermuda is the same size as Altoona, Pennsylvania in the United States and Wansbeck, Northumbria in the United Kingdom.

40. A useful way of comparing Bermuda with other countries is on a per capita basis. The population of USA is about 4,500 times that of Bermuda, UK is about 1,000 times bigger. This helps to understand problems such as the number of AIDS deaths. As at October, 1996 there had been 291 AIDS deaths in Bermuda, the equivalent of 1.3 million in the United States, and 291,000 in the United Kingdom.

4 See Part III 10 for greater details.
5 Employment Survey 1995, page 17.

11. WHAT IS THE BERMUDA MONETARY AUTHORITY ?

"Although in terms of its balance sheet liabilities and numbers of staff the Bermuda Monetary Authority is purportedly, the third smallest central monetary institution in the world, its size does not necessarily mean narrower legal definitions of less comprehensive objectives, or for the country it represents less financial stability, systemic soundness, balanced growth and so forth. On the contrary it has become evident that, philosophically and in many practical aspects, there is no real difference between the smallest and the largest."

THE CHAIRMAN OF THE BERMUDA MONETARY AUTHORITY, 1996.[1]

The Bermuda Monetary Authority (BMA) was created by the Bermuda Monetary Authority Act of 1969 and it is a body corporate, wholly owned by the Bermuda Government, with an independent Board of Directors who are responsible for policy matters, general administration and business decisions of the BMA. The capital and reserves of the BMA at the end of 1995 totalled $19.7 million and total assets amounted to almost $84 million.

The BMA has seven directors[2] none of whom can be members of the Legislature, that is the House of Assembly or the Senate. The Chairman, like the other directors, is appointed by the Minister of Finance and clearly has a greater day to day involvement in the activities of the BMA than the other directors all of whom are unpaid and have other jobs. The principal administrative officer is the General Manager and he heads a staff of seven senior professionals who are accountable to him for such matters as the Domestic Economy Division, Investment Services and Policy and Research.

The main objects of the BMA are:

1. To issue and redeem notes and coins - the amount of which at the end of 1995 was almost BD$63 million. An important policy objective is to meet the demand for Bermuda dollars by Bermuda residents. In addition, to issue coins and notes to service numismatic dealers in many parts of the world which also generates income for the Authority. The importance of the Bermuda dollar is discussed in the next section.

2. To supervise, regulate and inspect financial institutions such as banks and collective investment schemes (mutual funds and unit trusts) which operate both in, and from, Bermuda. This is an increasingly important objective as concerns are expressed and lessons were learned from the supervisory and control problems which led to the collapse in 1994 of the British merchant bank, Barings and the earlier fraud which arose from the collapse of the Bank of Credit and Commerce (BCCI) a few years earlier. The BMA requires periodic reports from financial institutions concerning their financial position, operations and policies and evaluates the information presented and takes appropriate action based on international standards of supervisory management established by the Basle Committee on Banking Supervision. Such responsibilities are carried out with the specific purpose

---

1 1995 annual report, page 5.
2 The author is a director of the BMA.

131

in mind of protecting the assets and interests of depositors and the investment public in general. The main statutes which govern oversight of financial institutions are the Banks Act 1969, the Deposit Companies Act 1974, the Credit Unions Act 1982, and the Trust Companies Act 1991. In addition, the BMA is affiliated with international organisations involved with supervising the banking industry, capital markets and financial services generally such as the Offshore Group of Banking Supervisors representing 19 international financial centres. In 1993 the BMA became a member of the International Organisation of Securities Commissions which has over a 100 countries as members. This organisation coordinates the regulation and supervision of securities markets.

3. Closely aligned with the previous object is the promotion of financial stability and soundness of the financial institutions in Bermuda by monitoring the performance of banks, credit unions, collective investment schemes and trust companies - much of this is accomplished informally by, for example, holding regular meetings with senior management of the supervised insitutions. The granting of Designated Territory Status to Bermuda in 1988 under the UK Financial Services Act of 1986, has provided international recognition of the importance of sound supervision of the Bermuda regulatory system.

4. The BMA supervises and approves the issue of financial instruments by both insitutions and residents of Bermuda. This additional object came into force in 1990 as collective investment schemes became increasingly popular and important.

5. Much of what has been said leads naturally to an increasingly important objective of the BMA which is to foster close relations between the various financial institutions which operate in Bermuda, and between Government and the financial institutions. The BMA arranges regular meetings, facilitates communications between institutions and encourages codes of professional conduct. It also acts as a focal point for government concerns and the concerns of the financial community and it smooths relationships between the two bodies. The close day to day working relationships between the BMA and the various private financial insitutions is an excellent example of how the much derided "old-boy network" works to the advantage of Bermuda.

6. The BMA also manages the Bermuda Government's exchange control regulations which are less onerous than they were three years ago. Such regulations apply only to Bermudians, and to non-Bermudians working for local companies but do not apply to international companies and their non-Bermudian staff who are designated non-resident for exchange control purposes. Exchange control is increasingly seen in the global economy as an irksome relic of a byegone age but its provisions in 1996 are not particularly onerous for Bermudians. The main regulation is that overseas investment by Bermudians of amounts greater than $25,000 per annum require special permission from the BMA. Most other regulations are administered in a sen-

sible way by the local banks to whom the BMA has delegated authority. The primary purpose of exchange control is to conserve Bermuda's reserves of foreign currency and to monitor foreign currency transactions by the public. As a by-product of this objective the BMA compiles the Balance of Payments statistics for Bermuda. The level of Bermuda's foreign exchange reserves - like that of most other countries - is highly dependent on what Bermuda earns from its trading activities and its earnings from tourism and international companies.

7. Finally, the BMA advises and assists Government (and other public bodies) on general financial matters. Government still determines general policy but can and does seek the advice of the BMA on such matters as interest rates, the investment of public funds, the financing of housing and government borrowing. The BMA carries out on behalf of the Ministry of Finance the processing of applications in respect of the formation of companies, partnerships, collective investment schemes and the granting of permits to overseas companies which wish to carry on business from Bermuda. It scrutinises the proposed ownership of organisations who wish to establish a presence in Bermuda and ensures that they are indivuals of integrity and sound financial standing. It pierces the veil of corporate ownership and requires information about direct or indirect ownership requiring for example a copy of the latest audited financial statements. Information provided to the BMA is protected by the secrecy provisions of the BMA Act of Incorporation.

It is generally recognised that the BMA has adopted a commonsense, flexible and practical approach to its role and responsibilities and it is rare for complaints of bureaucratic footdragging - so common to other parts of government operations - to be voiced against the BMA.[3] The result of this is that with rare exceptions a number of sensible goals have been achieved such as :

- The protection of the integrity of Bermuda as an international financial centre without compromising international standards.
- The application of standards of supervision and regulation in Bermuda are of an internationally recognised calibre.
- The maintenance of Bermuda as an attractive business environment.
- A vetting process for incorporation which is both rapid and flexible.
- The commitment of Government to the expansion of international business.
- The preservation of the reputation of Bermuda by the application of sensible regulatory methods.

Clearly being a regulator, supervisor, gatekeeper in the incorporation process and channel of communication between the financial community and government is not an easy balancing act to carry out. Differences of opinion and conflicts do, and will continue, to arise from time to time. There is no groundswell of opinion which wishes to change the present arrangements in any significant way and the absence of any major criticism of the BMA indicates that the present process is working well.

---

[3] Although this occurs from time to time.

A major issue facing Bermuda is that of money laundering. In 1994 the BMA promulgated a Code of Conduct which has been accepted by Bermuda's banks. It is a self-regulatory code but the United Kingdom government has implemented a European directive on money laundering which it has requested be implemented in Bermuda as soon as possible. Money laundering arrangements until recently were concerned with dealing with the illegal proceeds of drug trafficking but they have been extended to deal with the proceeds from a greater range of crimes. That process has gone even further with measures being put in place elsewhere to deal with the need to establish and verify the identity of every banking customer and the reason for opening the account. This will add to the supervisory burden of the BMA as each and every customer of the bank will need to verify his identity by for example having certified copies of current valid passports submitted when bank accounts are opened.

As Bermuda banks expand their operations to other jurisdictions the BMA will be viewed as the home regulator to ensure that appropriate regulation takes place and conforms to the standards of the foreign jurisdiction in which the Bermuda bank has an affiliate. If a Bermuda bank has a subsidiary in the United Kingdom or elsewhere in the European Union, like Luxembourg, the BMA will need to have in place a regulatory system which meets European standards.

Finally, the BMA is often likened to a central bank but in at least three major ways it does not satisfy the criteria. Firstly, it does not act as "a lender of last resort" as a central bank like The Bank of England would do in the event of an emergency in the private banking sector. Occasionally, private banks can suffer from liquidity and The Bank of England (for a price) will step in and provide the necessary cash to keep the commerical bank functioning. On other occasions, as was the case with Barings in 1994, it may decline to do so and the private bank collapses. The BMA does not function in this capacity in Bermuda.[4]

Secondly, the BMA does not possess the full arsenal of monetary control techniques available to most central banks. It cannot use its power and prestige to move interest rates and the availability of credit by such things as open market operations and direction. It exercises its limited powers in this regard by persuasion through informal meetings with the domestic banking industry and deposit companies. In any case Bermuda is too small a country to have an independent monetary policy. Its strategic monetary policy is essentially decided in the United States.[5]

Finally, the BMA does not manage the foreign exchange reserves of Bermuda. That is done by the commercial banking sector. In most countries this is a function of the central bank, particularly in countries where there is a shortage of foreign exchange - which usually means everywhere outside the developed world. Foreign exchange control is administered by the BMA but it is delegated in large part to the banking system. The management of Bermuda's foreign exchange reserves is not a matter of concern, provided the banks are financially sound and well-managed. The ability to be able easily to acquire foreign

---

[4] See Part I 13 and 14 for a discussion of what is money.

[5] See Part II 1 for a discussion on the importance of the United States economy.

exchange, which for Bermudians is U.S. dollars in the main, is dependent on the ability of the Bermudian economy to earn U.S. dollars from its two main industries.

In conclusion, the BMA is an institution which unobtrusively discharges its responsibilities of ensuring that Bermuda's financial institutions conform to the highest international standards of probity, and that they retain the confidence of the public of Bermuda and their customers.

12. WHAT IS THE BERMUDA DOLLAR AND HOW STRONG IS IT?

"Money is the most important thing in the world. It represents health, strength, honour, generosity and beauty as conspicuously and undeniably as the want of it represents illness, weakness, disgrace, meanness and ugliness."

GEORGE BERNARD SHAW (*WHO WAS A SOCIALIST*).

"A disordered currency is one of the greatest political evils."

DANIEL WEBSTER.

In day to day commercial transactions most Bermudians use the Bermuda dollar (BD$) without giving a second thought as to what it is they are using. The fact that they do so without thinking about it is silent testimony to the underlying value and confidence in the Bermuda currency. In this respect, Bermudians are not dissimilar to Americans, French or any other nationality for the bit of paper they exchange for their daily needs serves the same purpose as the American dollar or the French Franc.

All sound paper currencies have the essential ingredient of money, that is to say it is generally acceptable for payment of debts. If the grocery store is happy to accept Bermuda dollars for groceries why be concerned? You have the groceries, the store has the paper money which can then be used by exchanging it for U.S. dollars to buy further supplies. Yet behind this seemingly simple set of transactions many complicated forces are at work.

Bermuda dollars and American dollars are used inter-changeably in commercial life in Bermuda because virtually all Bermuda's foreign income arises in U.S. dollars. Most Bermudians are indifferent as to whether the Queen's portrait is on the currency or the head of George Washington, although perhaps they should be. Every Bermudian who carries and uses the American dollar is effectively giving Uncle Sam an interest-free loan and at the same time increasing the costs of the Bermuda government which is the same thing as increasing Bermudian taxes. Why is this so?

At the end of 1995, approximately $63[1] million Bermuda dollars and coins were in circulation. It is estimated by the Bermuda Monetary Authority (BMA) that about $40 million in U.S. currency is in circulation in Bermuda at any given time. In the vaults (or strictly speaking under the control of an independent custodian) of the BMA are investments equal to at least 115 percent of the value of

---

[1] BMA Annual Report for 1995.

the notes in circulation. In fact at the end of 1995 the international currency assets backing the Bermuda dollar notes in circulation were valued at $79 million, in excess of the 115 percent legally required.

The assets of the BMA means that in principle anyone can take a Bermuda dollar to the BMA and receive in exchange an American dollar. So long as the public remains confident that Bermuda dollars can be easily and quickly converted into American dollars there will be no difficulties for the Bermuda dollar being an accepted means of exchange. The BMA Act gives legal effect to practical reality by requiring that Bermuda dollar notes are legal tender for the payment of debts.

The reason why Bermudians are able to exchange Bermuda dollars for American dollars is that Bermuda earns sufficient American dollars from its two main industries. If Bermuda ever failed to generate sufficient foreign income the Bermuda dollar would degenerate into a worthless piece of paper wanted only by collectors, a situation which prevails in many countries. For example, in Guyana the Guyanese dollar has been devalued so many times that at the last count it was worth one-third of a U.S. cent.

Why bother with having a Bermuda dollar, after all it would be just as easy to use U.S. dollars in our commerical transactions? There are at least five sound reasons for retaining the Bermuda dollar.

Firstly, the portfolio of investments backing the Bermuda dollar earns income for the BMA which is ultimately paid as dividends to the Bermuda Government, its sole shareholder. Since the creation of the BMA in 1969 a total of $40 million has been paid to Government which effectively reduces Bermudian taxes by that amount. Unfortunately, the U.S.$40 million in daily circulation reduces the ability of the BMA to earn income and as a result Bermudians have to pay the income foregone in taxes. In addition, the entire operations of the BMA - exchange control, supervision of banks and deposit companies and all other activities conducted by the BMA does not cost the taxpayer one cent.

If there was no Bermuda dollar and we used American dollars as does, for example, The Republic of Panama we would effectively be paying taxes to the American government which is not a sensible thing for Bermudians to do. The U.S. dollar is the de facto common currency in the Western Hemisphere. I have never experienced any problems when travelling in Central and South America when I use U.S. dollars for tips, buying drinks or buying trinkets in the market place. In fact quite the reverse as discounts are often offered if payment is in U.S. dollars. Many tourists also take away Bermuda dollars as souvenirs and it is estimated that approximately BD$500,000 is removed from circulation in this way which means that tourists are effectively making a gift of this amount to the Bermuda treasury and paying taxes on our behalf.

Secondly, the existence of the Bermuda dollar makes it easier to capture the data necessary to compile Bermuda's Balance of Payments statistics. Compiling these figures would be immeasurably more difficult without the existence of the Bermuda dollar.

Thirdly, the Bermuda dollar allows the possibility of the Bermuda Government being able to introduce monetary instruments such as Treasury Bills should they ever consider it necessary to implement monetary policy.

Fourthly, the Bermuda dollar assists the police to control illicit transations in Bermuda, particularly those which relate to the drug trade and money laundering. The U.S. dollar is the favoured currency of drug dealers and money launderers, and replacing the Bermuda dollar with the US dollar would limit our ability to control such nefarious activities.

Finally, the Bermuda dollar is one of the factors which creates the individuality of Bermuda and provides an element of national pride. To give it up would be to give up some of Bermuda's history, identity and distinctiveness as well as relinquishing an element of control over Bermuda's financial affairs. Bermuda is already highly dependent on the U.S. economy and few people would wish us to become the 51st monetary state of the Union.

Bermudians can sleep easier knowing that the currency is as good as gold (in fact better as the BMA can earn income from its investments) provided our ability to continue to earn foreign exchange is not impaired and Bermuda banks continue to be well-managed. We have been good at doing just that for many years and there is no reason to expect otherwise in the future. The Bermuda dollar is as good as the U.S. dollar.

13. WHAT IS MEANT BY BERMUDA BEING DESCRIBED AS AN INTERNATIONAL FINANCIAL CENTRE?

"There is no sign that the rapid changes in the international financial system and markets that have been so marked a feature of the last few years will do anything other than continue. Indeed, the pace of growth seems certain to accelerate as technology and electronic communication continues to develop, bring financial markets closer together into what are, in effect, increasingly global markets."

MARGARET ALLEN.

"Nothing contributes more to world prosperity than the work of tax havens in preserving the savings of the rich from the hands of national tax collectors."
WILLIAM REES-MOGG (*FORMER EDITOR OF THE LONDON TIMES*).

The term international financial centre (IFC) is usually used as a shorthand to describe the various financial activties such as banking, insurance and foreign exchange dealings carried out at a particular location or city and the institutions which are involved with their execution. It is an all-embracing term which can mean different things to different people and, surprisingly, the term is not found in various dictionaries of economics and finance which I use.

Bermuda has been describing itself as a financial centre for many years because it has been utilised by many multinational companies since 1945 as a location for some of their financial activities the most important of which is insurance.[1] However, the use for some specific corporate purpose does not necessarily make Bermuda an IFC as such centres usually provide a vast battery of international services usually on a 24 hour basis.

There are three main ways in which the term IFC is used:

1.   To distinguish between activities which take place solely within Bermuda and are therefore localised, and those which are international in nature and scope. The most important international activities in Bermuda are those of Exempt Companies[2] and banking which generate much of the Island's foreign exchange earnings, estimated to be just over 50 percent of the total.

2.   To describe many of the services which are readily available to the public, customers and clients of firms involved in international business. Such services would encompass the purchase of foreign exchange, the investment of surplus funds in international stock markets or the provision of specialised professional advice on financial matters.

3.   To give Bermuda some standing, or status, in international financial matters in a way which allows it to compete with larger and more established IFCs such as London, New York or Zurich.

It is in this third category - as a competitor or rival of major centres in which the term is increasingly used as most of the services mentioned in point 2 can be obtained almost anywhere in the world these days. Point 1 is simply stating that as a constituent of Bermuda's economic activitiy its participation in international business is a major source of employment and foreign exchange earnings and without these earnings Bermuda would not be as well-off as it is.

A major IFC could carry out or facilitate all or most of the following activities for customers from any parts of the world :

• Making major cross-country payments.

• Attracting investment funds from all over the world and through its markets and contacts enable these funds to be invested in securities of all descriptions.

• Mobilising large funds in many different currencies.

• Providing of means by which industrial, trading and government projects can be financed.

• Providing venture capital for new commercial projects or the public offering of shares in a new corporate venture.

• Providing a wide variety of commerical and financial services on an international scale.

• Providing access to a large pool of talented specialists in international financial matters that is to say investment managers, bankers, accountants, entrepreneurs and international civil servants who are easily and quickly assembled for major projects and who are known to each other.

• Providing a wider and more innovative range of financial services than competitors and other jurisdictions.

---

[1] See Part II 7 for a discussion of this subject.
[2] See Part 11 6.

- Having a reputation for being able to accomplish complex financial deals at short notice.

- Providing 24 hour trading, 365 days a year, in such areas as foreign exchange, commodities trading or stock exchange transactions.

- Having the ability to innovate and bring to the market important new financial products, for example derivative products whose value and importance is "derived" from underlying products on which they are based such as commodities like oil or copper or contracts based on movements in important stock market indices like the Dow in the USA or the Nikkei in Japan.[3]

- Providing an economically friendly environment for international business.

- Providing custodial services for investment organisations. The Bank of Bermuda is the world's 21st largest global custodian[4]

- Allowing foreign financial institutions to establish a presence for the purpose of allowing them to compete with other jurisdictions.

- Developing new technologies to provide instantaneous global information and the ability to deal in the battery of financial products available worldwide.

- Providing a free competitive environment which encourages international competition at the highest level and the sweeping away of archaic restraints on trade such as exchange control, equity ownership or the ability to employ the best talent.

- Having in place a system of financial regulation and supervision which provides protection to depositors, investors and other interested parties and which will prevent major financial failures because of incompetence, fraud or other wrong-doing.

The above is a full, but not an exhaustive, list ; but it indicates some of the requirements and ingredients needed for a location to describe itself as an IFC of major international importance. Bermuda has clearly satisfied some of the above criteria - for example the provision of an economically friendly environment in which to do international business but it is nowhere close to making it possible for large 24 hour trading of equities or foreign exchange although increasingly the advances in information technology and communications allows firms established in Bermuda to deal with major centres like Tokyo, London and New York. The following table describes some of the major activities of an IFC and it can be seen that Bermuda has only a handful of the characteristics required to be a major financial centre.

---

[3] It was speculating in the Japanese stock market indices by Nick Leeson a trader in the British Bank, Barings, which led to its spectacular collapse in 1995.

[4] 'Institutional Investor,' September 1996 page 197.

SOME CHARACTERISTICS OF AN IFC

FINANCIAL ACTIVITY	London	Tokyo	New York	Bermuda
Major international economy	Yes	Yes	Yes	No
Central Bank	Yes	Yes	Yes	No
Modern legal and administrative system	Yes	Yes	Yes	Yes
Major banking centre with non-national banks	Yes	Yes	Yes	No
Effective supervision and regulation	Yes	Yes	Yes	Yes
Foreign exchange markets	Yes	Yes	Yes	No
Absence of protection in financial services	Yes	Yes	Yes	No
Ability to raise huge capital amounts	Yes	Yes	Yes	No
Large provider of capital in major currencies	Yes	Yes	Yes	No
Major stock market	Yes	Yes	Yes	No
Major insurance market	Yes	Yes	Yes	Yes
Provision of portfolio management	Yes	Yes	Yes	Yes
Futures and derivatives markets	Yes	Yes	Yes	No
Shipping and trading centre	Yes	Yes	Yes	No
Commodities markets e.g. gold, copper, oil, tin etc	Yes	Yes	Yes	No

Whilst Bermuda is unlikely to rival the large financial centres of Tokyo, Hong Kong, Zurich, Frankfurt, Amsterdam, London, New York, Chicago and San Francisco there is no reason why it cannot to continue its highly successful strategy of being a niche financial market in a manner akin to other small locations like Singapore, Manila, Bahrain, Luxembourg, Edinburgh and Charlotte. It is unrealistic to expect a small community of around 60,000 people to provide the range of major market-making services available in the large financial centres like London or New York. A critical mass generating huge volumes of business is essential and a Mid-Atlantic small island could never be in a postion to provide this.

What then should Bermuda do to continue to maintain and enhance its status as a minor, but highly successful player in the financial services game, and legitimately be considered by international businessmen to be an IFC? Several major strategies almost recommend themselves.

Firstly in the financial services industry, whose principal assets are knowledge and reputation, it is not possible to put a tariff or restriction around an idea or an electronic impulse in the same way as it used to be possible to impose barriers to physical trade. The removal of protectionist policies has the major benefit and advantage of strengthening every participant in the market as it is not a zero-sum game. Competition enlarges the pie to be shared out - it does not make it smaller - and as a result productivity is improved and everyone gains financially. This is a particularly hard message to get across not only to those who are financially sophisticated but it is extremely difficult to reach an electorate which has been weened on the milk of protectionism and the strong but naive belief that these protectionist policies are mainly responsible for the high standard of living which Bermuda enjoys.

It is difficult to maintain the illusion of Bermuda as a modern and innovative financial centre when it still, as a matter of government policy, continues to implement 18th and 19th century mercantilist and protectionist policies which have rightly been rejected and jettisoned by most other advanced economies.

Secondly, the reputation of Bermuda as an honest corruption-free environment which has a cooperative and understanding government has always been high in the international business sphere. It has avoided many unsavoury aspects associated with doing business in Cayman or The Bahamas, its supervisory and regulatory processes are reasonably effective and continuous efforts are being made to improve them. Reputation is at the centre of the effectiveness and acceptability of any IFC. Honest customers such as major insurance companies, pension funds and other institutional investors do not like dealing with countries whose ethics can be questioned. The Swiss reputation took a nose-dive in 1995 when accusations were made that Swiss banks were failing to repay money to heirs of Holocaust victims who had sheltered their assets in Switzerland in the 1930s to protect them from Hitler.

Today many financial markets are in a constant state of flux largely because of scandals and inadequate methods of regulation. The mess in the insurance markets at Lloyds of London, the huge fraud at the Bank of Credit and Commerce International (BCCI) in 1991 which led to depositors losing their money, the collapse of Barings in 1995 and the losses sustained in 1996 by the Japanese Bank Sumitomo on the copper exchange in London indicate that current methods of regulation may be inadequate to control the complexity and interdependence of international financial markets.

Bermuda has fortunately been relatively scandal free compared with its offshore competitors but its reputation could very easily be tarnished by some unfortunate sequence of events resulting from inadequate management controls, fraud or a failure by management to understand the nature of their business. The authorities are fortunately not complacement and several steps are being taken to improve the degree of supervision and regulation by, for example, the introduction in 1994 by the BMA of a "Code of Business Practice and Standards of Professional Conduct for Investment Advisers dealing with the General Public in Bermuda" and the extension in 1995 of Bermuda's Money Laundering Code of Conduct to domestic investment service providers. The downside to this is that compliance with regulations and supervision is expensive and could erode some of Bermuda's competitive advantage.

Thirdly, Bermuda will have to participate in greater international liaison with other governmental authorities such as the Bank of England and the Securities and Exchange Commission in New York. International financial interdependence is an established fact of life and there is increasingly a requirement for governments to work together. International bodies such as the Organisation for

Economic Cooperation and Development (OECD) based in Paris of which Bermuda is now a member is only one of a host of international organisations involved with ensuring that the financial world continues to have the confidence of international business. In recent years, Bermuda has made substantial progress in this direction and is contemplating an International Financial Institutions Act, a Companies Management Law and legislation for mergers and acquisitions in Bermuda as mechanisms to build on the substantial progress already made.

Whilst there has been much hype about the status of Bermuda as being an IFC, there is no doubt that as in the Olympics Bermuda has an importance in international finance disproportionate to its size and importance in the world economy. Whilst it can never rival huge IFCs like London, New York and Tokyo there is no doubt it can be a major player in niche markets such as insurance. To be big in the modern world does not necessarily mean that small rivals can be ignored or patronised, and to be a small player does not mean that you are unimportant in the big financial picture.

Bermuda has been remarkably successful in the past. There is no reason why it should not continue that success provided it is prepared to move with the times, remain competitive, maintain its focus, innovate, keep up to date with information technology, produce the right kind of people from its educational system and discard that which is no longer relevant to the modern world. Bermuda can continue to be a small but prosperous fish in a very large pool.

14. WHY DID HONG KONG COMPANIES WISH TO ESTABLISH A DOMICILE IN BERMUDA.

"I feel it would be desirable for British administration to continue because that is one of the elements that has made Hong Kong successful and prosperous until now. If that was not to continue, one would have to examine and reassess it very, very carefully."[1]

DAVID NEWBIGGING, THEN CHAIRMAN OF JARDINE MATHESON, 1983.

"Bermuda added up to more plus factors. Stability, reputation, quality of administration, local infrastructure, communications - it all added up to a package we couldn't find elsewhere."

RAYMOND MOORE - JARDINE MATHESON'S MANAGING DIRECTOR IN BERMUDA.

At first blush Bermuda and Hong Kong have very little in common and it is therefore something of a mystery as to why so many Hong Kong companies have established a presence in Bermuda over the past 12 years or so. The differences between Hong Kong and Bermuda are not difficult to document :

- There is a 12 hour time difference.
- One borders the Pacific Ocean - the other is in the middle of the Atlantic.
- Chinese is the dominant ethnic and social group in one (most of the population has close ties to Communist China), the other has a black and white population and a dominant Western culture.

---

[1] 'Hong Kong Business Today,' May 1984

- Hong Kong has a large population (5.5 million) by comparison with tiny Bermuda (less than 60,000).
- Corruption is not unknown in Hong Kong; it is rare in Bermuda.
- Hong Kong is the world's busiest port and has a huge entrepot trade whilst Bermuda is almost entirely a service economy.

The differences, however, in the economic sense are relatively unimportant. It is the common characteristics and common financial interests which are much more important.

- Each were barren rocks until the British arrived.
- Both are British Colonies - almost an anachronism in today's world. Hong Kong changes status in 1997 when it becomes part of the People's Republic of China. Bermuda voted in 1995 to retain its colonial status. Colonial status is important to business organisations in both jurisdictions because of the right of appeal under both legal systems to the Judicial Committee of the Privy Council in the United Kingdom. So long as a territory remains a British Colony this right of appeal cannot be changed. However, should the constitutional status change to that of an independent country, the legislature of the newly independent country can discontinue that right at any time as has already been done in many countries. It is the cement of the English legal system which binds the two very different jurisdictions to each other. Each jurisdiction probably could not maintain its standing as an international business centre without this right and its absence would affect the willingness of international business organisations to do business with Hong Kong or Bermudian companies.
- Following on from the previous point, each jurisdiction is dependent on retaining the confidence of the international business community in order to continue to prosper.
- Each ties its currency to the United States dollar (one HK$ = US$7.80) recognising the importance of having a stable currency and also the economic importance of the United States.
- Each is openly capitalistic understanding the significance of having low taxation, limited government and sound administration.
- Each is located close to an economic giant. Bermuda to the United States (and to a lesser extent Europe) and Hong Kong to China and the economic dynamism of the Pacific Rim countries.
- Most important of all - having few natural resources - each is dependent on the greatest natural resource of all, the skill and energy of its people.[2]

As an aside, each is a place or jurisdiction which should not in logic exist in the modern world. Hong Kong is a thriving, ultra-sophisticated and beautiful metropolis a few miles off the coast of Mainland China one the world's poorest and deprived countries. It is an oasis of capitalism run in the main by a small oligarchy of businessmen (many but not all of whom are European) in the midst of

---

[2] This is explored further in Part IV 2.

the largest Communist state the world has ever seen. The logical contradictions are immense and obvious but Hong Kong goes about its business very successfully oblivious of its contradictory status.

Bermuda has a freak climate, an almost fairy-tale atmosphere of pastel coloured housing and style of life which is different, but not too different from its large neighbour to the west. Each country should not exist in its present form in the increasingly homogeneous business environment which the globalised world has created. Yet almost inexplicably both do and both continue to do well in a world which should have left them behind.

The close financial relationship between Bermuda and Hongkong can be traced to the period before March 28, 1984 the date on which Jardine Matheson (a major trading and commercial house in Hongkong) announced that it would restructure itself under a Bermuda holding company.

Many Hong Kong businessmen had had business relationships with Bermuda - Y.K. Pao a large ship owner being the best known. The Keswick family whose ancestors had been involved with Jardines for years had established family trusts in Bermuda in the 1970s. Probably most important the business community in Hong Kong had long known that major changes could be expected when British colonial rule came to an end on July 1, 1997. Bermuda still a British colony was an obvious, if distant, safe haven from the potential storms of political change.

The announcement in 1984 by the Chairman of Jardines, Simon Keswick, of the decision to form a new Bermudian holding company for the Jardine Matheson Group and move its domicile to Bermuda was greeted with shock and disbelief in Hong Kong. It was described in the local press as a "bombshell", an insult to the Chinese people, arrogance, disloyalty, and as indicating a lack of confidence in the future - meaning the period after July 1, 1997 when Hong Kong reverts to Chinese rule. In phrases reminiscent of major military defeats, there were snide comments about rats (wearing kilts) leaving a sinking ship, the British running away from danger, and bumpy rides on the way to the Bermuda Triangle. The Financial Secretary of Hong Kong made light of the situation with the comment of "Who are they?" and the local TV station made it the last item of news that day.[3] Jardines were derided as being the first into Hong Kong and the first out.

However, the decision by Jardines emphasised the fragility of confidence of the business community in the future of Hong Kong and one immediate reaction was a drop in the stockmarket index of about 10 percent on the day following the announcement.

> "We want to ensure in future that our holding company is able to operate under English law and to have access to the Privy Council in Britain."
> Simon Keswick[4]

Any major organisation in Hong Kong making this sort of announcement would have had a profound effect on business confidence but Jardines' decision

3 'Far Eastern Economic Review,' 12 April, 1984.

4 'Far Eastern Economic Review,' 12 April, 1984, page 46.

was like a bolt from the blue as it was considered to be the doyen of European dominated (in this case Scottish)[5] Hong Kong businesses dating its connection to the territory to 1841 when it purchased its first plot of land. Jardines has been involved with China longer than any other company, it formed its first joint venture with China and in 1995 had 60 joint ventures there employing 10,000 people. It was at pains to stress that no company has a greater long-term interest in a stable and prosperous Hong Kong and to an open and sincere relationship with China.

Jardines commercial interests are commercially and geographically widespread.

- Restaurants - Ruby Tuesday in Hong Kong, Pizza Hut in Taiwan and Sizzler in Australia.
- Engineering and construction all over South East Asia.
- Aviation and shipping such as air cargo handling in Hong Kong.
- Security and environmental services.
- Sale and service of motor vehicles.
- Financial services such as life insurance, risk management, corporate finance and portfolio management.
- Widespread ownership of property such as hotels and office buildings - mainly in Hong Kong (ownership of real estate in Hong Kong alone is US$8 billion).
- It owns almost 5 percent of the Bank of N.T. Butterfield.
- In 1995 Jardines had a turnover of US$10.6 billion; a net income of US$420 million; capital employed was US$6.5 billion; and it employed 220,000 staff of which 58,000 were in Hong Kong.

The Far Eastern Economic Review in an article[6] stated that, "Jardines has thrown a brick through Peking's window, and did not trouble to wrap the missile in a way which would minimise the noise. By doing so, it may well have damaged its own reputation with the local community and its future relations with China."

Businesses do not like abrupt change or political instability and most organisations have tucked away in a bottom drawer contingency plans in order to position themselves for the future. A failure to make arrangements for the future prosperity of an organisation is a charge which no managing director likes to have levelled against him. Shareholders' money and employees' jobs are matters too important to be left as hostages of fortune. Repositioning a large and influential organisation in a politically sensitive area like Hong Kong at a critical time of potential political change cannot but help risk being misunderstood. Jardines were always at pains to state that they "are not sellers of Hong Kong"[7] which would be difficult given that it has over US$8 billion invested in real estate in Hong Kong. The decision to restructure in Bermuda was a rational choice for a multinational corporation.

---

[5] At lunches hosted by Jardines the St Andrew's cross of Scotland is draped across the dining table.
[6] Dated 12 April, 1984.
[7] Speech by Alistair Morrison, Managing Director, Jardine Matheson Holdings, 10 January, 1995.

There is always the unlikely possibility that the new Chinese government could seize the assets of businesses operating in Hong Kong so that business can no longer be profitably conducted. Many people do not believe the Chinese will adhere to the principle of "One country, two systems" set forth in the British-Chinese agreement over Hong Kong. If Hong Kong was to retain the rule of law, press freedom, the impartiality of the civil service and individual liberty it could retain its status as one of the world's major international financial centres. But if it was administered like the mainland of China it would be an unattractive place in which to do business. The rule of law and capitalism go against the communist Chinese mentality. Hong Kong could also be swept up in the political turmoil which is endemic to The People's Republic of China.

In a recent book[8] it is concluded by the authors that the day the UK hands over the city will be the beginning of Hong Kong's demise as a dynamic, free-market financial centre. Many in business are unwilling to give the benefit of doubt to the Chinese government and many (about 700,000) individual Hong Kong residents - most the cream of Hong Kong society - also took the trouble to acquire American, British, Canadian or Australian nationality as a precaution against the unthinkable. The decision by the Board of Jardines to establish a corporate home outside Hong Kong was as rational and as predictable as anything can be although it was portrayed in the Hong Kong press as something of a panic decision and an act of treachery.

The previous paragraph is probably too pessimistic about Hong Kong's future. After all in the first nine months of 1996 the stock market had risen by almost 22% - significantly better than the dismal performance of the Bermuda stock market. A visitor to Hong Kong is swept off his feet by the energy and bus-tle of the place. Hotels are full, shops are crowded and everyone is too busy mak-ing money to lose sleep over a change in government. It takes a real pessimist to believe that Hong Kong - so vibrant and properous in the late 20th century - will not be the same in the 21st century. However, the future of Hong Kong is totally dependent on the politics and economics of China. Politics could be the death of Hong Kong - that is why Bermuda still looks attractive.[9]

The question therefore was "why Bermuda"? And why did so many Hong Kong companies follow the example of Jardines?

The most important reason of all was the legal system of Bermuda. The Chinese legal system is rudimentary - almost non-existent - and is highly depen-dent on who you know and not on case law and established legal principles worked out over many centuries of practical experience. To place a modern multi-national corporation at the whim of politicians was a risk that Jardines did not wish to assume. To move to an impartial well-respected jurisdiction made a great deal of sense.

The legal system reason was not enough on its own, after all the move could have been made to Cayman, The Bahamas or The Channel Islands and others. Other factors which made Bermuda the domicile of choice were:

[8] "Red Flag Over Hong Kong," by Bruce Bueno de Mesquita, David Newman and Alvin Rabushka.
[9] Some say that politics could also be the death of Bermuda as a thriving economy.

- The English language which counted out places like Luxembourg.
- The well developed infrastructure of communications, power, harbours, roads and so on. Jardines subsequently entered into a joint venture with Edmund Gibbons Limited to build an office building on Reid Street, Hamilton where the St Andrew's cross is still displayed over the dining room table.
- Political stability and absence of corruption. The question of independence from UK was not a major consideration probably because the issue had been put to bed in 1977.
- Availability of professional services such as accounting and law.
- Bermuda is an attractive place in which to live with an excellent climate and good communications to the United States and UK.
- No direct taxation and no restraints on the repatriation of profits.
- The Channel Islands and Isle of Man were too close in a regulatory sense to the UK.
- The Cayman Islands was not such an attractive place to live as Bermuda and in the 1980s it did not have a good business reputation.
- Bermuda already had attracted quality corporations - mainly in captive insurance but also in other fields such as shipping and trading.

The decisions of other Hong Kong companies to come to Bermuda are not as well documented as that of Jardines who were the first to make the move. In 1996 about 50 percent of the companies listed on the Hong Kong stock exchange have a presence in Bermuda.

Why other Hong Kong companies came to Bermuda is probably because once a large and respected firm makes the decision to change, it is easy for others to follow. The legal work had been done, the political difficulties have been dealt with, and the idea is not as revolutionary as it had first appeared. It is too strong to say that other Hong Kong organisations behaved like sheep storming the exit but once a precedent has been established for sound commercial and business reasons it becomes difficult to resist.

For Bermuda, the conclusion is inescapable that potential political difficulties and uncertainties elsewhere in the world are good for business. It is when foreign governments behave as sensibly as the Bermuda government that business opportunities could dry up.

15. WHAT IS THE BALANCE OF PAYMENTS AND HOW IMPORTANT TO BERMUDA IS IT?

"The Balance of Payments statistics are, to a large extent, based on estimated and historical data. The reader is therefore advised to observe an appropriate degree of caution when interpreting the figures. A review by the Government Statistics Office of the estimates of imports and exports is continuing, and this may result in further revisions to the data."

BERMUDA MONETARY AUTHORITY, ANNUAL REPORT 1995, PAGE 26.

The International Monetary Fund's definition is "a statistical statement that systematically summarises, for a specific time period, the economic transactions of an economy with the rest of the world". Domestically the balance of payments is an annual statistical summary, an account, of Bermuda's transactions with the rest of the world - it shows the total payments made by the residents (which includes individuals, firms, and the government) of Bermuda to foreign countries on one side of the account, and on the other side the total receipts which Bermuda earns or receives from residents of other countries.

The balance of payments has two important parts to it, (1) the current account, and (2) the capital account. The current account deals with current transactions such as paying for imports like clothes or food for which Bermudians pay foreigners, or on the other side the selling of services like tourism or financial services for which Bermudians receive payments from foreigners. If receipts and payments taking one year with the next are approximately in balance the public would be unaware of the importance of this account. If there occurs a severe imbalance, by for example not earning sufficient foreign currency from tourist or international companies, the consequences of this for Bermuda and Bermudians would become readily apparent.

Importers would be unable to acquire from Bermuda banks foreign exchange to pay foreign suppliers, and suppliers would, when not paid, discontinue or reduce shipments to Bermuda. In extreme circumstances if the foreign currency reserves of Bermuda were exhausted, we would be unable to acquire food, spare parts for such things as power generation, or gasoline for cars.

Fortunately, Bermuda has never been in this position but a visit to a third world country like Pakistan will dramatically show the impact on a country which persistently fails to export sufficient to earn foreign currency. Dirt, poverty, disease and hardship are visible to even the least observant visitor. The reason is quite simple. Modern products which make life comfortable and enjoyable such as modern medicines, motor vehicles, television sets, oil for power generators or nutritious food are usually imported. On the other hand, a country which has a consistent trade surplus with the rest of the world will look remarkably like Bermuda - little evidence of poverty, well-fed and well-dressed people are common and everyday luxuries like cars, television sets and air-conditioning are readily available. A country which cannot pay its way because its exports and imports are not in balance rapidly falls into financial trouble.

The balance of payments, as its name implies, must balance. The total receipts must equal the total payments in very much the same way as an individuals trans-actions with the rest of the community must also balance. If a country exports more than it imports it is said to have a favourable balance of payments (the more accurate term is that it has a favourable balance of trade) in which case the excess is accounted for by lending abroad to other countries by, for example by Bermuda residents having deposits designated in United States Dollars or buying shares in foreign companies or mutual funds.

If there is a deficit (or unfavourable) balance of payments the reverse process takes place and Bermuda residents would have to borrow from foreign banks or sell previously held foreign assets. This would be a clear indication that Bermuda is living beyond its means and a warning that corrective steps need to be taken. Borrowing from foreigners and selling foreign assets on a regular basis is not a policy which can be continued for very long. Moreover, foreigners would be understandably reluctant to lend to a country which has little prospect of paying its debts. For many years (as the table shows below) Bermuda has earned a cur-rent account surpluses of between $10 million and $83 million which has per-mitted Bermudians to enjoy the good things of life and to invest abroad, for exam-ple, through their employer's retirement benefit fund.

The Balance of Payments figures for Bermuda are shown below and indicate that Bermuda is in the enviable position of paying its way in the world of inter-national trade.

Table 1 — Balance of Payments Estimates — $ million

	1987	1988	1989	1990	1991	1992	1993	1994
Merchandise trade	-390	-450	-478	-481	-389	-399	-480	-536
Shipping & other transportation	- 62	- 66	- 64	- 61	- 59	- 60	- 66	- 64
Travel	375	332	330	371	330	313	370	383
Investment Income	59	9	17	6	2	15	40	22
Professional, technical & managerial services	270	287	297	313	303	324	387	401
Other goods, service & income	- 85	- 75	- 80	- 99	-114	-104	-125	-103
Transfers	- 60	- 66	- 73	- 73	- 63	- 78	- 71	- 59
Current account balance	83	- 29	- 51	- 24	10	11	55	44
Capital account balance	- 69	26	81	- 24	- 116	- 61	- 75	- 42
Errors and omissions	- 14	3	- 30	48	106	50	20	- 2

Note: Positive signs indicate inflows and negative signs indicate outflows
A negative sign on the capital account represents an increase in assets or reduction in liabilities

Source: Bermuda Monetary Authority

Why is it that Bermuda does not have a Balance of Payments problem? The simple answer is that Bermuda is able to attract a sufficient number of tourists and international companies to Bermuda and these two industries generate sufficient foreign exchange for Bermudians to enjoy the good things of life which are imported from foreign countries. The amounts for 1994 for example show that Bermuda earned a net $383 million from tourism and $401 million from international business. Without these earnings Bermuda would be a very different place. It would not take long for Bermuda to change from being a society which enjoys one of the highest standards of living in the world to one which suffers from one of the lowest. Anything which prevents, or impedes Bermudians earning foreign exchange is a threat to our standard of living. Crime, high costs, poor service or political instability are examples of such threats.

The capture of data to compile the balance of payments is undertaken by the Bermuda Monetary Authority from a variety of sources. Customs data is probably the most reliable source of information as was until recently foreign exchange forms completed by residents who had to obtain consent to acquire foreign exchange of an amount greater than $100. Banks and deposit companies provide aggregate data for statistical purposes, and organisations like the Chamber of Commerce and the Bermuda Hotel Association are able to provide much of the information required.

Although the data gathering arrangements are effective, there are still 'gaps' in the information which results in a line in the accounts called errors and ommissions, or more simply the BMA does not know why the figures fail to balance. If this figure is insignificant there is no problem but if it is high, it was above $106 million in 1991, then something is clearly wrong with the data collection system. This is a problem which many countries have and considerable work is being done to try and plug this gap in information. The illegal drug trade is clearly one major source of the problem.

Bermuda is unusual in that the activities of its international companies are not recorded in its balance of payments statistics. The value of such transactions would swamp the puny figures on which Bermuda government policy decisions are made. The annual insurance premium revenues for Bermuda companies is $16 billion whilst the annual imports of Bermuda in 1994 amounted to only $536 million (3.35%). In addition, much of the data for corporate holding companies simply is not available - nor would the companies want that data to be publicly known.

This has created a gap in international statistics and the ICD is considering whether to recommend to its members that such statistics be furnished to the International Monetary Fund. If Bermuda wishes to participate fully in the international economy it has little choice.

16. IS BERMUDA A COMMODITY?

"Bermuda's product has not changed markedly since 1980. It is offering the same product it offered in 1980 at an effective rate (for the U.S. market) of twice the price."

COMMISSION ON COMPETITIVENESS, 1994 - PAGE 77.

"A Bermuda vacation simply costs too much, even for the affluent market. Bermuda must find ways to reduce its prices to visitors, and to offer more product without increasing costs."

IBID - PAGE 101.

Commoditisation is an inelegant and ugly word but for Bermuda it is also an ugly concept . Commoditisation means that the buyer of a particular product is influenced only by price and not by such things as service, location or beauty as these things are available from others suppliers of the product. Price is the factor above all which determines whether or not the customer is prepared to buy.

As with all products the market calls the tune. This means if a supplier wishes to succeed the price has to be right. There are many explanations of why price dominates in such businesses as tourism and allied industries like airline business (is American Airlines all that different from Delta?), shopping (why do Bermudians travel to the United States to buy things?) and to a certain extent restaurants (a major reason for the success of chains like Burger King and McDonalds):

- The main reason for market forces dominating the tourist business is that of increasing competition from other destinations. Countries like Belize, Thailand and Kenya which had never considered tourism as being a business option are now active in the tourist market place and new countries are joining each year - one of the major threats to Bermuda is Cuba. Not only has the number of countries competing increased, competition has changed the nature of the business so that what was successful in the past may not necessarily be successful in the future. Tourism is probably the biggest industry in the world, has become vital to the economic development of many Third World Countries and is growing at the rate of about four percent per year. To gain an understanding of the competitive threat to Bermuda the reader should glance through the Travel Section of the Sunday edition of the 'New York Times' newspaper.

- Consumers are much more price conscious than they were in the past. As inflation has been wrung out of the world economy and household incomes in the United States have stagnated over the past twenty years the customer has become more concerned about obtaining value for money.

- Not only are consumers more price conscious they are much better informed about the vacation options available to them and they are demanding more than good weather and beaches. The consumer is now a dictator when in the past he was nominally the king.

Many other industries have faced the same challenges - Cargills the grain trading company does not own farms it makes deals on the financial markets, Shell, the oil company also buys and sells oil products in the financial markets; banks do the same thing with financial products and have long ceased simply to take in deposits and lend them out. With tourism that choice is not available - no one has come with a futures exchange for vacations - but the two options are either:

1. drive down the price of a Bermuda vacation so that we compete with Third World Countries like Jamaica or the Dominican Republic and earn Third World wages; or

2. differentiate (another ugly word) our tourist product in such a way that the customer (the tourist) is prepared to pay a premium to the Bermuda brand over and above the cost of a vacation in say Jamaica.

As competitive forces gain impetus it is extremely difficult to justify that premium in the market place as the public does not stay loyal to a brand for very long unless they are convinced they consistently receive value for money. The Bermuda brand therefore must be built around reputation, quality and value. Bermuda has to find ways to differentiate itself from other destinations, manage its cost base in a more effective manner and retain the loyalty of its existing customers and visitors. This is not an easy task.

Commoditisation has not affected international business by anything like the same extent that it has affected tourism. Nevertheless a glance at the advertisements placed in the back pages of "The Economist" magazine by business developers in other offshore jurisdictions stressing price indicates that many of the forces which have affected the tourist industry could , and probably are, affecting our international business. Increasing competition is being seen from the Cayman Islands, Channel Islands and Luxembourg for example and many other new competitors are entering the field such as Mauritius, Belize and the Cook Islands all of whom are targetting Bermuda's client base or seeking to undermine its reputation as a sound location in which to do business.

The Bermuda brand in international business depends on a number of factors the most important of which are:

- Political stability - in part undermined by ourselves during the independence issue.
- A reputable and corruption free legal system.
- Absence of corporation and other related taxes.
- Widespread availability of professional services.
- Competitive cost base.

In the past many of the countries mentioned above who now compete with Bermuda did not possess the physical infrastructure and other societal and political attributes to compete effectively with Bermuda. They all now have modern telephone systems, good airline connections , modern hotels and the appropriate political, fiscal and legal structures in place. All of this suggests that price will pay an increasingly important role in the decisions of those who wish to establish international businesses in Bermuda. In addition, the costs of doing business in Bermuda is increasingly of importance. For example, many back office functions like accounting, claims handling and other routine clerical tasks can be transferred to low cost areas like Ireland and the Caribbean whose populations are highly educated.

Bermuda was a pioneer in the development of both the tourist industry and of offshore international business, and as a result it benefited greatly in financial terms by enjoying one of the highest per capita incomes in the world. In the early stages of development of these two Bermuda industries, there was limited competition from other countries, communications and technology were not nearly as well developed and as widespread as they are now, and customers were not as well informed or had as great a choice. Because of this favourable situation, Bermuda was able until fairly recently to charge high prices and therefore enjoy a high income. In short, Bermuda companies and employees were able to determine the prices charged to customers in these two industries. However, nothing lasts forever and circumstances have changed dramatically over the past five to ten years, as new competitors have entered both industries, knowledge about the skills necessary to be successful has been disseminated and the dramatic improvement in information technology and communications has made time and distance less important.

As circumstances changed, Bermuda has now become a price taker (especially in tourism) rather than a price determiner, and like many other international industries it can charge only what the customer is prepared to pay, not what Bermuda as supplier wishes to charge. This is a dramatic change in the financial circumstances and one which is not yet fully appreciated. This phenomenon has occurred throughout the world as competition has intensified and as inflation has been wrung out of the world's monetary systems. Despite the evidence before their eyes, many Bermudians still continue to believe that the customer will be willing and able to have to pay the price which Bermuda determines it has a right to collect based on the costs of its operations plus a percentage for profit[1]. The reality now is that the customer determines what he is prepared to pay, and the supplier has to produce the product at that price. If the supplier of the service fails to do what the customer wants business will go elsewhere, and jobs, and income will be lost.

If I am correct in my assessment that Bermuda in moving towards commoditisation, it means that Bermuda may have to change its economic strategy from being based on selling its two main industries at a price based on cost, to selling at a price which the customer is prepared to pay. Increasingly, customers are not prepared to pay premium prices for a branded product (which is what Bermuda is) unless they believe they are gaining clear additional value from the transaction. Bermuda cannot sell beer at champagne prices and hope to be successful long-term. If the product cannot prove in the marketplace that it has a distinct added value, there will be customer resistance and eventually a fall in the demand.

---

[1] Retailing is a good example of this.

To a very great extent this is what has happened in the tourist industry. Bermuda has charged premium prices even although market circumstances have changed dramatically. Customers have not believed that they have gained added value from run down hotels, poor service and a tired product. Customers have failed to return in their previous numbers and there has been a fall in demand, evidenced for example by a 60% or so occupancy rate in the major hotels for the past ten years. This phenomenon has happened in many foreign industries, computer hardware, motor vehicles, retailing and TV sets, to name only a few and it evidences a significant change in consumer behaviour with which Bermuda has yet to come to terms.

In the 1996/97 budget statement of the Finance Minister taxes were raised because government costs had increased.[2] Congratulations were expressed because of the relatively modest increases in taxation. In the old era this may have been an appropriate response, but in the new era government like everyone else will have to produce its services at a cost which taxpayers (who are customers) are prepared to pay. If it fails to do this, taxpayers will intensify their tax avoidance habit of shopping abroad (an example of where distance is no longer economically relevant) where prices as lower. When taxes are raised to the point at which taxpayers are unwilling to pay them government finds itself in very much same position as business - it has to reduce its expenditure as taxation cannot be as easily increased as it was in the past.

17. WHAT IS GLOBALISATION OF THE WORLD ECONOMY AND HOW WILL IT AFFECT BERMUDA?

"In the extremely competitive global environment in which we now live, we must constantly remind ourselves, as a bank and as a service community, the only thing we have to sell is ourselves. Success is solely dependent on providing excellent service at reasonable prices in a friendly way."

THE BANK OF BERMUDA.[1]

"It must be considered that there is nothing more difficult to carry out, nor more doubtful of success, nor more dangerous to handle than to initiate a new order of things."

MACHIAVELLI - "THE PRINCE."

Globalisation is one of the buzz words which is hard to escape at present. What it means is that a new era is now upon us, sometimes called globalisation, sometimes the service economy, sometimes the information age, and sometimes the knowledge society. The consequences of this new era are impossible to predict but most commentators believe that the changes we are now undergoing are as revolutionary as anything in economic history. We are lucky enough to be living in an age where the possibility to create new opportunities, wealth and interesting jobs is as great as it has ever been in the past. The world has become a huge electronic highway where money and ideas race along fibre optic cables or go up

---

[2] See Part III 7 for a discussion of this issue

[1] Letter to shareholders. April 15, 1988.

into the sky to satellites at the speed of thought not the speed of machines. In the globalised economy brains replace brawn and human ideas are more important than factories pumping out steel and chemicals.

A consensus has been reached about the value of open markets and government fiscal prudence. This has created a world which is clearly global and with the downfall of communism there is no real alternative ideological or economic model for Western democracies. In days gone by, countries could effectively build a tariff wall around themselves to keep out foreign goods. Radio and TV could be censored and foreign influences and bad political news kept to a minimum. Communications were fairly basic - a local telephone company with only a few people able to afford to call internationally. Many countries like the Communist bloc, India, Burma and China as a matter of policy deliberately excluded themselves from the world economy.

The rules of the game have now changed, and changed dramatically. There has been a revolution in the past ten years of earth shattering proportions in many industries, in national economic policies, and in technology some of the most important being:-

- New technology has expanded the capacity of the telecommunications industry to provide services other than just telephone calls.
- The General Agreement on Trade and Tariffs (GATT) has systematically led to reduced trade barriers, and following the Uruguay Round in 1995 the World Trade Organisation (WTO) was created and it extended international trade agreements to agriculture, services, investments and intellectual property.
- In information technology, both hardware and software, is more widely available. Hardware is smaller, less expensive and more powerful. Software is more flexible and is also less expensive. Capacity in data transmission is progressing at a bewildering pace.
- The costs of transportation have been reduced dramatically, and its reach has been extended: anywhere in the world can be reached from anywhere else in less than 24 hours.
- Formerly closed communist and socialist centrally planned economies are moving to more market orientated capitalist economies, putting a potential labour force of more than 2 billion people on to the labour market.
- Economic interaction through more liberal investments has dramatically increased market competition in virtually every industry.
- Residents of most countries are free to buy and sell foreign assets.
- Real time coverage on radio and TV of major political and economic stories brings events to homes of billions - CNN played a major role in the downfall of communism.
- Entrepreneurs like George Soros and Rupert Murdoch roam the world in search of opportunities for investment.
- Excess capacity and the intensified competition has increased competition from low wage countries which previously had not participated in the world

economy. Industries which are labour intensive and use standard technology are now competing with the old established industries of the rich countries. This results in the necessity of cutting costs by restructuring and shedding unproductive labour - or in extreme cases exiting from certain industries.

- With the reduction in rates of inflation, and in some cases such as the USA, cuts in real wages, consumers are now more price conscious and better informed than they were in the past. They are becoming more sophisticated in their demands and a decision to buy takes into account of product quality and convenience as well as price.

- In almost all the rich countries there has been a switch in employment from traditional manufacturing to service industries and knowledge based activities as knowledge is now the competitive advantage. One result of this is that the number of jobs for women has increased whilst those traditionally done by men has fallen. A more chilling result is that those workers without special skills required by the market will be unable to find productive employment.

The above changes have made it possible for rich countries to outsource jobs, make major investments and modernise poor countries, whilst at the same time the dismantling of tariffs and other trade barriers has made it possible for poor countries to export basic manufactured goods like textiles, motor vehicles (in Bermuda we can now buy a motor cycle made in India but not one manufactured in England) and shoes to rich countries. Access to pools of capital can be achieved easily provided the political risks are not too great as investors avoid governments who create budget deficits by overspending on things like the military, impose trade barriers or who are politically unstable or corrupt. Trade and investment flows make it possible for countries to use advanced technology and intensified competition forces governments to remove barriers to trade and to make sensible economic reforms.

Location is now no longer a crucial ingredient for production. A department store in London, for example, at the close of business by using computerised stock taking and pricing, knows exactly how many dresses of a particular design it has sold that day. It can then advise the supplier in say Thailand of its requirements and the manufactured dresses will on their way the next day by an international airline and be in the store's warehouse within 48 hours or less. Customers now make known their wishes from the market place in London to the place of production in Thailand in a matter of hours and this is happening in more and more industries. The customer is no longer king , he is dictator - and it is the customer unconsciously using modern technology and communications who now creates investment, productive capacity and wealth.

Political reforms and transformations taking place in large countries like India, China and Brazil have the potential effect of adding millions of highly literate, numerate and disciplined people on to the world labour market. When I visited India in 1995 I met a manager of a firm in Bombay which solves software problems for New York banks overnight and has the solution for opening business the next day. Being in another part of the world is an advantage not a disadvantage.

Money can move around the world in seconds moving from one personal computer in New York to another in Frankfurt and with instantaneous communications distance and time increasingly don't mean very much. The value of international securities transactions in the G7 group of countries is equal to $6 trillion per quarter, five times the value of international trade. Political borders are becoming increasingly irrelevant as governments can no longer control the flow of information and news - it is impossible to block out advertisements on satellite television from Los Angeles which is being watched in New Delhi. Designer tee shirts, Nike sneakers, and Sony walkmen are as much in evidence in Jakarta as they are in Johannesburg. The world can and does watch the same TV programmes, wear the same clothes, eat the same junk food (except in Bermuda)[2] and respond to the same advertisements.

Money and information do not respect national borders because their objectives go far beyond national communities as the economic reach of capital is immeasurably greater than the national influence from which it originates. Nominal political independence may have been achieved from London, Paris and The Hague but economic independence for any country, including the United States, just does not exist. People increasingly define themselves not by the state or nation of which they are nationals, but by clothing, lifestyles and their interactive network of friends and colleagues. An international lawyer from New York would find himself just as home in London or Tokyo as he is in his own environment. He would not be at home in rural Kansas or in the centre of large cities like Detroit or Chicago which are increasingly alien to the educated middle class. Traditional barriers between national economies have been pulled down by flows of hot money, electronic information, technology, ideas and industrial products.

There is a world market economy and the national economic systems are an integral part of it. The size of this new market economy is shown by a recent study by the United Nations' Center on Transnational Corporations who estimated that the combined sales of the 350 largest multinational companies amounted to one-third of the combined GNPs of all developing countries, including China.

It is now impossible to buy a pure American car, British suit or Japanese stereo. Hondas are made in America, Coco-Cola is made in scores of countries, Chrysler builds its best selling car in Canada. Corporations are almost stateless, dedicated to their shareholders and customers by moving their capital and technical resources to the most cost-effective location which they can find. Globalisation increases the power of capital relative to that of labour (and governments) and it increases its share of global income witness the massive increases in stock market prices over the past 10 years. Who will be successful in the global economy will be the companies and countries which produce the best products and are the most efficient. That still tends to be in North America, Western Europe and Japan because such countries were wealthiest first, but also

---

[2] See Part III 4 on the subject of Big mac.

because these countries still enjoy a major advantage in possessing the greatest body of knowledge which is now the essential resource not land, factories or the possession of coal and iron as in the past.

This is as great a structural economic shift as the move from agricultural economies in the nineteenth century to the mass production systems of the twentieth. It will leave beached many workers, especially those who do not possess marketable skills, even as it creates masses of new jobs in the knowledge based industries. Retail banking has seen major shrinkage as many tasks are now unnecessary because of new technology. Broadly similar things are happening in the insurance, telecommunications and retailing industries. Millions are unemployed in Europe and the USA because they make things for which there is no longer a market, or they possess skills which are no longer required. Highly skilled jobs still remain, they even multiply but there are fewer jobs for those who can only do simple tasks. The distinction between blue collar and white collar is becoming increasingly irrelevant as is the distinction between capital and labour; the more important distinction is between the knowledge worker and the service worker and understanding the difference will be the key to economic success.

Globalisation means that the world is now a single market. Increasingly there is nowhere to hide inefficiencies, provide subsidies to the incompetent, or tolerate bad government because capital, labour and knowledge and hence eventually the customer will go to where the price and quality are the best.

Bermuda will be affected by the above changes by:-

- A changing labour market as jobs in Bermuda will increasingly change from being basically clerical to be being high tech. Those who gain a sound education will enjoy satisfying careers ; those who do not will labour away at low paid service jobs and this will tend to exacerbate social problems especially if a large part of the black population is unable to secure its fair share of the these good jobs.

- Bermudians may have to spend some of their working career in New York or London in order to acquire modern skills before they can achieve senior positions in international companies. Only economies and countries with an educated, inspired and dedicated workforce can retain the competitive advantage essential for success in the global economy[3]. Someone, sometime will have to tell low skilled Bermudians that their "right" to a well paying job does not exist and this will be difficult as not everyone is educated, technologically adept and self reliant.

- The battery of protections which may have served Bermuda well in the past will become increasingly irrelevant. Banking can now be done by PC with any bank in the world. Knowledge workers will have to be employed in greater numbers, not because they are Bermudian but because they have the relevant knowledge and experience. New products as well as old can be purchased anywhere in the world and be sent by courier to Bermuda within 24 hours. Electronic shopping does away with government regulation of opening hours and control over ownership and distribution of goods.

---

[3] See Part III 18 for a discussion of competitiveness.

- Foreign tax laws and regulations may be changed to conform with the new realities and as a result this could have a major impact on Bermuda's international business.

- Bermudians may enjoy cheaper products from abroad because of increasing productivity brought about by globalisation. At the same time, increasing competition from abroad in both tourism and international business will compel Bermuda to provide services at a price the consumer is prepared to pay not the price Bermuda wishes to charge[4].

The world in the next few years will almost certainly prove to be more integrated, more unpredictable and probably more wealthy but it will require a change in Bermuda's approach to business. How Bermuda responds to this new world remains to be seen.

The world will be a more exhausting but also a more invigorating place and although it may look chaotic Bermuda has little choice but to join this hyper-competitive world. To do otherwise would be to stagnate and return to being an eighteenth century fishing village.

18. SHOULD BERMUDA BE A GLOBAL VILLAGE OR A FISHING VILLAGE?

"The island-nation of Singapore may be the first to totally immerse itself with the realm of placelessness. By 2005 Singapore expects to have every home, company, and government worker connected on a single fiber-optics information grid. Government records, customs bills, architectural blueprints, and even the precise location of each manhole cover will be reproduced electronically and available instantly. Every household will have terminals that combine the telephone, computer, television, video recorder, and camera."

WILLIAM KNOKE.[1]

At this moment Bermuda is very much a part of the global village and many years ago, probably when the Royal Navy established a base here in 1795, it ceased to be a simple fishing village. However, atavistic urges in Bermuda are very strong so we run the risk of regressing to the so-called "good old days" largely because of complacency and inertia. In addition, there are now many more countries who mistakenly adopted policies like socialism in the 1940s through to the 1990s who are now clamouring to join the global village of which Bermuda has been a part for many years because they can see, perhaps more clearly than ourselves, the many advantages of membership.

There has always been a degree of tension between those Bermudians who favour Bermuda being global or international, and those who prefer Bermuda to be an isolated parochial community quietly living a life which implicitly rejects many of the assumptions of the international community like freedom of capital to go where it can earn the highest return, reasonable mobility of labour, and new

---

[4] See Part II 16 for a discussion of commoditisation.
[1] "Bold New World," page 30.

and improved ways of doing things.

The internationalists in Bermuda, or those who prefer the global village, have usually won the day in the public debate because being a part of the global village is the major reason why Bermuda enjoys its enviable prosperity which has come at some cost to the xenophobic, isolationist and self-satisfied elements of the community.

The characteristics of the Bermuda global village are:-

- Having a significant proportion of foreigners in the labour force - usually in the region of 20 to 25 percent - which has led to a limited degree of social and racial tension between Bermudians and non-Bermudians .

- Many large businesses are foreign owned because of the importation of foreign capital particularly after the Second World War. Most major hotels are foreign owned and managed, as are some large important commercial organisations like Shell, Esso and Cable and Wireless .

- Large Exempt Companies are by definition also foreign owned and increasingly they are large employers of local labour.

- Local Bermudians have access to foreign TV and radio programmes which can culturally disrupt the conservative traditions of Bermuda.

Many black Bermudians see the Bermuda government as being under the thumb of foreigners often failing to recognise that this accusation (often overdone) has been levelled at many other governments because of world globalisation[2]. Paradoxically, the globalisation of the world's economies has brought about an increased desire for local identity and a greater emphasis on the distinctiveness of race and ethnicity - characteristics which are particularly relevant to Bermuda. This tendency can be seen elsewhere in the world where, for example, in the European Union nationalism has been weakened at the nation state level, but local nationalism strengthened at the peripherary in places like Scotland, the Basque country in Spain or in Normandy in France.

Many Bermudians are just as at home in the sophisticated capitals of the world such as New York, London, Paris or Tokyo or in the company of business and political leaders in other parts of the world as they are with their fellow Bermudians flying kites on Horseshoe Bay on Good Friday - indeed many of them are probably more comfortable in that atmosphere than they would be in the sand and sweat of the South Shore. There is now a truly international labour market from which Bermuda obtains major benefit, open to a small elite group of people whose skills, interests and experiences supersede cultural differences.

Increasingly, nationality and background mean less and less and professional and business interests mean more and more so that a Bermudian businessman travelling in a foreign country will associate with people like himself (or herself) rather than with the traditional local resident. I have often been to foreign countries like Peru or Thailand and seen only the local Hilton Hotel, the inside of a taxi and airport and met only people engaged in the same business as myself. I might as well have been in New York as Lima. Local issues, people and idiosyn-

---

[2] see Part II 17 for a discussion of this issue.

cracies become increasingly irrelevant - except perhaps to create a diversionary interest from business - but what is really important is the ability to get things done in an acceptable way and to be able to rely on the competence of local services like restaurants, accountants, public safety or even the electrical supply.

In Bermuda local chauvinism is most strongly shown in the policy of Bermudianisation where the opposition PLP persistently has raised the spectre of a conspiracy against Bermudians when sensible and much needed appointments of non-Bermudian staff are made. For example, there was huge criticism of the appointment of a new Police Commissioner and Deputy Commissioner when crime was increasing at an alarming rate. When the Marriott Hotel wanted to appoint a new general manager the local Svengali of Bermudianisation and conspiracy theories, Mr Alex Scott MP, was reported[3] as saying, "We want to know why Immigration has approved the work permit of a non-Bermudian when there is obviously a qualified Bermudian available."

The issue for him was not that the Police Service and the Marriott hotel required the best talent to lead them, but that only local Bermudians should be appointed, irrespective of how the job was done. The fact of the matter is that immigrants are a source of economic strength, advanced technology and bring valuable skills to Bermuda. They generate jobs and contribute to the cultural vitality of Bermuda. However, because they are highly visible, economically powerful and generally affluent it can create social friction with those who do not fully understand their economic contribution to the well-being of Bermuda, a fact which is often seized on by unscrupulous politicians. Put more bluntly, many of them prefer Bermuda to be a fishing village rather than a global village.

Clearly local sensibilities and aspirations cannot be ignored but then neither can the legitimate interests of the taxpayers of Bermuda who have an interest in minimising crime or the shareholders of the Marriott Hotel who clearly wish to see their investment protected. Dilemmas of this nature are increasingly important as the interests of foreigners can often conflict with those of locals. However, Bermudians cannot have their cake and eat it too. If they wish to enjoy the benefits of a higher standard of living arising from being a member of the international community, they must recognise (as many obviously do) that this involves giving up the belief that in every case a Bermudian should be appointed to a senior job.

The international world - or the global village - is not a place or a physical location in which we work, buy things, or even where we sleep or live but a concept which allows people, goods , capital and most important of all knowledge to be made available to the customer or the international business in a manner which allows wealth to be created in the most efficient manner and which has built into it processes for dealing with rapid change. Success will come to those who embrace constant change and improvement not to those who wish to eliminate them.

It is a characteristic of human beings to try and keep things the same but technology is fortunately immune to sentimental familiarity. Roadblocks placed in the way will at best slow the process down, or at worst signal to the rest of the world

---

[3] 'Royal Gazette,' April 4, 1996 page 5.

that Bermuda does not wish to be a real participant in the new world and that it wishes to be a fishing village with all the penalties which that involves such as a much lower standard of living, isolation from the exciting events taking place all over the world, and abdication of responsibility for the future of our children.

19. HOW IMPORTANT TO BERMUDA IS THE CONFIDENCE OF THE INTERNATIONAL FINANCIAL COMMUNITY?

"Confidence is the foundation for all business relations. The degree of confidence a man has in others, and the degree of confidence others have in him, determines a man's standing in the commercial and industrial world."

WILLIAM BOETCKER.

"True prosperity is the result of well placed confidence in ourselves and our fellow man."

BENJAMIN BURT.

Confidence is not a term found frequently in economic texts. The standard texts by authors like Paul Samuleson, Richard Lipsey and even The Fortune Encyclopedia of Economics do not contain references to the word confidence in their indexes although Fortune Magazine has a confidence index. This is not surprising as confidence can mean different things to different people and it is a difficult word to define. As to whether or not it exists is dependent on the circumstances in which it is used. For a small economy like Bermuda confidence is a vital ingredient for its continued success and for the Bermudian people to continue to enjoy their high standard of living. For larger diversified economies the question of confidence is not nearly as important as it is for economic minnows like Bermuda. This begs the question - confidence in what?

First of all confidence in the policies of government. If business investors believe that the government will pursue policies of envy, high taxation or division of the people according to class or race there will be diminished investment for the future. A good example of government policies having gone haywire is the former colony of British Guiana now known as Guyana. It was to Guyana in South America, a rumoured source of the famous El Dorado, that the Pilgrim Fathers had proposed to set sail to before settling on New England, a place which was described by Anthony Trollope as the "one true and actual Utopia of the Caribbean seas."

Like Bermuda, Guyana has two main racial groups, blacks and East Indians, and a small minority, the Portuguese. Blacks were originally slaves brought to work on the sugar plantations from Africa. When slavery ended in 1834, East Indians were brought to Guyana as indentured servants in order to provide the necessary agricultural labour and also act as means by which wages could be reduced in order to control costs. Almost immediately there was rivalry and distrust between the two groups which lasted until independence from Britain in

1966, after which the politicians exploited the historically bad relationship made worse by the increase in the wealth and numbers of East Indians.

The politics of envy was practised with energy and skill by Guyanese politicians which further divided the two races which were roughly equal in numbers, and extreme economic policies of nationalisation of private enterprise, self sufficiency, almost perpetual devaluations of the currency and high taxation led to exhaustion of the country's foreign exchange reserves and a complete lack of confidence in the future of the country by foreign investors and by the people themselves, many of whom emigrated to Canada, Britain and Bermuda.[1]

Relationships between the black population and the East Indian population became awful and racial stereotypes developed, taking hold of the political cultures. East Indians, many of whom specialised in commerce, were portrayed as Asian coolies, money-grubbing bloodsuckers who were Johnny-come-latelies to Guyana, whilst the black population was described as lazy, unintelligent and work-shy[2]. Blacks did not join the People's Progressive Party which was viewed as an arm of the East Indian population, and East Indians did not join the People's Progressive Party which was regarded as a black party of repression. This failure of confidence resulted in Guyana being one of the poorest and most miserable countries in the world and for Guyanese to be regarded as the beggars of Caribbean until recently.

Secondly, confidence about the future; investors are passionately interested in forecasts about the future of economies indeed they think of little else. Investments are made for the returns which can be earned and if the future is not reasonably assured with regard to such things as profitability[3], taxation, government stability and low (or nil) inflation investors will be tempted to go elsewhere. Money has no loyalty, no nationality and no fixed abode and it moves to those areas in which the highest returns can be achieved. No one, least of all economists, can predict the future because no one is able to forecast the future or even what will happen in a few years time, nothing is harder to acquire or easier to lose than the confidence of international investors.

If confidence is lost it is extremely difficult to regain it. Even large countries like Argentina, Brazil and more recently Russia are highly dependent on the confidence of international investors and are not masters of their own fate. Similarly, if their populations lose confidence in the future they do, as the Guyanese did in the 1970s and 1980s, they emigrate to other countries. In Hong Kong uncertainty about the future led to many Hong Kong companies establishing a holding company in Bermuda to limit the impact of adverse Chinese government policies on business. For a small country like Bermuda whose two major industries are largely controlled by outside interests, confidence about the future is even more essential.

Thirdly, sensitive markets like the real-estate market or the stock market are barometers of confidence. Prices of land and houses, and stocks tend to reflect immediately the underlying concerns of the population. The future prospects for

---

[1] Sir Edward Richards, Premier of Bermuda between 1972 and 1976 came from Guyana.
[2] Stereotypes which some Bermudians may recognise.
[3] see Part II 4 on the profitability of the hotel industry.

Bermuda suffered a substantial drop in confidence during the period of the independence referendum in 1995. In 1996 that confidence was not yet restored although independence as a political issue was dead. The Hong Kong stock market goes up and down depending on statements made by the Chinese government about the future of the British colony after 1997. Many investors believe the Chinese would not be foolish enough to enforce communist doctrines on what is probably the most capitalist place in the world but nobody knows for certain. If confidence falls the stock market and real estate prices fall in sympathy.

Fourthly, one of the fundamentals of the free enterprise economic system is that constant votes of confidence take place in the products or services which businesses offer for sale to the public. If the consumer is not prepared to spend his income dollars on the product this is a means of showing the public's lack of confidence in the management in the enterprise. In 1996, the 'Bermuda Times,' a weekly newspaper regarded as expressing black opinion, failed. The front page of one edition[4] contained comments by several notable Bermudians expressing their concern about the newspaper's failure. The word confidence did not appear once but the fact of the matter was that the buying public was not prepared to pay the 50 cents per copy largely because it was not confident that the newspaper would print news about subjects in which it was interested. An additional reason was the failure of business to place advertising in the paper. If sufficient members of the public were interested in the news the 'Bermuda Times' printed, advertisers would fall over themselves to buy space. However, they were not confident that the public could be reached through this medium. All sorts of businesses lose the confidence of the consuming public, restaurants, bars, retailers are classic victims but even large international corporations are subjected to the same forces. At various times giants of industrial America like General Motors, IBM, Apple Computers have looked over the precipice of financial failure which simply means that their customers have lost confidence and have gone over to another supplier.

Broadly similar arguments to the above about the importance of confidence in the economic system can be made about such issues as:

- **Education** - why do so many parents enrol their children in private schools in Bermuda?
- **Pensions**[5] - will pensions be paid when there are many more Bermudians over the age of 65? It really depends on your confidence about whether the future workers of Bermuda who are young adults or at school will be prepared to support older Bermudians.
- **Value of a currency** - Most currencies, including the U.S. dollar are highly dependent on what international investors believe about the future. In 1992, international bankers did not believe the policies of the British government made much sense and the British Pound lost much of its international value. Britain was forced out of the European Exchange Rate Mechanism. The U.S. dollar is the currency of choice in many independent countries as different as Jamaica, India and Guatemala largely because their citizens have

---

[4] April 26, 1996.

[5] See Part III 20 on the subject of pensions.

little confidence in the economic policies of their governments[6] who have inflated away the value of their citizen's savings. At the turn of the century the British pound played the role of the U.S. dollar but since 1945 successive British governments have inflated the economy and as a result have reduced the international value of sterling with the result that few foreigners have confidence in its future international value. When barmen treat a tip made in sterling with disdain, you know that confidence in the economic policies of the British government does not exist.

As world economies converge, globalisation intensifies and as markets become increasingly important confidence about the abilities of countries and businesses efficiently to function becomes fundamental and this is particularly true about very small dependent economies like Bermuda. Over the years those in authority in Bermuda have been remarkably successful about retaining the confidence of foreign investors[7] and the electorate about their ability to manage the economy effectively. Sound fiscal policies, the absence of corruption, sensible regulation, the common-sense of the Bermudian people and a reputation for fair-dealing established over many years are the main building blocks for the creation and retention of the confidence of those who wish to use Bermuda for business purposes.

Confidence (or trust) is a sine qua non of international business. Without it countries stumble into poverty and economic chaos as the example of Guyana vividly shows, or small businesses like the 'Bermuda Times' fail.

20. WHAT IS RESTRUCTURING AND REENGINEERING AND HOW WILL IT AFFECT BERMUDA?

"Reengineering is the FUNDAMENTAL rethinking and RADICAL redesign of business PROCESSES to bring about DRAMATIC improvements in critical, contemporary measures of performance such as cost, quality, service, and speed."

MICHAEL HAMMER AUTHOR OF "REENGINEERING THE CORPORATION."

The headlines in newspapers, magazines and television have contained over the past five years a regular refrain about lost jobs in large corporations all over the world. GM, IBM, Kodak, Exxon and AT & T are only a few examples of companies which have undertaken fundamental reorganisations since 1990. Every time one picks up a newspaper or magazine there is another story of another large corporation conducting a large-scale layoff of staff, including managers. The figures are difficult to absorb and comprehend for they change very quickly. For example, according to the New York Times more than 43 million jobs have been lost in the United States since 1979 and nearly 75 percent of households have been closely affected by job changes since that time.

---

[6] Bermuda is a happy exception to this rule.
[7] Standard and Poor's gave Bermuda an AA credit rating in 1995.

In the United States employment in the Fortune 500 Companies is down from 16.5 million in 1979 to 11.5 million in 1996. The single-minded pursuit of economic efficiency in the US, UK and other parts of the world has ended the concept of a job for life. Paternalism has been sacrificed on the altar of shareholder value - a policy which is increasingly being seen in Bermuda.

In Bermuda the publicity given to job changes has been patchy. Hotels closing for the winter and laying-off workers temporarily has been a staple of labour news for a number of years. But larger organisations like the Telephone Company and the banks have found it impossible to be able to provide their employees with life time employment as was the case in the past. Less conspicuous organisations do not make the headlines to the same extent but several local and international companies have undergone restructuring in recent years. Shell for example, reorganized its insurance arrangements and as a result eight people (about 10 percent of Shell employees in Bermuda) were made redundant because of this.

Increasingly white collar employees are affected, accountants, lawyers and secretaries - people who have traditionally thought of themselves as being immune to the ups and downs of economic life. Employees in the hotel industry and construction have lived with this uncertainty for years but it is only when the middle classes are affected that much is made of the fact. Added to this uncertainty is the fact that in the United States incomes for most people have at best remained stagnant and at worst have declined. This is important as most of Bermuda's customers - tourists - come from the Northeastern United States an area which has been particularly adversely affected.

Jobs are lost, jobs change, companies merge or go out of business, new countries difficult to find on an atlas enter the competitive arena. Everywhere change in business activity is the rule of the day and rapid change creates uncertainty and insecurity, even anxiety, as the bedrock assumptions people have grown up with are challenged and destroyed and life becomes increasingly unpredictable. One of these assumptions was that children would enjoy a more prosperous life than that of their parents and that as time went on prosperity would increase. The most important worry of anyone with dependants is that of losing a job. In society much of what we stand for stems from the job we do - young children are always asked by relatives what they want to do when they grow up. A person's identity, what he is, his status in the community and with his peers, his self-esteem and obviously his income are intimately tied up with his job. So great is the shock of losing a job that the terms being fired or dismissed are rarely used; instead a set of euphemisms like downsizing, rightsizing, layoffs, separations, delayering, severance, restructuring and reengineering are used to blunt the emotional damage caused to the individual employee.

Reengineering as the definition provided above indicates is not about adjusting, modifying or tinkering with a commercial organisation. It is a radical reformation of the way in which things done, the way in which management thinks about the business and, in part a reaction to the forces of change which are altering business. It means ripping up the rule book and starting afresh with an entirely new book. In effect saying that if we were to enter the business in which we are in how would we structure ourselves as opposed to saying we have done things this way for a number of years and been successful at it how are we going to improve our existing processes[1]. The answers result in an upheaval similar to the invention of the steam engine in the 18th century or the computer in the 1980s both of which changed the face of society.

Reengineering has become confused with the phenomenon of downsizing in which wholesale dismissals of the labour force take place in order to force down costs and make the organisation more efficient. The objective is not necessarily to reduce the employee body-count but to focus attention on what is essential to do within the organisation in order to compete effectively in the modern world. Companies are responding to the international competitive postion - something with which Bermuda has still to come to terms. However, the inescapable fact is that in order to be competitive it is often (although not always) necessary to reduce the number of employees on the books. Many companies have more staff than they require or can afford to keep on the payroll. At the end of the day reengineering changes the structure of the company, job skills, business process-es and employee expectations. A major question which arises is why has all of this happened in the past three years or so?

There are three major forces changing the face of Western capitalism (1) the behaviour of customers, (2) competitive forces, and (3) the rapid pace of change in the economic world.

Firstly, the key issue to understand is that it is the customer which is the dri-ving force in almost every business and commercial activity one cares to name, and they are compelling managers to rethink the way in which they operate their business. For as long as anyone can remember and certainly for the last 100 years, there has always, in general, tended to be more buyers than sellers. When Bermuda entered the tourist business in earnest in the 1920s there was only a lim-ited number of destinations available to the traveller from the Northeast. Now there are unlimited choices for the customer. Bermuda tourism has moved from being an industry in which the supplier can call the shots into one in which the customer has a bewildering choice. In the global economy, choices hand power over to the customer at the expense of the supplier. To get and keep business it is imperative to be the best. Being adequate is no longer sufficient.

Production capacity was limited, the pace of change was modest by today's standards, and probably most important of all inflation disguised changes in costs so that costs could be simply passed on to consumers by saying that inflation was the culprit. In essence the producer controlled the market and the customer could largely be taken for granted. Since the alleged end of inflation[2] this cozy world has ended. New and hungry producers compete for business and today's cus-tomers are much more knowledgeable about prices and markets, they are sophis-ticated and they are unpredictable. The customer is no longer simply king, he is an absolute monarch.

---

[1] Bermuda has been notoriously slow at making effective changes. See Part II 4 and 5.
[2] See the discussion on inflation in Part III 12.

Again if we turn to the Bermuda tourist industry, any Bermudian wanting to understand what choices the customer has available to him should look closely at the travel section of the U.S. Sunday newspapers. New, exotic destinations are available at very competitive prices. Customer loyalty is no longer an important factor in business as fickle consumers transfer their allegiance demanding more and better products for less cost. If Bermuda is too expensive there is always Guatemala or Ecuador, or if the consumer has had enough of the Americas he can always travel to the Orient and visit Malaysia or Hong Kong.

This means for example, that employees in Bermuda acting through the medium of the BIU can no longer come to management Oliver Twist style and ask for more because the customer is simply not prepared to pay more. Increasingly he insists on paying less. The customer has triumphed not only over the corporate supplier but also over the staff of the supplier. There has been a customer revolution and no one knows what customers will demand and no one knows for certain what the customer will pay except that he will not pay more than he did yesterday. The same worker who wants higher wages and benefits, shorter hours and more security is also the self-same consumer who demands better products for less money. The worker seeking higher wages during the week is simply the customer along Front Street on the weekend demanding lower prices from businesses. If he doesn't get lower prices he goes abroad. The Bermudian traveller who visits the shopping malls of the United States in search of cheaper products is also the same person who asked his employer for a raise the week before. A point which the BIU has yet to understand.

Secondly, competition has intensified beyond recognition of what it was even ten years ago. With an acceptable product or service customers were always available but competition has changed that cozy relationship. Niche competitors increasingly dominate the market. Costa Rica for eco-tourism, England and France for cultural tourism, Brazil for adventure and so on. New entrants have none of the institutional baggage which weighs down old competitors - strong unions, high wages or calcified organisations. The new entrants write new rules and can implement the latest technology, particularly information technology. Competition is not only intense it is unrelenting and brutal a fact with which many Bermuda businesses have yet to come to grips. If enterprises are able to compete, long-established businesses either go out of business - like Pan American Airlines or Archie Brown in Bermuda - or they are unable to earn adequate profits for their shareholders.[3] Companies which cannot compete are the ones which shed jobs or go into liquidation.

Thirdly, there is relentless and unsettling change. Customers and competitive forces have changed but change itself is accelerating at a bewildering pace. Banking used to be a staid steady industry tagged with the label 5-3-2. Lend at 5, borrow at 3, be on the golf tee at 2. This is no longer the case and banks now offer a bewildering array of products and services to their customers other than the traditional deposit or loan facilities. Credit cards, investment advice, management services, trustee services, on-line banking and so on are just some of the products introduced or significantly enhanced over the past few years. New companies cre-

---

3 See discussion on the profitability of retailing and hotel industry.

ate new products, technologies or business methods but they also threaten existing organisations. Corporate decline sometimes cannot be stopped or slowed down. More than 50 percent of companies listed in the Fortune 100 biggest companies in 1956 no longer exist.

> "In Bermuda, over the past five years, we have lost six percent of the jobs in retail, 15% of the jobs in construction and seen stagnation in other sectors."
> Sir David Gibbons, 1996[4]

It is a delusion to believe that growth and decay is something unusual or undesirable. If organisations are not expanding and changing there is no opportunity for the future. This is the process which is called "creative destruction."[5] Therefore, to stand still is to court disaster and any management which rests on its laurels would be out of business within a short space of time. Any established organisation which continues to run its operations on the basis of stability, predictability and being able to ignore the customer cannot succeed in the new world of fickle customers, intense competition and destabilising change[6]. Lloyds of London tried this and one result was the emergence of a significantly bigger Bermuda insurance market. Companies which continue to organise themselves around the old principles of division of labour and specified unchanging tasks will increasingly become obsolete.

The reader should look at the following table and pick out how many of the ten business characteristics on the left still apply to many Bermuda businesses like tourism, retailing and banking. Perhaps he may agree with me that the balance is still tilted too strongly towards the left hand side of the page.

TRADITIONAL VALUES	REENGINEERING VALUES
⇨ My job is 9 to 5 and what happens after that is not my concern.	⇨ I am prepared to work any time, any place.
⇨ My job is to tend bar - nothing else.	⇨ I am happy to take your food order
⇨ I am just a cog in a wheel: I lie low and don't get involved outside my responsibilities.	⇨ Each and every job is important, and each job adds value to the bottom line.
⇨ My boss sets my wage: I just keep him happy.	⇨ Customers pay the wages ; whatever it takes to keep them happy I will do.
⇨ If things go wrong, I pass it on to somebody else so no one can blame me for mistakes.	⇨ The buck stops here. I am responsible for getting things right.
⇨ This is not my department - I don't know	⇨ I'll find out immediately how this problem can be resolved.
⇨ This is the way we do things in Bermuda	⇨ Whatever you want me to do just let me know.
⇨ The more people I have working for me the more important I am.	⇨ I belong to a team - we sink or swim together.
⇨ Mr. Smith is not available, please call back.	⇨ I'll get hold of Mr. Smith immediately and he will call you back.
⇨ Tomorrow will be just like today - why change.	⇨ I have no idea what tomorrow will be like I just know it will be different and I will have to continue to learn and train as part of my job.

---

[4] 'Royal Gazette' July 22, 1996.
[5] Joseph Schumpeter mentioned in the discussion about productivity.
[6] This is the argument for privatising the Department of Tourism in Part III 17.

Even if Bermuda worked on the principle of only two or three characteristics on the left-hand side, it is two or three too many. Too often Bermudians look inward towards their department or colleagues, upward towards their management but not as frequently as they should outwards towards the customer. The world does not owe Bermuda a living and with changed customers, intense competitive pressures and new and improved ways of doing things it is not difficult to understand why Bermuda may have to reengineer or restructure the way it thinks about doing business in the modern world. Business reengineering means starting all over from the beginning. It means trying to forget how things were done yesterday and determining how things can be done best now and in the future. It means essentially doing much more with less resources.

> *"The complex dynamics of "globalisation" continue to challenge businesses, industries, and indeed whole economies around the world. The pace of change - technological innovation, fierce competition, freer trade - is relentless. We continue to witness the impressive and far-reaching results of the near-universal adoption, in recent years, of economic liberalisation, coupled with heady infusions of political freedom in previously-authoritarian countries, the new cyberspace frontiers of the Information Age, and with them the ever-dwindling significance of national borders. It is an environment where those businesses which are well-focused, carefully managed, soundly capitalised and global in their outlook, will flourish. Your Bank intends to remain among them."*
>
> Report to Shareholders on financial results at
> 31st December 1995.
> Bank of N.T. Butterfield & Son Ltd.

Many people may wonder why Bermuda firms should be affected by reengineering and restructuring, events which largely are externally generated. The short answer is that in a global economy it is not possible for Bermuda business organisations and employees to avoid or hide from pressures which are so prevalent in other parts of the world. Nor could they even if they wanted to as the captioned quotation from the Bank of Butterfield Report to Shareholders makes clear. If local skills and attitudes do not meet international standards the solution is not to build a wall around Bermuda and keep improved skills and standards at bay. The answer is to raise domestic standards and to do that requires redoubled effort on the part of both employers and employees.

The harsh facts of life are that hotels, banks, retailers and other businesses which operate in Bermuda are an irreversible part of the market economy and are subject to the same rules of the game as organisations anywhere else in the world. Failure to make the appropriate response will result in jeopardising the future of all Bermudians. The commercial world has changed in the last 10 years and it is impossible to avoid the consequences, uncomfortable as they may be. There is simply no choice.

Restructuring and reengineering are not heartless exercises in downsizing but a response to competitive pressures which will not go away. In more leisurely days many Bermuda companies were able to retain people who were not pulling their weight as their social conscience outweighed their dedication to making profits and international competitive pressures were not as great. Qualities like compassion, loyalty, obligations to friends and neighbours, and trust tended to dominate over crude commercialism. Many companies regarded themselves, and still do, as a family with responsibilities for employees which go way beyond paying a regular monthly salary. Employees often regarded their employer as "my company" although they may not have owned any shares in it. However, when profits are difficult to achieve or are non-existent carrying passengers is no longer possible. Banks, for example, compete in Bermuda not so much with one another but with banks from all over the world. It is a delusion to think that Bermuda can shelter behind its present protections and believe that Bermudians will not be affected by current events.

If foreign institutions are able to cut costs and hence prices to customers and improve service and products, for example, Bermuda banks which operate internationally have no real alternative but to follow suit. If overseas banks install the latest information technology Bermudian banks would soon be in trouble if they failed to respond. International business has to react to the demands of international customers and failure to do so is commercial suicide.

The logical and sensible reaction by Bermuda firms to improve productivity does not prevent, of course, newspaper articles 'Vietnam War' style about body-counts and casualties of corporate insensitivity. The pressures of technological change and competition are forcing (or will force) Bermuda businesses to make hard choices which will have an adverse impact on the labour force. Businesses exist to serve the customer (who is increasingly discriminating) and for making profits for shareholders not as a social welfare service or a baby-sitting service.

What Bermuda and rest of the world is living through is wrenching economic change, the net result of which will be that for every 100 jobs lost through reengineering another 100 jobs will be created in other areas. That has been the lesson of economic history for the past 200 years. The chairman of Procter and Gamble (the makers of Tide and other household products) put it succinctly when he stated "We must slim down to stay competitive. The consumer wants better value. Our competitors are getting leaner and quicker, and we are simply going to have to run faster to stay ahead."[7] The reader should ask himself if that statement applies to Bermuda and if he was honest he will answer "yes". Many people tend to put the blame on others but the fact is there is blame to be attributed it falls on the shoulders of you and me. Everyone is looking for a better deal be that in air fares, shoes or beer. The reader should ask himself if he would agree to pay twice as much for his beer if Goslings would promise not to make people redundant.

---

[7] 'Wall Street Journal,' May 4, 1995.

Rather than mourn the past, it is necessary for employees to understand that jobs are no longer unchanging, permanent and that education and training does not end in the early 20s but that it is essential for life-long learning to continue all through the working life.

If changing competitive conditions, new technology and customer behaviour simply took jobs from people and gave them to computers and machines the rate of unemployment would have been rising ever since the industrial revolution in the late eighteenth century. If we cast our minds back 30 years when most Bermudians either worked in tourism or tourist related businesses the economic changes which have occurred since have resulted in many Bermudians working in Exempt Companies in air-conditioned offices, being paid monthly salaries and not working evenings and weekends. I doubt if many would like to return to earlier days of shiftwork, low wages and tough working conditions. Changed economic circumstances simply takes jobs from one group of employees - say fishermen - and gives them to others - say computer programmers.

The real difficulty for Bermuda is that future job opportunities will not arise for the unskilled and relatively uneducated and this segment of the population will therefore have to do what teenagers never have been very good at, namely doing homework and becoming proficient in such boring but essential subjects as reading, mathematics, English, and foreign languages. Even then there may not be guarantees of life-long employment in one's chosen field or with one firm. The challenge is to cajole, implore, persuade, counsel and do all other things necessary to direct our young people to obtain a better education than their parents. This is not an easy task but it will be a necessary one. No nation can thrive in the modern economy unless it invests in its people and ensures that they are properly educated and trained. The data is very very clear about the relationship between economic success and educational standards and levels. If Bermuda fails to educate the bottom 20-30 percent we are likely to face all sorts of economic trouble. It is ridiculous that students starting courses at the Bermuda College do not have a grasp of basic English and math.[8]

Increasingly around the world major problems exist in being able to place those with few skills and limited education in rewarding jobs. The Department of Education would perform a valuable service if they were able to influence our young people[9] to go where future job opportunities will arise and parents would also help if they were able to destroy the employment assumptions which they grew up with. Although many educated and skilled people will have to deal with unemployment problems associated with restructuring, especially those who are older than 45, those who are resourceful will be able overcome what in retrospect will be seen as a temporary setback.

Irrespective of how well we have done in the past (and we constantly have to remind ourselves that we have done well) it is not possible complacently to stay as we are, doing what we have always done. The problems facing many organisations arise from their process structures not necessarily from their organisational structures. The pace of technological and marketplace change makes organisations with a complacent attitude vulnerable for the future.

---

[8] See 'Royal Gazette' March 7, 1996 page 1.

[9] Why are shcool hours still arranged as if we were a 19th century rural community.

Reengineering is involved with a fundamental, radical and dramatic redesigning of the work process in a business. It means doing away with obsolete practices which impede efficiency[10] and driving down change mechanisms into the body of the organisation. At present most work is organised inefficiently around specialists employed in "functional silos" such as accounting, sales and operations. In the new world work is best organised around results not tasks with the objective of keeping the customer happy, satisfied and willing to come back. The objective is to deliver continuous improvements in customer service at ever reducing cost. To fail to do this is to flirt with disaster.

---

10 In short, increasing productivity - see Part I 18 for a discussion of this.

THE ECONOMY AND GOVERNMENT

3

1. WHAT IS MEANT BY THE TERM BERMUDA INC?

"After all, the chief business of the American people is business. They are pro-foundly concerned with producing, buying, selling, investing and prospering in the world. I am strongly of the opinion that the great majority of people will always find these are moving impulses of our life. Wealth is the product of indus-try, ambition, character and untiring effort. In all experience, the accumulation of wealth means the multiplication of schools, the increase of knowledge, the dis-semination of intelligence, the encouragement of science, the broadening of out-look, the expansion of liberties, the widening of culture. Of course, the accumu-lation of wealth cannot be justified as the chief end of existence. But we are com-pelled to recognise it as a means of well-nigh every desirable achievement. So long as wealth is made the means and not the end, we need not greatly fear it".
CALVIN COOLIDGE, PRESIDENT OF THE UNITED STATES (1923-1929).

The above quotation is often, wrongly, shortened to "The business of America is business." The term Bermuda Inc. was coined by the present Premier Dr. David Saul when he was finance minister and was used by him as a metaphor to help the general public understand the importance of tourism and international busi-ness to the welfare of Bermuda and in particular to help the public understand that the only way to make money is to earn it. There are three meanings to the term:-

Firstly, Bermuda was compared, rightly, to a corporation upon which all employees are dependent for their daily bread. Anything which jeopardises the prosperity of the corporation has the effect of jeopardising the well-being of every other member whether they are employees or owners. Until 1968, Bermuda was run very much like a business by a white oligarchy collectively known as the "40 Thieves" and although politics was important the overriding philosophy was to run Bermuda in much the same way as a business would be run. This process was unsustainable when Bermuda acquired a new constitution and many of the polit-ical trappings of a larger society. Debates about public policy moved away from the board rooms to the House of Assembly where they rightly belonged. But Bermuda also acquired an administrative system which over the years has become "wholly disproportionate to Bermuda's limited needs."[1] In a particularly savage editorial[2] it was stated "Walt Disney was a cartoonist turned businessman who ran his enterprise like a small country. Bermuda leadership consists of busi-ness turned politicians who run their small country like a cartoon." Whilst I think this description goes too far - Bermuda is reasonably well governed - the essen-tial point to note is that the costs of operating Bermuda should be compared to the operating costs of a corporate venture named Bermuda Inc.

This leads to the second way in which the term may be used. The working population of Bermuda in 1995 was 34,133 of which 26,612 were Bermudian.[3] This is a reasonably small population by comparison with some of the large cor-porations of the world - IBM for example has about 220,000 employees world wide - almost seven times the size of the Bermudian working population. Large organisations like IBM which has been on the 'Fortune' most admired corpora-

---

[1] 'Mid-Ocean News,' April 12, 1996.
[2] Ibid.
[3] Employment Survey, 1995.

tions list for a number of years until recently, can run into financial and business trouble. Bermuda which is much smaller in scope than a corporation like IBM could similarly run into financial problems because our size does not permit the diversification of the economy possible in much larger countries. This vulnerability to unforseen economic events is a major weakness of the Bermuda economy and hence it becomes vital that our prosperity is not jeopardised by actions like strikes, violence or high crime[4] which would significantly affect larger economies.

A third way the term was used was to try and ensure that the Bermuda Government was run not on bureaucratic lines in a business-like way. This attempt was less successful than the first two because making a bureaucracy into a business is as hopeless a task as attempting to train a cat to bark. Public service and business are two different animals requiring different talents. Businessmen are by and in large decision makers and autocrats who want to get things done - they bark orders and expect everyone to jump in order to meet the expectations of customers and shareholders. Civil servants are by their nature more cautious, tending to avoid hasty decisions and are more involved in persuading people that it is beneficial to move in a certain direction. Their customers, meaning the general public, are usually regarded as something of a nuisance who must expect to wait until procedures and policies have been checked. By its very nature a bureaucracy marches to the beat of its own drum, not that of the public who pay their salaries. The key characteristics of bureaucracy are threefold:

- Unlike businessmen, they do not spend their own money but that of the taxpayer.
- They do not have a bottom line - the objective of making a profit - in the same way as business. Their bottom line is to become more powerful, increase their importance and also increase their salaries and pensions.
- They are difficult to remove from office. Only rarely is a civil servant dismissed or demoted and only after a prolonged period of inquiry. In business incompetents are removed as soon as possible because they costs the owner or shareholders money if they remain in place.

If as President Calvin Coolidge allegedly said that the business of America is business, it is not a bad motto for Bermuda to adopt for its own. The trouble comes when seeking to apply it.

---

[4] This issue is explained in Part III 10.

2. WHAT ROLE SHOULD THE BERMUDA GOVERNMENT PLAY IN THE ECONOMY?

"All governments like to interfere ; it elevates their position to make out that they can cure the evils of mankind."

WALTER BAGEHOT.

"Government is the great fiction through which everybody endeavours to live at the expense of everybody else."

FREDERIC BASTIAT.

"People and politicians are dominated by quite excessive expectations as to what can possibly, or practicably, be delivered by governmental economic policies."

T. W. HUTCHISON.

Governments are central insitutions in any economic system, even in primitive or agricultural societies where there are low levels of commerical sophistication and economic activity. If we look at the activities of the US, British or Canadian governments, it is readily seen that in such basic functions as being a major employer, formulating monetary, fiscal and other economic policies, or merely proposing changes in the law , the activities of government in day to day economic matters are critical to the efficient functioning of the economy. What applies to the US, UK and Canada also applies with equal force to Bermuda. A healthy functioning economy is dependent on an effective corruption-free government for its continued vigour and growth. If these conditions are absent the economy is likely to be as dead as that of Haiti. Governments exist to discharge tasks which individuals cannot, or will not, do for themselves such as providing for a system of public order. Informed opinion has long ago abandoned the idea that government's role in the economy is merely that of an interested spectator or referee although many neo-conservatives hanker for the day when government activity dwindles to what is was in the Middle Ages.

The health of an economy is a central issue in any election campaign and any political leader, such as President Bush, who forgets this will be punished at the polls. Governments role in society and the economy goes far beyond simply the collection of taxes and the spending of public money. The following is a list of activities which influence the economy and for which foreign governments have enacted legislation at different times:-

- Enacting an equal opportunity law for females.
- Declaring Karl Marx day (1st May) a public holiday.
- Establishing six months maternity pay for employees both male and female.
- Instituting a corporate tax.
- Prohibiting the dismissal of employees with five years' service.
- Expelling foreign employees.
- Introducing dividend, price and wage controls.
- Putting employee directors on the boards of public companies.
- Controlling domestic credit.
- Limiting pay increases for employees.

The conventional view of government is that it is an essential instrument for the promotion of the general welfare, the only institution which has the power and the ability to deal with intractable social problems to remedy the adverse social outcomes of the free enterprise system and of producing consistent and measurable economic progress for everyone. Reality however has been something quite different as politicians in different countries have promised and promised and failed and failed to deliver results. This extravaganza of political promises has resulted in disillusionment and even cynicism on the part of the public in countries like Britain and the United States and is increasingly the case in Bermuda where disappointment with the results of government action is also widespread. Government intervention has made such a mess of things economically over the past 50 years or so, that many of its advocates have now targeted such things as family life, education and social objectives. Such matters are difficult to measure and accordingly there is no accountability in the process - which is what governments prefer.

Everyone has an example of government incompetence, inefficiency or heavy-handedness and everyone has a solution to the problem. Unfortunately, the solutions remain very much in the hands of government which created the problem in the first place.

The question of whether government is a benevolent uncle or is a foolish spendthrift is emerging as one of the major issues in politics in Bermuda, just as it has done in other countries. Many want government to be smarter and more efficient, but at the same time the electorate also see government as a force for good, as a means of improving society as everyone favours a strong, resilient and expanding economy. The opposite point of view is that government is a collection of self serving politicians (too many) and bureaucrats (overpaid and inefficient) and that smaller government is better government.

The evidence from other countries is that government does not have the ability, tools or the talent to deliver on promises of making the economy healthy and self-sustaining whilst at the same time maintaining full-employment, stable prices and a balanced distribution of income and wealth. According to a recent United States Congressional Research Service Report, the American Government has spent US$4.5 trillion on poverty programmes in the past 35 years but the poverty rate is greater in 1996 than it was in 1960. There is mounting evidence that individuals and private organisations do a much better job of using economic resources more efficiently than government. This view was summed up by President Reagan who said "Government is not the solution; it's the problem." The facts are that active government involvement in the economy does not result in a better functioning economy but in bureaucratic imcompetence, unintended consequences, uncertainty, worse economic performance and short-term thinking.[1]

Many also believe that the role of government is withering away under the assault from the forces of globalisation of markets and from the vast flows of capital which can move from country to country in the period of time it takes to strike a computer keyboard key. Such global forces are imposing stricter limits on gov-

---

[1] See Part III 16

ernment power and many see this as a mechanism for making government an economic ananchronism. The Japanese author, Kenichi Ohmae believes that global forces have meant that "traditional national interest is becoming little more than a cloak for subsidy and protection" and he dismisses government as "a mere merchant of pork." This is something of an extreme view, for the state is very much a major player in the economy although its ability to act capriciously or foolishly is, fortunately, being eroded. Once a government loses the confidence of the financial community it becomes very costly in terms of lost business and it is very difficult to regain that confidence. It takes many years to establish confidence, but only a few short weeks or the threat to introduce a few foolish economic policies to lose it.

That was the major lesson of the independence debate Bermuda experienced in 1995. Politicians wrongly believed that this was simply an issue between them as elected representatives and the voters, but what they failed to appreciate was that capital and foreign investors whilst not having a vote can still exercise significant political influence. At that time the local stock market, the real estate market, and international business experienced declines and voters became unmistakably nervous. The Bermuda economy had functioned so well over the past 50 years that many politicians and voters had taken its success for granted.

Readers of the international press know that fundamental questions are being asked about the levels of activity undertaken by governments, their capability of being able to discharge some of their tasks, and most fundamental of all how much they should extract from the economy in the form of taxation or other charges. In early 1996 the Congress and the President of the United States were locked in combat over the budget and how and who should exercise control over the level of the budget deficit. Politicians (and civil servants) behave very much like consumers in a market place and act primarily to promote their own self-interest and not to serve some higher public ideal.

Over the past twenty years or so, there has been increasing involvement in the economy by governments, including the Bermuda government. The percentage of GDP spent by governments has steadily increased although there is widespread and world-wide resistance by voters and taxpayers to paying more taxes. Many governments have been incapable of bringing government expenditure within budgetary disciplines. In the Netherlands and Scandinavia government expenditure exceeds 50% of GDP. In UK despite 15 years of Thatcherite policies government expenditure still exceeds 40% of GDP. In only a few countries like New Zealand, Argentina and the Czech Republic is government economic activity retreating. In countries like Bermuda which traditionally has had governments which kept their hands off the economy it is not quite as easy to push back the frontiers of government intervention which has been growing over the past 20 years.

Bermuda has been fortunate in that historically government has taken a very limited role in its stewardship of the economy. It is a large employer, employing about 24 percent of the labour force, and it is estimated that it will spend about 25 percent of GDP in the fiscal year 1996/1997. The truth is that the ratio of government spending to GDP does not reveal the whole truth about government's influence on the economy. In 1996, American businesses complained that the economy suffered more from excessive regulations than it did from high taxes. Bermuda has traditionally been highly regulated; no fast food, exchange control, tight planning regulations are only a few examples of the many ways in which governments exercise control over the economy and influence over commerce. In the period prior to 1960 the Bermuda Government was seen as a wholly-owned subsidiary of the two major banks and of the then reigning oligarchy of Front Street merchants known collectively as the '40 Thieves.' This is a caricature of how things were in those days but like many caricatures it contained a large measure of truth, but today banks and Front Street merchants are unable to exercise any real clout with government.

Historically Bermuda has avoided many of the strategic blunders committed by other governments, particularly that of the United Kingdom. Bermuda never had nationalised industries and its utilities, The Bermuda Electric Light Company and The Bermuda Telephone Company, were privately owned organisations from inception. Nor did government intervene in the same way as other governments by erecting complicated welfare structures (mainly because it didn't have to), it avoided (until recently) public debt like the plague, and it basically allowed private enterprise to get on with the job of supplying goods and services to the public. It established a broad framework of rules, set the strategy and allowed private enterprise to get on with day to day management of the conomy. That policy is consistent with much modern thinking about the role of governments in the economy which is to loosen the shackles of political power and allow free enterprise to bring home the bacon. As Kenichi Ohmae puts it "No policy can substitute for the efforts of individual managers in individual institutions to link their activities to the global economy."[2]

Governments, including the Bermuda Government, have now accepted overall responsibility for the well being and functioning of the economy and the electorate holds them accountable, for their stewardship. The governing UBP has always maintained that it is the only party capable of managing Bermuda's economy and if the PLP was elected major economic catastrophe would result. This is something of an exaggeration as the economy of Bermuda, like economies elsewhere, functions best when government intervenes least and when it restricts itself to setting the rules and allowing individuals and private enterprise to make commercial decisions.

Economic ideas like the sanctity of contracts, the stability of prices or the absence of corruption are much more important than the political process. If the ideas and policies are correct in the first place bad politics are not important. A recent study into government intervention in the economies of 102 countries over 20 years concluded that the more economic freedom a country enjoyed the greater its level of economic growth and the wealthier its inhabitants became.

The lesson for governments is that there are certain tasks which are the concern of private enterprise and that imposing limits on businesses results in lower than optimum outcomes. This is simply a restatement of what Walter Bagelot said more than a hundred years age namely "that a government which interferes with

---

[2] "The End of the Nation State", by Kenichi Ohmae

any trade injures that trade." For Bermuda it means that if the PLP kept its hands off the economy, and this is a very big "if", the economy would function just as effectively and as efficiently as it does now under the guidance of the UBP.[3]

The main strategic responsbilities of the Bermuda Government in 1996 can be summarised very briefly as follows:-

- Controlling inflation as measured by the Consumer Price Index.
- Maintaining full employment.
- Promoting tourism through the Department of Tourism and encouraging international business.
- Maintaining of the value of the Bermuda dollar against that of the U.S. dollar.
- Encouraging economic growth.
- Providing equal opportunity and a degree of social justice for those who perform badly in the market economy.
- Providing services which individuals cannot easily provide themselves and for which no provision is made in the market economy such as police protection, public health and environmental planning.
- Providing a corrupt-free economic environment and setting the rules of economic game.

President Reagan used to mock the traditional Democratic Party reactions to any economic problem which was, "don't just stand there - do something" by proposing the slogan "don't just do something - stand there." However, governments believe they are elected to accomplish great economic feats but if they are smart they will recognise that there are great limitations as to what government can achieve within the economy.

3. WOULD IT MAKE ANY ECONOMIC DIFFERENCE IF THERE WAS A PLP GOVERNMENT?

"THE MISSION : To ensure a steady, balanced expansion of Bermuda's economy especially in the areas of tourism and international business ; to provide meaningful employment, investment and ownership opportunities for all Bermudians ; to provide Island-wide upgrading of Bermuda's infrastructure, facilities and services without the introduction of income tax.
THE COMMITMENT : The United Bermuda Party will utilise its experience to continue leading Bermuda's economy through the perils of world events : provide a stable, reliable environment for living, working and investing ; ensure the sustainable growth of services which meet Bermudian needs, visitor expectations and international business requirements."

UBP PLATFORM FOR THE 1993 GENERAL ELECTION.

---

[3] This issue is explained in the next question

"We will develop a long-term national plan which coordinates options affecting land use, housing, transport, immigration and labour, education, training and youth development."

PLP PLATFORM FOR THE 1993 GENERAL ELECTION.

The United Bermuda Party (UBP) has been the governing party of Bermuda since 1968 and during that almost 30 year period it has presided over an economy which has performed in a manner which is the envy of almost every other democratic government in the Western world. The characteristics of the Bermudian economy are full-employment, a high standard of living, a high quality of life, an absence of corruption, political stability and healthy foreign exchange earnings. Most Western governments, including those of the United States, Canada and the United Kingdom, would be prepared to do almost anything to be able to copy Bermuda as their lacklustre record, particularly with regard to unemployment. This does not speak well of foreign government economic management.

Notwithstanding these remarkable achievements Bermuda still has several economic problems such as a poor record of economic growth over the past decade, uneven racial distribution of jobs in the private sector, allegations of a 'glass ceiling' for women and blacks, a decline in tourism revenue and numbers, a bad record of profitability in the hotel industry, poor labour relations, a growing and intractable illegal drug problem, a patchy public education service and since 1994 an unusual lack of business confidence mainly arising from the decision to hold a referendum over political independence from the UK.

One of the major international economic themes in recent years is that governments have limited abilities to control, direct and influence the economy. Limitations on their power arise from the globalisation of the world economies, failure to produce concrete results, disillusionment with active government management of the economy and the growing recognition that the tools of economic management such as fiscal and monetary policy are not as effective as they were once thought to be. This is not to say that government's influence is not important, the share of spending of GDP for example shows how important the role of government is. To see the negative and destructive effect on the economy of having a weak or incompetent government one has only to spend a few days in countries like Bosnia, Haiti or Brazil.

Whilst it may be argued that the UBP over the past 30 years has provided Bermuda with sound stable administration, the question is would the same thing happen if the PLP was to gain political power. Put another way would the PLP deviate significantly from the sound and sensible (for Bermuda) policies advocated and implemented by the UBP. The main economic policies pursued by the UBP over the past three decades are:

- No direct taxes on income and corporate profits.
- Government spending limited to around 20 percent of GDP[1].
- Sound public administration in such areas as police, education and public works.

---

[1] In the fiscal year 1996/1997 it is estimated to rise to 25% of GDP about the same as U.S. Federal, State and local governments spent in the 1930s in the midst of the New Deal.

- Absence of corruption in the public services.
- Commitment to the preservation of the physical environment.
- Commitment to equality of opportunity in employment.
- Policies which foster racial harmony.

Such policies have been popular with the electorate and together with a reasonably talented group of individual Members of Parliament the public has believed the UBP to be the best manager of the Bermuda economy and the party most likely to preserve their high standard of living. Thirty years of economic and political success is no mean achievement.

A comparison between what economic policies are proposed for the future by the two parties shows surprisingly little divergence. The following table is based on the political platforms advocated by the two main political parties prior to the 1993 general election and shows the degree to which there is now overlapping agreement. The main areas of difference are mainly related to means rather than ends.

COMPARISON OF 1993 UBP AND PLP POLITICAL PLATFORMS

POLICY OBJECTIVES	STATEMENT OF POLICY	
	UBP	PLP
A. No Significant differences		
Equality of economic opportunity	Yes	Yes
Active policies on racial discrimination	Yes	Yes
Environment	Yes	Yes
Commitment to human rights	Yes	Yes
Drugs and alcohol	Yes	Yes
Youth development	Yes	Yes
Improve tourism	Yes	Yes
Improved transportation	Yes	Yes
Improved education	Yes	Yes
Limited granting of Bermudian status	Yes	Yes
Greater role for Small Business Corporation	Yes	Yes
Housing subsidies	Yes	Yes
Preservation of the family	Yes	Yes
National pension scheme	Yes	Yes
B. Some philosophical differences		
Tougher immigration policies	No	Yes
Constitutional change	No	Yes
Income tax^2 and other direct taxes	No	?
National service scheme	No	Yes
Independence	?	Yes
National training agency	No	Yes
National economic plan	No	Yes
Introduce welfare state	No	Yes

---

[2] The PLP is very sensitive about this subject. My own view is that they favour direct taxes.

Since the 1960s many of the policies advocated by the PLP - such as the moratorium on the granting of Bermudian status to those whose parents are not Bermudians - have been embraced by the UBP, and many of the electorally unpopular positions of the PLP - such as the mild advocacy of income tax - have been quietly jettisoned. The UBP at first opposed many strongly held PLP positions such as providing financial assistance to the economically disadvantaged, then reluctantly implemented some of them, and then eventually claimed to have been the party which first thought of them. The PLP on the other hand in its early days opposed many of the long-standing policies of the UBP such as a balanced and realistic approach to immigration but then recognising economic reality (one expatriate worker tends to generate two or three local jobs) modified their position and stated they never had been xenophobic.

In 1996 there is not as great a difference in economic policies between the political parties as is commonly believed or as the parties, particularly the UBP, would like the public to believe, a situation which applies in most other economically advanced democratic societies. One of the most baffling things about foreign politics for Bermudians is to distinguish between Democratic or Republican Party economic policy, and in Britain it is almost impossible to spot a socialist in the new Labour Party, just as it is difficult to locate a Thatcher Conservative in the present Conservative Party Cabinet. The political centre acts like a magnet on economic matters preventing immoderate policies from gaining widespread political support. The underlying reality is that the electorate is invariably more centrist than the politicians and extreme positions on economic issues are usually disliked by the public at election time.

There are four major differences between the UBP and PLP. First, is the question of whether income tax (and almost by implication corporate profits tax) should be implemented in Bermuda. The UBP is unequivocally opposed to income tax as the quotation from their 1993 platform clearly shows. The PLP pussy-foots around the subject calling for "a review of the entire tax system with a view to making the system more equitable."[3] This is not really a policy but a mechanism to confuse or to buy off any criticism from the general public. What happens if after a review of tax policy a recommendation is made to implement income tax? What is meant by making the tax system more equitable? Income tax is supposed to be more equitable (in fact there are serious doubts that it is in an offshore financial centre like Bermuda) so would the PLP adopt a tax policy which is more equitable but which will lose elections? The public has a right to know where the PLP stands on the issue and hiding behind a proposal to review the tax system is not informing the public. Most people do not trust the PLP on tax policy and for that reason would not give them electoral support.

Secondly, the PLP put great store on the establishment of a National Economic Plan - as the quotation above illustrates - despite the overwhelming evidence from other parts of the world that no one has yet devised an efficient mechanism for implementing such a plan. The examples of the many economic plans in the former USSR, the great leap forward in China or the National Plan set up by the Labour Government in Britain in 1965 are not encouraging. Smaller

---

[3] See page 6 of the PLP 1993 election platform.

countries have tried economic planning and all have been major disasters. What hidden skills do the PLP possess which would allow them to be successful when economic planning everywhere else has been such a dismal failure?

Thirdly, immigration in a small community is a highly sensitive subject. The PLP has wisely suggested that it will "provide security of tenure to long-term residents of Bermuda who have made a contribution to our country" pretty much along the lines of the green card arrangments in the United States. The United Bermuda Party is silent on this issue - mainly I suspect because being in power they may have to do something about it. The UBP on the other hand understands that the importation of skilled labour is one of the major reasons why Bermuda has been so successful in maintaining economic health. Many voters believe that Bermuda's prosperity would be jeopardised if the PLP implemented more draconian immigration policies.

Fourthly, the PLP in its role as representing the poor, the unskilled and the less influential wishes to introduce an unemployment insurance programme but without specifying how such a programme would be paid for. The welfare state has never been a major issue of political debate in Bermuda but the PLP generally favours programmes sponsored by government to mitigate the consequences of economic insecurity or for those who are unable to function effectively in a modern economy. The UBP has shied away from formal government programmes recognising the disincentive effects which such programmes have had in other parts of the world. Again the electorate is worried about the extension of government power over the economy and the long term costs of such programmes and their effect on taxation policies.

It is in the area of government intervention in the economy that the differences in policy between the two parties is highlighted. The UBP tends to favour individual or market solutions, whilst the PLP favours government interventionist solutions to economic problems. Examples of PLP policies in this regard are:-

- Encouragement of small business by extending the powers of the Small Business Corporation - a government organisation.
- Introduction of unemployment insurance.
- Increased tax incentives to improve hotel profitability.
- A new Ministry of International Business.
- Giving the Government Employment Office a greater role in job placement and training.
- Limiting job categories which are open to non-Bermudian employees.
- Creating a national youth corps.
- Improving pensions for senior citizens.[4]
- Subsidising housing costs for the poor.
- Instituting studies to develop new energy sources such as biomass, solar and wind.

---

[4] Without specifying how this will be paid for.

Many of the above programmes have been tried elsewhere with a conspicuous lack of success and the PLP does not provide any evidence to the electorate that they possess the additional skills which have eluded foreign governments. There is wishful thinking in the PLP platform.

Too much should not be read into political platforms which tend to be 'wish lists,' emphasising what will be done but neglecting any mention of how things will be paid for. Statements like "A PLP Government will demonstrate its ability to manage the economy by inaugurating a new era in which employers and employees will cooperate in a joint effort to provide for the future well-being of Bermudians both born and unborn."[5] are dreams not economic policies.

The UBP has similar dreams by, for example, stating that the party will target "overall economic growth at 2% each year through the next decade, thereby ensuring improved job opportunities and a continued high standard of living."[6]

Both of these statements encompass worthy objectives and everyone would be delighted if they were achieved. The reality is that political parties are not really able to play a central role in their achievements. Economists are not certain of what policies make for successful economic growth. Investment, implementation of new technology and a sound educational system help but increasingly it is believed that government policies which emphasise property rights, enforcement of contracts, an independent judiciary, low taxes, low government spending, a hands-off government, red-carpet treatment for foreign investors, and an open and free society are the key to economic growth and stability. In other words policies akin to what has been in place in Bermuda for many years. The evidence from other countries is that policies which permit producers and consumers to respond to economic incentives are the best way for politicians to run an economy. Both political parties in Bermuda are astute enough not to blunt economic incentives, although on balance the UBP favours individual initiative.

The electoral difference between the two parties is not great nor are the philosophical differences wide, would it then make any difference economically to Bermuda if there was a PLP government? The answer is heavily dependent on the answers to two important questions.

Firstly, would the PLP pay any attention to their political platform after they were elected? Some of their MPs have stated publicly that they entered politics in order to settle old scores[7] and many other public statements made over the years leave question marks over just how genuine some of the PLP members are about putting aside historic grievances, real or imagined. On the other hand many UBP members, both inside and outside the House of Assembly, have made extreme statements but rightly and wisely have forgotten about them when in a position of responsibility. Political reality and what the electorate are prepared to tolerate provide considerable safeguards against hot-headed policies. In addition, the PLP leadership understands only too well that if they pursue economically foolish policies the main and primary victims will be their own membership who would be unlikely to continue to give them overwhelming support at the next election. Self-preservation is a strong incentive not to act foolishly.

---

[5] See page 6 of the PLP 1993 election platform.

[6] See page 2 of the UBP 1993 election platform.

[7] Ewart Brown and Alex Scott are examples.

Secondly, does the PLP have sufficient administrative talent to run a government? A cursory review of the abilities, financial and otherwise, of many of the PLP candidates does not inspire much confidence. In the 'Royal Gazette' editorial of June 14, 1996 it was stated that, "It is always shaming when PLP members whose personal affairs are in chaos rise to speak on the Country's budget." Management experience in private life of MPs is not widespread, many of their policies lack credibility and have not been spelled out in sufficient detail. But frankly speaking similar comments could be made about UBP policies and political talent. Meetings of professional bodies like accountants, lawyers or engineers generate much more intellectual fire-power than meetings in the House of Assembly or the Senate. Anyone who has listened to broadcasts of or attended the House of Assembly is usually appalled by the low calibre of debate and the absence of substantial ideas.

The conclusion is that the United Bermuda Party has a track record of about 30 years successful government and no one really knows what would happen if the PLP gained political power. It is very much a case of preferring the devil you know to the devil you don't know especially when the latter is unclear about unpopular issues like income tax, the welfare state and government planning.

If there was a PLP government it is hard to believe that policies would be pursued for long which would damage the long-term interests of the Bermudian economy. However, it is as well to recall the Argentina example. In 1940 it had the sixth highest per capita income in the world - ahead of countries like Australia and Canada (and Bermuda). In 1990, it was 40th - just behind Iran. In the 50 years Juan Peron and his successors had pursued socialist economic policies such as price controls, expropriation of property held by foreigners and class warfare against the middle classes. The PLP is not the Peronistas but in economic matters some of their members have strange ideas.

Nevertheless with a PLP government mistakes would be made, there would be some idiotic policy decisions and there would be a degree of government inefficiency. But these things also happen with a UBP government. Would it make any difference if there was a PLP government in Bermuda? Probably "yes" and most Bermudians would suffer financially as a result, but it would not be a catastrophe for Bermuda. The PLP would quickly learn that governments have only limited influence over economic events and would have to modify its policies and actions.[8] Reality would set in very quickly and in order to retain credibility with the electorate and hold on to power unpopular unworkable policies would have to be abandoned with the result that the differences between the PLP and the UBP would be as fuzzy and confused as the differences between the Democrats and Republicans in the United States. A PLP government would be uncomfortable for most Bermudians but it would not be the end of the world.

---

[8] See Part III 2 for discussion of this issue.

4. SHOULD MCDONALDS BE ALLOWED TO OPERATE IN BERMUDA?

"The government sets policies which regulate its actions. If Ministers contravene them, it brings government into disrepute."

LETTER TO THE EDITOR OF 'THE ROYAL GAZETTE,' APRIL 11, 1996.

"McDonald's is, of course, synonymous with a certain tawdriness Bermuda has sought to avoid for decades."

'MID-OCEAN NEWS' EDITORIAL, MAY 3, 1996.

"There was a time when political favours were frowned upon and anyone caught seeking a favour would have departed in shame. Once people went into politics to make a contribution, today some people go into politics to help themselves."

'ROYAL GAZETTE' EDITORIAL, JUNE 14, 1996.

For many years Bermuda has had a policy of not permitting fast food franchises like McDonalds on the grounds that their existence could jeopardise the different and high class ambiance of Bermuda which is believed to be important to the American tourist. The question of whether McDonald's should be allowed in Bermuda is not as frivolous a question at it appears but one which crystallises a number of important issues.

Firstly, it raises the issue of protectionism in a very direct way. Should Bermuda consumers be prevented from buying an innocuous product like a hamburger which is popular with millions of people around the world? If they are not allowed to buy a McDonald's hamburger why are they allowed to buy a chocolate bar manufactured by Cadburys? The official reason, which has been given for many years, is that Bermudians are being deprived of the opportunity to buy a big Mac because of a larger more important principle, namely that by allowing McDonalds and other fast food chains to operate in Bermuda would be detrimental to the long term interests of the tourist industry and the greater public good of preserving Bermuda's style of life and heritage. One can legitimately quarrel with the preservation of the tourist business argument but it is a policy which has, as far as anyone can tell, served Bermuda well.

The policy government has established, is in one which should determine its future actions until such time as it is changed. If a senior minister in government decides to change a prevailing established policy that should be done only after a period of debate about the reasons for changing the policy. If there is no open debate, government runs the risk of having its reputation being brought into disrepute.

Secondly, the main promoter of the proposed new enterprise is a company two of whose main shareholders are prominent politicians. Sir John Swan, a former Premier of Bermuda, and Mr. Maxwell Burgess a former Minister of Transport. The licence to open a McDonalds is being issued by the Minister of Finance who is a Member of Parliament representing the same constituency as Sir John (Bermuda has two-member constituencies) and who would probably be his running mate in the constituency of Paget East at the next general election. Questions have been raised by the public as to whether this is a political payoff by one politician to another and by extension it raises the question of whether Bermuda is run by means of openly discussed policies or by political cronyism.

One of the reasons why Bermuda is an attractive place of incorporation for international companies is that there is a government which is able to rise above petty favouritism and corruption. Bermuda is not Nigeria (believed to be the most corrupt country in the world) and neither does it wish to be. In all its actions government needs to be purer than the driven snow otherwise its reputation for honesty and impartiality will suffer. It is impossible to separate good sound government from moral standards and the appearance of duplicity on the part of government is one which makes the public uncomfortable. As Abraham Lincoln said many years ago "with public trust everything is possible; without it nothing is possible." Government is a trustee and it violates that trust at its peril.

Thirdly, there is also the question of the value of a McDonalds franchise in which the average annual sale is about US$1.5m in the United States.[1] Anyone who has a McDonalds franchise almost has a licence to print money. The public believes that there is something wrong with a system whereby a fellow politician can give to another politician the right to print money. An arrangement like this smells to high heaven and the question really is should a government have this power to reward its supporters. Government policy should be based on clear objective principles not on the personality of the beneficiary of government policy. There is a major conflict of interest in this tawdry case, the equivalent of Caesar giving a piece of Rome to Caesar's wife. This is a power of patronage which should not be exercised by a twentieth-century government.

Fourthly, the policy like any other government policy should be subject to review, change and public debate but no review process was undertaken when the decision to grant the licence was made by the Minister of Finance. What seems not to be understood is that if government intervenes in the economic process it cannot simply change its policy without a degree of openness and public discussion without allegations of favouritism. It is not good policy in a democratic country to determine such financially sensitive matters behind closed doors and make a decision in favour of someone who is a political supporter. It raises important issues of public corruption, ill-considered policies and a contemptuous regard for public opinion.

If the policy on fast food franchises can be changed without adequate public debate and in a manner which benefits former government ministers, it means that other government policies on more important issues can be similarly changed. That is to say in secret, without prior debate, in a manner which smacks of political cronyism and corruption and which totally disregards public opinion. This is not a smart or a moral way to govern a country which is dependent on its reputation to attract high calibre international business or which has its fair share of self-respect. "To recognise error, to cut losses, to alter course, it the most repugnant option in government."[2] The Bermuda government should cut its losses and admit it made a mistake.

---

[1] 'Wall Street Journal' April 17, 1996.
[2] "The March of Folly" by Barbara Tuchman, page 481.

5. SHOULD BERMUDA HAVE A NATIONAL LOTTERY?

"If you bet on a horse, that's gambling. If you bet you can make three spades, that's entertainment. If you bet cotton will go up three points, that's business. See the difference?"

BLACKIE SHERRODE.

"I think the primary motive at the back of most gambling is the excitement of it. While gamblers naturally want to win, the majority of them derive pleasure even if they lose."

JOSEPH P. KENNEDY (FATHER OF PRESIDENT KENNEDY).

The public intensely dislikes paying taxes and there is, in the absence of imposing income tax which I believe works against Bermuda's best interests, few opportunities for government to dream up new taxes. An exception would be a national lottery. Many people believe that buying tickets in a national lottery is a lot of fun and who knows they may become wealthy beyond belief if they select the lucky numbers. Moreover, many countries have national lotteries - UK, Germany and 36 states in the United States and it does not result in major problems - so why not Bermuda? Why not indeed.

A lottery is a form of voluntary taxation, but it is by definition a bad investment. The participants are acting in an irrational manner as much of the lottery revenue generated is retained by government and there clearly has to be many more losers than winners. Insurance, an industry which Bermudians should know something about, is based essentially on an understanding of probabilities. So are lotteries. For members of the public it is an investment which will never pay a return (unless you are fantastically lucky) for it is specifically designed to make the chances of winning negligible. If a private individual marketed a product like a lottery he would rightly be accused of organised cheating and fraud.

In any rational society, moral principles suggest that government should prohibit such a product, not promote it. However, we do not live in a wholly rational society - after all many people smoke knowing that it is slow motion death, abuse alcohol and take illegal drugs - and if the public and the financially naive wish to throw away their money why should government object to this especially as no one is forcing the public to participate and government needs the money to spend on socially desirable projects. One could be cynical and state government wastes some of our money on foolish projects; why not let foolish people pay for foolish projects by foolishly buying lottery tickets.

There are many precedents for having a lottery, after all the sailing of the "Mayflower" to the New World was financed this way as were the founding of the Ivy League universities of Yale, Harvard and Dartmouth. Lottery funds were used to pay George Washington's armies during the American revolution because money could not be raised by taxation.[1]

The public already participates in similar activities like bingo, football pools and betting on horses and few people object to these activities, churches for example often sponsor bingo games. Indeed life itself is a lottery, genes deter-

---

[1] "Inside Las Vegas." by Mario Puzo (the author of the Godfather).

mining economic essentials like intelligence, physical attributes like health, looks or race. Other critically important matters such as country of birth (Bermudians are especially lucky to have been born or live in Bermuda with its beauty and high living standards), wealth of parents and being born at the right time (being born in the 20th century is surely better than the 16th century) are all very well matters of luck. I would love to have been born with the looks of Tom Cruise, the voice of Luciano Pavarotti, the athletic skill of Pete Sampras but I wasn't. I did not win any of life's lotteries.

There are three main arguments for having a lottery:

1. State sponsored gambling replaces illegal gambling.

2. Gambling is fun and a painless way of raising revenue for government.

3. There are no victims as there is willing participation.

The essence of the argument for or against a lottery is really where should the state stand on questions of financial morality. It makes those in authority and in the church uncomfortable that government approves gambling as a short cut to wealth, that speculating is fun and that it is an appropriate mechanism for financing socially approved projects like education, hospitals and public parks. The widespread acceptance of government lotteries gives credibility to undesirable social behaviour. Should it spoil what many people would call harmless fun or should it step in like a benevolent nanny and protect the financially unsophisticated from their own foolishness - after all there is something which is not quite right by fooling the public and making the average Bermudian poorer. Evidence from elsewhere suggests that gamblers come disproportionately from the poorer parts of the population, they usually cannot afford to gamble as they have no savings on which to draw and that they are particularly susceptible to dreams of instant wealth.

Gambling (for that is what a lottery is) is a socially undesirable way of speculating and it teaches people that becoming wealthy is divorced from the process of making and selling goods and services in an economically acceptable way. One of the weaknesses of capitalism is that many believe wealth is obtained from exploiting others not from honest endeavours. However, argument for protecting the public from their own stupidity is based on the Marxist premise of false consciousness which holds that the mass of workers are easily misled into believing things their betters know to be against the best interests of the poor.

There are some convincing economic arguments against a national lottery:-

- it is disguised taxation.
- it redistributes wealth from the poor to the rich.
- it undermines important concepts like thrift and hard work.
- it trivialises the state.

The contra argument is that money is freedom - and if the public wishes to use that freedom to act irrationally and voluntarily tax themselves for the common good - why should anyone prevent them from doing so. After all it is an economically irrational act to give money to a charity although it may make the donor feel better and provide help to someone who is badly off.

Morality or fun - where should government stand? My own view is that life is dull enough and if the public can have fun and dream of great wealth and get pleasure from buying a ticket in a national lottery, is this any different from enjoying music, a walk on the beach or playing with your dog? In order to get pleasure you sometimes have to pay so why not do so by having a national lottery? I will continue to buy lottery tickets when I visit UK and USA but I would prefer to buy them in Bermuda and contribute to the financial improvement of the Bermuda treasury.

6.   WHAT IS THE BUDGET AND WHY IS IT IMPORTANT?

"Inevitably there's going to be a downturn in national income sooner or later. And when income no longer matches expenditure we'll have to start borrowing to pay the civil service. Just a couple of years of that, and the UBP - the party that took us to almost unrivalled prosperity - could dump us firmly into the Third World."

'MID-OCEAN NEWS' EDITORIAL. MARCH 4, 1988.

The former Prime Minister of UK, Mr Harold MacMillan, once described the budget as "rather like a school speech day - a bit of a bore." However, almost everyone loves the Bermudian tradition of budget day, even the word budget is dervied from the French world "bougette", meaning little bag. The budget of the Bermuda government is a numerical expression of the government's priorities and policies which sets forth in considerable detail its overall programme, expressed in dollars so that the public may understand where the priorities lie. The budget sets out in detail estimates of the revenue to be raised, the main taxes which will be levied and the expenditure of various government ministries and departments making a distinction between current and capital expenditure. It is prepared annually by the Minister of Finance, usually in February, and deals with the next financial year which runs from April 1 to March 31. Failure to approve the government budget (this has never happened) in the lower house, The House of Assembly, would lead to a loss in confidence in the government and would require it to resign and call a general election. The budget therefore is not only an economic event of major importance it is also the political showpiece of the year.

The budget statement which is tabled in the House and read by the Minister of Finance, is also a report on the state of the economy and invariably contains self-congratulatory statements about the wonderful way government has run the financial affairs of Bermuda. As with most political statements such messages should be taken with a grain of salt in recognition of the well known political axiom that 'politicians tend to avoid drawing attention to things which are going wrong and for which blame could be attached to themselves.' When reading budget statements a healthy degree of scepticism should be retained.

The following quotations from previous budget statements give an indication of how unreliable or how optimistic self serving statements of Ministers of Finance are:-

- *"Looking ahead to 1986, there is every cause for optimism. First, the decline in the dollar will improve Bermuda's competitiveness[1] against Europe, Mexico and some of the Caribbean countries which have enjoyed a substantial increase in American visitors in recent years. Second, the planned opening of Club Med in March of this year,[2] and the Marriott-Castle Harbour in April with the prospect of good occupancies in both establishments, should boost the total of regular arrivals."[3]*

- *"In the coming year the Government will also examine how the public sector can be streamlined, for example through privatisation or by putting some services out to private tender."[4]*

- *"The Government has clearly demonstrated its determination to control current account expenditure more tightly. Sufficient revenue will be raised to give a substantial surplus once current account expenditure and debt interest payments have been met."[5]*

The opposition has many opportunities to criticise the financial proposals and economic policies of the governing party, and they are therefore given a major opportunity to put forward their own ideas as to what they would propose if they had the reins of power. Unfortunately, that opportunity is frequently wasted and the following selection of recent opposition responses to government proposals shows that the Opposition party has consistently showed a regrettable and limited grasp of economic matters. For example, the Opposition spokesman on finance in 1990 stated that Bermuda should seek

- *"a monetary contribution from the US Government for the right to retain a US base in this country." Going on to say, "It is a powerful economic argument for pursuing independence for Bermuda, since in this event the relevant treaty arrangements for these bases would have to, as a matter of course, be renegotiated."[6]*

Apart from the major benefits accruing to Bermuda from the presence of the US military (which amounted to about BD$50 million) which the Opposition has not always appreciated this was an invitation to the US Government to close down its facility which was in fact done in 1995 following a major review of foreign bases. There has never been a coherent policy of the Opposition on budgetary matters and it is widely recognised by the electorate that financial matters are its Achilles' heal.

That being said, the Opposition is at a severe disadvantage in dealing with budgetary matters largely because they simply do not have the resources to do the

---

[1] In fact it didn't as the Government appointed a Commission on Competitiveness in 1992.

[2] Club Med closed about four years later.

[3] Budget Statement, 1986/1987, page 5.

[4] Budget Statement, 1990/1991, page 4.

[5] Budget Statement, 1991/1992, page 13.

[6] 'Royal Gazette,' page 4 - Thursday, March 1, 1990.

research necessary to draw attention to flaws in Government proposals. Government has the benefit of being able to utilise the resources of the Ministry of Finance as well as all other Government departments and is therefore able to anticipate many of the Opposition attacks and successfully fend them off.

A major achievement of the Bermuda Government over the past 10 years or so has been to achieve a balanced budget which, in simple terms, means that, taking one year with another, the amount spent by government is roughly equal to the amount raised in taxation. This is a major achievement as many larger governments until recently were not unduly concerned about balancing the budget but viewed government expenditure as a means of stimulating the economy (by spending more than was collected in taxation) or by cooling down the economy (by spending less than was collected in taxes). A major exception to this rule is the commitment made by Government in respect of pensions for which totally inadequate provision has been made.[8]

Government deficits should be regarded as a sign of financial recklessness and any government which consistently runs a deficit (like the United States) deserves the punishment increasingly handed out by international capital markets by having to pay higher interest rates than would otherwise be the case. However, the creation of national debts has led to major political and financial difficulties in many countries and added to the fact that stimulating or cooling the economy does not work in practice most governments are now seeking to run a budget surplus or keep public expenditure and taxation roughly in balance - an achievement which has eluded many of them, but one of which successive Bermuda governments can be proud.

One of the major achievements of the Bermuda Government (and one for which they are rarely given credit) is that the percentage of GDP spent by government is one of the lowest in the world, and is the lowest in what is called the rich man's club, the Organisation for Economic Cooperation and Development (OECD). The OECD average for 1994 is 41.4% - almost twice as much as Bermuda for the same year - and Bermudians although rightly concerned about the increasing levels of government expenditure should be content that their government is not as profligate as others. Of the smaller countries only Switzerland at 25.8% is reasonably close to the Bermuda level of around 25% of GDP.

Only one-quarter of the country's income is spent by government who provide quality and levels of service which can only be expected in wealthier nations. However, when one takes into consideration the absence in the Bermuda government budget of such major items of government expenditure as defence, social security benefits like unemployment insurance, and foreign affairs the gap narrows considerably.

A distinction is always made in the budget between current and capital expenditure, the latter relating to fixed investment in infrastructure projects like roads, waste disposal, schools, airports and so on. Spending on such important matters as education and training is still classified as current expenditure when there is a strong argument that such spending should more accurately be regarded as a cap-

---

[8] See question III 20.

ital investment in human capital, which is just as (or more) important than investment in roads and buildings. This classification however is a historical hangover from a period when individuals were not viewed as important capital investments in themselves. In the new global economy brain power is increasingly seen as the key investment for future economic success.

The distinction between current and capital expenditure is conceptually important because budget deficits are often justified on the grounds that capital investments made by government should be thought of in the same way as capital investments made by individuals or by private enterprise. Such public investment it is asserted is made for the long term good of the country and will benefit future generations more than current taxpayers. The sums involved should be borrowed and therefore be notionally written-off over a period of time in much the same way as when an individual buys a house the cost is amortised by means of a mortgage over a period of twenty or thirty years. This notional justification for borrowing for capital expenditure assumes that there is a moral justification for government borrowing.

Taxpayers should always be on the alert when government invokes morality as traditionally this has meant that they should clutch their wallets more tightly. Politicians live in the present and for them the long term does not stretch beyond next week. If a current benefit can be achieved credit is immediately given to the political party in power. Borrowing means that costs can be transferred to future taxpayers, or to future generations and the politicians involved will either be out of office or dead, and blame can be transferred to their successors.[9]

The crucial difference between capital investment made by individuals or governments is that individuals tend to have only two or three major capital expenditures during their lifetime, mainly housing and education of children. Government, on the other hand, has a constant requirement to make public investment in schools, roads, harbours and so on. Individuals have limited long term investment expenditure; governments have almost unlimited requirements. It is therefore highly questionable as to whether government should borrow to meet its capital obligations and thus impose a debt cost on future generations, or whether it should recognise that there will be continuous requirements for capital projects and that they should be prudently funded from current taxation.

It is pretty obvious that taxation has to be levied on the public to pay for government expenditure. Unfortunately, but not unexpectedly, the electorate is unhappy about this obvious fact of life but governments everywhere have learned that whilst government expenditure tends to be popular (although not always) taxation is always extremely unpopular unless the governing party can convince voters that they, the beneficiaries of the spending, are not paying for the services rendered.

The essence of a good Finance Minister is to convince everyone that they benefit from government expenditure but that no one, particularly the voters, has to pay for it. Incredibly many voters both in Bermuda and abroad fall for this nonsense. Nailing down who actually pays is often a difficult process and the only tax which is universally applauded by the electorate is the one which the other fel-

---

[9] Pensions is a perfect example of this; see Question III 20 for a discussion of this issue.

low has to pay. A cynical politician from Louisiana, Senator Russell Long, put it thus "Don't tax you, don't tax me, tax that man behind that tree." Unlike countries which have income tax, confusing the electorate is much more difficult in Bermuda than in countries abroad, where politicians are often able to convince the electorate that the rich will pay the bulk of taxes whilst the poor will be the beneficiaries of government spending.

One of the key issues in the budget, at least for the taxpayers not employed by government, is the percentage of total government expenditure attributable to civil servants' salaries. For reasons which baffle and annoy the electorate, no explanation is given as to why this percentage continues to increase at a pace faster than any other level of expenditure. For example, in the early 1980s employee salaries and benefits accounted for about 50% of government expenditure; by 1996/97 that percentage had increased to an estimated 55%. In the fiscal year 1995/96 the actual cost of salaries was 49.69% of government revenue. This percentage does not include benefits such as pensions (which are very generous by comparison with the private sector), cost of health plans, or deemed payroll taxes. A conservative estimate of such costs would be 15%. A major reason for the phenomenon of high public service benefits was attributed as long ago as 1776 by Adam Smith who noted that public servants, like any other group of people, primarily tend to act in their own self interest. Professor James Buchanan, who was awarded the Nobel Prize in economics in 1986, confirmed Smith's observation and in slightly more elegant prose than the following quotation from Sir Richard Marsh, (a former minister in the British Labour Government of the 1960s) who stated, *"You can cut any public expenditure except the Civil Service, those lads spent a hundred years learning to look after themselves."* In this connection, the Standing Committe on Public Accounts reported in June, 1994[10] "Your Committee had serious concerns about the high salaries of department Heads and other senior Civil Servants, and about their level of performance as managers." It continued, "Concerns were expressed that Government's retirement and pension policies actually encourage senior civil servants to retire from the Public Sector with full benefits just at the time when their expertise and experience are at a peak, in order to enter the private sector."

One of the major differences between government accounting and the way in which private enterprise maintains its financial records is that Government operates on a cash in cash out system of accounting, not very different from the way a small businessman like an odd job man would operate or in the way which children would operate a lemonade stand. More sophisticated businesses use the accrual system of accounting, in which provision is made for the non-cash costs and benefits of running an organisation. For example, if a business invests $10 million in a project the cash required for the investment is spent that year. However, the asset will be depreciated over a period of time, say 10 years, and a charge of $1 million each year for depreciation will be made to the profit and loss account. At the same time, if the enterprise wishes to remain in business for the long term it will have to retain a proportion of its profits for future expansion and working capital. Therefore it cannot, as a matter of prudence spend all income

---

[10] See Report of the Auditor for the Financial Year 1990/1991 issued in April, 1995.

earned during the year, otherwise it runs the real risk of being out of business in the future.

The government budget does not account for the public's money in the same way as the management of a private business accounts for its stewardship to shareholders. There is no published government balance sheet showing the assets of the Bermuda Government ; and there is no system of creating reserves during years of economic prosperity for use when there is a period of hard times. The tradition has grown that governments determine expenditure as a result of the political process and then scramble to raise sufficient funds in taxation to meet that expenditure. Expenditure is the driving force not prudent financial management and the cash system used by governments allows imprudent financial management to rule. Some would go even further and say that there is an iron law of democratic politics, namely that government spending will always be greater than government revenue.

If private companies ran their operations in the same manner as government currently does there would be a strong likelihood that they would be out of business within a relatively short period. Only a few countries use the accrued method of accounting for public finance, New Zealand, being the best example. For large countries this would be a huge task, but for a small community like Bermuda additional discipline could be brought to the budgetary process if business accounting methods were applied. It is unlikely that such a process would arise in Bermuda, for very much the same reason as it is rarely applied elsewhere, and that is because politicians and civil servants would be held to a higher standard of accountability than they are at present. The current system allows for many smoke and mirror tricks to be played on a gullible public, misrepresentations of the sort which would not be permitted by shareholders in a private organisation.

Whatever valid criticisms may be made about the budget process in Bermuda, there is much to be said for the efficient and competent way in which it has been dealt with in recent years. The United States and Britain constantly run budget deficits, there is manifest incompetence in the provision of public services and government costs continue to rise. Whilst improvements can be made in Bermuda, we are, by comparison with most countries in a very enviable position. Government deficits are small, revenue and expenditure is roughly in balance with a minimal national debt (except for pensions) and the process works well by concentrating the attention of the electorate on the way in which government spends public monies. The budget plays an important role in retaining the confidence of foreign investors and international business in the future of Bermuda. Government spending is under control, it is presented in an open and transparent way and in the main it is spent on objectives with which the electorate agrees. Clearly there can be criticisms, many of which are made in this book, but it is fair to say that the process retains the confidence of most Bermudians and it works effectively. Bermuda is a long way from one opinion of a recent budget of President Clinton "The budget that Bill Clinton is presenting today is not lean ; it is not efficient; it is not frugal. It is a monstrosity. It should be greeted with heaps of ridicule and scorn."[11]

---

[11] 'Wall Street Journal,' 2 April, 1995.

7.   WHAT DID THE BUDGET SAY TO BERMUDIANS IN RESPECT OF THE FISCAL YEAR 1996/1997?

"The art of taxation consists in so plucking the goose as to obtain the largest possible amount of feathers with the smallest possible amount of hissing."
JEAN-BAPTISTE COLBERT, FRENCH FINANCE MINISTER IN THE 18TH CENTURY.

In the 1996 Budget Statement in support of the Estimate of Revenue and Expenditure for the financial year 1996/1997, the Finance Minister drew attention to the impact which globalisation of the world economy is having on Bermuda, restated the underlying financial philosophy of government, and the way in which his budget conforms to government priorities. In doing so he made six points:-

1.   The current budget was viewed as part of a continuation of government policy towards the general welfare on the population of Bermuda with particular emphasis on such major areas of public concern as safety, education and drugs.

2.   Cash would be provided for new programmes which would enhance Bermuda's competitive position.

3.   Departmental restructuring would enable government to improve the competitiveness of the labour force.

4.   Money would be provided to enhance the partnership which government has with Bermuda International Business Association (BIBA) by financing (with BIBA) an overseas marketing programme.

5.   Funds would be devoted to capital allocations for education and the base lands redevelopment.

6.   Non-payroll expenditure would be frozen on current government programmes.

Obligatory mention was also made about the importance of overseas investment to the welfare of Bermuda, the importance of tourism and international business and the "formidable" challenges of developing the land which was previously occupied by the military. Other comments were made about economic conditions in the United States and the impact these have on the Bermudian economy, the dangers of wages being increased beyond the levels of increased productivity, government revenue for the current year being somewhat less than forecast, the economy performing less well than had been expected all of which was laced with cautious optimism government has about the future.

His optimistic comments seemed to be at variance with some of the views expressed in a document published by the Ministry of Finance[1] (issued at the same time as the Budget) entitled "1995 Economic Review" which amongst other things stated that:-

"The problems facing the tourism industry are not merely cyclical. There has been a trend decline in real visitor expenditure of around 1% a year since the beginning of the 1980s. Bermuda faces an ever more competitive tourist market

---
[1] In February, 1996.

200

and must continue to ensure that it markets its product effectively and provides visitors with added value commensurate with the price of a holiday in Bermuda. The major hotels have already taken steps to control costs and enhance value added, but further adjustments in cost structures may be required within the economy. The 1996 Olympic Games in Atlanta - which is likely to be a considerable attraction, particularly for US holiday makers - will be yet another challenge for the industry in 1996."[2]

The review further stated:-

"The world economy is becoming increasingly integrated and Bermuda's tourist and retail market are becoming more exposed to more intensive market forces from which they have historically been sheltered. Bermuda's residents still enjoy an enviable standard of living, but if this is to be maintained business and labour practices must change to recognise the new economic environment in which they are competing. This is likely to require increased focus on cost control and reduction. The failure to adapt will cause firms to close down and employees to lose their jobs."[3]

Many of the statements made by the Minister are the show-biz part of the 1996 political act and their inconsistency with the facts notwithstanding, are a prelude to the softening up of the public before tax and expenditure plans are revealed. This is the part of the budget process which had greatest immediate interest for the general public. This is when the public learns to its horror that, for compelling reasons, at least in the eyes of the governing party, government expenditure will have to be increased and, that in order to finance the rise in expenditure, taxes will also have to be increased. The public rarely has the benefit of a Minister of Finance saying that government expenditure will fall and that as a happy consequence of this event taxes will be cut to allow the electorate to enjoy the money which they have earned through their hard work. The 1996/1997 budget was no exception to the general rule of increasing taxation and taxpayers are required in 1996 to pay about a quarter of their incomes, directly or indirectly, to the Consolidated Fund, the term used to describe the public treasury.

The main expenditures of the Bermuda government increased in 1996/97 to $508 million (approximately $8,700 for each person living in Bermuda or getting close to $10 million per week) from an estimated $458 million in 1995/1996 an increase of $50 million or almost 11 percent. The main expenditures are shown clearly in the following table:-

---

[2] Page 15.
[3] Page 19.

Government Department or Ministry	Expenditure 1996/1997 BD$ Million	Percent of Total Expenditure
Health and Social Services	96.5	19.0
Capital Expenditure	71.7	14.1
Education & Human Affairs	63.5	12.5
Finance	55.9	11.0
Works and Engineering	53.5	10.6
Labour and Home Affairs	45.5	9.0
Tourism and Marine Services	40.2	7.9
Transport and Aviation	31.5	6.2
Interest and Sinking Fund	12.8	2.5
Environment	9.5	1.9
Judicial and Legal	9.4	1.8
Administration	8.0	1.6
Youth and Sport	4.8	0.9
Community and Cultural	3.6	0.7
Technology and Information	1.6	0.3
TOTAL	508.0	100.0

Revenue on the other hand is expected to raise only approximately $452.6 million a shortfall for the year of just over $50 million. The amount of revenue raised by the various taxes are shown in the table which follows:-

TAX	AMOUNT BASED BD$ MILLION	PERCENT OF TAXES
Customs Duties	138.2	30.5
Payroll Taxes	115.0	25.4
Company Fees	36.1	8.0
Land Tax	24.1	5.3
Passenger Tax	20.2	4.5
Stamp Duties	15.0	3.3
Vehicle Licences	14.9	3.3
Hotel Occupancy	14.0	3.1
Immigration Fees	11.7	2.6
Post Office	8.3	1.8
Bermuda Monetary Authority	0.5	0.1
All Others	54.6	12.1
TOTAL	$452.6 Million	100.0%

A major issue is that import duties - the main source of government revenue - which raise just over 30 percent of government revenue have declined as a proportion of revenue for many years. Ten years ago, in the fiscal years 1986/1987, customs duties brought in just over 42% of government revenues.[4] The main argument against import duties is that it has a disproportionate impact on those with low incomes and they impose a huge burden on the retail sector (and indirectly on tourists) whose current financial health is poor - in some cases terminal. The budget statement studiously avoided discussion of the retailers predicament apart from paying lip service to the problem by reducing or eliminating taxes on minor, almost irrelevant imports like costume jewelry, kitchen ware and tableware.

Debates on government expenditure can be wearying. They always tend to centre around priorities - should education have more money than health and welfare (the answer is less) , how important is the environment relative to money spent by the Ministry of Works and Engineering (also less) and how much should be devoted to capital expenditure for the benefit of future generations. Or should that tax be lowered or that tax increased? I will spare the reader this tedious exercise although it should always be borne in mind that budgets are a numerical and financial expression of political priorities.

The decision to increase Employment Tax from 11.5% to 12% of salary from which 4.5% may be recovered from employees. Many equate Employment Tax with income tax and in many respects they are correct. It cannot be stressed too strongly that companies and employers are merely legal abstractions through which taxes are collected by Government but that the burden of paying taxes always remains with individuals in their capacities as employees, shareholders or customers. Employment Tax is no exception to this rule.

Like public gossip, the most interesting thing about budget statements is what is not mentioned or is referred to only in passing. There were a number of key issues missing from the 1996/1997 budget statement and it is the points which are not made which are the really important message to the public of Bermuda.

Firstly, there is an implied assumption that each year government expenditure should rise in response to the wishes of the voter. The reality is that voters are not demanding new programmes; in fact many would like government programmes to be reduced. Government expenditure continues to rise because there is an inbuilt tendency, almost a rule of bureaucratic bloat, for it to increase constantly because governments always seek to expand their powers. Parsimonious politicians, even of the calibre of Prime Minister Thatcher and President Reagan are virtually powerless to prevent the creep of government power. Power creep arises because the public is lulled into believing that government can actually achieve positive results in areas of public concern such as education, tourism development and rent control. The harsh reality is that government rarely achieves success but seeks to give the appearance of success. For example, almost every study of expenditure on social services in large countries like UK and USA has shown that the money is used to make life better for the staff rather than to improve the service delivered to the taxpayer.

---

[4] In the mid 1960s it was just under 60 percent.

The implications are that the Cabinet and the Minister of Finance believes government can continue with its bad fiscal habits, the taxpayers will stoically continue to stump up, and that there is no requirement for government like the rest of the public to live within its means. Government expenditure has more than doubled over 10 years - in 1986/1987 it was estimated at BD$231.5 million - in 1996/1997 it is estimated at BD$508 million.

The two vital questions voters should be asking their representatives are:-

• Do we want more government programmes and greater expenditure? and

• Are we better governed today than we were 20 years ago?

Most would answer in the negative.

Secondly, there is no accurate costing of government activities. A statement to the effect that government will spend on education in 1996/97 the sum of $63.5 million does not tell the electorate anything very much. However, if a statement was made that the cost of educating a child at government schools was over $7,000 compared with under $7,000 at a private school, or that the cost of maintaining a prisoner at Westgate Correctional Facility is $42,337 that statement would be much more informative and greater relevant information would be conveyed to the public. Expenditure on education when expressed in millions of dollars per annum does not convey anything to the electorate which cynics say is precisely the reason why it is couched in this way. In addition, if some international comparative costs were included, for example, by providing the cost of education per child in Canada or the cost of maintaining a prisoner in prison in the United States the voter would have a much better understanding of how well (or how badly) his money was being spent.

Thirdly, the costs of government per capita (or per head of the total population) is approximately $8,700 per annum (over $700 per month) - almost six times greater than the per capita income of Jamaica which is $1,500 per annum and greater than the Federal Government per capita expenditure in the United States of about $5,600 per annum. It would be helpful to taxpayers if the Minister tabled a statement showing how much is spent per head of the population in several other countries of the world. This would provide some guide to taxpayers on how much value they are obtaining from the current arrangements. Unfortunately over the years government has got into the business of promising more than it knows how to deliver.

Fourthly, payroll costs of the civil service are increasing. Some years ago the Premier (then Minister of Finance) expressed concern that civil salaries were approaching 50 percent of government expenditure; that figure is now about 55 percent. If voters take into consideration the non-pecuniary benefits which arise from civil service employment like inflation proof pensions, an additional car (if your are sufficiently senior) and little chance of being dismissed or demoted for incompetence it is difficult to escape the conclusion that taxpayers are subsidising a bureaucracy which enjoys conditions of service which are currently not available to the rest of the population. One reason why this state of affairs continues is that a government with a small majority of four cannot afford to offend an influential segment of the population and it is only too painfully obvious that civil servants vote.

Fifthly, Government will need to increase its borrowing during the financial year 1996/97 as expenditure is estimated to exceed revenue by approximately $50 million (or almost $1 million per week, $137,362 per day, or $5,723 per hour, or almost $100 per minute). For a population of under 60,000 these amounts are not chickenfeed in fact just under $1,000 per annum each. The lesson to be learned from elsewhere is that when government expenditure exceeds government revenue, the population is being fooled into believing that they are better off than they really are. The real problems begin when borrowings have to be repaid and interest costs have to be met.

Previous Bermuda government budgets, at least until the early 1990s , tended one year with another to balance the country's books, and this was a major factor in the Bermuda Government being considered a sound prudent fiscally conservative organisation thus allowing for the rating of AA by Standard and Poor's a financial rating organisation in the United States. The long term disadvantage is that future taxpayers have to pay the interest charges for current borrowing and, just like an alcoholic taking another drink, borrowing does not improve the financial health of the community - quite the opposite. The debt problems are compounded by the off-the-budget deficits of over $1 billion (BD$1,000 million) in the Central Pension Fund and the Public Service Pension Fund.[5]

Bermuda has fortunately been a happy prosperous island for many many years, which means that the majority of the population have little concept of understanding what it is like for a country to encounter financial difficulties. Government expenditure is equivalent to Bermuda Inc incurring an annual overhead of $500 million or so per annum and this heavy burden would be impossible to carry in the event of a major financial downturn. This is unlikely to occur but Bermuda, unlike many larger communities elsewhere in the world, does not have a diversified economy and a large fall in earnings from either tourism or international business could lead to considerable difficulties for the public in being able to support government expenditure at present levels.

In larger rich countries it is not at all unusual for areas of the country to encounter economic decline because of structural changes in the economy, examples being the Maritime Provinces in Canada, the rust-belt of the mid-western United States, or the former mining and shipbuilding areas of the United Kingdom. Diversification of the economy in large countries allows the central government to provide relief, and the physical size of the country allows the population to move elsewhere - options which are not available to Bermuda. It is unfortunate during our period of major prosperity in the 1970s and 1980s that we did not make provision for the possibilities of economic adversity but rather, in my view, rashly expanded government activities and increased costs.

Although the Bermuda Government spends a smaller proportion of GDP than almost any other economically advanced country, there is little scope for govern-

---

[5] See Part III 20 for a discussion about pensions.

ment revenue to be increased without the introduction of new taxes. Bermuda's prosperity depends to a very great extent on it being a low tax country, otherwise international business would not locate themselves in Bermuda. A major reason for international companies coming to Bermuda in the first place is that corporate taxes are low and in addition government has given undertakings under the provisions of The Exempted Undertakings Tax Protection Act, 1966 not to impose for 30 years corporate, income or capital gains taxes on exempted companies. This restricts the ability of government to raise additional funds from the tax base.

In conclusion the 1996/97 budget studiously avoided most of the long term difficulties mentioned above - problems associated with increased government spending, accurate costs, benchmarking, a bloated public service, borrowing and overhead costs of government. A recent pessimistic newspaper editorial stated in its conclusion, "No one capable of balancing a chequebook is willing to buy into his (the Minister) ludicrous business plan for Bermuda Inc. The Finance Minister should start preparing 'Going out of business' signs."[6] This is an exaggeration but Bermudians should remember that in the 1950s the standard of living in Jamaica was not very different to that of Bermuda. It is now very significant lower, the per capita income in Bermuda being $27,500; in Jamaica it is $1,500. Most of this decline was accounted for by poor financial management by the Jamaican government and steadily increasing government expenditure. This is the path Bermudians do not wish to travel but there is little evidence that the Government is about to take another direction.

8. DOES GOVERNMENT DO A GOOD JOB?

"The theory of bureaucratic displacement is that an increase in expenditure will be matched by a fall in production. Such systems will act rather like black holes in the economic universe, simultaneously sucking in resources and shrinking in terms of emitted production."
DR MAX GAMMON (QUOTED IN THE 'WALL STREET JOURNAL' NOVEMBER 12, 1991).

"He (George III) has erected a multitude of new offices and sent hither swarms of officers to harass our people and eat out their substance."
AMERICAN DECLARATION OF INDEPENDENCE, 1776.

Most people are puzzled by the fact that government often fails to act in an efficient manner and those who work in business and commerce are often compelled to ask - why does government fail to work as efficiently as private enterprise? Leaving aside for the moment that private enterprise itself often fails to work efficiently, it is important to understand that seeking to improve the day to day performance of government is usually an exercise in superficial tinkering. Government bureaucracies are inefficient because they are designed that way.

Private enterprise needs to focus on the bottom line (or profitability) because shareholders and institutional investors demand, (usually in private) a satisfacto-

---

[6] 'Mid-Ocean News,' Friday March 15, 1996.

ry level of performance and a failure to comply results in action, frequently the jobs of management. On the other hand a government department has its focus on such things as pleasing the minister (who is a politician) which means looking good in the press. It is also concerned with fairness, avoiding favouritism in awarding contracts, avoiding arbitrary decisions, publicity and responding to the demands of elected representatives or the requests of the public. All of these factors tend to militate against efficiency. If there is, for example, a clash between looking good in the press and efficiency the former will always win. There are no kudos for a government department in being efficient - salaries are paid irrespective of performance and it is almost impossible to lose one's job. In government, it becomes important not to make mistakes; if there are successes hardly anyone notices but make one mistake and everybody pounces on it.

In business it is easy to determine if an organisation is successful. You simply look at the profits for the year. In government, the measures of success are not easy to identify. Indeed the focus tends to be on inputs - how much money is spent on education, fighting crime or on public health measures. Little attention is paid to outcomes or results. If a government department is not successful the standard response is to spend more money; not much attention is paid to results because the focus tends always to be on budgets and how much money is allocated to the problem. Because results are not measured to the same extent as budgets, bureaucratic government does not achieve the results the taxpayer wants. Politicians and bureaucrats spend much of their time explaining away why things have failed to work. The Department of Tourism has been dubbed by Graham Outerbridge of the NLP as 'the Ministry of a thousand excuses.'

When modern governments were established in the nineteenth century great things were expected from the civil service bureaucracy. Max Weber the German sociologist stated that "the fully developed bureaucratic mechanism compares with other organisations exactly as does the machine with the non-mechanical modes of production. Precision, speed, unambiguity, knowledge of the files, continuity, discretion, unity, strict subordination, reduction of friction and of material and personal costs - these are raised to the optimum point in the strictly bureaucratic administration."[1] Somehow the efficiency got lost and self-interest began to dominate.

As a result a bureaucracy is an organisation created for a purpose such as the provision of an educational system, but which establishes its own rules, procedures, priorities goals and agenda which may, or frequently may not, be consistent with the reason for its existence. In the main decisions are made which serve the bureaucracy's own interests and the personnel in it NOT the people the bureaucracy is supposed to serve.[2] This is a major assumption of public choice theory which states that politicians and civil servants behave in a way which furthers their own self-interest - not that of the public. This differs from the usual civic text book view that they always act for the benefit of the public. This is why, at the TCD, despite huge numbers of customers public servants behind the counter discontinue service at 4.30 p.m.. TCD exists not for the benefit of the public but to provide jobs for those who work there. This is an extreme statement

[1] Quoted on page 28, The New Palgrave "World of Economics".
[2] The view of Economics Nobel Laureate, James Buchanan.

but if anyone doubts its validity they should ask themselves the following question. Why is it possible to rent a car from Avis or Hertz anywhere in the Western world in a period of less than 10 minutes, yet it takes about 4 hours to re-licence a motor vehicle in Bermuda?[3]

After a period of time the bureaucracy seeks not to solve the problems for which it was set up but to preserve and protect its own existence, to stifle criticism of it, and to extend its influence and power in order to provide bigger and better paid jobs for those in the department. In short, bureaucracy looks after itself first and foremost, not the public for whose service it was originally established.[4] When the question of civil service incompetence arises the answer is not to convene an investigation into the specific grievance which is usually the action taken. A more original and fruitful act might be to ask the question - do we wish our lives to be increasingly subjected to civil service control by people who are, in the main, often incompetent and cannot be removed in the event of proven incompetence. The same principles tend to apply in large private organisations like banks and oil companies but the principle of operating for a profit tends to prevent organisational inefficiency getting out of hand.

In addition, to all of that, governments are established with all sorts of constitutional checks and balances designed expressly for the purpose of ensuring that quick and efficient decisions cannot be made. Bermuda is a happy exception to the general historical rule that governments have been the oppressor of the public - just recall the evils of France before the French Revolution, or Britain under the Stuarts, or America under George III. After suffering from arbitrary government (which usually means quick decisions and efficiency) reformers established a structure which make it difficult, if not impossible, for efficiency to flourish. Bermuda inherited that structure when its constitution was established in 1968. One of the recurring themes of this book, is that economic efficiency means distancing economic decision making from the political process.

With the above caveats in mind there can be no correct answer to the question I have posed. It all depends on the department of government which is under discussion. In my view, government departments like Works and Engineering do a reasonable job - I believe trash collection a function of this ministry which is not exactly a glamorous objective of government works extremely well - but a visit to the Transport Control Department would not leave a good impression with the taxpayer.

It is extremely difficult, almost impossible, to make generalisations about whether Government or the civil service provides value for money although this does not discourage people from making them. One rough and ready test which can be applied to organisations which are not affected by the discipline of profits (money tends to concentrate the mind particularly if it is your own or you are rewarded by how much money the company makes) is the "broken window theory"[5] which signals that no one cares.

---

[3] It should be noted that TCD has recently improved its performance and that the above comments may be unfair.
[4] In the 'Economist' publication "The World in 1997" a former editor Mr Norman Macrae described modern government as "The Thieving State".
[5] see page 292 of 'Dumbing Down Our Kids,' by Charles J. Sykes.

This theory states that if a window on a building is left unrepaired, the rest of the windows will soon be broken. An unrepaired window is a signal that no one cares and so the breaking of the rest of the windows costs nothing. The broken window test can be applied to other situations where signals are sent that no one cares. Examples of the broken window theory as it applies to government are:

- Check your children's homework book. If spelling and bad handwriting are not corrected this is the educational equivalent of a broken window.
- At the Transport Control Department do the attendants go out of their way to please the public when they re-licence a vehicle. If not, this is the equivalent of a broken window.
- Are customs officers polite and helpful at the airport. If not, this is the equivalent of a broken window.

Government is so big (at least for Bermuda) - it employs about 4,600 people or about one quarter of the labour force - so that statements of efficiency or inefficiency can be corroborated with many examples. In addition, in a small country like Bermuda, public administration costs are more likely to be high because the economies of scale which can be found in larger countries like the United States or the United Kingdom are not present here.

It is not difficult to find egregious examples of government inefficiency and the following three examples could be multiplied by many members of the public:-

1. In 1991 a German tourist was murdered by a prisoner on work detail who was clearly improperly supervised - no one was dismissed from the Prison service as a result.

2. In 1995 three civil servants went to New Zealand at a cost of BD$20,000 to interview one potential recruit to the teaching profession who was allegedly an expert on a Reading Recovery Programme. No one was hired.

3. In 1988 the Departure Terminal at the Bermuda Airport was significantly over budget and the Minister of Finance stated that the estimated cost of expenditure had been pulled out of the hat and that nothing could be done about the additional cost.

The reader should not be left with the impression that today's Bermuda Government has a monopoly of sloppy management - in fact its record by comparison with elsewhere is quite good - so let me give three examples of poor government management in other countries:

1. In England between 1974 and 1985 annual expenditure on the National Health Service increased from approximately $6 billion to $25 billion and the staff from 674,000 to 817,000 whilst the number of beds available for patients fell from 406,000 to 345,000.[6] A good example of Parkinson's law to which I will return later.

2. In the United States a restaurant owner was inspected by a government officer who ordered that the fans were making too much noise and had to be turned off. As a result the kitchen overheated causing the fire alarm to go off

---

[6] 'The Times,' London 8th June, 1987.

costing the owner $10,000 in lost business and $60,000 in legal fees and fines.[7]

3. The United Nations Disaster Relief Organisation spent more money on its airconditioning system in New York than on sending staff to disaster zones.[8]

In historical times Bermuda featured as an example of government profligacy. Commissioner's House at Dockyard was built in 1824 as a residence for the Senior Naval Officer West Indies. It cost £40,000 (a fortune in those days) and questions were raised about the extravagance in the House of Commons. It fell into disrepair from the 1950's and is now being restored, I hope with a plaque to honour the tradition of government waste.[9]

On a happier and less critical note, one of the key issues in discussing how well government functions is the degree of corruption which exists. I am quite convinced that there is very little government corruption and that the standards of public life in Bermuda can be favourably compared with any other country in the world. When one compares Bermuda with countries like Nigeria, Brazil or even the United States, Bermuda is refreshingly free of the corrosive effects of corruption. This is a major achievement for which the Bermuda government is rarely given credit and, in my opinion, it arises from four main sources:-

- Government intervenes in the economy only to a limited extent and this severely restricts the opportunities of politicians and public servants to receive under the table payments.

- The traditions of British colonial government were extremely high and it was rare for officials to be 'on the take.' These traditions were continued in Bermuda after the British Government granted responsible constitutional government in 1968.

- The high level of income enjoyed by Bermudians, and by public servants, is such that it is not necessary for them to seek illegal payment from doing their job.

- There is a high degree of professionalism and integrity in the personnel employed by the Bermuda government and personal standards are such that anyone associated with wrongdoing would be ostracised. In addition, the tradition of political impartiality is an ingrained feature of the civil service culture and is an integral part of the professionalism of public life.

One of the major criticisms is that the civil service lives in a world of its own, free from day to day concerns about being profitable and efficient, and relatively free from worries associated with a downturn in the local economy. It is top heavy, is unable to make decisions and is weighed down by bureaucracy.[10]

Indeed, civil servants are not paid for making decisions (theoretically they are made by the politicians) but more important the power of a public servant arises from his ability to delay.[11] The more a problem is deferred and circulated for further comment, the more power accrues to the bureaucracy and the more impor-

---

[7] 'Wall Street Journal,' April 8, 1996.

[8] 'The Economist,' December 2, 1989.

[9] See "Your Bermuda", by George Rushe, page 46

[10] See "The Demand and Supply of Public Goods" by James Buchanan.

[11] Ibid

tant the bureaucracy becomes. Making a rapid decision moves the problem from a desk and therefore from the control of the bureaucrat. None of this surprised Professor C. Northcote Parkinson who in his classic book "Parkinson's Law"[12] made the following statements

- *Work expands so as to fill the time available for its completion.* Two key assumptions underline this law:-

1. An official wishes to multiply subordinates mainly because his job responsibilities, and hence his salary will increase - a major reason why numbers in any bureaucracy continue to rise.

2. Bureaucrats make work for each other by, for example, sending memos to one another, delaying decisions in case they make a mistake, holding meetings and so on.

Parkinson proved his case by showing that when the Royal Navy had 542 ships under its control the Admiralty staff was 4,366. In 1967 when the number of ships had fallen to 114, the Admiralty staff had increased (wait for it) to 33, 574 and the technical staff had increased more slowly than the clerical staff.

- *Expenditure rises to meet income.* This should be a familiar statement for the Bermudian taxpayer, the more naive of whom probably assumes that when government expenditure goes up the government needs to increase revenue by increasing taxation. It is really the other way round. Government and bureaucracy decide what they can extract from the public in taxation and they then decide on what to spend. Government expenditure cannot be reduced piecemeal it can only be done by across the board reductions - something which the politicians and bureaucracy will strongly resist.

- *Expansion means complexity and complexity decay.* What this means is that as things get bigger things get worse - a lesson which we in Bermuda have learned to our cost over the years. Now that restructuring and reengineering is all the rage it shows that Parkinson was way ahead of his time.

- *Delay is the deadliest form of denial.* Parkinson described bureaucrats as the "abominable no-men" who delay and delay until the public gives up in disgust. It is the ability to delay which gives the public service their power and power is what attracts many to the public service in the first place. It is easy to think of examples of this in Bermuda, taxing your motor vehicle for the next year, asking for a response on your social security payments or applying for immigration consent to hire an employee. The list is endless.

All of this is not very surprising as similar criticisms are made about government costs and civil servants everywhere. However, public service is not all that different from private enterprise. You hire the right people, control costs and meet the needs of the public. Public service should not be designed to provide and secure, well-paid, non-productive jobs to Bermudians - it is designed to provide the services which are paid for by taxes. Increasingly the trend is that when costs go up the civil service automatically assumes that it is the job of the Minister of Finance to increase taxation and for the public quietly to pay for such additional costs.

---

[12] Published by Penguin.

A leading critic of the civil service was reported as saying "Businesses have had to take a hard look at themselves and find ways of trimming fat and adjusting to change, and there is no reason why Government should not do the same."[13] It is regrettable but it is most unlikely, if the experience of elsewhere is anything to go by, that government will trim much fat from their present operations.

I must be careful not to give the impression that everything in the private sector is good and everything done by government turns to dust or that government is always inefficient. The world is not that straightforward. Long queues at a bank, repeated failures to repair motor vehicles or a failure by stores to keep in stock imported goods are only a few examples of how private enterprise could improve its performance. The way in which the Bermuda Government has dealt with operations at the Bermuda Airport, the development of the insurance industry or the way in which the budget is prepared are only a few examples of how competent government is.

Nevertheless the conclusion reached by many is that government is not structured in a way to respond to the changing needs of its customers or to provide the drive and originality necessary to make the economy function more effectively.

9. HOW IMPORTANT IS EDUCATION TO THE JOB PROSPECTS FOR AN INDIVIDUAL AND TO THE BERMUDA ECONOMY?

"There is little doubt from our research that education and training are decisive in national competitive advantage. They constitute perhaps the single greatest long-term leverage point available to all levels of government in upgrading industry. The majority of students must be given the foundations that will allow them to be trained in industry or on the job. Math, computing, writing, basic sciences and languages are particularly vital. The minimum standards necessary have been rising continuously as technology advances."

PROFESSOR MICHAEL PORTER - "THE COMPETITIVE ADVANTAGE OF NATIONS."

Education provides many obvious benefits like greater enjoyment of literature, history, and culture as well as providing a greater degree of confidence in meeting life's difficulties because of the trained ability to analyse and think through problems. It has much greater utility than just being thought of as a means of improving the economy or as a passport towards achieving a high status job, as education adds immeasurably to one's enjoyment and understanding of life.

Apart from opening a window to the world, educational attainment is the most important factor in determining how much money an individual will make during a working lifetime. The data is very clear about the relationship between education levels and economic success even when adjustments are made for the fact that individuals with the best education tend to have higher IQs and more influential parents. The monetary benefits from a university or professional education

---

[13] 'The Bermuda Sun,' March 8 , 1996.

has risen sharply over the past 30 years and it is estimated in the USA that the wage or salary premium on acquiring a college education is over 65 percent. At the same time, real wages have fallen for those in unskilled manual jobs and this trend from the United States and elsewhere is becoming increasingly obvious in Bermuda. The message is unmistakably clear that the best investment anyone can ever make in his lifetime is the acquisition of a good education; it is more important than buying a house or investing in the stock market.

Access to education is the key to success in a world where well-paid jobs for those with a basic education are vanishing and being replaced by managerial and professional positions. If you are educated there is real opportunity available to you, and opportunities to achieve something, be it a high income or prestigious job, only arise if you generate opportunities for yourself. This cannot be done for you by anyone else. The challenge for Bermuda is to ensure that everyone understands that the world has changed dramatically and everyone has the opportunity to obtain the education and training they need.

If Bermuda fails to educate the one-third or so of the population at the low end of the educational tree, we are going to face considerable problems in the future. We have already seen the social problems which can arise when a large proportion of the population are effectively shut out of the international company business because their educational standards (and social skills) are not high enough.[1] No country can prosper or enjoy harmonious social relations in the future unless it invests effectively and efficiently in its young people. All of this does not mean to say that only the educated will earn high incomes, or even if you are educated you will be guaranteed a high income (there are many educated poor people) but it is the most important factor in forecasting who will earn most.

One of the major problems in acquiring an education is that you have to forego immediate pleasures. It is no fun to do homework like writing an essay on the history of Greek civilisation whilst there is a movie on television called "Showgirls." Yet giving up immediate gratification is by itself an education, something which has to be done in the real economic world as there would be, for example, no money to borrow if some people did not save i.e. forego immediate pleasure.

Combined with other variables such as experience, luck, health, choice of occupation, initiative, entrepreneurial flair and so on education accounts for between one-third and one-half of the variations in earnings across many countries, both poor and rich. Increasing the skills and capabilities of individuals is the single most important key to successful economic development. Investing in people, not surprisingly, raises living standards by providing opportunities to gain skills in areas which require high standards of basic education, it raises the productivity of the existing labour force, attracts foreign capital for further expansion and development and leads to substantially increased earning power. The importance of investing in education has led to children and young people spending longer periods of time at school in almost all countries of the world.

---

[1] Major structural changes to the Bermuda system are in the process of being implemented. It is hoped that the new system will resolve the issue of the bottom 20 percent.

General education gives young people basic skills like reading, counting and reasoning which they can later transfer to the adult world but also use as a platform to undertake further learning. It also provides an increased investment return by taking most advantage of new ideas, methods and procedures. Investments in human capital also tend to coincide with general improvements in health and nutrition both of which are important factors in raising productivity. Given these obvious advantages to an individual who takes the opportunity to obtain a sound basic education it is not surprising that world wide enrolments at all levels of education have increased fivefold.

"Improving education requires not doing new things but doing (and remembering) some good old things. Thomas Jefferson listed the requirements for a sound education in the Report of the Commissioners for the University of Virginia. In this landmark statement on education, Jefferson wrote of the importance of calculation and writing, and of reading, history, and geography. But he also emphasized the need 'to instruct the mass of our citizens in these, their rights, interests and duties as men and citizens.' Jefferson believed education should aim at the improvement of both one's morals and faculties."

William Bennett, former US Secretary for Education.

The spectacular economic growth in the Asian countries of Japan, Taiwan and South Korea dramatically emphasises the importance of human capital to the growth in living standards. Worldwide in 1960, 33 percent of the world's population was literate and this increased to just over 50 percent in 1990. So important is education and training that economists have estimated that it accounts for more than fifty percent of the wealth of industrialised countries like USA and UK. Productivity is highly dependent on it, yet national income statistics do not yet record expenditure on education and training as investment.

In many respects corporations have access to the same technology, the same information systems, the same networking systems and the same software. The only way they can gain a competitive advantage is by enabling their workforce - usually called in the annual report of companies their greatest asset - to be more innovative, more efficient, more resourceful and more flexible. This requires better training programmes and from the employees requires greater adaptability to the needs of the modern world marketplace. Hanging on to old techniques and old ways of working simply slows up the process of necessary change.

In Bermuda 30 years ago, children could and did leave school as early as 13 with only a basic elementary education and only in exceptional cases did young people go on to higher education and acquire professional status. Even in Scotland, where I was born, although education was valued, almost revered, the bulk of the population left school as I did at 15 to become unskilled office and factory fodder for an industrial age which has now almost disappeared. A large percentage of Bermudian children stay on at school beyond the compulsory legal of 16, and after 18 years many go on to further education at university, college and other training.

Bermuda's literacy level is equal to the best in the world, at around 99 percent although a disappointing number are considered functionally illiterate which places them at a severe disadvantage in the labour market. In a speech to Hamilton Lions on 6 March, 1996 the former Bermuda College public relations officer, Jan Doidge, stated that "we definitely find that schoolchildren coming to us do not have all the skills" meaning that there were severe limitations in basic knowledge of math, English and science. It has always been something of a mystery to me how children can spend about 12 years at school and yet leave to go to the Bermuda College with inadequacies in basic subjects.

Public education for the black population was seen to be the way to work their way up in the economy and society. Unfortunately, despite some innovative and necessary reforms the educational system is viewed, by many, as a major impediment to black mobility and progress. One area of concern to employers is that many children are wrongly counselled by the Department of Education and go on to sub-standard universities.

For most people capital means money in the bank, shares in large organisations like the Bank of Bermuda Limited or physical assets like office buildings or factories all of which make a return for the owner of the asset. Such tangible assets are not the only investments, or even the most important ones. An educated population which understand differential calculus, the eloquence of Shakespeare or the wonders of science is as much an asset as a building or factory.

In the 1990s we are living increasingly in an intangible economy in which the great sources of wealth are not physical like oil wells or gold mines, or factories and office buildings. Consumers have access to the quantities of food, shoes, clothing and gadgets they require. Increasingly, they want the ability to buy experience and time - the intangibles of life which are now the growth areas of the 1990s economy. Why? Because educational knowledge increases earnings of everyone over the long term, improves health and adds to commercial virtues like honesty and punctuality. They are best thought of in terms of human capital, which does not appear on the balance sheet of an organisation in the same way as furniture and fittings, but which nevertheless are key ingredients to economic success.

If am right in my assessment that there is a simple equation - education = knowledge = money = power = influence = security = status then it is remarkable how few people are prepared to seize the opportunity to enjoy that which everyone wants. It would be appropriate in this day and age for any 16 year old who is doing poorly at school, and his parents, to sign a document certifying that they understand the implications of not studying at school. Such a document could read something like this:

"I, the undersigned student, accept full responsbility for failing to study at school. I recognise that I will not have the necessary job skills to survive financially in the 21st century and that I will be a burden to my parents and fellow-Bermudians for most of my life."

10. IS ECONOMIC THEORY OF ANY ASSISTANCE IN DEALING WITH CRIME IN BERMUDA?

"The only purpose for which power can be rightfully exercised over any member of the civilised community against his will, is to prevent harm to others. His own good, either physical or moral, is not a sufficient warrant. In the part which merely concerns himself, his independence is, of right, absolute. Over himself, over his own body, and mind the individual is sovereign."

JOHN STUART MILL.

"I lost a precious son to street heroin in 1993. Since that awful night I have been reading all I can about the 'drug problem'. I have come to the conclusion that my son died because drug-prohibition laws made it impossible for him to know the quality and potency of the heroin he ingested."

LETTER TO THE EDITOR OF 'THE ECONOMIST MAGAZINE,' 11 FEBRUARY, 1995.

One of the major selling points to potential tourists to Bermuda is that of safety and that levels of crime are very low. In a 1996 Hilton International Survey 47 percent of American travellers put safety and security as their greatest concern when travelling abroad. By international comparison crime levels in Bermuda are ludicrously low but a worrying trend over the past ten years or so is that not only are crime levels in Bermuda increasing,[1] but also the nature of crime has changed from innocuous crimes against property, like petty theft, to more vicious crimes like serious assault, robbery, handbag snatching and burglary. The fear of crime and its economic consequences have grown dramatically in recent years and for a tourist resort this fear is a real one as the following table showing crime figures shows:

BERMUDA'S SERIOUS-CRIME FIGURES

CRIME	1984	1985	1986	1987	1988	1989	1990	1991	1992	1993	1994	1995
Murder	0	2	2	2	6	3	1	3	2	3	6	3
Attempted Murder	4	3	5	3	4	2	1	2	2	5	2	5
Serious Assaults	234	233	227	204	262	310	358	323	349	307	364	347
Rape	9	8	13	14	10	20	16	16	16	18	21	10
Robbery	34	11	33	33	11	26	49	41	54	60	95	90
Firearm Offences	20	14	17	22	27	10	22	7	9	17	28	8
Home Breakings	779	638	452	520	567	692	644	870	754	877	1,151	902
Business Breakings	385	277	326	300	269	275	369	387	389	387	675	454
Handbag Snatches	34	29	37	47	46	37	17	60	30	20	83	48
Bikes Stolen	1,818	1,214	1,161	1,164	1,466	1,380	1,334	1,255	1,168	1,284	2,536	1,910

(Source: Bermuda Police Annual Reports)

---

[1] Although in 1996 with the appointment of two new senior officers crime has shown a welcome drop. Total offences in 1994 were 8,409 and in 1995 dropped to 7,143.

Crime would not normally feature in a book about the economy but increasingly economists are examining crime policy and applying economic techniques in an effort to reduce the frightening increase in crime in countries like USA. This is not an easy process as economists are used to explaining human behaviour by reference to such objective matters as rational behaviour, prices and incomes and they are ill at ease when prescribing remedies for criminal behaviour which are commonly[2] thought to be caused by social and psychological factors. It should also be noted that crime is big business. The London 'Sunday Telegraph' reports[3] that according to experts at the United Nations crime represents about 4 percent of the world economy - about twice as much as the global oil business.

Bermuda has two major advantages over many other countries when it comes to containing the criminal explosion. Firstly, it has wisely enforced a ban on firearms, including imitations, which takes away one of the criminal's major tools and severely reduces its violent impact on the public. Secondly, it is a small community where people have many relatives, almost an extended family, and tend to know their neighbours well. This makes for greater social cohesion unlikely to be found in large cities in other countries. The problem is therefore much more manageable than elsewhere and accounts in large measure for Bermuda's reputation for being a safe destination at least until recently.

Drugs are seen as a major factor in the increase in levels of crime over the past thirty years. The laws of Bermuda on drug use are very similar to those which exist in the USA and Canada and many of the same social factors at play in those countries are also applicable to Bermuda. Increasingly, young people are attracted to trafficking in drugs as the profits to be earned in importing and selling drugs can be enormous. So great is this scourge that many countries have sold out to drug cartels.[4] The influential Washington Post reported[5] that drug traffickers have infiltrated the highest levels of society and government institutions in Antigua, Barbuda, Trinidad, Aruba, Jamaica and the Dominican Republic and that about 150 metric tons of cocaine go to the United States from the East Caribbean each year. The amount of money to be made from drugs has corrupted many of those societies to the point that impartial and legitimate government is in peril.

The impact of drugs on the black community is especially severe and the widespread use of illegal drugs has contributed markedly to the high incidence of AIDS in Bermuda. As in the United States the numbers of dealers or pushers has increased and gangs violently compete for market share. The profits can be enormous and provides an incentive to recruit younger and younger users.

The laws of economics whilst not well understood in an academic way are extremely well understood by criminals when it comes to the profits which can be made from the drug trade. Drugs are one of the largest multinational enterprises in the world. In Bermuda cocaine and marijuana for example are roughly four times the cost of similar narcotics in New York. They are imported by pseu-

---

[2] Mistakenly in my opinion.

[3] November 17, 1996.

[4] Bermuda has not sunk to the level of many small West Indian Islands like St. Kitts as reported in 'Time' Magazine February 26, 1996.

[5] September 23, 1996.

do tourists and professional couriers, through cruise ships or simply hidden away in legitimate cargo imports. The police in Bermuda, as well as the professional counsellors have been unable to make much of an impact on the problem.

It is estimated that roughly 60 percent of the crimes against property are drug related. One of the remedies economics can propose is that of legalisation[6], which largely takes out the super profits to be earned in the trade[7], but that option has been ruled out on moral grounds on many occasions by the authorities in Bermuda. In any case, legalisation of drugs would be impossible for Bermuda unless legalisation was also enacted in the United States - otherwise every pot-head and his mother would swell the tourist numbers. If the United States unilaterally legalised drugs Bermuda would have little alternative but to comply.[8] It is therefore difficult not to conclude, that as far as drugs are concerned, Bermuda is unable to take any major steps on its own to alleviate the problem. Drug use along with its glamourisation and violence in films on TV are some of the most pernicious cultural exports of the United States.

One factor usually put forward by the caring professions and politicians is that crime is caused by poverty and hence by society. However, in Bermuda per capita incomes have gone up by a factor of about four since the 1960s when crime was modest and as a consequence if that theory had any validity there should have been a reduction in crime. Although the facts are in contradiction to this theory the caring professions have never been a group to let facts get in the way of a great theory. Poverty has never really been a major factor in Bermuda, at least not since the Second World War, but that fact is blithely ignored by those who support the poverty cause of crime.

The opposite view to that of the caring professions is that criminals should be locked up in prison and given harsh treatment. Prison is unlikely to make a bad citizen a good one, and indeed there is a considerable body of evidence that the professional law-breaker comes out of prison more proficient at his trade than when he went in. Prison is frequently seen as a mechanism for the public showing its disapproval and seeking revenge rather than as a mechanism of deterrence.

Professor Gary Becker a quarter of a century ago put forward the proposition that criminals are rational individuals who act in their own self interest, pretty much like the rest of us in other occupations. When they decide to commit a crime they instinctively weigh up the costs and benefits. In this decision there are two factors.

Firstly, there is what is known as opportunity cost, that is the alternative income given up by devoting time and effort to crime. This factor is not usually an important consideration as most criminals are not well educated and sophisticated concepts like opportunity cost are unlikely to cross their mind. In addition, they are not highly skilled so that the legal alternatives for earning money like driving a bus or waiting at tables are not sufficiently highly paid to appeal to them.

---

[6] A position advocated for some years by "The Economist" and Professor Milton Friedman.
[7] Especially is supplying drugs to minors.
[8] Perhaps another example of Bermuda's limited economic independence.

The second, and by far the most important cost, is the cost of being caught and convicted, the social stigma of being regarded as a criminal, and of the unpleasantness of spending time in prison. Prison in Bermuda used to be called "Casemates" which was the name of an sinister looking building, (resembling Dracula's castle) and to which was attached a highly negative image. In 1994 a new prison was built to house prisoners and later called not "Casemates" but "Westgate Correctional Facility" a euphemism for prison which tends to take away much of the social stigma of incarceration. Many economists would argue that if the chances of being apprehended and convicted in the courts are not high[9], a rational criminal quickly understands that the costs of being a professional criminal are also not high.[10] On the other hand, the revenue benefits from crime are high so instead of waiting on tables a reasonably competent criminal could make a much better living robbing potential diners. The costs of crime in Bermuda for the criminal have been reduced considerably. Apprehension, conviction rates, the unpleasantness of prison and social criticism of criminals are all down, which as a consequence brings forth an increase in crime. What is surprising is that many people are surprised by the consequences of our criminal justice policies for the past few years.

There is always considerable debate within the political system to determine what are the "root causes" of crime as if it were possible to gain an insight into the criminal mind which would then permit government to implement the necessary benign social and criminal policies necessary to reduce the rate. Too often such policies are judged by the intentions of those who propose and promote them and not by the actual results and consequences for society of such policies. The road to hell is paved with good intentions as Charles Dickens noted over one hundred years ago. There are, as best I can determine, no root causes of crime only the rational economic decision of an individual that the rate of pay for being a criminal is better than working for living as a waiter or labourer. The sad fact is that in making this judgement the criminal is acting more rationally and logically than those in authority.

Crime is not only a social offence in Bermuda but it has the potential to threaten in a direct way the livelihood of many of those dependent on the tourist industry.[11] Rarely is street and violent crime viewed as an act of economic sabotage similar to insurance fraud. For a country highly dependent on safety as a selling point the government has been notoriously slow at recognising the threat to our economic well-being. The unimaginative way of concentrating punishment on fines, probation and prison has not worked effectively; a more innovative approach to dealing with the problem would help to alleviate the situation.[12]

Crime is largely the prerogative of the young male, aged between say 16 and 28, although there are many criminally inclined males who fall outside this arbitrary boundary. Nature blundered badly when she designed the young male in that they are not particularly attracted to the middle class, highly disciplined and intellectual type occupations which increasingly are the source of Bermuda's pros-

---

[9] An incompetent or lazy police force is the best recruiting sergeant for crime.

[10] Of the 7,143 offences in 1995, 2,181 were cleaned up - a success rate of 31%. In 1994 the success rate was 33%.

[11] So does the marked deterioration in driving standards.

[12] Such as tagging offenders to restrict their freedom without the necessity of prison.

perity. Being on time, dressing in a conservative manner, paying respect to one's elders, acknowledging the importance of tradition and applying rigorous standards of intellect to such matters as accounting, computer programming or investment procedures is not a process which comes naturally or easily to the young male. Male traits of hyperactivity, shows of physical strength and aggressiveness are useful qualities during war or when hunting wild animals required for food. Modern technology, communications and the white collar industries have little need for a strong back, physical power or a sensitive male ego. The great irony for the young male is that the qualities which give him respect from his peers are the very qualities which make him so useless to the modern Bermuda economy.

The qualities required for success in Bermuda's economy are those which require careful nurturing from an early age and to which great care and attention needs to be paid. Such qualities used to be called character and they tend to be rigid, hedged with moral warnings, surrounded with old fashioned virtues such as sportsmanship, initiative, intellectual curiosity, concern for others, good table manners and etiquette and most important of all require an almost unquestioning obedience to authority and to established precedents.[13] In many ways crime is a moral problem because individuals make wrong moral decisions although they make correct and logical decisions (low chances of being caught, and high rewards). The answer is only that of morality by making the wrongdoer understand the merits of a more responsible lifestyle. Economics has few moral lessons to teach in this respect.

Unfortunately no one has the answer to the problem which is to bring a minority of young males[14], especially young black males within the rubric of the modern economy and to produce more employable and socially conditioned individuals. Crime appears to be one of the few options available to young males who have been unable to gain widespread respect and understanding or find an important role in society other than that of juvenile career criminals. This is a struggle between reason and passion, between long term aspirations requiring hard work and study and immediate gratification, between now and later, between the long view which requires the deferring of appetites and short term which sees next week as too far into the future for which to make plans.

The financial costs of the high crime society are enormous The prison service costs $12.2 million according to the 1996/1997 budget which means that the cost of maintaining a prisoner behind bars is BD$42,361 per annum[15], but that is only part of the costs of crime. The cost of the police force for the same year is about $30 million. At least 20% of the Health and Social Services budget (excluding prisons) of $80 million is applicable to crime. Almost $4 million worth of property was stolen in 1995.[16] In addition there are almost the same number of private security guards as police to help businesses avoid the immediate consequences of crimes.

---

[13] One reason why sport is a good builder of character.

[14] Except to lament that parents are unable to bring up children effectively because both parents are working, or that there are an alarming number of one parent homes.

[15] based on 288 prisoners (male and female, young and old) at 31 December 1995

[16] 1995 Police Report, page 54.

The financial overhead of crime is horrendous as the following rough calculation shows:-

		$M
1)	Prison costs	12.2
2)	Police costs	30.0
3)	Share of Department of Social Services costs	16.0
4)	Private costs of security (50% of police)	15.0
5)	Property stolen	4.0
TOTAL		$77.2 million

This translates into BD$1,290 per annum for each person in Bermuda or more than $5,000 per family of four. An incredible waste of money.

Whilst by comparison with other countries Bermuda has a negligible crime problem, compared with what the position was say 30 years ago we have created a police state but the opposite of what the politicians in Parliament believe to be a police state. Increasingly, the law abiding population, especially the old and infirm are imprisoned in their own homes, often afraid to go out in the evening, spending large sums on burglar alarm systems and paying higher insurance premiums on their property.[17] Probably most important of all, the reputation Bermuda rightly established in the tourist business for being a safe friendly place is gradually being eroded which in the increasingly competitive tourist business puts Bermuda at a relative disadvantage.

11. HOW IS INCOME REDISTRIBUTED IN BERMUDA?

"When someone has something to distribute, he rarely forgets himself."
LEON TROTSKY.

"No society can surely be flourishing and happy of which by far the greater part of the numbers are poor and miserable."
ADAM SMITH - "THE WEALTH OF NATIONS."

The Bermuda Government has never given the redistribution of income a high priority in its budgets or policies, largely I suspect because the redistribution of income is very much associated with the introduction of income tax. Policies to create wealth have rightly been more important than policies to redistribute it recognising that what people earn roughly measures what they put into society.

In other parts of the world one of the main objectives of government is to redistribute income from the high income and wealthy towards the low earner or those who may be disadvantaged in some way through no fault of their own, or

---

[17] Not included in the above costs.

to those who are unemployed. In USA and UK recent governments have begun to question the effectiveness of such policies, one economist in the USA noting that "in spite of massive increases in federal government taxes and spending, we are about as unequal in 1988 as we were in 1950."[1] However, there are redistribution policies in place in Bermuda not all of which arise through the tax system.

With regard to the tax system it is generally agreed that where the main sources of revenue arise from expenditure taxes the system is regressive in that the poor pay a greater proportion of their income in tax than the wealthy.[2] Nevertheless certain taxes like land tax, a tax on the value of property, is heavily weighted towards those with more modest accommodation like the poor. For example, in Bermuda a residence with an assessed annual rental value (ARV) of $29,000 will pay tax at the rate of 27% whilst one with an ARV of $14,000 will pay tax at the lower rate of 5.3%. This however is offset by the payroll tax where someone earning over $100,000 will pay the same rate as someone earning $30,000 provided the employer is prepared to tax all employees in the organisation at an assumed rate of $66,000.

Income is also redistributed on the basis of age. Most Bermudians, irrespective of income, receive at the age of 65 a social security payment from the government of BD$750 per month, although there may be in the future some question about the long term viability of the Central Pension Fund.[3]

In addition, there are benefits for senior citizens of subsidised bus fares and most important of all subsidised medical care at the hospital where government pays about 80% of the cost of treatment for those over 65. The assumption is that the elderly are poorer than the general population because many of them are retired. This assumption may well be wrong, as many of those over 65 in other countries are generally more wealthy than the working population. In addition, they tend to be more assiduous about registering to vote and exercise the ballot more frequently than the active population, hence the desire on the part of the politicians to ensure that they are not forgotten.

The poor tend to be greater users of various government services such as counselling, various health and welfare programmes and perhaps most of all education - mainly because the wealthy middle class has lost confidence in the policies of the Department of Education and can afford to pay private school fees.

A less obvious way of redistributing income arises from legal restraints and government regulation. For example, when the interest rate ceiling was in force prior to 1993 it was calculated by the government economist in 1991 that this law created windfall profits to the three Bermuda banks of BD$37 million at the expense of local depositors (the widow who keeps a savings account).

Restrictions on the foreign ownership of Bermuda companies[4] shield Bermudian businesses from competitive forces. The result is that consumers invariably have to pay more for goods and services than would be the case if there was international competitive pressures. More often than not, protectionist mea-

---

[1] see "Starting even : An Equal Opportunity Program to Combat the Nation's New Poverty" by Robert Haveman.

[2] see Part III 14 on the subject of income tax.

[3] See Part III 20

[4] But obviously not Exempt Companies

sures redistribute income away from the average consumer (the poor) to those who own businesses (the rich) whilst, at the same time, harming economic efficiency into the bargain. That is why economists of whatever political persuasion tend to be free traders in recognition of the fact that protectionism is a conspiracy of a few against the many - a conspiracy theory which the PLP has yet to discover.

An even less obvious way of redistributing income in favour of the rich is the government confidence trick of inflation.[5] Inflationary policies invariably benefit the powerful, who tend to be wealthy, who can protect their assets against the depreciation of the purchasing power of the currency. The poor and the elderly tend to hold their modest assets in cash, or in savings or deposit accounts which pay a rate of interest much lower than the rate of inflation. Inflation is the pestilence of the middle classes. It is somethings which threatens anyone who works hard, who plans, who saves to invest or who is prudent. To pay debts on time is foolish, to borrow and spend as fast as possible is prudence. It has been said of inflation that it is the cruellest tax of all.

Finally, government programmes which allegedly bring financial and other benefits to the poor are generally poorly run. The evidence from abroad is compelling and Bermuda is undoubtedly little different although there have been no studies of which I am aware to determine their effectiveness. The major beneficiaries of such programmes are not the poor and afflicted but the administrators who recognise that when the poor are studied and administered they have literally discovered a money machine.

The caring professions have played on the guilt of society as an excuse to increase government programmes which coincidentally increases the number of job opportunities for themselves. As Thomas Sowell, the economist has said *"To be blunt the poor are a gold mine. By the time they are studied, advised, experimented with and administered to, the poor have helped many a middle-class liberal to attain affluence with government money."* Statements like this promote heretical thoughts that perhaps the greatest redistribution of wealth in Bermuda is from the general taxpayer (who may or may not be poor) to the civil service which is protected from many of the uncertainties of this world by job security and subsidised pensions.[6]

Bermuda is very much like other parts of the world in that income redistribution through government policies, legislation or regulation does not take place from the rich to the poor, but from the poor to the rich. Government economic policy tends to take money from the ill-informed or unorganised , mainly the general taxpayer, and transfer wealth, benefits and jobs to highly organised interest groups such as the "caring professions" or the retired. The most important factor in determining the redistribution of income is not need but organised political power.

[5] see Part III 12 on the subject of inflation

[6] See Part III 7 on the share of GDP taken by government in taxes

12. WHAT HAPPENED TO INFLATION?

"There is no subtler, no surer means of overturning the existing basis of society than to debauch the currency. The process engages all the hidden forces of economic law on the side of destruction, and does it in a manner which not one man in a million is able to diagnose."

JOHN MAYNARD KEYNES (1920)

Prior to 1914, it was the norm for prices to be stable, rising slightly in good years falling back in bad years, for interest rates to cluster around 3 percent, house prices and rents to be fixed in price with the main interest in the price of goods being centred on whether or not there had been a good harvest that year.

Any Bermudian whose adult life spans the years after 1945 has lived in a very different world. Since 1945 prices have risen steadily, and have sprinted since about 1968, although they have levelled off in the past three years or so. For most adults continually rising prices (and constantly rising property prices) has been their life experience and, as is common in human nature, there is a wide-spread belief that this will continue be the case in the future. Just as many middle-aged people in the 1960s believed that the world would be very much as it was in the 1930s, 1940s and 1950s. They were wrong of course and it may be that those who have lived through the inflationary era may be just as wrong about the future.

Inflation arises when there is a continuous increase in the general (not just specific goods) price level which means that there is a corresponding fall in the value of money. Inflation, at least until recently, was the economic equivalent of multiple sclerosis, a wasting away of the vital sinews of the economy. From the mid 1960s through to the early 1990s the value of money continuously fell which meant that using money to measure the value of goods and services was like using a piece of elastic to measure a piece of wood.

Inflation arises essentially from the activities of Central Bankers - the Federal Reserve and the Bank of England being the best known - in providing more money to the economy that can be used productively whilst maintaining a stable price level. Milton Friedman, the Nobel Prize winner in economics, and the man most responsible for the current diagnosis of the causes of inflation has stated in unequivocal terms *"Inflation is always and everywhere a monetary phenomenon."* In the United States (and because Bermuda is essentially a part of the United States for financial purposes[1]) this is the work of the Federal Reserve System who from the mid 1960s at the request of President Johnson, who was fighting the Vietnam War, pumped more money into the economy than the system could productively use. The quantity of TV sets, cars, clothing and other goods and services produced could not be increased at the same rate as the supply of money and the result was that the world suffered from inflation for a period of just under thirty years. This is simply a complicated way of saying that there was too much money chasing too few goods - the definition of inflation which has stood the test of time.

---

[1] See Part II 1 on the importance of the United States to Bermudian economy.

Most people who have vivid memories of the 1970s and 1980s came to believe that it is normal behaviour for prices to increase each and every year, indeed many are having difficulty adjusting to the fact that this may now no longer be the case. For example, a house may not be an investment which grows in value each year but simply a place in which to live. Employees can no longer expect regular annual wage increases. This results in the general public suffering from what is called the "money illusion" as stable prices may make them believe they are worse off . This is true for the rich as when inflation subsides there is no longer subsidisation of the rich by the poor

In the 25 year period prior to 1992, money lost its value as goods such as real estate which is relatively fixed, particularly in a small place like Bermuda, rose in price. This was something of an illusion because in many cases the value of property was not rising - it was the value of money which was falling. There were many losers and gainers in this process. I was one of the beneficiaries as, like many people my age, I was able to borrow almost one hundred percent of the buying price of my house in 1972 which was a time when prices were increasing at about 10 percent per year. The money cost of my mortgage went down as the value of money fell by 10 percent, and the money price (but not necessarily the real price) of my house went up. At the same time, being in a secure job I received cost of living increases to my salary to compensate for the fall in the value of money. Many of us in that happy combination of circumstances, believed that we were very smart but the truth was that we were lucky in that we were able to convert a set of circumstances which were basically unfair to others in society into an opportunity to grow more wealthy.

This was achieved at the expense of those who were on fixed incomes, those whose salaries did not increase as fast as the increase in the cost of living, those who could not borrow from the bank because they did not have a secure job or did not understand the confidence trick governments were playing on them and those too old to continue playing the economic game. It was a period when wealth was redistributed from the poor to the rich.

The Bermuda Government was very much a passive player in all of this, as Bermuda was too small to have any effect on what was happening in the United States and elsewhere. The only serious error made by the Bermuda Government was to maintain the interest rate ceiling at seven percent - later increased to nine percent - when inflation was running at between ten and seventeen percent. This was a subsidy to the rich and powerful and was paid for by those who could only save by keeping their money in institutions like a savings banks. There was a massive redistribution of wealth from the poor to the rich which ironically was supported by the PLP whose constituency was the poor. However, much of this is history and not all that relevant to the present.

What is of importance to the present is that inflation has been recognised as a monetary phenomenon - thanks largely to President Reagan and Prime Minister Thatcher - although the Germans and the Swiss had known this for many years and had acted accordingly. This was one of the major reasons why the German Mark and the Swiss Franc appreciated so much against the U.S. dollar and

Sterling. What happened to inflation was that the British and American governments under new leadership understood the mistakes which their predecessors had made from the 1960s to the 1980s and pursued policies to correct them. This belated understanding by politicians when combined with greater competitive forces both at home and abroad, globalisation of the economy, weaker trade unions and improved technology has made it much more difficult for producers to generate price increases. Bermuda being small is simply reflecting economic decisions which have been made elsewhere. People like me will no longer be subsidised by the poor.

Many commentators believe that inflation has disappeared forever[2] but the financial markets, particularly the bond markets who reflect the collective views of millions of investors hate inflation with a passion, are not so certain as any news which indicates a general increase in the price level results in the financial markets taking a beating. At the end of 1996, the Boskin Commission in the United States reported that the rate of inflation had been overstated by about one percent because insufficient allowance had been made for such things as improvements in the quality of products or the ability of consumers to buy at discount stores. In addition, governments are still able to create money through the banking system and the belief that inflation has ended depends very much on the extent to which you are prepared to accept the promises of politicians. The death of inflation may be as premature as the famous premature death of Mark Twain.

13. WHAT IS THE NATIONAL DEBT?

"The financing of current government spending by debt is equivalent to an 'eating up' of our national capital value. By financing current public outlay by debt, we are, in effect, chopping up the apple trees for firewood, thereby reducing the yield of the orchard forever."

JAMES BUCHANAN (NOBEL PRIZE WINNER IN ECONOMICS IN 1986)

In "Hamlet" by William Shakespeare there is a warning that one should *"neither a borrower nor a lender be"* although most people, including governments, don't pay much attention to that injunction. Over the past 20 years or so the national debt of governments as diverse as Belgium and Brazil has soared - I doubt if Brazil has a good handle on the size of its national debt. As with any binge, the day after is the moment when people make a resolution not to sin again and the same sorts of arguments are used by repentant politicians and applied to the national debt.

In the United States the President and the Congress have been embroiled in a battle for many years to try and reduce (note not to eliminate) the size of the debt which President Eisenhower in the 1950s described as "our children's inherited mortgage." In the European Union one of the long term objectives is to have a

---

[2] See "The Death of Inflation" 1996 by Roger Bootle.

common currency and in order to the join the monetary union it was agreed some time ago that the National Debt should not exceed 60 percent of GDP and annual budget deficits not to exceed 3 percent of GDP[1].

Net Public Debt as a % of 1995 GPD	
Belgium	130
Italy	110
Canada	70
U.S.A.	50
Germany	45
U.K.	35
France	30
Japan	10
Bermuda	10[2]

Government debts impose heavy burdens on an economy long after the reasons why the debt was incurred in the first place have been forgotten. The main burden clearly is the interest which has to be paid on the debt which requires that taxes have to be increased over and above that which is necessary just to finance day to day expenditure. Higher taxes are usually unpopular[3] but they can also reduce incentives to work - after all why work and pay more taxes when you can have the day off? Taxes can also distort the market economy leading to a degree of inefficiency. There is also the future pain when principal repayments have to be made. Indeed so great is the pain that governments rarely get round to paying off the principal preferring for future administrations to handle the problem or using inflation to reduce the real amount which has to be paid back. In addition, if governments are major borrowers on the capital market they may "crowd-out" more productive private investment as has happened in the USA although this is not really an issue for the Bermuda Government. Another major argument against borrowing is that government borrowing tends to stoke the fires of inflation, although this can benefit the government by reducing the real burden of the debt.

The strong argument for the national debt is that often governments have reasonably compelling reasons for spending money which is the nature of an investment and in the future it may provide a return to the community so increasing wealth. Education is usually cited as a good example of this. At times incurring a national debt can be of major benefit to the community as for example when the British national debt during the Second World War was more than twice as much as the GDP. A strict adherence to the principle of not incurring debt would probably have led to defeat which would have been a worse fate for the unborn than having a generation or so later having to pay for the debts incurred by their parents and grandparents.

---

[1] Bermuda is one of the few countries in the world which would qualify to join the common currency, mainly because it is soundly managed.
[2] Excluding pensions.
[3] See Part III 6 and 7 which deal with the budget.

Bermuda has been a country which has incurred very little in the way of a national debt and for many years it had a highly commendable policy of balancing the budget (compared with the USA which has had only one balanced budget in the past 30 years) and mainly for this reason Bermuda was given an AA rating - a mark of sound financial probity. If however one looks at the statistics for the period between 1990 and fiscal 1997 the picture in Bermuda is not quite as rosy.

Debt outstanding has increased from zero to around $180 million or just under 10% of GDP, and this does not take into consideration the deficit on the Public Service Pension Fund[4] or the unfunded promises made on social security.

Spending is easy, getting income is difficult. A simple way to overcome this gap is to borrow, and if the Bermuda Government borrowed mainly from other Bermudians the national debt would be, in effect, some Bermudians lending to all Bermudians as represented by the Government. Most of our borrowing comes from foreign sources so we are in effect increasing our present living standards at the expense of the future when the amounts due have to be paid.

If the borrowing was used for productive purposes which could be measured, a reasonably strong case could be made for borrowing. In many cases borrowing is used for productive purposes, improving roads or widening educational opportunities for example. Indeed public investment may well yield a higher return than some private investment decisions. Spending on increased salaries for civil servants, or for visits by Department of Education officers to New Zealand should not be considered productive uses of resources. When we borrow for purposes which either allow us to catch up with what we should have spent on community projects in the past, or such projects that do not lead to increased economic growth we are borrowing from the future to finance the present. I would not describe this as a sensible economic decision. Moreover, when the economy was strong in the 1980s we should have run a budget surplus to offset periods when business is weak - as it is in 1996.

This failure to take advantage of the good times is compounded by the fact that in the forseeable future, within the next 20 years, many of the people born in the baby boom will be retiring and this will place an added burden on our children and grandchildren. If there is no major change to our productivity, the rising dependency ratios as the population ages (with its increasing costs of pensions and health care to the growing elderly population) may threaten to push government deficits to unmanageable proportions. What is likely to happen is that a combination of bigger deficits, increased taxation or a reduction in benefit to those who retire will be necessary neither of which will be popular with the taxpayer.

The unfortunate thing about government deficits is that government has the power to tax and therefore by coercion obtain the funds it wishes from taxpayers. Individuals can only spend what they earn or borrow. If they do not earn sufficient money or cannot borrow because they are a credit risk they have to work harder or reduce their expenditure accordingly. Such constraints do not apply to government to the same extent and hence benefits which go to the present generation will be paid for by future generations. The key issue on the national debt is not so

---

[4] See "will I collect my pension" Part III 20.

much its absolute size, although that is important, it is the use to which the money is put after it is borrowed. If future generations of Bermudians are much richer than the present generation the current level of debt may be trivial. If on the other hand they are poorer the sins of the father will truly be visited on his children.

Creating a national debt is rarely a good policy, except in times of dire emergency. It is not recommended for Bermuda.

14. SHOULD BERMUDA LEVY INCOME TAX?

"From each according to his abilities, to each according to his needs."

KARL MARX.

"It is fairer to tax people on what they extract from the economy, as roughly measured by their consumption, than to tax them on what they produce for the economy, as roughly measured by their income."

THOMAS HOBBES.

It is remarkable how few people would disagree with the above quotation from Marx but it is equally remarkable how few people disagree with the commonplace observation that income tax - which is the way of putting the quoted principle into effect - is one of the most hated instruments of modern government. There are not many people I know who have ever lived under a system of government which levies income tax who would wish to return to it. They much prefer a system where "from each according to his abilities, to each according to his needs" is replaced by "from each according to his abilities, to each according to his work and productivity."

Contrary to what many people think, income tax is neither efficient nor equitable. It imposes penal rates on the most productive people in the economy and is a unique combination of severity and inefficiency. In countries where doing things and creating jobs is punished with penal tax rates, and where just registering as poor is rewarded with generous benefits it is not surprising that very little is accomplished.

Bermuda is a beneficiary of the foolishness of foreign governments who imposed high direct taxation, as wealthy people tend to shelter their assets and income in stable off-shore countries like Bermuda. One of the most flourishing industries in the United States and Britain is tax avoidance (which should be distinguished from tax evasion which is illegal) which employs armies of accountants and lawyers (one reason for there being so many lawyers and accountants in Bermuda) who battle it out with an equally large army of tax collectors who try and enforce unpopular and economically distorting tax laws. Bermudians are very fortunate to have never experienced income tax although there are many who believe that the current employment tax is a very close cousin.

Income tax is the most notoriously complex tax ever devised by man, producing a million reasons for dispute and disagreement with government tax departments. Experience from the United States and the United Kingdom suggests that it is impossible to devise an income tax which can meet the conflicting objectives of being simple and fair. The complexity which surrounds income tax prevents it from being a mechanism for fiscal fairness as is often claimed by its proponents.

Income tax was first used in Britain as far back as 1435, but its founder is popularly believed to be William Pitt the Younger who imposed it in 1799 as a temporary measure to pay for the Napoleonic wars. It was levied at 10 percent on incomes over 200 pounds and was dropped in 1815 when the wars ended. It was revived by Robert Peel (who also introduced the concept of regular policing) in 1842, again as a temporary expedient, to pay for the abolition of import duties and since then has been a permanent feature of the British tax system.

In the United States it was used to finance the Civil War (it is amazing how close the connection between wars and taxation is) and was abandoned in 1872. An attempt to introduce it again in 1894 was unsuccessful when the Supreme Court declared it unconstitutional. The 16th Amendment to the U.S. Constitution was approved in 1913 and since then income tax has been a permanent part of the American tax system. It is now so complex that no individual can possibly know what it means and it is estimated that one-third of the inquiries made to the Internal Revenue Service 800 help-line are answered incorrectly.[1] This is one reason why the great Chancellor of Prussia, Otto von Bismarck, is reputed to have said that the two things you don't wish to see being made are tax laws and sausages. The tax laws of most countries can reasonably be described as legislative sausages. It is therefore fiscally ironic that the United States, a nation born because of a revolution against unfair taxation by the British, should now join Britain in implementing income tax thereby guaranteeing the prosperity of three of the few remaining British colonies, Bermuda, Cayman and Gibraltar. Patrick Henry, the author of the cry "no taxation without representation" must be turning in his grave.

In all countries income tax tends to be levied on all wages and salaries above a certain level and incomes from dividends, property and businesses. Until the beginning of the Second World War tax reliefs - such as the payment of mortgage interest - were few and tax rates were low by today's standards. Today very few people are exempt from its influences which is the main reason for income tax being unpopular and hence the fleeting popularity of the flat tax movements spearhead by Malcolm Forbes in the 1996 U.S. presidential election.

Income tax is also regarded as being economically inefficient, as an individual who enjoys his wealth privately by spending it on yachts or works of art pays little or no tax but anyone who puts his wealth to work by investing in industry or creating jobs is penalised. Probably the most economically efficient tax system is one which is based on expenditure and where savings are exempt - a system not all that dissimilar from that in Bermuda. In foreign countries the real burden of income and related taxes tends to fall most heavily on those with the least political power as rich individuals avoid payment either through the use of their political power (even in socialist regimes wealth tends to translate to political power) or by utilising offshore financial centres like Bermuda and the Cayman Islands.

---

[1] See "American Taxation" in the May/June 1996 issue of 'American Heritage.'

If income tax is effective in obtaining revenue from a reluctant public there invariably arises a degree of unfairness and within a short space of time a huge industry of tax avoidance is spawned. In fact, the whole concept of offshore islands like Bermuda playing a prominent role in international business originally arises from the actions taken by individuals and corporations in high tax areas taking steps to avoid paying levels of taxation (in the 1970s in the United Kingdom it reached the preposterous heights of 98 percent of income) a level which would make the average Bermudian have nightmares.

The subject of income tax in other countries is one which raises the blood pressure of the average taxpayer and it is usually a central theme in any election. The 1996 Presidential election in the United States was fought against a backdrop of major reform of the present tax structure with radical proposals (at least within the United States) being made for a flat income tax of around 18 percent.

That being said however there is a logical case for stating that income tax is simply a method of raising revenue for government and whether it is appropriate for a country depends very much on the social and economic structure, the nature of its industries, the sophistication of the taxpayer, the administrative structure and the general acceptance by the electorate. In 1971 the Bermuda Government requested an eminent tax lawyer, W.A. MacDonald Q.C.,[2] from Canada to examine the tax structure of Bermuda and his report in 1973 did not recommend the creation of income tax structure for a small community like Bermuda whose economy was heavily influenced by external events particularly those in the United States.

Many of his arguments for rejecting income tax are still very relevant more than twenty years later.

1. Bermuda has a legal, accounting and banking community which is fully conversant with the latest developments in tax avoidance and knows many of its most accomplished practitioners - this is one reason why international business has flourished in Bermuda in recent years - and this community would be able to put into practice tax avoidance mechanisms which would make the imposition of income tax ineffectual. Or it would be borne disproportionately by those unable to pay the fees of expensive lawyers and accountants. There would, perversely, be a real risk that the Bermudian poor would effectively subsidise the Bermudian rich who would be able to avoid paying their fair share of taxes.

2. More than fifty percent of Bermuda's economy is dependent on international business corporations, many of whom have been attracted to Bermuda because of its low personal and corporate taxation.[3] The imposition of income and related taxes would discourage future business and would almost certainly lead to many existing organisations leaving Bermuda for more attractive jurisdictions like Cayman.[4]

3. Many businesses like tour operators, taxi drivers, or handymen do not keep records of the quality required by income tax authorities. Indeed apart from

---

[2] Report on Tax and Fee Structure of Bermuda, 1973.

[3] But increasing - it is now 25% of GDP.

[4] It would also be a breach of the undertaking given by government under the provisions of The Exempted Undertakings Tax Protection Act, 1966.

a bank statement many businesses have no records at all except for a few invoices and receipts kept in a shoe box. The introduction of income tax would require a cultural leap which many small businessmen would be unable or unwilling to make. Maintenance of complex records and accounts would almost certainly put many of them out of business as professional accountants are expensive employees. This would be inconsistent with the government policy of encouraging the development of small business.

4.   Many employees are dependent on such things as tips, work in tourist related businesses is seasonal and the absence of documentation for small businesses would make it easy for many to evade income taxes. The success of income tax collection is highly dependent on having large numbers of employees in regular, well documented and white collar environments - conditions which apply to only about 60 percent of Bermuda's working population.

5.   The costs of establishing a sophisticated tax department within government would be high and would require staff of the calibre of the best tax accountants and lawyers. This would be very expensive and the costs involved may not be worth the cost of collecting the additional revenue. It may even be a task well beyond the resources of any government department no matter how dedicated or efficient. An anonymous citizen of Lagash, a city state which existed about 6,000 years ago in what is now Iraq is reported to have said, *"You can have a lord, you can have a king, but the man to fear is the tax collector."*

6.   Income taxes tend to be paid by the middle classes because the rich can avoid them, and the poor are unable to earn sufficient to pay them. Soaking the rich has never appealed to Bermudians who are mainly middle class, in part because he hopes to be rich himself, and in part because he understands that when the rich get soaked, the middle class gets drenched. Experience from elsewhere suggests that this has a negative impact on the desire to work and to improving productivity the basis on which growing prosperity depends. Taxpayers make rational choices to benefit themselves and those choices are strongly affected by the economic incentives (or disincentives like income tax) they face. Income taxes reduce incentives by taxing what people put into the economy as distinct from taxing what people take out of the economy by way of consumption. People act from enlightened self-interest and government's role is not to stifle that but to allow everyone the freedom to choose how they wish to spend, or save, their income.

7.   Since the end of the First World War there has been in Western society a push to redistribute income from the rich to the poor. This has proved to be something of a wild goose chase. Vilfredo Pareto, an Italian economist, in a study of income distribution concluded that governments are unable in any meaningful way to affect the distribution of incomes - what determines the distribution of income is the productivity of the economy. The more productive is the economy the less the inequality of income and vice versa. Bermuda has played a significant role in frustrating foreign government policy to redistribute income by playing host to owners of assets seeking to

---

[5] Page 51.

shield them from the grasp of the tax authorities. It would be something of an irony if Cayman, or some other business centre, did the same thing to the Bermudian tax authorities.

Mr MacDonald in his report stated "In my view, the case against an income tax for Bermuda is compelling."[5] Twenty-three years later it is hard to disagree with what he said then.

15. IS THE BERMUDA TAX SYSTEM FAIR?

"No man in this country is under the smallest obligation, moral or other, so to arrange his legal relations of his business or to his property as to enable the Inland Revenue to put the largest possible shovel into his stores."
LORD CLYDE IN AYSHIRE PULLMAN V THE COMMISSIONERS OF THE INLAND REVENUE.

"And it came to pass in those days, that there went out a decree from Caesar Augustus, that all the world should be taxed."
NEW TESTAMENT, LUKE 2:1.

"The moment you abandon the cardinal principle of exacting from all individuals the same proportion of their income or their property, you are at sea without rudder or compass, and there is no amount of injustice and folly you may not commit."
J.R. McCULLOCH.

When commentators speak about a tax system being fair it is important to understand that tax systems to the taxpayer are never fair as everyone seeks to minimise their tax burden whilst secretly hoping that others will foolishly maximise theirs. What is fair is dependent on who you ask and the fairest tax is that which somebody else pays. What is really meant when politicians speak about fairness is the proposition that those who earn more than average should pay more in taxation than someone who earns less and that the tax system should be used as a means to redistribute income from the rich to the poor. This is predicated on the well-known fact that there are more poor people than rich and the poor have a greater number of votes. In politics there seems to be a law against talking economic sense when the subject of taxation comes up. Not only should the rich pay proportionately more but they should pay a higher percentage of their income. In tax terminology this is known as advocating a progressive system of taxation, progressive being a word which has a pleasant ring to it meaning in non-tax speak as being related to or characterising progress an objective to which few are opposed. However, there is an additional meaning of progressive which is more relevant to the subject of taxation and this is "increasing in extent or severity." As long ago as 1294, when King Edward I increased taxes on the clergy by a severe 50 percent the Dean of St Paul's collapsed and died upon hearing the bad news. This is an extreme example of a tax protest.

Taxes can be classified accordingly to the proportion they take of a person's income. These classifications are threefold, (1) progressive, (2) proportional or (3) regressive.

A progressive tax takes a higher proportion of income as income increases beyond a certain level. Not only does that individual pay more in absolute terms he pays much more in percentage terms. Economists in the 19th century used the concept of marginal utility as the underlying justification for the concept of progressive taxation. Marginal utility means that the last dollar earned becomes less important as incomes increase so that in order to be "fair" high incomes should be taxed at higher rates.

A proportional tax system takes a given proportion of an individual's income, say 20 percent no matter what the level of income. This was the system favoured by Adam Smith who wrote, "The subjects of every state ought to contribute towards the support of government, as nearly as possible, in proportion to their respective abilities; that is, in proportion to the revenue which they respectively enjoy under the protection of the state."[1]

A regressive tax system takes a higher proportion of the lower paid individual's income than the progressive or proportional systems of tax. Regressive taxes therefore fall harder on the poor than on the rich because they are consumption based and the poor necessarily consume much more of their income than the rich. Whether Madonna earns $500 more or less per year would not change her life style one jot. But if one of her homeless fans earned $500 less it would make an enormous difference to what could or could not be afforded by the poverty-stricken fan.

Let me give examples of what is meant by the different systems in the following table:

1. PROGRESSIVE TAX SYSTEM		
Income	Tax paid	% of Income Paid
$1,000	200	20%
$2,000	600	30%
$4,000	1,600	40%

2. PROPORTIONAL TAX SYSTEM		
Income	Tax paid	% of Income Paid
$1,000	200	20%
$2,000	400	20%
$4,000	800	20%

---

[1] "The Wealth of Nations."

3. REGRESSIVE TAX SYSTEM		
Income	**Tax Paid**	**% of income Paid**
$1,000	200	20%
$2,000	300	15%
$4,000	400	10%

Under a progressive tax system - the type which exists in USA, Canada and UK - not only does the high earner pay more in absolute terms, proportionately the tax payer pays more of his income so that the person earning $4,000 per month pays $1,600 in tax which is 40% of income whilst the person earning $1,000 per month pays only $200 which is 20% of his income.

Under a proportional tax system, the high income individual who earns $4,000 per month pays more in tax ($800) which is 20 percent of his income ; whilst the person who earns $1,000 per month pays less in absolute terms ($200) but still pays 20 percent of his income.

From the above table it may be seen that in a regressive tax regime although the person earning $4,000 per month pays more in tax ($400) than the person earning $1,000 per month ($200) as a percentage of income the tax payer is paying only 10 percent whilst the low income person is paying 20 percent. This is considered unfair by those who believe the tax system should be about redistributing income not just raising revenue for government.

Bermuda does not impose income taxes and as a result the tax system is considered to be regressive and unfair because of its reliance on customs duties and as a result the poor pay more of their income in taxation than the rich. The philosophical divide arises when the electorate has to determine which is the fairer system. This is discussed when the question is asked whether Bermuda should introduce income tax.

One frequently heard criticism is that there are no taxes on companies operating in Bermuda and that commercial organisations like TELCO and BELCO should pay their fair share of taxes. The fact is that companies do not pay taxes they only collect them. The sources for the collection of taxes are :

- from shareholders by means of smaller dividends.
- from customers in the form of higher prices.
- from a company's retained earnings by not investing in the future.
- from employees by cutting wages or by failing to pay increases in wages.
- from higher productivity, the benefits of which do not go to employees or shareholders.

Thoughtful people know that a company is merely a legal construction built around a set of human beings. That legal entity must shift costs imposed on it like taxes, either forward to customers or backwards to the firm's owners or its employees. The most effective way to deal with tax increases is to improve productivity in which case the increased cost is more than offset by the increased efficiency which benefits all - shareholders, customers, employees and government.

There is a curious omission in the political debate about the fairness of the tax system and it is this. Everyone is familiar with the rallying call of the American Revolution "no taxation without representation." Yet for about 25 percent of the population, non-Bermudians, there is no political representation for the people who continue to pay their fair share of taxation - a burden which tends to increase as government continues its bloated growth. In all the reports I have read about public debates on the subject of the fairness of taxation there has been no call to remedy this omission. The PLP quick to note, and rightly so, any transgression of human rights are conspicuously silent on the subject. As far as the PLP - a political party which was established in part to correct civil rights injustices in Bermuda in the 1950s and 1960s - is concerned non-Bermudians do not exist as taxpayers. Non-Bermudians tend to receive fewer benefits from their taxes than Bermudians - no rent subsidies, frequently no old-age pensions and no scholarships for their children. Patrick Henry (the author of the revolutionary slogan and one of the Founding Fathers of the United States) must be wondering what happened to ideas of fiscal justice and fairness.

One final comment on fairness. The most efficient tax system is considered to be one which is largely based on expenditure (such as Bermuda) and under which savings are exempt (on which investment and hence future prosperity is based). The tax base is determined by what is spent not on what is earned. As a result thrift is rewarded whilst expenditure is penalised. Many studies have shown that thrift which leads to savings which leads to investment is one of the major keys to future prosperity. Using that argument the present Bermuda tax system is fair because it rewards those who are prudent enough to refrain from consumption and save thus making it possible to generate the standard of living we all currently enjoy.

There are two unintended consequences[2] of imposing direct taxes:

1. Incentives to work are blunted and as a result the country is invariably worse off.
2. Requiring people to report their incomes to government results in ordinary decent people being turned into liars and cheats.

There is a third consequence of trying to make the tax system "fair". The Italian economist Vilfredo Pareto (1848 - 1923)[3] reported that the unequal distribution of income was a constant between different countries and at different times. He concluded that this "constancy of inequality in the distribution of income reflect inequality of human ability, which is a natural and universal category."[4] What this means is that government through the tax system is unable to redistribute income from the rich to the poor. Differences in income arise not from the tax system but from levels of productivity and are largely the result of the skill and motivation of the individual. The more efficient and productive the economy the less the inequality of income.

---

[2] Unintended consequences arise when actions, particularly those of governments, lead to results which are either unanticipated or unintended.

[3] See page 66 and 67 of "The New Realities." by Peter Drucker.

[4] page 453 of "The History of Economic Thought." by Sir Eric Roll.

Bermuda is a productive economy as evidenced by its high per capita GDP and this is the major reason for there being little inequality of income. Both the rich and the poor earn high incomes. The search for a fair system of taxation is therefore an exercise in futility. Increasingly the evidence shows that high tax rates serve no revenue purpose at all, the only purpose being served is to create the illusion of soaking the rich. Higher taxes do not automatically mean that there will be more government revenue. That was the old way of UK, US and New Zealand and it simply did not work. It is important not to be deceived by the perception that Bermuda is awash with wealth but that it is wrongly distributed. An obsession with its distribution leads to contempt for the process of wealth creation and dislike of those who have the initiative to create incomes and jobs.

As a consequence, the quotation by J.R. McCulloch stated above leads to the conclusion that injustice and folly tend to be two words which one immediately associates with the current progressive and redistributive tax systems in place in USA, Canada and the UK - a conclusion with which few people who live in those countries would disagree. Unfortunately, in a democratic society there are more poor people who have never heard of Pareto than there are rich and as George Bernard Shaw put it so bluntly, "A government which robs Peter to pay Paul can always depend on the support of Paul."

16. SHOULD ANY GOVERNMENT FUNCTIONS BE PRIVATISED?

"It has taken long decades of empirical experience to discover that government failure is often so much worse than so-called market failures."

LORD HARRIS.

Countries all over the world, from Chile to Thailand to France are discovering - almost to their surprise - that government provided goods and services can be handed over to the private sector with a significant improvement in the quality of service or product provided and at a much lower level of cost to the consumer. On top of that the taxpayer does not have to fund the massive losses which are a conspicuous characteristic of government owned organisations. Privatisation is a revolution which is sweeping the world and is affecting major industries and every government no matter what its philosophy is. According to 'The Economist' there were a total of 1,300 privatisations pending in 1994 ranging from airlines, electric power, telephones, railways, gas supply, oil companies and a host of others.[1]

For almost 200 years and until recently, the debate about the role of government in the economy has been controlled by the question, 'What should government do?' In the last 15 years or so the question has been framed differently and now is, 'What can government do efficiently?' In economic[2] terms the answer is not very much and not very efficiently. The evidence tends to suggest that when assets are owned and operated, even indirectly, by government a strange alchemy takes place. Concern for efficiency and value for money goes out the window

---

[1] 'The World in 1994.' page 131.
[2] I stress economic because in other areas governments are effective.

because there is inadequate financial discipline, a discipline which is exerted on private companies by market mechanisms. Most government organisations tend to be insulated from market pressures, financial discipline and sound management practices. Even Adam Smith did not spend much time on the issue of government involvement in the economy, taking it for granted that in economic matters (and education) there was not much government could do efficiently.

Privatisation is the process whereby government owned organisations are sold to the public by means of a share offering in the enterprise. It first gained popularity and acceptance in Britain when Margaret Thatcher was Prime Minister and was done to achieve a variety of objectives:

- to free commercial organisations from bureaucratic control.
- to improve government revenues.
- to widen share ownership in private enterprise.
- to increase competition.
- to improve efficiencies.

Most of these objectives have been attained and privatisation has progressed at an enormous pace almost everywhere in the world; airlines in UK and Malaysia, telephone companies in Germany and UK, car factories in France, provision of pensions in Chile and UK, and oil companies in France and Argentina.When the Chinese privatised their farms output shot up in a very short space of time. The programme has been highly successful and has provided benefits to customers, taxpayers and employees as well as to private investors.

Probably the best example of an impact on Bermuda was the privatisation of British Airways in the late 1980s which was wholly owned by the British Government. Ten years ago British Airways treated their customers with contempt, was perpetually late and the whole financially incompetent operation was subsidised by the British taxpayer. After privatisation British Airways was consistently ranked as one of the best in the world, treated its customers like welcome guests and made piles of money into the bargain. For Bermudians who travel regularly to London this was like a breath of fresh air. It was and is a text book example of how a large organisation can be transformed for the benefit of almost everyone - except the lazy and incompetent employee. It was no accident that Bermuda was chosen as the location for the first board meeting of British Airways after privatisation.

The concept of privatisation, in the eyes of many, has only limited relevance to Bermuda because there are only a few services provided by government or by government owned organisations. Bus services, ferry services and trash collection are some of the minor services which could be privatised, but they are relatively unimportant in the larger scheme of things. Bermuda, unlike many other countries, was shrewd enough many years ago not to involve government in the ownership and provision of services in major industries like electrical power generation and supply, telephones and airlines.[3] Bermuda therefore does not have the financial baggage of a large government owned and operated business sector. Or does it?

---

[3] The PLP have always been keen for Bermuda to own and operate its own airline despite the fact that such airlines have been financial disasters for years.

Let me give you three examples of where there has been surreptitious privatisation, almost a silent revolution against the failure of government to fullfil its obligation to meet the requirements of the public.

Firstly, all over Bermuda, during the day, as well during the evening any observant person can see large numbers of security guards. They are present in stores, banks, and hotels or simply guarding property like golf courses or oil installations. The number of private security guards is estimated in 1996 at 412 people, just 77 less than in the Police Service.[4] Twenty years ago there were only a handful of security guards but the upsurge in crime in Bermuda has made it necessary for private organisations to make their own arrangements to protect their property or the persons of their employees to the extent that private police services are almost equal to the government police service.

Of course, we pay taxes for the police service (the cost for fiscal year 1996/97 is almost BD$30 million), but over the past 20 years the number of security firms and guards has increased at a much faster pace than we spend money on the police (or the general economy for that matter as crime is now one of the few growth industries in Bermuda). The reader has to ask himself the question - if the police service was really doing an efficient job would we require as many people providing private security? There is also the financial burden which at the end of the day is borne by the consumer. Not only is the public paying for a service, they are also paying for additional service because government is not doing its job. However, critical one can be about the police no one would argue that the police service should be privatised because one of the essential functions of government is to provide for the safety and security of the public. In addition, there has been a major reorganisation of the police service which, in part, has resulted in a fall in the crime rate[5].

> There are functions which are clearly governmental which no one but government can be allowed to perform. Among them is the governmental monopoly on defence and arms. There is also the governmental function of maintaining law, order and justice so that citizens can sleep peacefully at night and can walk the streets without fear - something governments a century ago did a good deal better than most governments do today.[6]

Secondly, like private security, one of the boom industries of the 1990s is private education despite the fact that government expenditure on public education has been increasing for years and for the fiscal year 1996/97 is almost BD$60 million or about BD$1,000 per capita. Government states that children must be educated and rightly so for reasons so obvious that it needs no further explanation. Government also states it will supply education, but in the eyes of many parents it does a poor job and many opt out of the government system.[7] The implied assumption of government is that education is too important to be left to the market place and that government is a superior supplier.

---

[4] See page 60 of "Employment Survey 1995," published by the Statistician's Department.
[5] The total number of offences in 1995 was 7,143; in 1994 it was 8,409
[6] "The New Realities," by Peter Drucker, page 63.
[7] 34% of parents sent their children to private schools. In the UK it is 7%, in the USA 12%.

Why should parents who are already paying taxes decide to pay additional fees for their children to attend private school? One answer is clearly the decision of government to build one giant secondary school, the mega school, at Prospect thus severely limiting parental choice at secondary school level. The black population has rightly demanded equal opportunity in the field of education; sadly what I think will be produced is segregation because of bureaucratic bungling. Another reason is that many parents believe The Department of Education is failing to provide many young Bermudians with what their parents consider to be an adequate education for the future. The standards of performance are either non-existent or are not enforced and no one is held accountable. The public has lost confidence in the abilities of the educational bureaucrats and teachers to do their job well and achieve acceptable results.

If the Department of Education was in private business and gave away its product free[8] (a product which parents passionately want for their children and are anxious to acquire) and 34 percent of parents said they didn't want the free product and would prefer to pay for a higher quality product provided they were able to choose the school their child attended, the Department would probably go into liquidation. The three uncomfortable questions which the Department of Education has to ask itself are surely these:

- Am I really providing my customers with what they want"?
- Why does the present system prevent children from learning the 3 Rs?
- Why do I resist excellence and accountability?

A particularly odd way of emphasising the poor job the Department of Education does for some of its customers was a piece of news in 1996[9] which stated that a BD$750,000 programme (ironically known as BEST STEPS) to provide remedial education in the reading, writing and maths could be in jeopardy. The news was the risk to the programme - the real news was, why do potential college students need remedial education and what had been going on in the educational system for the previous twelve years with those who require remedial assistance?

It is the degree of responsiveness to the customer or the client which is the essential difference between the effective provision of services by government and the provision of services by private enterprise. Government is relatively indifferent to the wishes of their customers - in the case of education to the wishes and aspirations of the parents of young children - because there is no penalty suffered as a consequence of the loss of market share of education to the private sector. Teachers and administrators in the Department of Education are paid irrespective of what the customer thinks, whether a good job or a bad job is done and no one is fired, no salaries are reduced and life goes on very much as before. Except that children do not receive the education to which they are entitled in this modern age. And some administrators at the Department of Education send their own children to private school recognising that many public schools are not up to scratch.

---

[8] At the point of use - for there is nothing free.

[9] "The Bermuda Sun." August, 30 1996.

When one settles for state monopoly of supply one is legitimising over manning, indifference to the consumer, financial laxity and minimising customer choice. More taxpayer's money is not going to make a bad system better. The fact is that government should be encouraging the growth of more private schools because they do so good a job of providing a decent education and promoting academic skills. The parents of the poor and those with little influence care just as much about the future of their children as the rich because they know that education is the main way out of poverty.

Thirdly, everyone is familiar with the fax machine, a machine which was invented by private enterprise, despite the fact that governments had had a monopoly over every mail system in the world for more than 160 years. In Bermuda, it is cheaper to send a fax, about 10 cents, than it is to send a letter which costs three times as much at 30 cents, and there is instantaneous and reliable delivery - which is more than can be said for mail deliveries. Post offices all over the world are models of incompetence, the only Western country which has a reliable postal service is Switzerland which is why Federal Express does not have an operation there.

In Hamilton it is easy to spot private delivery vans all over the place. They are not delivering supplies to stores or offices but delivering mail. Federal Express, United Parcel Service, International Bonded Couriers are just a few of the companies engaged in this business. A few years ago nobody in Bermuda had heard of them. The growth of international business has made it essential for letters and other important documents to be delivered on time if they cannot be faxed. The Post Office has shown itself to be unreliable and indifferent to the wishes of its customers and this has allowed the private delivery service to be established.

There are obvious absurdities in government running of the postal service. If the customer takes a post office box and collects his own mail he has to pay the post office for not doing its job. Logic dictates the Post Office should pay the customer because there is no need to hire postmen to deliver the mail thus saving the Post Office money. To add insult to injury, many customers want to rent mail boxes but there are not sufficient of them and so a private company (not the Post Office) fills the gap by making additional boxes available to the public. Again the uncomfortable question which has to be asked is, 'Why does the Post Office fail to meet the requirements of its customers?' If it was a private business and did not have the legal protections it has it would surely be out of business by now. Fortunately, the international customer has a choice - use Fedex - and the Bermuda customer can use the fax. However, for magazines, payment of local bills and other routine correspondence the public is in the hands of an organisation which overcharges for its services.

When spending decisions are made through the political process and implemented by civil servants, powerful vested interests determine how the tax dollars are spent and the least influential voice in that process is the customer, usually the taxpayer. It is no accident that government spending results in neglect of the customer and ends up in the pockets of the people who are supposed to be providing the service. As government sponsored organisations face no real market-place competition they can, and do, spend public money in wasteful and inefficient ways, fail to meet objectives (like delivering the mail, arresting criminals and educating children) and generally pay little attention to efficiency without fear of losing customers to competitors.

With a ballooning government budget and widespread dissatisfaction with some (though by no means all) government services, there is considerable scope for privatising many government tasks. One answer is not to spend more and more of the taxpayer's money in Government departments which have failed because that produces only more and more expensive mistakes. Yet that is what has been happening at the Department of Education, Community and Cultural Affairs and the Department of Tourism - a department which has presided over a decline in our main industry for about 15 years. It is to the question of privatising this government department that I turn next.

17. SHOULD THE DEPARTMENT OF TOURISM BE PRIVATISED?

"All successful businesses make constant adjustments to their management process as the requirements of the marketplace change. The existing organisational structure (The Department of Tourism) often impedes decision making and implementation of decisions at a time when the pace of change in the business is demanding that more informed judgements be made and more tactics be completed efficiently (sic). No single area of the marketing mix of Bermuda Tourism is more deficient than the product."

THE COMMISSION ON COMPETITIVENESS, PAGES 16 AND 17.[1]

In private enterprise one of the hallowed principles, often ignored in practice, is that the man (or woman) at the top carries responsibility for the success (or otherwise) of the organisation. President Truman put it most succinctly when he stated, "The buck stops here." Success in commerce is evidenced by sky-high salaries, luxurious offices, or first-class air travel and accolades in business magazines. Failure is accompanied with swift removal followed by a corporate reorganisation. It is often said, 'That to err is human.' In corporate life, to forgive is not usually company policy.

The recent history of big business is littered with the bodies of people who did not cut the mustard in private enterprise. John Akers at IBM, Robert Stempel at General Motors, and Tiny Rowland at Lonrho (which owns the Princess Hotels) are only a few examples of the those who were ignominiously and publicly fired because under their leadership the company performed badly. Contrary to public perception, the more senior an executive is the less secure he is in his job. He is paid for dealing with different issues, resolving dilemmas, and forecasting the future. Failure is punished quickly and without mercy. It is a heartless brutal system and rightly so because thousands of employees and suppliers are dependent for their jobs and security on the abilities of the people at the top.

---

[1] The Commission's Report on tourism is a superb analysis of what is wrong with our tourism industry. I am baffled as to why so many of its recommendations have been ignored.

In government employment the system is quite different. It is rare for some-one senior to be appointed from outside the civil service. If an individual is talented he gets the same as the half-wit next door. People at the same level are paid at the same rate. Being innovative is a risky business so risks are rarely taken. Success and failure are treated in the same fashion. Incentives, benefits and accolades are rarely given except perhaps at retirement. The system operates on a basis of "buggins turn". If things do not work well the taxpayer can be coerced into paying higher taxes to keep the system going.[2]

A government Ministry, The Department of Tourism (DOT) presides over the success or failure of the Bermuda Tourist Industry. There are no prizes for guessing what system is used. It is not that of IBM or General Motors and the "buck does not stop here."

The decline and crumbling of Bermuda tourism is depressingly laid out in only a few stark facts:

- Air arrivals have declined from about 450,000 to under 400,000.
- Visitor spending has declined by a like percentage.
- Bermuda's competitors have increased the number of visitors and tourist expenditure.
- Major hotels are losing money.[3]
- Young people believe, rightly, that the hospitality industry offers a limited future.
- Customer complaints about value for money and poor service have increased.
- Labour relations have been nothing short of dreadful.
- Hotel occupancy rates have declined.
- Our competitors have expanded; we have shrunk.
- No major hotels have been built in Bermuda since 1972.

The litany can continue but the conclusion is inescapable - tourism is in a very bad way.

Bermuda is still a wonderful place to vacation. There are wonderful sports facilities, great beaches, superb climate, the people are friendly. There is little crime (though it has increased during the past decade) and it is close to its prime market. With advantages like that it is hard to get things wrong. IBM had great computers, and GM had superb cars but each company got it wrong and had to change. Bermuda Inc. is in the same position. Most people know what is needed to remedy the situation - keener prices, improved service, warmer welcomes and so on. At present, we give our visitors what we think is good for us and ask them to pay through the nose for it. The reverse needs to be the case but that cannot be achieved through our present organisational structure.

If the DOT was a private organisation some significant changes would have occurred by now. They may not have resolved the situation but action would have

---

[2] One of the main redistribution effects of the last 10 years has been from the private sector to the public service.
3 This issue is explored in Part II 4.

been taken and the organisation and people in it would have been shaken up. The sad fact is that Bermuda tourism is organised along exactly the same lines as it was 15 years ago, namely that the Minister of Tourism is responsible to Cabinet and Parliament for the industry's well-being and that day to day management is carried out by tenured civil servants most of whom have been in place for years. In marketing a product like tourism, which has to be constantly revitalised, security of tenure for the person in charge is the kiss of death for the product. Flair, imagination and innovation are not qualities easily found within the realms of government. Government has been compared to, "an overcrowded banquet where you have to fight to get a seat but can feast in peace once seated."[4]

Success in any operation is dependent on being able to do two things simultaneously:

1. In the short term it requires incremental innovation and small, almost imperceptible, changes in strategy, culture, people and processes. Such improvements in efficiency are not by themselves sufficient - they require a second technique.

2. Organisations need to manage well not just for today but also for tomorrow. Tomorrow will not be like today as the DOT has so often assumed. As happens with many successful organisations, inertia sets in. The DOT was very successful in the 1960s and 1970s but from the 1980s things started to go wrong. Structural inertia evidenced by political direction, resistance to change, bureaucratic complexity, and general indifference to the customer set in. The bureaucratic culture was able to strangle any desire to keep up with the times.

It is as if General Motors and IBM had ignored in their management practices all the market and other changes which had shaken their world since the 1980s. If fundamental reform and action had not been taken to reverse the decline in their performances IBM and GM would have been consigned to the corporate graveyard and rightly so. Why was not similar action taken in the Bermuda Department of Tourism? The answer must surely be that no pressure can be brought to bear by the customer, the public or the taxpayer when things go wrong.

It is important to distinguish between politicians and civil servants. In theory policy is determined by the Minister, and is carried out by the civil servants. In a commercial type activity this distinction has little or no validity. Just as the Chairman of the Board is different from the Chief Executive Officer, so the Minister differs from senior civil servants. When things go wrong in business both are accountable but government is forever and there is no effective mechanism for dealing with tectonic change and penalising incompetence.

The sad brutal facts are that:-

1. The present Department of Tourism appears to have lost its way.

2. Because of restrictive civil service regulations (mentioned earlier) the pool of talent from which to recruit is limited.

---

[4] "The Culture of Bureaucracy", by Charles Peters, page 105.

3.   Governments are concerned about such issues as fairness, how a decision will look in the press, what vocal elements of the electorate will think about it, how will the opposition criticise the policy and so on. A business organisation, on the other hand gets on with the job and make decisions irrespective of political considerations. Governments operate by persuasion, compromise, education and the consent of many parties with different points of view. This invariably means delay, inefficiency and compromise. Business leaders tend to be autocrats who are impatient to get things done and are cut from a different cloth than our civil servants.

4.   The civil service traditions are not normally in accordance with commercial imperatives. Bureaucracy, which in many ways is a desirable thing, is not good at making rapid business decisions or coping with change. Civil servants tend to have their own rules and procedures and are uncomfortable with the unknown or non-routine. The reverse also tends to be the case. Businessmen are not good civil servants because they are too impatient, too autocratic and do not mind being unpopular.

The quality and educational qualifications of people who work for government are probably higher than what will be found in private enterprise. At senior levels the work-load is heavy and the hours can be long. Civil servants are invariably better educated, more cultivated and certainly more diplomatic than their counterparts in business. Civil servants compared to businessmen are urbane, charming and are always prepared to compromise and understand another point of view. Business people tend to be single-minded, often ill-mannered, brusque, direct, indifferent to what people think of them, unpleasant and authoritarian. They want action not talk, results not a contented public, they are motivated by money (or greed) not the alleged long-term benefits to the community. One is fish the other is fowl. Businessmen generally are not good public servants, public servants are not good businessmen.

To be fair to the DOT, it does not have total responsibility for the tourism industry, its main objective being to bring visitors to Bermuda. Its main responsibilities lie in :

- determining cruise ship policy.
- coordinating airlift policy.
- licensing and inspection of hotels.
- regulating the number of hotel beds.
- marketing of Bermuda including supervision of overseas offices.
- advertising and public relations.
- collecting statistics.

The Department spends most of its budget of about BD\$40 million[5] on marketing and promoting Bermuda. However, it is not specifically accountable for crucially important strategic issues like product planning, development, overall investment in tourism and general management. In addition, the DOT has not sat

---

[5] About \$80 per tourist

idly by passively watching the decline. But the acid test is success and if you are not successful in the business world you are a failure no matter how hard working, dedicated and innovative you are.

> "It is disconcerting, even shocking, that in the fact of the enormous growth in world tourism, Bermuda is losing its tourism, both absolutely and relatively.
> 'The Commission on Competitiveness' page 45.

However, the fact of the matter is that a government organisation under the traditional civil service structure cannot convert itself into a business-like day-to-day decision making body. The civil service is established not for the purpose of initiating innovative policies but to concern itself with process, procedure, precedent and public response to government policies. It is concerned with perceptions and making politicians look good, not with making hard decisions whose eventual success is not immediately apparent. It is concerned with building consensus and relationships not with action, pleasing the customer and getting value for money. Management does not have the tools to do the job efficiently. They cannot transfer, promote, pay more or dismiss staff all of which are handled by the Public Service Commission or by trade union negotiation. This process may work well in an environment which is not concerned with day-to-day business decisions like say Home Affairs or Cultural Affairs. It does not and cannot work in the commercial world.

If the Ministry of Tourism had the qualities needed to deal with the problem of tourism it would have dealt with it years ago before it reached crisis proportions. The reality is that it has not dealt successfully with the issue. As a practical matter civil servants cannot be easily changed and cannot be dismissed or demoted. In 1995 the Deputy Director was suspended on full-pay for alleged misconduct pending an investigation into his activities. At the end of 1996 this investigation has not concluded. Moreover, many of the current staff are not tourism professionals but career civil servants. A civil servant has property in the job, a benefit which does not exist in the commercial world.

It will take a major effort of time, original thought, and an understanding of the realities of the modern world to revitalise the industry. Many innovative steps are being taken by an energetic and imaginative Minister and everyone wishes him success in his task but frankly, it is unrealistice to expect success from an organisation which has failed to perform over the past 10 to 15 years.

In October, 1996 an organisation called "Coalition For Change" announced that it was seeking to get government to review the operations of the DOT stating that business had had "enough of excuses and why we're in this state."[6]

Given the situation that:-

1. The Department of Tourism is charged with running a business;
2. it has not successfully managed the tourism industry in the past few years; and

---

[6] 'The Royal Gazette,' October 16, 1996 page 1.

3.	it cannot by definition function like a business for the reasons stated above,

the conclusion must surely be to privatise its operations as was recommended by the Commission on Competitiveness three years ago. To remain a moribund organisation is to court disaster. The head of a privatised DOT would then have to prove he can do the job. If he can, he is paid accordingly. If he can't, he is replaced and someone competent is found to replace him. Payment by results and performance undermines the confederacy of mediocrity which dominates the civil service and which sucks out the lifeblood of motivation and innovation which are the forces of success. The principle of reward of individual merit is a key fundamental of dynamic industry - and also of a free society. It is that easy and it is that difficult.

Privatisation is like business. You hire the right people, control costs, and give them freedom to innovate and meet the needs of the customer - the tourist.

## 18.	WHAT WAS THE COMMISSION ON COMPETITIVENESS?

"It is also important to stress that both tourism and international business are sensitive to changes in Bermuda's competitiveness and that even the fairly pessimistic picture I have painted so far may prove to be overly-optimistic if Bermuda allows her competitiveness to deteriorate much further. Competitiveness is to a large extent about costs and value for money and the message has been preached often - though not I believe really understood or appreciated - that Bermuda is becoming far too expensive a place to choose to visit or to conduct business in. But competitiveness is also about intangibles: the quality of life and the stable political and economic environment. It is always possible to do something to offset or counteract worsening cost competitiveness but it is much more difficult to deal with non-cost factors simply because they are so intangible. A period of labour unrest, for example, can do far more serious harm to Bermuda's image than a much longer period of excessive inflation. Bermudians in their quest to better themselves need to be careful not to kill the goose that laid the golden egg."

NICHOLAS WEINREB, FORMER GOVERNMENT ECONOMIC ADVISER, 1988

The Commission on Competitiveness was established early in 1992 by the Premier, Sir John Swan, and chaired by Mr. Mansfield Brock - who was Chairman of the Bermuda Monetary Authority. Its mission was broad in scope - to analyse the competitive position of Bermuda, review international trends and most important of all to formulate concrete actions plans to assist Bermuda in meeting the demands of today while preparing to address the challenges of tomorrow.

The Commission was established because of:-

• Concern about the poor economic performance of Bermuda during the 1980s and early 1990s.

• Bermuda's lack of competitiveness which could jeopardise the high living standards to which the community had become accustomed.

- Major changes which had taken place in many world economies, and the impact such changes could have on Bermuda's capacity to continue to earn sufficient foreign exchange to maintain living standards.

Several hundred people participated in the project by analysing data, producing ideas and making recommendations to improve economic performance. It was an exercise of major proportions and community input was sought for innovative proposals from which it was hoped that Bermuda would take the appropriate path and continue its prior stellar economic performance. Over a period of two years the Commission prepared five major reports which dealt with the key areas of Bermuda's economy:

1. A strategic plan for the tourism industry.

2. A report by the Bermuda International Business Association (BIBA) which had three main components:-

   - orientation towards the customer;

   - marketing proposals;

   - encouraging the development of new business to achieve sustainable real growth.

3. A report on future opportunities for the development of new business.

4. A strategic assessment of protectionism in Bermuda.

5. A report on local costs such as shipping, government charges and other costs as well as the comparative costs of operating in other jurisdictions.

The report is a mine of information about the Bermuda economy and it brings together in a coherent fashion many statistics with some penetrating observations about the performance of the economy.[1] As a minor criticism the final report could have used some prudent editing to avoid repetition, to improve the structure of the presentation and to provide an index of the several hundred recommendations made.

The Commission made it clear that Bermuda, if it wished to continue to be a economic success story, needed to recognise that since the early 1980s fundamental, even chronic, malfunctions occurred in the Bermudian economy, examples being:-

1. Economic growth has been an anaemic 0.21% p.a. between 1981 and 1993.[2]

2. In the period 1968-1992, Bermudian inflation was 26% higher than USA.[3] In essence this means that Bermudians paid themselves 26% more than they earned during this period, a form of gratuitous pay rises which belongs to the world of "Alice in Wonderland."

3. Major hotels in Bermuda have lost $41.6 million over the past 5 years - a situation which is clearly unsustainable.[4]

4. Our labour relations are not the best, and accounts for a large share of the blame for points 1 through 3 above.

---

[1] The Report on Tourism is particularly good.

[2] Page 8.

[3] Page 9.

[4] Page 62.

Clearly, the Premier recognised that this state of affairs could not continue otherwise Bermuda faced a dramatic and unacceptable fall in its enviably high standard of living and quality of life. Accordingly he established the Commission to make recommendations for the purpose of making the Bermuda economy more competitive.

Competitiveness is now something of a virility symbol. Major companies have undergone major reorganisations, or downsizing to meet the demands of their shareholders and the stock market and many governments, like that of Bermuda, have established commissions to see how well or how poorly their country's compare with the rest of the world recognising that future prosperity is highly dependent on being competitive and increasing productivity. For others it is the economic equivalent of a military campaign and the enemy - the foreign competition - must be vanquished. For others it is much ado about nothing. Professor Paul Krugman in an article in the 'Harvard Business Review'[5] has stated that national competitiveness does not mean anything. Competitiveness, however, is not all that difficult it is about the ability of a country to add value to the economic process thereby improving the standard of living of the inhabitants.

The Commission used the Professor Michael Porter[6] definition of competitiveness namely:-

"The only meaningful concept of competitiveness at the national level is productivity. A rising standard of living depends on the capacity of a nation's firms to achieve high levels of productivity and to increase productivity over time. A Nation's firms must relentlessly improve productivity in existing industries by raising product quality, adding desirable features, improving product technology or boosting production efficiency. At the same time, an upgrading economy is one which has the capability of competing successfully in entirely new and sophisticated industries. To sustain advantage firms must achieve more sophisticated competitive advantages over time, through providing higher quality products and services, or producing more efficiently. This translates directly into productivity growth."

Other meanings of the word competitive are perhaps more relevant to the problems which Bermuda faces and get to the point quicker. For example:

1. How well is Bermuda doing compared to other countries?

2. How well has Bermuda done in the growth of international tourism?

3. Is Bermuda performing at the optimum level?

As noted, Bermuda's economic performance over the past 15 years is not impressive and is in marked contrast to previous decades. Steps therefore need to be taken to reverse this mediocre performance, re-invigorate the economy and increase productivity. Failure to take such steps will inevitably depress living standards, may create social unrest which in turn will make Bermuda a less attractive place to visit and do business, which in turn will produce a listless economy. This downward spiral is not pleasant to contemplate.

---

[5] See January-February 1996 edition.
[6] See "The Competitiveness of Nations" by Michael Porter.

This rather bleak picture must be viewed against a backdrop of quite remarkable success in the 1960s and 1970s, and even since 1981 the international offshore business has flourished, and continues to do so. It is the tourist industry and related businesses such as retailing which has continued to perform badly and where success at making Bermuda more competitive is so essential. There are disturbing underlying long-term problems which are crying out for remedial action. Although it is important not to exaggerate Bermuda's economic problems it is important to recognise that it has been moving in the wrong direction. It is important to change direction but in a manner which will retain the reasons for Bermuda's earlier success such as political stability, favourable business environment, low taxation and so on.

Bermuda is not as fortunate as many other advanced economies (with whom we compare ourselves) as we are wholly dependent for foreign exchange earnings on only two industries, tourism and international business. We therefore do not have the resilience of large countries like USA, Canada or UK who have immense industrial diversity. Indeed, it may well be true to say that we are similar, structurally, to developing countries and economies which are dependent on one or two agricultural or mineral products. If and when market conditions change, the economy can be blown off course. The task, simply stated, is for Bermuda to take steps to avoid the economic gales and adjust behaviour accordingly.

A further analogy may be appropriate. The former Minister of Finance speaks of Bermuda Inc.[7] as a means of impressing on the public how important our basic industries are to our standard of living. Bermuda Inc. can be compared to the three large automobile companies in the United States who eight years ago were in a similar predicament to Bermuda. Poor financial performance, bad labour relations, old fashioned products, tired management and so on.

Their answer, which is the correct one, was to cut costs, raise quality and improve their product. The automobile companies adopted new technologies and business methods. They adapted and evolved into more enterprising organisations and whilst not yet out of the woods their future looks bright. Bermuda faces exactly the same sort of challenges. The temptation is to tinker with more protections, give subsidies or impose restrictive regulations. This does much more harm than good, and delays the process of improvement.

A recommendation made by The Commission, but not acted upon, was the formation of an Institute of Economic Development whose objectives would be to focus on long-term strategic economic and human resource issues and to act as a focal point for the establishment of new industries in Bermuda. It was also proposed that the Institute monitor progress made on the Commission's recommendations, sponsor studies on economic matters and arrange forums for discussion purposes. It was never really clear how this Institute would function - would it have executive powers for example and how would it coordinate its activities with the Ministry of Finance? The main flaw in the proposal was that such planning organisations have never really worked in other jurisdictions and at the end of the day there is the belief that somehow or other a group of wise men are able to sub-

---

[7] See Part III 1 for the meaning of this term.

stitute their ideas for those of entrepreneurs and that their wisdom is somehow greater than the billions of decisions made daily in the market place.

Economic planning tends to be a euphemism for substituting the wisdom of the politicians and bureaucrats for consumers' choice. History demonstrates the folly of government programmes which tend to distort investment and prevents the market from making continuous small adjustments to changes in technology and consumer tastes. Advocating a greater government role in the economy is based on a deep-rooted fallacy of confusing "some" with "all". Some may benefit from government programmes but most do not. No computer or circle of wise men can predict the emergence of new knowledge, innovations or ideas and the reaction of consumers to them.

Social and economic realities are so complex, composed of so many exquisitely interrelated variables that no planner can forsee the results of the billions of decisions made by ordinary people. The decisive advantage of market systems is that they decentralise power away from the politicians and political considerations and move it towards individual businessmen and consumers. Defects are intrinsic to arrangements which permit political constituencies to dominate economic ones. One of the major lessons of the past fifty years is that centrally planned economies do not work as the tragic example of the failed USSR clearly shows.

Western experience shows that government bodies who spend taxpayer's money tend to make worse investments than private investors who spend their own money. It is tempting to think that organisations like the proposed Institute of Economic Development would work, but the fact of the matter is that private business creativity is the fundamental source of wealth creation. This partly explains why nations rich in natural resources like the former USSR remain poor, whilst others with almost no natural resources like Hong Kong become wealthy.

Apart from the reports of the various task forces The Commission made three major points made about the performance of the Bermuda economy:

1. The only real way to improve living standards over the long term is to increase productivity.[8] This can be achieved either by adding value to the service provided or by reducing the costs of doing business. Both are difficult and both involve making changes to the existing ways of economic behaviour.

2. The economy only grew at the rate of 0.21 percent between 1981 and 1993 and this failure to grow at an acceptable rate is one which must be dealt with if Bermuda is to prosper in the future.

3. During the period 1968 to 1992 the rate of inflation in Bermuda increased by 26 percent more than the United States. *"Visitors returning to Bermuda in 1992 after visiting in 1968 would find that they would need to pay $509.90 for the same $100 of goods and services.......in their own country they would be paying $403.70."*[9]

---

[8] Final Report of 'The Commission on Competitiveness' page 6.
[9] Ibid, page 9.

An understanding of these three facts is at the centre of the poor performance of the Bermuda economy for the past fifteen or so years. Poor productivity, low growth and high inflation are symptoms of something seriously wrong. The level of protectionism with its attendant limited competition is identified as a major cause of the malaise but yet inconsistently the report goes on to say that, "It would be inappropriate for Bermuda to throw out all of the carefully crafted set of protectionist rules which have been designed to ensure that future generations of Bermudians may enjoy a continued high standard of living."[10]

This recommendation was in direct contradiction to many of the proposals made in the Report by the London Business School "Protectionism in Bermuda". Costs in Bermuda will continue to grow at a rate faster than many of our competitors because many suppliers to goods and services within the Bermuda economy are protected from outside competition and can therefore increase prices easily (labour costs are the best example of this) whilst many of our revenue generating institutions, particularly the hotels and guest houses, are in direct international competition and can only increase prices to their customers (the visitor to Bermuda) at the risk of losing business. They are therefore caught in a vice of seeing their costs increased by Bermudian suppliers - mainly labour, government, utilities and local merchants - whilst they cannot pass on such increased costs without losing business. This is a short cut to financial disaster.[11]

The Commission made six major recommendations which unfortunately fell very short of dealing with the problems diagnosed in the report:

1. Increase the value in two basic industries of tourism and international business.

2. Encourage the development of new industries.

3. Eliminate exchange and interest rate controls.[12]

4. Improve the efficiency of government services as government expenditure in 1993 was 23 percent of GDP. In 1996 this percentage had edged up to 25 and there had been no noticeable improvement in the efficiency of government.[13]

5. Proposals were made to improve the competitiveness of local business - yet the main competitive impulse of removing protections has been left uninterrupted.

6. Improve the flexibility of labour through improved training and better labour relations.

No one would disagree with any of the above recommendations - or with many of the plans to implement such recommendations. Yet two years later there has been only limited progress towards these desirable ends. Many of the tourism recommendations (which were sound and sensible and were by far the best part of the report) have yet to be applied. No new industries have been established, government efficiency still remains something of a fiction, increased competition

---

[10] Ibid, page 11.
[11] See Part II 4 on the issue of hotels losing money.
[12] this was effectively done in 1995
[13] See Part III 8 on government efficiency.

leading to reduced costs is still elusive, and labour relations are still fragile although improvements can be expected after 1996 following the retirement of the former President of the BIU, Mr. Ottiwell Simmons. However, the underlying structure of labour relations remains untouched.

Since publication of the Report in 1994, international business has continued to flourish and now generates a higher proportion of foreign exchange earnings than tourism. Military bases are now history, the decisions about them having been made in Washington, London and Ottawa largely without reference to the wishes of the Bermuda Government. Government spending, labour relations and the tourism industry are areas which are mostly within Bermudian control. But not a great deal has been done to make necessary reforms except to change the marketing of tourism in the United States and Canada.

The Commission on Competitiveness found, as did the survey published by the World Economic Forum and the International Insitute for Management Development,[14] and hosts of other studies that competitiveness is dependent on:

- open markets.
- low taxation.
- high savings.
- a sound educational system, especially at secondary level.
- flexibility in the labour market.
- openness of the financial system.
- quality of government - those who tax less, spend less and intervene least.
- respect of the rule of law and the absence of corruption.

The conclusion is get these fundamentals right and everything else will tend to fall into place. My personal view about the work of the Commission is as follows:-

1. Remove as many restrictions of the use of land, labour and capital as possible. The burden of proof should be with those who wish to retain such restraints rather than the other way around.

2. It is essential to avoid Bermuda being seen by our visitors as a commodity tourist destination, or for international business to regard us as a commodity place of residence.

3. The Department of Tourism should be privatised.[15]

4. Unless steps are taken to reverse the disastrous financial predicament of our large hotels we shall face continued deterioration in industry standards and further closures. Shareholders invest in Bermuda to receive dividends from their capital commitment; they will not for long tolerate financial losses.

5. Labour and management relations, particularly in the hospitality industry leave much to be desired. For too long Bermuda has failed to find a solution. Until that is done there will be continued decline and financial losses in the industry. It is entirely possible, indeed probable, that the BIU and other labour

---

[14] Published in 1996.
[15] See Part III 17 for a discussion on this issue.

organisations will negotiate not about wage increases but wage reductions, a process which is increasingly common in the United States and elsewhere.

6.   Bermuda requires a policy of benchmarking by comparing local and government costs with its main competitors. Bermuda costs will always be high because of our small market, isolated location and high standard of living but it is vital for them to be controlled.

7.   One of the main objectives of government is to give their citizens a rising standard of living. That has been done very successfully over the past 30 years or so. To continue to do so depends on continual gains in productivity which are largely provided by Companies that search constantly for fresh sources of competitive advantage. Our banks, to use only one example, are doing that. Other organisations including government need do the same thing. Our past economic environment helped in this upgrading process; there are questions about whether our present economic environment helps or hinders this process. The Commission did a good job of suggesting reforms which would allow Bermudians to work for the best possible environment. The tragedy is that many of its major recommendations have been ignored.

19.   WHO REALLY RUNS THE ECONOMY OF BERMUDA?

"The intangible duty of making things run smoothly is apt to be thankless, because people don't realise how much time and trouble it takes and believe it is the result of a natural and effortless unction."

A.C. BENSON.

"Knowledge, money , power. That's the cycle democracy is built on."

TENNESSEE WILLIAMS.

Bermuda is a community which is rife with conspiracy theories. This is, and always will be, a characteristic of a country which has a small population, a degree of suspicion between the two main racial groups and an opposition party with a very limited understanding of economic matters. This belief partly arises because in the past Bermuda was run very much by a small oligarchy, collectively known as the '40 Thieves,' many of the decisions of which were made informally, often, if rumours are to be believed, over drinks in some of Bermuda's exclusive clubs. However, this cosy arrangement - and I have doubts as to whether it was as true as many people claim - came to an end in the early 1960s and although the public should not underestimate the power of old money and influence, public policy decisions are now made in a much more structured formal, and constitutionally correct way.

Power no longer rests with the old oligarchy, most of whom are dead anyway, and Bermuda like most other Western countries has a clear line of responsibility which run from the electorate to the Government, and in certain areas of decision making run from the British Government to the Governor of Bermuda. Nevertheless many believe that the objective decision making structure which has worked well and has been in place for about 30 years is something of a sham and that Bermuda, and in particular the Bermuda economy is controlled and run by a small group which has never been clearly identified and who are accountable to no one but themselves.

A variation of this theme is one of the most persistent theories (or fantasies) is that there is now a small clique, somewhere, which somehow runs Bermuda and meets to determine who will get paid, who will get what job, whose mortgage will be called in if there is any criticism of the way in which Bermuda operates, or if there is opposition to fundamental economic decisions. The fact that no one ever attends such meetings, no one has reported to the press of who is involved and where they meet (other than at the Yacht Club), or that as a practical matter it is almost impossible to get a large group of people to agree on anything for very long does not seem to faze the many people who fervently, and honestly, believe that there is a conspiracy somewhere out there.

Running a small sophisticated individualistic place like Bermuda is not an easy matter. In fact running anything is not easy although to the outsider it appears that way. To Fred Astaire dancing was easy, to Greg Norman playing golf is easy, to Pavarotti singing is easy and being President of the United States is easy - no need to wait in queues at the airport or get stuck in a traffic jam and you live close to the job. As a general rule anything which looks easy, usually turns out to be difficult. Bermuda is not any different from anywhere else and running a successful economy is dependent on the skills, good sense and cooperation of many individuals.

Analysing the formal constitutional structure of Bermuda is not difficult. There is a Governor who looks as if he has a lot of power - after all he lives in a big house on the hill. The reality is that apart from foreign affairs which are limited, defence (nobody is about to attack Bermuda) and internal security (in which he has some say but perhaps not a decisive one) he does not have that much power and influence over the economy. There is not much for him to do other than attend events like the Agricultural Show and inspect the Bermuda Regiment from time to time. In economic terms his influence is very, very limited.

The House of Assembly (Bermuda's parliament) has 40 members of which 22 (at last count) belong to the majority party, the United Bermuda Party (UBP) the senior membership of which forms the Government. Executive authority is vested in the Cabinet, appointed by the Premier, and the usual list of ministries which exist in other countries are also found in Bermuda. There is a Minister of Health and Social Services, Minister of Education and Minister of Works and Engineering all of whom have a host of civil servants and well-paid well-trained permanent secretaries to recommend and carry out policy. Yet people in Bermuda still become ill, they have difficulties in their private lives - teenagers get into trouble with the police for example - some children go to school for 12 or more years but end up being functionally illiterate and roads have potholes. If these ministers ran their departments efficiently, and were all that powerful these sorts of things simply would not happen.

Perhaps the most powerful Minister, other than the Premier or the Finance Minister, is the Minister of Labour, Home Affairs and Public Safety, the ministry which is responsible for labour relations and immigration. Labour relations are poor, it is probably the second greatest problem which Bermuda faces.[1] As far as immigration is concerned there are too many non-Bermudians in the opinion of many so that does not quite seem to work in the manner it should. The less well-known ministries like the Minister of Community Affairs is not all that successful in getting the community to work together, and women still complain that the 'glass ceiling' is still firmly in place. So it is difficult to conclude that cabinet ministers and civil servants are able by themselves to run the economy.

Finally, there is the Premier and the Minister of Finance. If anyone really ran Bermuda it would be these two gentleman who on the face of it have all the power to do what they think is best for Bermuda (even allow McDonalds to operate). Both are PhDs, supremely self-confident, experienced, humorous, honest, capable, knowledgeable about the economy of Bermuda and generally the sort of people to whom you would trust your life. Yet as of 1996 the Premier is battling to keep the governing party together, the Minister of Finance is at his wit's end to raise enough taxation and they may both be out of a job in about a year's time if the voters continue to be unhappy with them. With all the authority vested in their offices few could say that they between them, or even individually, run Bermuda.

If we examine the banking system we find that The Bermuda Commercial Bank has downsized to such an extent that it does not want anybody to open a bank account with them, so there is no real power there. The two established banks The Bank of N.T. Butterfield and The Bank of Bermuda are large and conservative institutions who on a quarterly basis issue a shareholder's letter complaining about Government and the state of economy whilst continuing to earn a healthy income although that has not yet translated into higher share prices on the Bermuda stock exchange. The senior management of both banks are honest, industrious employees whose full-time job is to run a commercial operation for the benefit of the shareholders. In a highly competitive global economy being in charge of the day to day operations of a bank is not a picnic, and the commercial challenges are more than enough to make it impossible for the bank management to run Bermuda in their spare time. In addition, periodically, both banks get taken to cleaners when borrowers default on loans - if they were that powerful customers would make sure they paid back their loans on time. Who ever heard of defaulting on a loan from the Mafia?

There are a number of other influential public officials in Bermuda who are not wholly accountable to the House of Assembly. The Commissioner of Police is responsible for keeping crime under control and the most recent appointment of a British police Commissioner in 1994 led to enormous opposition from the PLP despite the fact that he has been reasonably successful in reducing the amount of crime and hence the indirect burden on the economy. However, crime is still significantly higher than it was 10 years ago, many of the public pay little or no attention to the speed limit and the drug problem is as insoluble as ever. The Chairman of the Bermuda Monetary Authority (BMA) exercises considerable influence over the financial system of Bermuda but he can be removed by the Minister of Finance. But influence is not power and you need power to run things.

---

[1] See Epilogue which deals with Bermuda's strengths and weaknesses.

The judicial system in Bermuda is as good as you would find anywhere in the world and judges cannot be removed. They exercise significant power but only after the event and have little direct influence over public policy.

In Bermuda's two main industries the chief executives do not wield as much power as one would think and I doubt if more than one in twenty Bermudians could identify the heads of our large hotels or international company organisations. Even if they could, power and considerable authority within them rests with specialist managers who have the knowledge, skill and training to make independent decisions. If there ever was a powerful or dominant personality this has been largely replaced by the dull anonymous management team which by definition prevents concentration of power. The Exempted Companies are varied, relatively small and as a result power is diffused. In addition, many of them are non-Bermudian and as a result are careful not to become embroiled in local squabbles. Managers of major hotels and hotel owners are unable to exert much concentrated power - if they were able to do so the hotel industry would be more profitable than it is.[2]

The arch rivals of the hotel owners are the unions and in particular the Bermuda Industrial Union (BIU).[3] Strikes and labour unrest in the hotel industry (and elsewhere) were rife in the 1980s and the local press tended to demonise the President of the BIU, Mr Ottiwell Simmons, as being the most powerful man in Bermuda. However, the dimishing importance of the hotel industry as well as the realisation by the BIU that ill-considered strikes hurt their membership has resulted in the BIU's alleged ability to run Bermuda being considerably diminished.

The Editor of the 'Royal Gazette,' the daily newspaper, is often credited with being able to exercise considerable power over events in Bermuda and on occasion politicians are heard muttering that Bermuda is being run by the editorial page. Many Bermudians and members of the opposition PLP allege, wrongly, that the Editor is simply the daily voice of the UBP Cabinet and that he seeks support for Government policies. Members of the Government refer to the Editor as a 'loose cannon' who does not understand the complications of exercising power. The Editor and those members of the public who use the "Letters to Editor" page are simply using the power of free speech to influence events and their influence is as good or as bad as their powers of expression or powers of persuasion. Clearly the Editor is able to make his point of view known but it strains credulity to believe that he exercises real power over economic events in Bermuda.

If we examined in any detail the power and influence of such organisations as The Chamber of Commerce, The International Companies Division of the Chamber of Commerce, Employer's Council, senior executives of major commercial organisations, partners in the main law and accounting firms , and a host of the other influential organisations similar conclusions would be reached about the limited abilities to run the economy of Bermuda.

All of this is a long-winded way of saying that many public figures exercise some influence, exercise some power and have an important voice in the formulation of public policy. No one person has the ability and probably more important

---

[2] See the discussion of hotel profitability in Part II 4 .

[3] See the discussion on the power of unions in Part IV 16.

there is not sufficient time in the day for any individual or clique to run Bermuda. None of the people mentioned above individually, or even collectively run Bermuda for the most important interest group or power bloc has yet to be mentioned. That is the public. In democratic systems power flows from the people to those in authority ; power does not flow from those in authority to the people, which is one reason for the furore which arose over the McDonald's affair in 1996.

In a small community a few dozen votes can swing an election and in some Bermudian constituencies a handful of votes can end the career of even the most experienced and respected politician. In the capitalist system power rests with the consumer - they vote with their income dollars and seek to obtain the best bargain. If producers fail to meet the tests of the market or if they take their customers for granted, whether domestic or international, they will go elsewhere, as we have seen when discussing the issue of retailing and the tourist industry. Customers are very conscious of how they spend their money and are constantly seeking the best value for their dollar. However, individuals are not only customers they are also employees and decisions they make in one area may possibly conflict with decisions made in another. In the employer/employee relationship although the balance of power rests with the employer - commercial organisations are one of the few authoritarian institutions left in society - that balance is changing as Bermuda and the world moves to a knowledge-based labour force. In the banking, insurance and international company business, management cannot instruct or order its labour force to come up with winning ideas. Employees are not snow to be shovelled around and reshaped in the way management would like.

There is a third economic element involved with individuals other than as consumers and employees. Bermudians are voters as well and if the Government wished to pursue more rational economic policies, by for example reforming the immigration law to make it more responsive to the economic forces, it requires an ability to persuade the electorate that in the long run everyone will be better off when irrational protectionisms are removed. The experience of elsewhere is not encouraging. Mrs Thatcher faced turbulent miner's strikes in the 1980s when she pushed through necessary labour reforms, public spending reductions and deregulation of the country's economy. France endured violent strikes in 1995 as it tried to reform its welfare state and public service.

Success can only be achieved at the cost of unnerving social disruption which by itself is bad for business on a tourist island like Bermuda. The individual's power and influence within the economy whilst paramount is often hedged with ambiguity. As a consumer he will buy in the cheapest market - hence the popularity of shopping sprees by Bermudians to the United States, as an employee he may be able to prevent his organisation from becoming more efficient, and as a voter he may also act against his own best interests an the interests of Bermuda by desirable reforms of labour law. The creation of a national lottery is a good case in point. Bermudians gamble (itself an irrational act) by buying foreign lottery tickets; they could reduce the burden of taxation by supporting a Bermudian lottery but as members of a church they may well oppose the idea. Bermuda has a small electorate and a tiny minority can often thwart rational economic policies.

In 1995 the "Bermuda Sun"[4] published a list of people who had supplanted the old '40 Thieves.' They ranged from the Premier to senior partners of law and accounting firms to senior Ministers in the Government to labour leaders to newspaper editors to senior business figures.[5] At first I dismissed the article as idle speculation and gossip, but the more I began to examine how the Bermuda economy worked the more I began to realise that Bermuda, like other capitalist democracies, works only when there is a division of power between government, voters, business, labour, customers, and the media.

The only important sector of the economy which was neglected by the 'Bermuda Sun' was the most powerful of all - the consumer, the individual who by using his income and labour wisely determines the success or otherwise of the economy. There is no doubt that individuals who occupy positions of authority can individually exercise more influence over the economy than the ordinary worker making the average wage of around $36,000 per annum. Wealth, high incomes and positions of authority mean that those fortunate enough to be in that position are more influential than those who are not. But over a period of time, the various coalitions of interests shift as economic changes work their way through the system, people's opinions change, individuals become older or change their minds and the list of 40 to which I have referred will no doubt be very different in three years time when old blood falls by the wayside to be replace by new young Turks.

Units of political and economic influence are not, and never have been, distributed equally across the population and between interest groups, and in a capitalist system that can never be the case, but in the pluralist economic system which Bermuda is fortunate enough to enjoy no one individual or group is able to muster anything close to a majority of units of economic influence - not even the Premier or the Minister of Finance as they would readily attest if they were honest about it.

The question of who really runs Bermuda is answered by responding that everybody does directly or indirectly, but there are many who because of their wealth, position, intelligence or reputation are more influential than the average citizen who may not be aware of the power and influence he could exert. Power and influence is not concentrated in Bermuda but is diffused, is sometimes exercised inconsistently and the power structure is much more transparent by comparison with other prosperous societies.

---

[4] 'Bermuda Sun,' June 16, 1995 page 7.

[5] To my surprise I was also included, Ibid.

20. WILL I BE ABLE TO COLLECT MY PENSION?

"As we grow old we work, produce and earn less, and therefore need a secure source of income to see us through life. Societies and governments have developed mechanisms to provide income security for their older citizens as part of the social safety net for reducing poverty. Today, as the world's population ages, old age security systems are in trouble worldwide. Income insecurity in old age is a worldwide problem."

"AVERTING THE OLD AGE CRISIS" - WORLD BANK POLICY RESEARCH REPORT, 1994.

"Other countries have been debating the very real problem of financing their national pensions schemes into the next generation of pensioners and contributors. In Canada and the United States, for instance, revelation of actuarial estimates in relation to the Canada Pension Plan and Social Security, respectively, has at least brought discussion to bear on the subject. In the opinion of the Auditor, it is time that discussion started in Bermuda."

REPORT OF THE GOVERNMENT. AUDITOR FOR THE FINANCIAL YEAR 1990/1991.

The answer to this question is that it all depends - not so much on whether you live to be 65, the age at which legally you can collect your state pension although that helps enormously - but on whether firstly, the fund in which you participate will be able to pay you when you retire, and secondly, whether Bermuda continues to enjoy the economic prosperity it has enjoyed for the past 50 years. Let us consider three of the most important retirement benefit funds in Bermuda - (1) The Contributory Pension Fund ; (2) the Public Service Pension Fund; and (3) Retirement benefit funds for employees who work in private enterprise.

(1) **The Contributory Pension Fund (CPF).**

The CPF is what is known in other countries as the state pension fund, and is administered by the Social Insurance Department in the Ministry of Finance. This fund was established in 1968 (very late by comparison with the rest of the world - the United States established its equivalent in 1935) and membership is compulsory; by law all employees and employers are obligated to make weekly contributions. The main objective of the CPF is to provide pensions (and certain other benefits like disability payments) when members reach retirement age of 65. It is an income-insurance programme, a safety net for the elderly, widows, orphans and for those who become disabled. Those who live for a long time or are widowed at a young age get a huge payout by comparison with what they pay in, whilst those who die young receive very little if anything. In 1995 approximately 7,500 people were receiving benefits from the CPF with pensioners accounting for 80% of benefits.[1]

All over the world government pension schemes are in trouble, for much the same reasons as the problems which confront the CPF in Bermuda. Firstly, gov-

---

[1] 'A National Pension Scheme for Bermuda,' Green Paper published 30 June 1995

ernment pension schemes are not pension funds in the sense which most people understand that term or what retirement professionals usually mean when they talk about pension funds. Pension funds are separate and independent entities into which employers and employees contribute at a rate which is sufficient to meet current and future obligations. This means that there are sufficient assets in the fund to meet all obligations incurred to date.

As of 1996 there are insufficient assets in the CPF to meet current pension liabilities (or obligations) accrued to date. The latest actuarial report on the CPF is as of 31st July, 1990 and at that date the accrued pensions and benefits (the liabilities of the CPF) amounted to BD$1,236 million. The assets of the CPF amounted to BD$149 million at the same date. The difference between the liabilities of the CPF and the assets amounts to BD$1,087 million and is called the unfunded liability.

This immense sum, which amounts to over BD$18,000 per resident of Bermuda is the difference between what has been promised to Bermudians and what has been provided for. If the CPF was a business organisation it would be bankrupt, but as the CPF is a government-sponsored organisation the pensions and other benefits promised will have to be paid for by taxpayers at some future date. This means that the burden will fall on the shoulders of those who today are children attending primary school. It is a form of child abuse which rarely makes the headlines or which is a subject of the Oprah Winfrey Show. The deficit of over one billion dollars should be identified as a major component of the national debt of Bermuda but is nowhere mentioned in the annual budget.

I doubt as of the date of writing (1996) that the financial position of the CPF has improved to any extent since 1990; in fact I would be on fairly safe ground to state that the position has probably deteriorated. Most people should be understandably alarmed, shocked and appalled when they learn these basic facts. When the CPF was created in 1968 it was unfortunately and recklessly established as a pay-as-you-go arrangement which means that residents who now receive a pension at the age of 65 are paid from the monies which younger people presently contribute on a weekly or monthly basis. The prudent and conservative way of making provision for pensions is by means of advance funding from contributions, a mechanism which would allow for the creation of an independent asset base which could be invested to earn income to meet future liabilities.

The problem with establishing a fund with financial assets which produce income is that it increases the current tax burden. For reasons to be mentioned later this prudent system of funding is unpopular with politicians. A pay-as-you-go arrangement only works provided the amounts paid in by younger workers continues to exceed the amounts paid to older people receiving pensions and other benefits. This has been the position in Bermuda since 1968; it still is and it will continue to be the position until about the year 2010 when the number of younger Bermudians relative to the elderly falls and the amounts which have to be paid to older Bermudians will exceed the inflow of funds from younger Bermudians. Around that date some hard decisions will have to be made.

The main reason why there has been little public comment or evidence of discontent with the system is that the year 2010 seems comfortably distant and that pensions is a difficult subject to understand. In addition, most other financially sound countries operate their state pension funds as pay-as-you-go arrangements and if that system is acceptable to the United States, Canada and Britain the public believe that it should be good enough for Bermuda. The counter argument is that if those countries pursue foolish policies that is no reason for Bermuda to follow suit.

Under pension scheme arrangments organised by private employers the benefits to be paid in the future are calculated based on such relevant criteria as the ages of members, prospective investment returns and forecast rates of inflation. An actuary then calculates on a regular basis, usually every three years, what contribution rate is required to be paid by employer and employee to meet future obligations. In such a situation the assets of the fund plus future earnings approximate the accrued liabilities to members so that prospective pensions are properly secured.

The method of funding private pension arrangements is therefore very different to a government sponsored pay-as-you-go arrangement. As liabilities are created (promises to pay future pensions) so are assets in the form of employer and employee contributions which are then segregated (separated from the assets of the business) in an independent pension fund. The trustees invest the monies to earn income which will ultimately be used to pay employee pensions.

In 1995 the CPF had assets of BD$270 million but unfortunately this amount will disappear in the early part of the next century when payments from the Fund will be greater than receipts. In an unusual expression of frankness in a government document, the Green Paper entitled "A National Pension Scheme for Bermuda" stated that "the CPF may face a condition of insolvency." This means in plain language that unless the contribution rate is increased or benefits are reduced or the age of retirement is raised (or a combination of all three) there will be insufficient funds available to pay pensions except from the proceeds of general taxation. When this occurs it means that for young Bermudians taxes will have to be increased steeply to confiscatory levels in order to pay pensions to the elderly. In the opinion of many financial commentators, it is wrong for the payment of pensions to be dependent on contributions from future generations. Each generation should make provision for its own retirement benefits otherwise there is a redistribution of income from the young and poor in favour of the old and rich.

In the 21st century old people dependent on the contributions of the young for their incomes will become increasingly unpopular with the young who will understandably be preoccupied with their own financial problems. Economics is often described as a form of financial warfare; sometimes it is the rich versus the poor, sometimes it is black versus white, but in the future increasingly it will be young versus the old. Put bluntly, if you are going to be 65 in the early part of the next century you will not be able to depend on your pension from the Bermuda Government unless the working population willingly accepts a savage increase in taxation.

The CPF has all the ingredients of an empty promise and many of the features of a Ponzi scheme. A Ponzi scheme is named after a Charles Ponzi, a native of Boston in the 1920s who concocted a fraudulent plan to pay investors 50 percent profit on their investment in 45 days. Foolish people rushed to invest but it was impossible to earn a return equal to the promised rate and when an occasional smart investor wanted to withdraw funds he was paid with money received from new investors. Eventually Ponzi was unable to meet all demands for withdrawal and the scheme collapsed like a ton of bricks. Ponzi went to prison for three and a half years. It is unlikely that the designers of the pay-as-you-go CPF will suffer a similar fate as governments do not go to jail and governments can change the rules when it suits them in order to keep the CPF going.

Let me mention three other relevant facts:-

1. In Bermuda, we have grown accustomed to full-employment and prosperity but difficult questions will have to be asked about the security of pensions if the future economy does not continue to function at maximum efficiency. For example, the tourism and retail industries are not in good shape in 1996 and major hotels still incur financial losses. It would be prudent for Bermudians to prepare for the worst, not assume that the current prosperity will continue indefinitely. If Bermuda was to suffer from extended unemployment for any reason the young may not be able to afford to pay the taxes necessary to meet the cost of pensions.

2. As the population ages, the requirement for medical attention will grow significantly. At present those over 65 have their hospital costs subsidised 80 percent by government. In addition to paying pension costs the young will increasingly have to pay the medical costs of an ageing population whose life expectancy is increasing and whose requirements for medical services will increase dramatically.

3. Like most advanced countries the population of Bermuda is getting older, or "graying" if we use the popular euphemism for the onset of old age. As life expectancy increases a larger proportion of the population no longer works and each working person will have to support more people who are collecting pensions. Probably for the first time in the history of Bermuda it will have a privileged class of economically inactive elderly voters who have been promised a government income and expensive health care provided free of charge. Added to which there is continuing political pressure to improve benefits for the old, a pressure many politicians are reluctant to resist as pensioners politically tend to be 'one issue' obsessionists.

The bad news is not quite over. In the Report of the Auditor[2] for the Financial Year 1990/91 it was reported that:

"My examination indicated serious deficiencies in the accounting records and in the systems of internal control. As a consequence, I was unable to satisfy myself that all contribution receipts of the Fund (the CPF) had been recorded, nor was I able to satisfy myself that the recorded transactions were proper."

---

[2] Issued January 8, 1993.

What this means in plain language is that the public cannot rely on the records of CPF and that there is serious risk that all contributions to the CPF have not been collected.

There is a final reason for criticism of pay-as-you-go CPF. Many members of the public in Bermuda wrongly regard[3] the government scheme as a substitute for making their own private provision for retirement. As a result they tend to save less and when this occurs it results in less investment which means ultimately lower incomes.[4] A recent American study suggests that if social security contributions had been invested in wealth creating assets in the private sector, U.S. GDP could have been increased by 3% per annum and it would make every American reasonably secure in his old age. One study in the U.S. concluded, "The bottom line is that Social Security hurts almost everyone. It's a bad deal for today's seniors, an even worse deal for baby-boomers and a sick joke for generation X."[5] Tomorrow's workers are likely to see their tax burden increase faster than their incomes.

So much for the unhappy story of the CPF as we turn to the pension fund of the civil service.

(2) Public Service Superannuation Fund.

If you are a civil servant it is common knowledge you don't have to worry about the security of your pension as there is a funded pension scheme on which there is an independent actuary's report every three years This is only half right - the good news is that there is an actuary's report but the bad news is that the pension fund is not fully funded. As at 31st March 1992 (the latest actuary's report) the accrued liabilities for current members and pensioners amounted to $203.7 million. The value of the assets in the fund amounted to $114.6 million. There was therefore a shortfall or a deficit of $89.1 million or just under 44 percent of liabilities. Since 1992 returns on investments have been excellent but civil servants have also had their salaries increased in the meantime which means higher public liabilities. Although much less serious than the deficit on the CPF, the public of Bermuda is faced with a similar problem in that promises of future benefits have been made but they have not been matched by adequate provision through the creation of an independent asset base.

Civil servants should ask to see the latest actuary's report as your future pension is at stake. If you are a taxpayer also ask to see the report - it is your money - because in the future you will probably have to pay higher taxes to pay for civil servants pensions in addition to paying higher taxes to meet the pension costs for those over 65. Being young in the next century in going to be expensive.

(3) Private Pension Funds.

If you are not a civil servant, you may be fortunate enough to be a member of the retirement fund operated by your employer. Most private retirement funds are independently managed by trustees whose obligation is to ensure that the assets

---

[3] This misconception was a major reason for issuing a Green Paper in 1996 on the subject of pensions.

[4] Chile is a good example of where privatising pensions have revitalised the whole economy - the reverse of what is being done in Bermuda.

[5] 'Fortune Magazine,' September 30, 1996, page 36

of the fund are sufficient to meet future liabilities, prudently invested, and segregated from the employer's business assets. An independent actuary examines the fund and makes recommendations to the trustees about the level of contributions needed in order to keep the fund solvent. If your pension meets the above criteria count your blessings, but also take the time and effort to read the annual report of the trustees of the fund and examine the statement of accounts and the latest actuary's report. I am a trustee of The Bank of N.T. Butterfield & Son Ltd., Employees Retirement Fund Trust and several other pension funds and I am satisfied that they are properly and prudently funded and managed.

Unfortunately, many members of the labour force may be members of a retirement benefit scheme[6] which is not independently funded and is therefore dependent on the future prosperity of their employer's business. If this is the case the protection or security you enjoy for collecting your pension is substantially less than that of independently managed and funded schemes. If the business falls on hard times or goes into liquidation there will not be sufficient money to meet the cost of pensions. Employees in the position are unable to call on government revenues to meet the costs and they could end up with nothing.

It is estimated that about 16,500 members of the labour force, or about half of all employees in Bermuda do not enjoy the benefits of an occupational retirement benefit scheme. Most will therefore retire with only a pension from the CPF and as a consequence will have inadequate funds to maintain their standard of living - not a very happy position to be in.

The recent Green Paper to which I have referred above was tabled in the House of Assembly on 30th June, 1995 and it sets out in realistic terms (a sharp contrast to the Independence Green Paper) the problem which Bermuda faces with half the labour force not covered by a retirement scheme and an ageing population. Proposals are contained in the paper to deal with the future problem but for a great many employees this may be too little too late.

The issue of providing adequate funds to maintain an income in old age is one of the key problems facing Bermuda as we enter the 21st century for during the fat years of the 1970s and 1980s little thought was given by government, or by the public, to the provision of savings for pensions. Most people thought the good times would roll forever, that they would never grow old and that a rainy day would never arrive. Tomorrow would take care of itself. The fact is that after retirement people can live for more than 20 years and to have an enjoyable life after ceasing to work it is necessary to have an income. The public has unfortunately deluded itself by believing that they would never grow old and that somebody somewhere would look after them. There is no Santa Claus, Easter Bunny or Tooth Fairy. It is hard to escape the conclusion that income insecurity in old age is a major social and economic problem for Bermudians in the immediate future.

---

[6] See Green Paper page 6.

BERMUDIAN SOCIETY AND THE ECONOMY

4

four

1. IS THERE AN ECONOMIC DIMENSION TO MULTICULTURAL-ISM?

"Each human culture is so unique that no one of them is higher or lower, greater or less than any other."

RENATO ROSALDO.

"But does study of the glory that was Greece and the grandeur that was Rome improve the academic record of Greek-American and Italian-American children? Not so that anyone has noticed. Why is it likely to help black children, who are removed from their geographical origins not by 50 years but by 300?"

ARTHUR M. SCHLESINGER, JR.

Multicultural education is one of the current educational policies receiving widespread attention in Bermuda in 1996. It is difficult to go through a month without some multicultural celebration taking place at some school or another. To most people this is a welcome reform as it implies recognition of the valuable contributions made to the progress of our civilisation, including the economy, by many previously unacknowledged individuals, groups or nationalities.

The economy has been a dominant force in multiculturalism for centuries long before the term was even thought of. As I write this piece I am listening to a CD produced in England, played on a Japanese CD player, played through an American receiver, of an Italian opera (La Traviata) set in France, and the main tenor is a Spanish-Mexican. It is a beautiful Bermuda Sunday morning and already I can see the Dockyard built by convict labour from England and the West Indies, several boats probably built in the United States and fuelled by petroleum products imported from Venezuela and Curacao. When I get round to breakfast I will probably drink Indian tea manufactured in England, cereal produced in the United States, using cutlery and china made in who knows where. As the reader reads this piece the letters come from Ancient Rome, the numbers from India and the Arabian Peninsula, the paper was invented in China and I was born in Scotland, using ideas which originated in Scotland, Russia, France, Austria and America. It is hard to imagine an activity which is more multicultural.

However, it easy to go even further. Sports in Bermuda like tennis, football or golf originated in UK but the top practitioners can be American, Russian or Bosnian. Our system of government originated in UK but British democracy has been exported all over the world. The products we use in everyday life come everywhere one can imagine and places of which many have never heard. Rubber from Malaysia, cocoa from Ghana, coffee from Brazil, and so on - the list is endless and fascinating.

Two hundred years ago it would have been impossible to write what I have written as many of the products, countries and ideas did not exist. Further, as an individual I would probably have spent my working life labouring on a farm or fishing in Scotland instead of using a personal computer made in USA on a beautiful Sunday morning in Bermuda whilst listening to opera. The chances are I would probably be dead as the life expectancy in those days was about 40 years - if you were lucky enough to survive childhood.

The reason why all the products mentioned have moved from their origins is quite simple. They were and are the BEST that could be produced and consumers and customers tend always to buy the best products they can at the most reasonable prices. One of the great achievements of the 20th century is that many cultural and economic gaps have been bridged through the medium of television (there have been many adverse consequences of this). National borders are porous because money, ideas and products can cross borders without the consent of bureaucrats or government and this enhances the power of the public and the consumer and leads to multiculturalism.

I doubt very much if the education process describes multiculturalism in the terms I have done, as being a reflection of the best that the world can produce. In fact nothing could be as different from the present multicultural philosophy as the international economy. The educational establishment in public education leans to the belief that the traditional school curriculum is biased because it asserts the superiority and stresses the cultural arrogance and achievements in science, literature and economics of Western democratic societies like France, United States and Britain at the expense of other societies. They allege that this Eurocentrism is the major reason why white males are able to dominate the financial and cultural world and hence squeeze out other racial groups and women. Western civilisation, it is asserted, is a conspiracy against other cultures and the application of the multiculturalism ideal will deal this conspiracy a death blow and correct historical injustices and inbalances.[1] It is European men who produced such "isms" as racism, sexism, and colonialism all of which were designed to impose white male values on the rest of the world.

Consumers select what they want from the wide variety of products and services and reject what is inferior. Who ever heard of Swiss opera, British cooking, the Iraqi insurance industry, Indonesian literature, Brazilian education or Austrian cars being described as "the best available?" Yet multiculturalism does not make decisions or judgements like this - as it is about celebrating diversity and stating that nothing is better or worse than anything else just different. The constant theme running through this philosophy is that nothing critical can be taught if it offends members of an officially sanctioned underprivileged group. Nothing should be taught unless it makes people feel good about themselves (whatever this means) and has a positive effect on self-esteem or pride of the group. It is as if self-esteem or character does not have to be earned or comes from flattering attention of teachers rather than from real life experiences. Lack of self-esteem, it is asserted, prevents large numbers of black students from reaching their full economic potential. Unfortunately, the cart is before the horse. It is achievements which create self-esteem; it is not self-esteem which underwrites achievement.

If this philosophy was applied to the financial world our standard of living and quality of life would plummet. Multiculturalism has clouded the minds of many children in the United States by deliberately stroking paranoia. Far from being an educational reform which benefits the public it has become yet another reason for the underprivileged being unable to achieve their potential. .

---

[1] There is more than a passing similarity to Marxism and Communism discussed in Part I 4

When the public has an economic choice (this is what free trade is all about) politically correct concepts like muticulturalism imposed on the unsuspecting public by ideologically inspired bureaucrats become totally irrelevant as individual consumers express their multicultural preferences by spending their hard-earned dollars. Multiculturalism is one of these luxuries which indulgent bureaucrats can impose on innocent children and complacent parents because they are paid by the public purse.

Much of what I have written might be enlightening but irrelevant except that through default many of the distortions which multiculturalism creates are being absorbed into Bermudian mainstream thought. The most pernicious doctrine is that there should be "representation" of each group in important facets of our economic life. For example, rather than having the best talent in jobs there should be equal representation of women and black males in decision making jobs, irrespective of skills and experience. This conclusion arises because of the unspoken and unexamined assumption that all cultural experience is neutral (neither better nor worse than any other) and each culture is equally effective at producing the blend of knowledge and experience needed to run a modern economy. Multiculturalism involves demographic diversity - a precise number of blacks, Indians, Hispanics, women etc. - that it disguises its ideological conformity and emphasis on mediocrity. For many proponents of multiculturalism the present concept of equality of opportunity and merit is a smokescreen for policies which result in the exclusion of the black race and women from positions of power and influence.[2]

At present we all practise multiculturalism in our day-to-day economic lives by seeking out the best products, but we should understand that the brand now on offer in our educational system is flawed. It may well turn out to be not an educational reform but an educational tragedy with a disproportionate adverse impact on the poor. For young Bermudians to succeed there must be a clear focus on the essentials of education - reading, writing, arithmetic, mathematics, history, geography, discipline and time-keeping - the old-fashioned virtues which make it possible for an individual to reach his potential in society.[3] We should not confuse cultural differences, which quite clearly exist, with artificially induced barriers to economic advancement.

---

[2] This idea is explored further when discussing institutional racism and the glass ceiling in Part IV 11 and 12.
[3] See, for example, "The Schools We Need," by E.D. Hirch, Jr.

2. IS BERMUDA TOO SMALL TO DO WELL ECONOMICALLY?

"The success of the United States is often attributed to its generous natural resources and wide open spaces. They certainly played a part - but then, if they were crucial, what explains the success of nineteenth century Great Britain and Japan or twentieth century Hong Kong?"

MILTON FRIEDMAN.[1]

For most people the ability of a country to do well economically is associated with bigness and plentiful natural resources like gold or copper mines, wide open spaces like the pampas in Argentina or the presence of oil and natural gas. If this was the case it does not explain the dreadful economic performance of large countries like Ghana (with gold), Argentina (with excellent spacious agricultural land) - until recently, or Venezuela from which Bermuda receives its oil. Clearly the bounty of nature is important - as it has been for Canada and the United States - but increasingly economists are recognising the importance of the general economic environment and allowing individuals to be given freedom to make the most of their lives.

In addition, there is compelling historical evidence that there is no relationship between high per capita income and the size of a country, whether that size is measured by reference to area or population. In a 1996 book[2] Kenichi Ohmae concludes that the future rests with small countries not large states. Indeed, if California was free of the remainder of the United States it would enjoy a standard of living higher than the others. One could go further and state that if Bismarck had not united Germany Barvarians would be richer, or if Cavour had not united Italy Piedmont would be richer than the remaining Italian provinces. To be a small country wide open to international trade, with strong social cohesion and with limited government has been a recipe for economic success for centuries.

Size and the supply of natural resources is not much of an advantage in determining financial performance. Monaco, a small independent tax-haven famous for its royalty, gambling and grand-prix motor race is much wealthier than the country of France which surrounds and dominates it. Some of the richest countries in the world are very small by comparison with their neighbours. Little Luxembourg is the richest country in the European Union, and small Switzerland the wealthiest country in Europe. Little Bermuda is the richest country in the Americas.

Grand Cayman, whose structure and policies are similar to Bermuda, is a model of economic efficiency by comparison with Jamaica which governed Cayman until 1962 when Jamaica became independent. Caymanians then opted to remain a British colony and prospered. Jamaica, whose living standards were about the same as Bermuda in 1962, went on to substantial economic decline evidenced, for example, by the value of the Jamaican dollar which at independence was J\$1 to US\$2; in 1996 it is 29 Jamaican dollars to US\$1. Put another way a Jamaican dollar in 1962 equalled 200 US cents, it is now worth about 3.5 cents.

---

1 "Free to Choose," page 37.
2 "The End of the Nation State," Kenichi Ohmae.

The story of successful small states is not a new one; cities like Venice were an oasis of wealth amongst the poverty of a much larger medieval Italy. Tiny Singapore and Hong Kong are very much the exceptions in Eastern Asia where their per capita incomes dwarf those of much bigger countries like India, China and Vietnam. In 1996, The World Economic Forum (WEF) and The International Institute for Management Development (IMD) issued a list of countries ranked by which were the most competitive. Of the top 25, only 10 could be classified as big countries and the other 15 were small countries like Singapore. The top 10 rankings from WEF were instructive and were as follows:

1. Singapore
2. Hong Kong
3. New Zealand
4. United States
5. Luxembourg
6. Switzerland
7. Norway
8. Canada
9. Taiwan
10. Malaysia.

Big countries suffer from the penalties of size, what economists call diseconomies of scale[3] and by far the biggest diseconomy is politics which all too often blocks prosperity and the freedom of individuals to utilise their talents to the full. The miraculous success of the Chinese outside China - in Malaysia, United States and Brazil - is in vivid contrast to cultural revolutions of great leaps backward in the homeland. Small countries, like small people, are usually quicker off their feet and more able to take advantage of opportunities which their larger brethren either cannot see or are unable to grasp because of their bureaucratic turn of mind.

Bermuda writes about 9% of global reinsurance.[4] Monte Carlo has a casino, Liechtenstein makes false teeth, Singapore is an offshore-trader following the example of Hong Kong, and Switzerland became the world's banker many years ago. Even tiny New Zealand, once dubbed the most inefficient economy in Christendom dumped its high tax protectionist policies and is now leaving its much bigger neighbour and rival Australia in the dust.

On the other hand, a large country like India with its mystifying, stultifying and sweeping financial and bureaucratic controls has resulted in most of its 850 million people living in abject poverty, many of whom die of diseases which were eliminated long ago in the West, and they have a shorter life expectancy than citizens of most other countries. This is a terrible waste of human potential to do good. One of the modern mysteries of economics is why Indians who emigrate to UK, Canada, Australia and USA do so well whilst their stay-at-home cousins stagnate in poverty.

---

[3] At one stage economies of scale, the ability to spread costs over a large output, was viewed as an essential ingredient of economic health.
[4] "1995 Economic Review," page 12.

It is not difficult, except perhaps for politicians, to reach the conclusion that being small, opening the economy to world trade, respect for the rule of law, keeping taxes low and specialising in some niche product is a much surer way to prosperity than protectionism, high taxes, intrusive and bureaucratic government. If a country has other merits such as a good infrastructure of telecommunications, roads and education, a flexible labour force and effective political and legal institutions it will be well placed to benefit economically.

Looking at the matter in a slightly different way, how would an international bureaucrat based in London or Washington view the economic prospects for a mid-Atlantic Island of 20 square miles of barren rock, 700 miles from the nearest land mass, with a population density several times that of UK and USA, which is two-thirds black, voted in a referendum in 1995 to retain its colonial status, imports everything from energy to electrical plugs, has no opera house or concert hall, no central bank, no national airline, no university, is dependent on rainfall for its water, apart from a benign climate and natural beauty has no valuable natural resources, and whose government has had a hands-off policy with regard to economic matters for centuries?

Sitting in UK or USA an imaginary bureaucrat would either write the place off or regard it as a typical speck of insignificance dependent on handouts from governments of the developed world. Indeed anyone who follows international news and the financial press, or is naive enough to believe the propaganda published by the United Nations, would be hard put to contradict this conventional wisdom particularly as it is evidenced by the poverty and marginal financial importance of such places as The Seychelles, Antigua, Grenada, the Cook Islands and many, many more small island communities.

If, however, the reader landed on an island by the name of Bermuda, which is still a British Colony, he would learn that the per capita income is about US$27,500[5] per annum compared to $24,753 per annum in the USA and $20,664 in Canada.

There is no income tax, no capital gains tax, and modest inheritance taxes. Until recently Bermuda had a consistently balanced budget, operates under a government system reminiscent of what was in place in the American Colonies before 1776, has an almost Elizabethan welfare system, negligible unemployment, minimal crime, comparatively little social unrest, is host to almost every large multinational company in the world, has eight golf courses and has never received a penny in aid from the UK, US or anyone else. In addition, there is an enviable quality of life - no traffic jams, few fast food outlets, clean streets, excellent sports facilities, and a wonderful climate.

Surely this is not possible in the 1990s when the description given in the previous paragraph sounds more like the hype from a tourist brochure or a party political manifesto than a sober description based on the dismal science of economics? How can a microscopic isolated barren island produce enviable success when so many larger more powerful countries who have a seat at the United Nations, large military forces and are endowed with greater natural resources are conspicuous

---

5 "Facts and Figures about Bermuda," 1996.

failures and spend much of their time rattling the begging bowl for aid or development money, whilst simultaneously cursing multinational companies for exploiting their natural resources or people, or insulting their sovereignty?

The fascinating question for the reader and for many Bermudians is, how is this possible and what is the secret of Bermuda's success? If there are no oil wells or hand-outs from Uncle Sam or the British Government what is the magic formula? Is it drugs or money laundering? And is it really the land of milk and honey the tourist brochures make it out to be? How can Bermuda with all its supposed inherent disadvantages be so successful when there are so many other conspicuous failures in the world?

The reasons for economic success in most countries are often difficult to determine and are dependent on many factors, some obvious - most not. There are certain fundamentals necessary for economic success to which Bermuda has traditionally paid a great deal of attention. Most of the following key success factors are discussed in other parts of this book but it is important for this particular essay to take note of them:-

- general acceptance of capitalism and public confidence in the system of private enterprise[6];
- respect for the rule of law, and in particular the absence of serious crime;
- respect for private property and contract rights;
- the right of appeal from the domestic legal system to the Judicial Committee of the Privy Council in the United Kingdom;
- tight controls on Government spending;
- Bermuda dollar tied legally and commercially to the U.S. dollar[7];
- modest levels of Government debt;
- no central bank to expand the money supply and create runaway inflation;
- no income, withholding or corporate taxes;
- access to foreign capital;
- access to foreign technology and labour;
- political stability and absence of corruption;
- sensible regulation of financial institutions[8];
- careful oversight of international organisations establishing a presence in Bermuda;
- excellent infrastructure of roads, ports, telephones and powers;
- heavy investment in education, both public and private;
- no welfare dependency[9];
- few state owned enterprises;
- a legacy of peaceful development and political stability;
- limited government intervention in the day-to-day economy.

---

[6] See Part I 9.
[7] See Part II 12.
[8] See Part II 11.
[9] See Part IV 15.

To sum up, it is politically stable, market-friendly institutions and limited government which provide the necessary ingredients for economic success. Although the pursuit of many of the policies mentioned above are important for the continuing success of the Bermudian economy, or indeed for any economy, it may be appropriate next briefly to examine Bermuda's history which is fundamental to an understanding of the present Bermuda economy.

3. HOW IS BERMUDA'S HISTORY IMPORTANT TO THE ECONOMY?

"When I want to understand what is happening today or try to decide what will happen tomorrow, I look back."

OLIVER WENDELL HOLMES JR.

"History is a pact between the dead, the living, and the yet unborn."

EDMUND BURKE.

It is said that history is to the nation as memory is to the individual and for Bermuda, our history is a major key to understanding how our economy works and why it works so well. Assume for the purpose of this question that Bermuda instead of being settled by the British had been inhabited by the Spanish, not too far-fetched an assumption as it was the Spanish who discovered the island. If that had been the case our history would have been vastly different and that would have had a significant impact on our economic structure.

First of all we would have spoken Spanish and not English and this is a crucial difference. The financial services world uses English exclusively as the language of international commerce. Whilst Spanish is used all over the Western Hemisphere, Bermuda would never have been able to create an international business industry without the population of Bermuda using and understanding English language. Our relationship with the United States would have been vastly different; similar say to that of the Dominican Republic and there would have been only a tenuous relationship with the United Kingdom whose importance to Bermuda in the early days of economic development was fundamental.

Until the late nineteenth century the economy of Bermuda revolved almost entirely around the British military, mainly the Royal Navy. There was some agriculture and fishing but reliance on these two basic industries for foreign exchange earnings would not have given Bermuda a high standard of living or a sophisticated style of life. With the loss of the American Colonies in the late eighteenth century, Bermuda became the historical equivalent of a large aircraft carrier permanently anchored in the North Atlantic. The repair, servicing and provisioning of the British naval vessels as well as catering to the needs of the large British garrisons - who were the eighteenth and nineteenth century equivalents of modern tourists or international companies - provided Bermudians by the standards of the day with well paying secure jobs, modern training in such things as welding, shipbuilding and management skills.

Even today there are many older Bermudians who learned their commercial and technical skills as apprentices or employees at the Royal Naval Dockyard which closed in 1951.[1] There may well have been the Spanish equivalent of Dockyard but the decline of the Spanish Empire in the Western Hemisphere took place more than one hundred years before the major changes to British military strategy. The Spanish effectively left the hemisphere after the Spanish American war of 1898 although their presence had been considerably reduced since the loss of their South American colonies in the 1830s. With the departure of the Spanish at the end of the nineteenth century Bermuda may well have become an American colony similar to Puerto Rico so that our life today would be vastly different and in many ways financially much poorer. The 1995 per capita income of Puerto Rico is US$6,360 per annum, less than one quarter of that of Bermuda.

The British brought not only a military presence but the British system of government and law. Government was by historical standards liberal, enlightened[2] and most day-to-day decisions in the Colony were delegated to the House of Assembly and the Crown appointed Executive Council - the historical equivalent of the Cabinet. The adoption of English law (strictly speaking there is no such thing as British law as Scottish law is different from English) is also of fundamental importance because one of the major reasons international companies decide to locate in Bermuda is because of the application of English law in the Bermuda courts and the right of appeal to the appellate courts in UK. Spanish law would not be attractive to international companies.

In terms of government Spanish colonial rule was much harsher and more authoritarian than that of UK. There was little delegation to the local population, the social structure was more hierarchical and the Spanish did not take kindly to any deviation from policies established in Madrid. The Catholic Church was similarly authoritarian and there was no tolerance of other religions. Commercial activity was not encouraged and even today countries with a Spanish heritage tend to be economically backward by comparison with the former English, Dutch and French colonies. I have little doubt that had Bermuda been a Spanish colony not only would we have spoken Spanish and been Catholic, but we would be financially much worse off. Although the British Crown did little to subsidise economic development, apart from their military presence, the liberal trade practices of the British permitted the local population to participate in trading activities and encouraged commercial innovation in growth industries like tourism and international business.

There are several other historical factors which have a bearing on today's Bermuda which could be explained in greater detail; the absence of corruption, high public health standards, the range of educational opportunities and many more.

Slavery is clearly a major historical issue for the majority black population in Bermuda who are the descendants of slaves as this was a practice of both Spanish

---

1 Mr Eugene Cox, the shadow finance minister is a good example.

2 The obvious exception to this was the treatment of the black population which by current standards was indefensible. However, by comparison AT THE TIME with other countries it was enlightened.

and British colonial rule.[3] Negroes were by far the biggest racial group enslaved although they were not necessarily the first. It is popularly thought that only the black population was subjected to slavery but in his book "Slavery in Bermuda", James Smith reports that, "A large section of the early labour force consisted of boys and young men, who were sent out to Bermuda as apprentices or indentured servants, sold to the highest bidders, and virtually held in a state of slavery for a period of years. Some had been unwillingly impressed from the streets of London and other English seaports before being shipped out to the colony." In addition, many Indians from North America were imported as slaves and in the second half of the seventeenth century 80 Pequod Indians from Massachusetts were imported and sold as slaves. This was followed by Scottish and Irish prisoners of war from the military expeditions of Oliver Cromwell. The unfree whites, Indians and blacks freely intermingled and interbred but were looked down on by the free white population.

Because of its remoteness and size Bermuda practised a form of slavery which was different in scale and style from that practised in a West Indian Island like Jamaica where large sugar and agricultural plantations were the norm. The duties and work of Bermuda slaves tended to be of a domestic nature or involved simple agriculture or fishing. The small numbers and the absence of plantations led to a milder form of slavery than practised elsewhere but which by modern standards was still brutal and degrading and which cannot be condoned because of the moral wrong of ownership of other human beings. It is more than likely that if Bermuda had been Spanish, treatment of slaves would have been much harsher.

Slaves were freed in the British Empire (which obviously included Bermuda), effective 1st August, 1834 by Bermuda's Act of Emancipation about thirty years before slavery was abolished in the United States and 50 years before it was abolished in Brazil. Most Bermudian slave-owners did not oppose the Emancipation Act and they received compensation from the British Crown for the loss of their "property" at the rate of £27.4.11 3/4 per slave. Thus came to an end in Bermuda the evil and degrading practice of slavery but it was replaced by a Bermuda "Jim Crow"[4] system which still regarded the black population as second-class citizens.

The bitter legacy of slavery and the long legacy of overt racial discrimination which was practised in Bermuda until the mid 1960s meant that opportunities for the majority black population to gain financial security and wealth were extremely limited in this oppressive system. It is clearly a major factor in the day-to-day relationships between white and black Bermudians and it is probably the most important historical factor which today affects the smooth functioning of the economy.[5] The black population still tends to occupy the poorest land, the worst housing, has lower earnings than whites, is less wealthy, has less commercial influence, and is employed in greater numbers in low status jobs. Much of this is rightly attributed to slavery and the disgraceful racial discrimination which took

---

[3] Slavery is a practice which existed in nearly all societies. It was common in Asia, pre-Columbian America, nearly all of Africa, and in most of Europe before 1400. Britain and United States were unusual in stamping out a practice which had existed from time immemorial. It was not peculiar to the relationships between whites and blacks. What was peculiar about slavery in the British Empire and the United States was that there were forces working to end this evil practice.

[4] This was the nickname given to the practice in the Southern U.S. of treating blacks as second class citizens with few political or economic rights.

5 See Part IV 8.

place after slavery was abolished and which continued until the mid 1960s. Even today it is widely believed that there are still overtones of racial discrimination which results in the black population being economically penalized.

On balance the history of Bermuda has been a peaceful one and together with its key location in the North Atlantic has allowed Bermuda to enjoy a standard and quality of life which, despite its shortcomings, is the envy of the rest of the world.

> "The study of history is a powerful antidote to contemporary arrogance. It is humbling to discover how many of our glib assumptions, which seem to us novel and plausible, have been tested before, not once but many times and in innumerable guises; and discovered to be, at great human cost, wholly false."
> Paul Johnson.

History clearly has a major impact on the modern economy and had Bermuda's history been different there is little doubt that it would be a vastly different place today. Men and women make history as things don't happen by chance - it is people, their energy, their resourcefulness and their vision which make things happen. Bermuda has been very fortunate in that it produced many men who dedicated their life to improving Bermuda. Examples are Sir Howard Trott, John S. Darrell, Sir Henry Vesey and A.W. Bluck in tourism and in the development of international business Sir James Pearman, Sir Dudley Spurling, Mr. William Kempe, Sir Bayard Dill, Fred Reiss, David Graham, Sir Harry Butterfield and Sir Henry Tucker.

There is nothing that can be done to change what happened in the past - the only thing we can do is learn from our mistakes and hope that some of the evil things which occurred can never take place again. But it is also important to understand that many old-time Bermudians were very far-sighted and set Bermuda on a road which has produced a life-style which allows present day Bermudians to prosper.

4. CAN BERMUDA CONTINUE TO GROW ECONOMICALLY?

"Be not afraid of growing slowly, be afraid only of standing still."

CHINESE PROVERB.

"Emphasis must be placed on improving the quality of services, increasing the productivity of man's effort, wringing higher returns from the use of land and buildings, and choosing activities which will allow Bermudians to share in the rewards of new technology, while avoiding some of its wasteful side effects."

'THE REISMAN REPORT ON BERMUDA,' NOVEMBER, 1977.

A leading trade union leader in the United States at the end of the 19th century was asked by a newspaper reporter what the workers of the United States wanted. Samuel Gompers answered "More." The average individual in Bermuda is immensely much better off than the 19th century American worker but if that question was asked of many people in Bermuda I would be surprised if the answer did not also boil down to an unambiguous "More".

Bermuda enjoys a standard of living and a style of life which is one of the highest in the world. Why not, therefore, forget about economic growth? After all we can only eat so much, wear so many clothes and watch only a limited amount of television. This view, appealing to some - usually the very wealthy or fanatical environmentalists, neglects the very human tendency of not looking at absolute standards or comparing ourselves with poor countries in other parts of the world, but comparing our relative position with others in Bermuda. There are many, probably a large majority who believe that they are doing badly by comparison with other Bermudians[1] and wish to increase their share of the economic pie. Besides a stationary society is not an attractive proposition to people involved in business. An economy is like a bicycle - it can only work by moving forwards.

In order to have more or for the community to become more wealthy it is necessary for Bermuda as a whole to earn more. This can be done in one of two ways. Firstly, increase prices so that tourists or companies which incorporate in Bermuda are compelled to pay more to the Bermudian labour force, service providers like accountants and lawyers, or to the Bermuda Government in the form of taxes. This was a soft or bogus option which we resorted to in the past. However, competitive forces both in the tourist industry and the international company business and the end of inflation make it increasingly difficult if not impossible to increase prices. To increase prices means running the risk that tourists will stay away or international companies will migrate to more financially friendly locations. Indeed, that has already happened in the case of the hospitality industry and a major challenge for Bermuda is not to increase costs but to reduce them.

The second way is to improve productivity, mainly of the labour force, so that greater incomes are earned because people work smarter and more productively[2] but this is not an easy process in an economy which largely provides services. Increases in productivity are easier to attain in a manufacturing environment where washing machines are produced on an assembly line but are difficult to

---

[1] See the Swain report as an example of this view.

[2] See Part I 18 for a discussion of productivity.

achieve when trying to raise the productivity of a waiter in a restaurant whose patrons demand personal service. In the final analysis, increases in productivity - that is output per employee per hour - are the only sustainable way in which Bermuda (or anywhere else) can raise its standard of living.

It should be kept in mind that Bermuda presently enjoys full employment (probably the only advanced economy in the world which does) so that increases in economic activity may well result in an increase in immigration by importing additional labour. In addition, Bermuda is one of the most densely populated countries in the world[3] and that problems of overcrowding on the roads and a shortage of housing could well be counterproductive to improvements in the performance of the tourist industry.[4]

The question for Bermuda is from where can future economic growth come? Tourism is a difficult and fiercely competitive business in which the main investors in Bermuda do not make money. If investors do not make money, it is unlikely that they will be prepared to throw good money after bad, although there is always the hope or the consolation that potential new investors will be convinced or naive enough to believe that they know more about the tourist business than prior investors. It is difficult to believe that tourism without the benefit of new hotels and significant investment can grow beyond its current level, particularly as it is struggling to maintain even its present level of business.

> "What Bermuda needs in the future is a growing share of the world's activities in insurance, banking, international trade, ocean transportation, management consulting and their related fields. It is these endeavours which best suit Bermuda's space constrained economy. They can be undertaken with modest demands on office space, but with a maximum of soft-ware support and intelligent manpower. Manpower plannning, education and training in and outside Bermuda should be slanted towards the provision of well-trained young people who can pursue opportunities in these rewarding occupations."
>
> The Reisman Report 1977.

Increasing productivity in tourism is clearly one route to follow but unless labour relations take a significant turn for the better not much progress can be expected. Tourist expenditure is unlikely to increase because of continued economic pressures in the United States and besides there is not much on which the tourist can spend his money. Whilst tourism will continue to be the major employer of labour, its prospects are such that it would be unwise to rely on that industry for any major income growth in the future.

International business is another matter. New ideas, new products and immense resourcefulness have been a trademark of that industry for the past 10 years during which the industry insurance premiums have almost doubled to $1.6 billion and major new organisations have chosen to locate or incorporate in

---

[3] See Part I 19 on the issue of population.
[4] This was the view of a former Economic Adviser, Nicholas Weinreb, and was the subject of a speech made by him in September, 1988.

Bermuda. The main problem with that impressive growth is that it is believed that insufficient numbers of Bermudians, mainly male black Bermudians, have participated in the benefits which flow from that growth and this has created social tensions. As in many discussions about the future of Bermuda, we return inevitably to the question of education and training. The qualities required for success in Exempted Company operations are those which are in chronic short supply all over the world.[5]

It is believed by many Bermudians and by many of those in the international business community that Bermuda is hard-pressed and simply too small to produce the quality and numbers of people necessary to operate sophisticated international companies. To dispel this gloomy prediction, it is essential that the educational system improve its productivity and efficiency (which has not occurred in many other countries) but many are equally gloomy and believe that this is unlikely to occur. The examples of Hong Kong and Singapore give credibility to the idea that the only resource which is not limited is that of the human mind. As the world enters the post-industrial phase it is in those areas which require trained intelligence that provide the greatest opportunity for continued economic growth.

In the short term, any expansion in international business will arise from attracting able business executives from elsewhere. As more and more non-Bermudians are hired to fill executive positions one result may be to create large numbers of non-excutive jobs but there are two disadvantages to this process. Firstly, the non-Bermudians add to population, environmental and social pressures by for example using residential accommodation, adding to the number of private cars or pressure for places at private schools. These pressures have been accommodated within the economy over the years without creating undue strain but there are limits to the social costs which can be absorbed by the community whilst seeking to generate ever higher incomes for the working population. Secondly, there is also the problem of pushing up the cost of local labour in those areas in which there is already a shortage of the trained and the educated.

This is not an easy dilemma to resolve because of the philosophical battle between those Bermudians who like Samuel Gompers have not fully enjoyed the benefits of past economic growth and who want 'more' and a vocal wealthy minority of Bermudians who say we have enough. The difficulties of the debate between the pro and and anti growth arguments are compounded when the racial dimension is factored into the equation. Creating a consensus is a difficult task.

One unknown factor about future growth is how the additional land made available by the departure of the military forces in the early 1990s will be utilised. There are many proposals for development which are currently under study as well as proposals, for example, to establish an Oceanarium at the old Royal Navy Dockyard. These issues are being examined in 1996 and the utilisation of the Base lands may provide a launching pad for additional economic growth or for reducing social and other pressures. At this stage it is too early to say how effective they will be.

---

5 See Part IV 18 for a discussion of this issue.

5. WHY DO WE HAVE SO MANY FOREIGNERS WORKING IN BERMUDA?

"Bermuda uses up and spits out these people with a degree of casual cruelty that is an affront to basic human decency."

'MID-OCEAN NEWS,' DECEMBER 15, 1995.

Firstly, there is a chronic shortage of skilled labour in Bermuda, especially in the newly established international companies industry. However this is also true about many positions in government and the hospitality industry. A casual review of the job columns in the Royal Gazette contains many advertisements for positions many of which could only be filled by a limited number of Bermudians with the necessary skills, experience and temperament. Many such Bermudians are already gainfully employed. The jobs either have to go unfilled, the salaries and benefits to attract a suitable applicant have to be raised, or a non-Bermudian has to be recruited from overseas.

Here is a sample of jobs culled from the 'Royal Gazette' of June 14, 1996 :

- Corporate lawyer with 6 years experience of international finance, mutual funds and capital markets transactions.

- Senior accountant with 5 years experience in an insurance related field.

- Vice President, Claims with a minimum of 20 years experience and outstanding track record.

- Senior Manager of Technical Support with CNE or MCNE qualification and 4 years experience.

- Portfolio Manager in private client asset management, Chartered Financial Analyst with 3 years experience.

The message is clear. There are a great many highly skilled, lucrative positions in Bermuda particularly in the sphere of international business and there are clearly insufficient Bermudians available to fill all of them. If these jobs remain unfilled Bermuda runs the risk of losing business and the opportunity to enjoy the benefits (and also the penalties) of economic growth,[1] and the opportunities for support staff are diminished. By support staff I mean the lesser skilled positions such as secretaries, receptionists, accounting and general clerical support which are needed to assist professionals. Such positions are often stepping stones to future executive positions. Being able to attract talented and productive people from around the world is one of Bermuda's greatest strengths, not a weakness. Those in favour of restraints argue that expatriates are "stealing" Bermudian jobs. This simply does not stand up to rational economic analysis as it is estimated that each experienced professional expatriate generates, directly or indirectly, between two and three jobs for Bermudians. Skilled expatriates enhance the competitiveness of Bermuda and make it a more productive place.

---

1 See Part IV 4 for a discussion of this subject.

Secondly, the international company business is one which requires a disproportionate number of professionals to discharge its many and varied responsibilities. Accountants, lawyers, actuaries, insurance underwriters, computer programmers, portfolio managers and a host of other professionals are required to maintain the business. This has a secondary effect on the economy in that an additional number of professionals are required to provide specialist services from the legal and accounting professions as well as from local banks and government.

There is in effect a transfer of technology from the highly developed financial sector, mainly in the United States and Britain, to Bermuda and Bermudians but which cannot be wholly accomplished through hiring local staff. It is therefore necessary to bring to Bermuda the current expertise in such critical areas as accounting, insurance and banking. It would not be possible for Bermudians to have enjoyed their high incomes had it been impossible to bring professional skills directly to Bermuda.

The public often thinks of Exempted Companies as being a homogeneous group of organisations. This is not the case, as they are involved in such diverse activities as insurance, banking and investment management but also in lesser known fields as oil trading, personal and corporate holding companies and pharmaceuticals. Frequently, knowledge of one industry cannot be easily transferred into knowledge of another. The recent origins of this business have simply not made it possible for Bermudians to acquire all the necessary skills, experience and knowledge required to fill all of those positions. And this will increasingly be the case in the future, because there is no way of being able to determine what business activities will be attracted to Bermuda in the future or even if international business will continue to come to Bermuda. In order to continue to service this vital industry it is essential to attract and retain a sufficient number of non-Bermudian professionals.

Thirdly, many Bermudians are understandably not attracted to jobs which either are low paid, have unattractive working hours or involve unpleasant and distasteful tasks. Examples of jobs which over the years have traditionally failed to attract sufficient numbers of Bermudians are gardeners[2] and agricultural workers, policemen, nurses, teachers or labourers in the hotel industry. This behaviour is to be expected of a prosperous modern day economy. Germany, UK and USA are also countries the citizens of which have not shown any great enthusiasm in recent years for lowly paid or hard physical work. Increasingly the wealthy countries of the world are immigration targets for the citizens of Third World Countries eager to escape harsh economic conditions or political repression at home. The Azores is a case in point. Traditionally Bermuda has recruited its gardeners and farm labourers from the Azores which is part of Portugal. Over the years many Portuguese Bermudians have prospered and made more than a significant contribution to the growth and welfare of Bermuda and their descendants now occupy many influential financial, political and other positions in Bermudian society.

---

2 Half of which are non-Bermudian.

Fourthly, Bermuda as a small community could not generate sufficient numbers of skilled people to operate its modern economy. For example, there are presently working in Bermuda approximately 600 Chartered Accountants of which about 110 are Bermudian.[3] The precise figures are not known because many accountants are not members of the professional institute. The estimated cost of educating a CA is approximately $60,000 (including university) an amount Bermuda could not possibly afford, so that the total investment in CAs comes to a staggering $36 million an investment which could not be met by Bermuda. If Bermuda had to pay the costs of education of other professionals such as engineers, lawyers or insurance underwriters the costs would be enormous. Foreign labour is therefore an investment on which no interest has to be paid.

Fifthly, as we have seen in the discussion of productivity[4] the key to sustained economic growth and an improved standard of living for Bermudians is improved productivity. Many people studiously avoid discussion of the subject but the fact of the matter is that some non-Bermudians are considered to be more productive than some Bermudians and as a result many Bermudian employers prefer to employ non-Bermudians. These are decisions dictated by entrepreneurs who know their business and its requirements and such decisions can be at odds with the politically popular policies in force at the Department of Immigration.

February 29, 1996

Dear Office Co-Worker,

I arrived at my desk late this morning - it was 8:55 - I'm normally seated, with my coffee, and working by 8:50, sometimes by 8:30 (our office hours are 9 to 5). I said good morning to your cheerful face as you came through the door at 9:10. You went to the kitchen, made some coffee, and on the way back to your desk stopped to tell two friends about your boyfriend's new car.

During the day as you chatted on the phone to your mother, boyfriend, auntie, child, garage mechanic, girlfriend, I took incoming messages for your boss, my boss and you.

There was a sale on at Trimingham's so you took an extra 15 minutes at lunch, then took another ten minutes when you got back to show your bargains to your friends.

Around 3 o'clock I helped you out by putting together a report for your boss that you didn't have time to do.

With your jacket on and purse in your lap, you shut your computer down at 4:59 and cheerfully said good night as you left.

At 5:45 I typed the last memo your boss had asked me to do. Your boss always stays late - did you know that? I left work at six and was glad to be home before seven for a change.

You were born in Bermuda. I'm a foreigner, here on a work permit. I just wanted to let you know - when you are let go and I apply for your job and get it, keep this in mind - I didn't take your job. You gave it to me.

A Different Work Ethic
City of Hamilton

---

3 Figures from the Institute of Chartered Accountants.
4 See Part I 18 for a discussion of this subject.

It can be seen therefore that at both ends of the economic spectrum there are simply not enough Bermudians available to do all the jobs generated by a modern successful economy like Bermuda. The conflicting pressures of shortage of skilled labour, education and training, the unattractiveness and low pay of many

September 24, 1996

Dear Sir,

I have been reading the letters submitted by Dr. Clark Godwin for some time now. However, it was not until today that my anger was fuelled enough to leap to Dr. Godwin's defence and to throw my support behind him.

Firstly, to all those who have been publicly lashing at Dr. Godwin via this newspaper column, I can only say that it is obvious that you do not know what this man is about, know his beliefs and all that he stand for, which first and foremost is the truth! They say that the truth hurts, and it has become quite apparent that there are a lot of people out there in intense mental agony because they cannot handle it!

I personally find it an abomination that we blacks, instead of throwing our support behind Dr. Godwin, are actually gleefully joining in his persecution. Here it is, we have a messenger, a man who has the guts to speak the truth, yet whenever he tries to help us, as he has many times in the past, we want to throw him to the wolves! Wake-up, speak up, people before it too late!

What finally got me riled up was the letter from Anonymous Expatriate. I am really not surprised that they don't see any racism in Bermuda. However, since they don't, perhaps they would like to explain a few things to me. Perhaps they can explain why the white woman sitting next to me, doing the exact same job, is paid more than I am. Perhaps they can explain why the ex-pats are driving brand new cars while I ride the bus. Perhaps they can explain to me why the white woman is sitting at home, painting her toenails, while the nanny looks after her children, and my black children are in day care while both parents struggle to make a living equal to her one white husband. Perhaps they can explain to me why my black brothers are thrown into jail left, right and centre and the white boy's cases don't even make it to courts. Yes contrary to popular belief, white boys do commit crimes, you just don't hear about it. Oh, I forgot! Maybe it's because when little Tommy gets into a spot of trouble suddenly Mommy and Daddy decide to send him away to a posh boarding school in England! End of story.

Mrs. L. Burgess
Pembroke

P.s. Let me get one thing straight. In no way am I a covetous or materialistic person. I consider myself very blessed and grateful for what I do have. However, I do feel that many of "our" problems stem from lack of equal social-economical opportunities.

jobs, the unlikelihood and costs of producing sufficient highly skilled people, and the level of productivity provide answers to the question of why there are so many non-Bermudians working in Bermuda. Given those facts it is something of a mystery as to why official Bermuda is not more welcoming. The answer, I suspect, is contained in the close association of the economics and politics.[5]

Except for a very small group of non-Bermudians, namely British subjects resident in Bermuda for five years and on the voting register before 1976, expatriates do not vote. If you are not allowed to vote your political influence is considerably diminished. Immigrants are usually disliked as a group by local residents although individually they are usually highly regarded. The two captioned letters to the Editor are examples of the different ways in which non-Bermudians are viewed by Bermudians. Both tend to be extreme but they illustrate the ambivalence shown by the general public.

Playing on irrational fears has long been a staple of unscrupulous politicians as myths can be more potent in economics than truth. Enoch Powell in the UK, George Wallace and Pat Buchanan in the USA and Jean-Marie Le Pen in France are only a small example of a political world-wide phenomenon of so-called political leaders picking on someone because they are different. Logic and truth are not characteristics of zealots. It would indeed be suprising if some of Bermuda's politicians failed to follow these examples and take advantage of the opportunity to earn votes by playing the fear and race cards. Bermuda is fortunately a very long distance away from the poisoned politics of countries like UK, USA and France although some vocal academic critics speak disparagingly of "imported foreigners" as if they were a virus. Dr Eva Hodgson[6], for example, is convinced that the white non-Bermudians recruited in UK in the 1950s through to the 1970s were participants in a conspiracy to change the racial balance in Bermuda.

International businessmen tend to view the world as one market place, and as a consequence of this approach Bermuda enjoys a very high standard of living thanks in no small way to the contributions made by non-Bermudians. Local politicians increasingly take the opportunity to play on people's prejudices and as a result fragment the social scene. Individual Bermudians are not usually that foolish. Their commonsense, sense of decency and sense of justice are often in refreshing contrast to that of the political leadership.

The often ambivalent approach to non-Bermudians should be kept in proportion. What would be the reaction of Americans in New York to having about 25 percent of the population of Korean nationality, or in Britain 25 percent of the population of Birmingham was Jamaican, or in Canada if 25 percent of the population was Indian. I doubt very much if the average American, British or Canadian would be as welcoming as that of the average Bermudian. The sour blight of economic prejudice is best exposed to the strong Bermuda sunlight where perhaps it may disappear.

---

[5] This is explained further in Part I 5.
[6] Who writes extensively in local newspapers about race relations and human rights.

6. DOES IMMIGRATION POLICY WORK?

"If a business can justify the expense of hiring a non-Bermudian on economic criteria, the immigration laws should allow that entry."

COMMISSION ON COMPETITIVENESS, PAGE 334.

The most highly controversial area of the labour market is immigration which joins together two highly inflamable emotions, race relations and nationalism. Immigration in most countries tends to excite passions, even in USA a country of immigrants,[1] but in Bermuda many normally placid individuals tend to lose their objectivity when the subject is raised. Why should this be so? A major reason is that in 1995, over 20% of the working population was non-Bermudian. This is very high by comparision with other countries - in the USA for example the comparable figure is 6%.

One reason is the matter of race, always a senstive issue. Most immigrants are white collared white males, largely from UK though with substantial numbers from Canada and USA (black immigration is relatively modest - mainly from the West Indies, usually Jamaica or Barbados). Unfortunately, the subject of immigration and its impact on the labour market and Bermuda society tends to generate more heat than light.

There is clearly a limit to the number of immigrants Bermuda can comfortably absorb before problems of crowding arise. The problems are manifested by the number of motor vehicles, a shortage of affordable accommodation and a shortage of places at good schools. There is a strong non-economic argument to place limits on the numbers of non-Bermudians.[2]

The most important policy of the Department of Immigration is Bermudianisation. It is a clear policy which briefly states if that if a qualified and experienced Bermudian applies for a position, the employer must appoint the Bermudian applicant. In the vast majority of cases this policy creates few difficulties and business generally is satisfied with the impartial way in which work permits are handled by the Ministry. To a certain extent, this is a suprising conclusion because the Board of Immigration which adjudicates on applications is not in a position of knowledge with respect to applictions which it considers. The employer on the other hand, knows his business, knows what knowledge and experience is required and is able to determine after an interview whether the personal attributes of the applicants (like punctuality, enthusiasm, dress and speech) meet his requirements.

The process starts when an employer seeks to hire someone to do a skilled job, say an accountant, one of the most loosely defined job titles in Bermuda. He will then place an advertisement in the 'Royal Gazette' for three days, stating amongst other things the desired qualifications, length of experience needed, and a brief description of the duties (salary is rarely mentioned). Potential candidates then submit their resumes, and the employer begins the selection process. If the employer decides on a Bermudian applicant and the intereview process goes smoothly the matter is then ended. The Bermudian is then hired and everyone is happy.

---

[1] Bermuda is also a country of immigrants.

[2] See Part I 19.

A broadly similar conclusion is reached if there are no Bermudian applicants. If that is the case and the employer can show that he followed the requisite Immigration Department procedures properly, such as advertising three times in the local press, the employer is basically free to appoint whom he wishes and an work permit application is submitted to the Immigration Department and will be approved after review by the Board. There is usually a nail-biting period of waiting for the successful applicant but after a period of say a month or so the work permit is approved, the applicant takes up the job for the approved period, say three years, and again everyone involved is happy.

A welcome innovation introduced in recent years is in respect of senior positions with international companies. Many companies wish to appoint their own experienced employees to top jobs and would be reluctant to incorporate in Bermuda if that option was not available to them. The procedure is now that exempt companies are able to appoint whom they wish and no longer have to go through the process of advertising. This is a sensible approach which indicates that the Bermuda Government is sympathetic to international organisations and as a result business thrives.

Problems invariably arise in difficult cases of what "qualified" and "experienced" mean. The problem is made more complicated because a proportion of the population do not believe that the procedures employed by the Immigration Department are fair.[3] Bermudians turned down for a job believe that employers have inflated the qualifications and experience required and there are sufficient examples of this to be a reasonable belief. Employers who have applications to hire non-Bermudians turned down by the Immigration Department believe that officials do not understand their requirements and that they are being forced to take on someone who does not match their standards of efficiency. Again there are several examples of this which makes the belief reasonable.

If there are a handful of Bermudian applicants, some of whom meet the basic requirements of qualifications and experience, but for one reason or another are not of the standard required by the employer, the position becomes much cloudier. Under Immigration law the employer should hire the applicant. If he does not wish to make the appointment, he could re-advertise and hope someone better turns up - which is unlikely, or he can apply to the Department of Immigration to hire a non-Bermudian. The employer then has to state why he does not wish to hire any of the Bermudian applicants, and a Board of the Immigration composed of local worthies adjudicates on the employer's decision. This is when the process becomes decidedly murky. Are the employer's reasons for rejecting the Bermudian applicant reasonable in the circumstances, or are they simply an excuse to appoint an outsider? Making decisions on such matters requires the wisdom of Solomon and the political sensitivity of Machiavelli. All too frequently such qualities are not in evidence and difficulties arise.

The most puzzling question to be asked about the Bermudianisation policy is why should it be necessary in the first place? The cost of a Bermudian employee is often (though not always) less than the cost of an expatriate and there is no bur-

---

[3] See the Swain Report, for example.

densome bureaucratic approval process to go through. In addition, in many cases the individual making the appointment is himself a Bermudian and therefore any existing bias would tend to be exercised in favour of a fellow Bermudian. Given the natural bias towards Bermudians, is a civil servant who knows little about the business in which the employer is engaged in a better position to know what qualities are required for the job especially when the civil servant (or the Board) has not interviewed the job-applicant? In other words, is there greater wisdom in a bureaucracy than in the free-enterprise system?[4]

Does the existing system work well? The answer is yes, reasonably so, but it really depends on to whom you are addressing the question. For unsuccessful Bermudian applicants to a job will give a different answer to the successful one. To an employer who is able to hire the expatriate employee he wants, the answer will probably be that the system works well. if the employer is faced with taking someone with whom he is not entirely happy, a less enthusiastic response would be given.

The subject is clearly a very sensitive one affecting what is probably the most important part of an individual's life, namely the quality of his job and the size of his income. And opinions of the success, or otherwise, of the system will vary from time to time. It is difficult to create a system which will satisfy all of the parties involved by they employers, employees, politicians and the general public. There will invariably be difficult and sensitive cases where it is difficult, almost impossible, to strike the right balance between the interests of the employer to employ whom he wants, and the interests of a Bermudian who quite genuinely believes that he is qualified for the job on offer.

Critics of the system say that many employers are faced with substandard employees, particularly in the international busienss sector of the economy, and that this raises costs which in turn affects Bermuda's competitive position. Others will say that some employees are often promoted beyond their capabilities in order to avoid difficulties with the Immigration Department. There is some truth to such criticisms but very difficult to replace the existing system with another which adquately balances the interests of employers and potential employees and which commands widespread public support.

Clearly there has to be some give and take in an economy which in 1995 had 34,133 jobs but only 26,612 Bermudians to fill such jobs.[5] Unless the economy is to contract or to function less efficiently, it is necessary to import labour to bridge the gap between the availability of jobs and applicants. It is in the sensitive areas of senior well-paid jobs that the tricky balancing act has to take place.

One method of avoiding the inevitable subjectivity that arises when the Board of Immigration or the Minister makes a decision about work permits and filling jobs with non-Bermudians would be to implement a market system by having a defined number of work permits, for which employers could bid on a periodic basis. If that number was 7,500 (the difference between the number of Bermudians and the available jobs) employers who were prepared to bid the highest price for a work permit could employ whom they wanted and those who were

4 This issue is discussed in Part I 7 to 9.
5 Employment Survey, 1995 page 7.

unwilling or unable to pay the market cost of acquiring a permit would be forced either to employ a Bermudian or not hire. The total number could be raised or lowered according to policy decisions by the Government on such things as housing and schools. Such a system could be further refined by allocating work permits according to Government policy or by industry; say 30% to tourism, 30% to international business, and the balance to other sectors of the economy such as government, retail and construction.

If government policy was to encourage international business the percentage allocated could be raised to 35%, and that allocated to another sector correspondingly reduced. Creating a market place for work permits would be an impartial way of making immigration decisions, and would do away with much of the bureaucracy and paper required by the Immigration Department. Its greatest flaw is that it would not be easily understood by the public and it would be open to constant political (and irrational) criticism in Parliament which could inflame social tensions.

Anyone who has worked in a business environment will know that bringing to a position the qualities of experience, honesty, reputation, interpersonal skills, decisiveness, and so on are just as important as a formal qualification or degree from a good university. Selecting a successful applicant for a job requires more than a fair degree of subjectivity. Deciding not to hire a Bermudian but a non-Bermudian can often be justified in an employer's mind by qualities which cannot be acquired at a good university such as punctuality and the ability to get along with others. An absurd situation arose in December, 1996 when St Paul's Church in Paget were unable permanently to appoint a Priest acceptable to the Church Committee because Government were unwilling to grant a work-permit to an English candidate. A Solomoneque comprise was reached whereby the Church was able to have a temporary permit and therefore remain open at Christmas. The Department of Immigration cannot sensibly rule on such matters.

It is not surprising that allegations of favouritisim, bias against Bermudians, racism or nepotism arise when some of the top jobs in terms of salary and prestige are filled by non-Bermudians. More remarkable, in my opinion, in how infrequently such allegations are made indicating that the Board of Immigration despite its limitations is able to do a creditable job, or that many qualified Bermudians are sufficiently candid about their own limitations to say that it is important to get the best man for the job rather than prefer a Bermudian. This area is a highly sensitive one and given the ruckus which could arise from making sensitive appointments it is remarkable how little fuss there is.

The question then is to what extent does the government's Bermudianisation policy work? The answer is much better than it has a right to expect. There are circumstances where Bermudians are in jobs which are beyond their capabilities; there are Bermudians who if this was a perfect world would occupy better positions; and there are many Bermudians who are in jobs which perfectly match their talents and aspirations. It is a question which can never be resolved to everyone's satisfaction.

7. WHY DON'T WE HAVE AS MUCH LIVE MUSICAL ENTERTAINMENT IN HOTELS AND NIGHTCLUBS AS WE USED TO ?

"Without music life would be a mistake."

FRIEDRICH NIETZCHE.

"Far from being the 'Vegas' of the West, the local entertainment scene started to resemble that of the city's outlying desert ghost towns."

'MID-OCEAN NEWS' EDITORIAL AUGUST 16, 1996.

When I was young man about town, the live entertainment in Bermuda was excellent - at least to my simple and innocent tastes. The 40 Thieves Club[1] on Front Street was the centre of attraction for both locals and tourists and it featured world class acts like Tom Jones, Dionne Warwick and Anthony and the Imperials.[2] The competition from the 40 Thieves Club also forced large hotels to feature top class acts like Cab Calloway - my favourite being Gordon MacRae[3] - but the point was that tourists and locals were able to enjoy live entertainment of famous international artistes. The local newspapers had sections devoted to entertainment, something which does not happen now. The night scene was bustling and exciting. Now it is drab, even non-existent. What happened?

Firstly, tourism has gone into a tail-spin and local business needs to be augmented by visitors in order to attract an audience large enough to support high-class performers. Secondly, competition from other resorts pushed up the prices of artistes and Bermuda could no longer afford the going rates. Thirdly, government bureaucrats interfered with market practices and this is usually the "kiss of death" to those who wish to meet the demands of the customer.

One of the most bizarre practices in the Ministry of Labour, Home Affairs & Safety relates to the procedure for hiring Bermudian musicians for employment at Bermuda clubs, hotels or other places of entertainment. Whenever an employer seeks to employ a foreign musician the practice has been established that a local musician (or group) must also be employed and that that musician be given equal time with the foreigner.

One of the problems in determining whether someone is qualified as a night club musician is that there are no formal musician qualificiations similar to those of say a doctor, lawyer or engineer. Who is a competent musician, or more important acceptable to audiences is simply a matter of taste, and in the case of an employer simply a matter of judgement as to whether audiences will pay the price of admission, buy drinks and return in the future to watch and hear the act in question. To teenagers Pavarotti is just a noisy fat Italian who sings funny tuneless songs called arias. To those who are middle aged Snoop Doggy Dog is incomprehensible. Anyone can set himself up as a musical act and when the general public has the bad manners not to attend performances, appeal to the Department of Immigration on the grounds that audiences have such poor taste that they require protection from hypercritical audiences.

---

[1] named after the oligarchic group which allegedly ran Bermuda before the 1960s
[2] All names from the 1960s.
[3] The star of the films "Oklahoma" and "Carousel."

Local musicians have formed a powerful and influential union for a membership which has limited talent and the Bermuda Government has imposed unacceptable conditions for hiring foreign musicians on local establishments, so much so, that it has virtually destroyed live entertainment at local hotels and clubs. Nevertheless, there is still live entertainment at large concerts for the Bermudian public. The "Jazzscape" jazz festival held in October, 1996 is an excellent example of this, as is the Bermuda Festival and numerous other outdoor concerts.

Two problems arise in this situation which are of major concern to the employer and his customers. Firstly, the cost of hiring an additional group, which neither the employer nor the customer wants in the first place, can be expensive as the two groups are being paid for when only one is required. Secondly, the customers may not wish to listen or watch the local group but that judgement is taken away from the employer or manager of the institution, and given to someone (the Department of Immigration) who has limited knowledge of what is required by the customer, or is given to the musicians' union who has a vested interest in the outcome.

The additional cost, and the ignoring of the wishes of the customer and employer indicate that business is being driven by interests which are not consistent with those of the paying customer. As a result, Bermuda provides not what the customer wants but what is more convenient for the supplier and at a higher cost. The result is that there has been a collapse in the provision of this service to tourists. One of the problems Bermuda faces is being competitive with other resorts, but the existing, unwritten and unknown policy is at variance with the best long term interests of Bermuda.

This rather frivolous example illustrates 4 fundamental economic issues:

1. Neglecting what customers want is dangerous - they are smarter and more powerful than commonly thought.

2. Interest groups, in this case the Musician's Union, usually work against the public interest and the customer especially when they align themselves with a Government policy.

3. Alleged benefits to a small group such as musicians invariably result in penalties to the wider public by reducing choice. Protection nearly always benefits a small group at the expense of a much larger group but is justified on the grounds that benefits to some are a benefit to all.

4. Whenever Governments interfere with the workings of the market economy things work less efficiently and the public gets shafted.

8. WHY IS RACE CENTRAL TO DISCUSSIONS ABOUT THE BERMUDA ECONOMY?

"No one can remain long in Bermuda and read its newspapers without becoming aware of the strong aspirations for achieving professional and management status. This is especially so in the black population. The incentives are strong - power, prestige and good pay. Furthermore, the target jobs are in the fastest growing employment sphere, and, for blacks, their unequal distribution represents status unachieved and often denied in a country where they are the majority."

DOROTHY K. NEWMAN.[1]

The dilemma of monumental proportions for the Bermuda economy and society is race. It has poisoned our past and casts a cloud over the future, despite the fact that to many visitors (and residents) Bermuda is a model of racial harmony by comparison with many other countries in the world. Underneath that peaceful exterior there is often a lethal brew of envy, blame, criticism, frustration, even hatred which leaves both white residents and guest workers puzzled that in a community blessed in so many ways with a high income and beautiful environment there is massive resentment and great misunderstanding. Resolving this dilemma has been the major challenge for many years but for many whites the more the situation seems to improve the more critical the black population becomes and for the black population the more things change the more they seem to stay the same.

Economic and financial issues such as employment, promotions, lay-offs, income, pay increases, labour unrest, scholarships, housing, loans, mortgages, statistics and economic power which are not, on the face of it, anything to do with race are easily and quickly converted into racial matters by those involved and by the press, politicians or community activitists. If race is not near the surface it is certainly lurking not so quietly in the background.

The facts behind this concern are easy to come by :-

- blacks do not occupy many positions of power in the private sector.
- black incomes are lower than white.
- black ownership of assets is lower than whites.
- life expectancy for blacks is lower than whites.
- black children are more likely to live in single parent homes.
- proportionately more blacks are in prison than whites.

Just one of the above injustices or handicaps would indicate that things are not as they should be; taken together they point to something which is drastically wrong. If the two races could not be distinguished, or inherited advantages were evenly distributed between blacks and whites the racial issue might be nothing more than a statistical aberration but that is not the case and it partly explains why race often becomes the central issue in financial matters.

The adversarial racial situtation in the 1990s is in sharp contrast to what was

---

[1] "Bermuda's Stride Toward the Twenty-First Century," by Dorothy K. Newman - published by the Bermuda Statistical Department.

expected or anticipated when Bermuda, like the United States, in the 1960s ended highly offensive and overt methods of racial discrimination. Blacks have gone to school with whites for about 30 years, have worked in the same offices or companies, lived in the same residential areas, played in the same football teams, gone to the same movies and have shared in many other experiences of life. Bermuda, despite its faults has never been less racist than it is at present, yet for many in the black population things have not improved but have become worse. The guts of the issue is that as things improve, as they have done in Bermuda, the remaining grievances are viewed as intolerable even although they are minor by comparison with past wrongs. People respond to expectations about the future, not what has happened in the recent past. Whites tend to have a historical perspective; blacks a vision that looks to the future.

There is probably no subject which diverges more from privately held opinions and public utterances than the relationship between the black and white populations. Race relations is a festering sore on the body politic and a potential threat to the economy which requires healing but somehow does not respond to treatment.

Those who questioned the system in Bermuda prior to the 1960s fought against the assumption that race determined or had anything to do with character, ability and ambition. Now paradoxically some of their successors subscribe to the argument that race does indeed determine character, ability and ambition. When race is used as a proxy for disadvantage it wrongly implies that to be black is to be inferior and underprivileged. Race based thinking is divisive to society and is particularly harmful to those who are disadvantaged, because it reinforces the negative attributes that characterise that society.

The essence of the problem , in my opinion,[2] is that the white population sees the problem from one perspective and the black population from another. Whites believe that if only the black population would stop blaming whites for their failure to make progress, and get educated and work hard they would be as successful as anyone else in Bermuda. The continual complaints made by blacks against whites because of historical prejudices and practices results in some whites losing respect for the black population many of whom are seen as using historical wrongs to justify present failures. Many blacks, on the other hand, firmly believe the system is stacked against them and no matter how hard they work the system which is controlled by whites and many of the whites are non-Bermudians working for international companies will not allow them to achieve more than token gains.[3]

[2] that of the white middle-aged middle class male who tends to see things through rose-coloured spectacles.

[3] See the Swain Report discussion.

> "Top managers must dispel beliefs that nepotism and old boy networks still thrive in Bermuda : they must dispel beliefs that blacks and women will still encounter barriers to how far they can go in the corporate world : and they must dispel beliefs that white expatriates are often hired when qualified Bermudians are clearly available. In short, they must convince those who are now skeptical that Bermudian companies are really committed to what they are are committed to i.e. to a policy of non-discriminatory inclusion in which Bermudians from diverse racial, ethnic, and gender backgrounds can all feel part of a common corporate enterprise, and can advance just as far as their abilities and their performance will take them."
>
> The Swain Report, page 25.

To make matters worse many businesses in Bermuda were established generations ago - "established in 1844" is proudly displayed on the Front Street store of Trimingham Bros. - which tends to reduce opportunities for those outside the old white families to make economic progress. Small businesses, like stores, however are becoming less important for job opportunities than they once were.

It is something of a caricature to talk in terms of embittered blacks and all powerful whites and it is also something of a bad anthropological joke. People are not members of undifferentiated mass as if they are walking and talking peas in a pod. The reality of human existence in Bermuda is of course much, much more complicated than that. There are many hardworking and well educated blacks who have earned their success who have faced the problems of life often against great odds and have defied the stereotypes and caricatures described above.

However, as in other parts of the world, there are some influential people whose careers and power base depends on maintaining the myth that blacks can never achieve economic success because of an oppressive white power structure. Most whites are not part of the "power structure" - whatever that means - and are therefore unable to influence forces which allegedly hold back the black population. Rumours, conspiracy theories and occasional facts feed the resentment and frustration of many in the black population and those in authority who wish to eliminate legitimate grievances are prevented from speaking out in fear of having their motives questioned or being branded racist if they say or write something controversial.[4]

A case in point arose early in 1996 when the Chief Executive of the Bank of Butterfield spoke to the Chartered Institute of Bankers. In a wide-ranging and thought provoking speech about the need for economic efficiency he stated, almost as an aside, that "many of us are still puzzled by the whole concept of 'institutional racism' and quite what is expected of banks and other major institutions."[5] The rest of his speech was ignored by the press, politicians and the public and he was taken to task for not understanding what the term meant.[6]

---

[4] A point of which I am highly aware.

[5] "Royal Gazette," March 26, 1996 page 1.

[6] There are many meanings of the term as discussed in Part IV 11.

When the bias-victimisation hot-button is pressed logical thought and rational debate flies out the window, people become intimidated and the debate is frequently confined to avoiding statements which can be construed in any way as being controversial or original. It becomes increasingly difficult to express a divergent opinion or a dissenting point of view on the subject of race or be frank and think out loud as happens when other problems demand resolution. As a consequence the gap between the races becomes wider and does not get closed.

In the economic system described elsewhere in this book[7] profits accrue to the firm which can not only maximise revenue but can reduce costs. In the market economy the only reason for employment and promotion within an organisation should be that of individual merit. To use any other criteria would result in an organisation consciously working against its own self-interest - something no rational profit-maximising organisation would choose to do. In strictly economic terms it does not make sense to discrimate racially - indeed in the Southern United States in segregationist days and in South Africa during apartheid commercial organisations were constantly in trouble because they placed profit ahead of the political objectives of the state which was to discriminate against the black population. Racial discrimination is not only morally wrong but commercially foolish and one of the most effective weapons against racial discrimination is a free labour market which highlights the fact that it costs organisations money (in the form of lost profits) to discriminate. Indeed the issue may be made more complicated in the future as competitive forces[8] outside Bermuda compel Bermuda business to be more efficient. Inefficient discriminatory practices may well be prohibited because of competition not because they are judged to be morally wrong.

More controversially, there are constant references to the ways in which commerical organisations discriminate against the black population but rarely is any hard evidence presented except to show that blacks fail to be appointed or gain promotions in proportion to their numbers in the general population. One of the great dogmas of the racial debate which is gaining a foothold in Bermuda is that racial groups would be evenly distributed in jobs, education, and mnagement positions if it was not for pervasive racial discrimination practised by the current decision makers in Bermuda. Those who believe this fail to supply any concrete evidence of their assertion and those who want to challenge this dogma can supply as much evidence as they can without making any impression on those who hold different opinions. The fact is that much of the public debate taking place is centred on the unproved assumption that talent, abilities and hard work are distributed evenly without regard to race and gender and that differences in outcome are not due to individual responses to opportunity but to malign societal forces not open to the usual rules of academic evidence. The result of all this is that people constantly confuse the statistics produced by looking at end-results and conclude that the process is biased.

The subject of race is so pervasive and so politically senstive that it cannot be openly discussed or questioned except in a handful of politically approved cliches. Cliched thinking does not lead to the resolution of difficulties it only makes

---

[7] See the discussion on the capitalist system, in Part I 9.
[8] See the discussion on globablisation in Part II 17.

them worse. If there is one thing the economics of race produces it is doublespeak - a language which pretends to say something but which hides, evades or misleads. To question the established orothodoxy automatically opens the questioner to accusations of being a racist with the result that the debate goes nowhere and little is achieved in dealing with the problem. The last thing anyone in authority wants is to be accused of being a racist because it is a charge which is almost impossible to refute and it immediately closes minds to rational debate. The promiscuous use of the word racism is a club which is used to silence opposition and to prevent constructive thinking. The whole subject could usefully benefit from some detached and rational economic arguments and debates.

The main assumption of the current orthodoxy on race relations is that the black population is not responsible for things which happen to go wrong and that all responsibility rests with the white population who wield all economic and political power. The implication of this nonsensical assumption is that blacks are helpless pawns of fate who will be unable to improve their situation in any significant way unless and until whites transform themselves from being brutal and insentive racists. Put another way what this means is that blacks are not responsible for their own lives, whites are.[9] If blacks commit crimes it is because of white oppression. If they fail at school it is because of racist teachers. If blacks are not promoted it is because of white institutional racism. This is inverted racism and is complete nonsense. Whites as a group are not that smart and not that powerful. The black population is not the equivalent of a class of young children who require the guidance, permission and blessing of adult whites. They are as responsible and accountable for their own lives as anyone else but it is this refusal to accept this fact by many black leaders which makes race central to discussions about the Bermuda economy.

9. IS THERE EQUALITY OF OPPORTUNITY IN BERMUDA?

"The reason a lot of people do not recognise an opportunity when they meet it is that it usually goes around wearing overalls and looking like hard work."

CHRISTIAN SCIENCE MONITOR

Equality of opportunity means that no individual should be prevented by unfair or arbitrary obstacles from realising his full potential or prevented from using his energy, natural gifts and hard work to pursue what he thinks are in his own best interests. This needs to be distinguished from what is now known as equality of outcome. This means that everyone should have the same level of income or should finish the economic race at the same time. Equality of opportunity is tied very firmly to freedom of the individual, whilst equality of outcome is clearly at odds with the right of an individual to achieve the best he can for nature has determined that individuals are not the same in talent, energy, application or skill. Some individuals are great sportsmen, others talented in music, others again have natural skills in mathematics or painting.

---

[9] A view with which Karl Marx would agree.

No one would argue that everyone has the talent to sing well or hit a cricket ball. What equality of opportunity states is that no obstacles such as birth, skin colour, nationality, religion, sex or any other economically irrelevant characteristic should be placed in the way of an individual to achieve the best he can at whatever objective he chooses. Performance is the criterion for success - not accident of birth, skin colour or religion. Bermuda's history and the history of other countries is littered with examples of where this ideal was not, and is not being met. The main injustice as far as Bermuda is concerned is that if someone was black he (or she) was automatically excluded from certain professions because of an irrelevant factor like skin colour.

In 1996, there are no formal or legal barriers to the ambitions of an individual but many believe that the ideal is being thwarted because of actions or attitudes or procedures the effects of which are to deny equality of opportunity to many in Bermuda, especially those who are black and those who are female. Equality of opportunity is denied because of the wish of the dominant group - white males - to preserve either consciously or unconsciously their favoured position in society. So seriously is the sabotage of equality of opportunity taken by government that a "Commission for Unity and Racial Equality" (CURE) has been established to ensure that no Bermudian is prevented from realising his (or her) potential.

The objectives of CURE, which is responsbile to the Minister of Human Affairs, is to achieve the following:

- Equality of opportunity for all persons.
- Meaningful race relations between persons of different racial/ethnic backgrounds.
- The elimination of all forms of systematic discrimination.

To achieve these objectives eight commissioners with experience in the field of human rights have been appointed with the authority to carry out research, identify and analyse major issues of discrimination. How effective CURE will be remains to be seen.

In a modern economy equality of opportunity can be provided in two basic ways. Firstly, government can ensure that within the free market system every individual will be given an equal opportunity to improve his economic status within a broad framework of impartial rules which provides maximum choice for the individual. This is the way in which the free enterprise system works and elsewhere it has provided the social and economic progress which people seek. There can be no expectation that all will receive equal rewards, the objective being to give everyone the chance to succeed. This method is the way proposed for CURE.

The second and competing philosophy, arises from a instinctive distrust of the average individual being able sensibly to make the best choices for himself within the market system. There is a strong belief that some superior group, say the civil service, can more equitably counsel or direct the talents of individuals. In this ideal society, everyone receives the same rewards and satisfactions no matter what the level of their individual contribution. There is equality of outcome. The job of deciding what is, or is not, equal achievement is so fiendishly difficult that it conjures up huge armies of bureaucrats writing regulations. Indeed, something like the civil service itself. This was the method allegedly tried in Communist countries and it was a dismal failure.

It is extremely difficult to achieve the literal objective of equality of opportunity. The economic prospects for the son or daughter of a wealthy executive are considerably brighter than they are for a poor child from a broken home. In addition, the blatant historical discrimination by race and by sex has sabotaged the hopes of many over the years. The denial of equal opportunity in the past was always as economically foolish as it was morally wrong.

Perhaps it is impossible to achieve the purest form of equality of opportunity yet it is still possible, as I hope to show, that those with capacity, determination and hard work can advance in modern Bermuda, and that most Bermudians will continue to work together to eliminate the remaining barriers to equality of opportunity for all. It is not in our long term interests to scrap a policy which is successful elsewhere simply because it has some flaws; the way to go is to try and eliminate the basic flaws.

There is a close and compelling link between equality of opportunity and economic progress which requires constant change. The most striking thing about the free enterprise system is that it promotes constant change by itself. It is the constant generation of change which is at the heart of providing opportunity to those industrious enough to benefit from it. Economic progress can only take place when newer and better processes, and greater and better education and training occurs and when there is a strong commitment to hard work and improved productivity, commitments which are often hard to get from those who are the main critics of the failure to provide equality of opportunity.

Many companies in Bermuda have a publicly stated Equal Employment Opportunities Policy and reproduced below is that of one of Bermuda's largest employers:

THE BANK OF BERMUDA LIMITED
EQUAL OPPORTUNITY POLICY

PURPOSE:

An integral part of the management policy at The Bank of Bermuda is to provide equal opportunity for all persons currently employed, and those seeking employment, within the parameters of Government Legislation and company laws in each and every jurisdiction in which we operate.

STATEMENT:

- With that in mind it is our practice to administer our hiring, working conditions, benefits and privileges of employment, compensation, training, advancement, recruitment, transfers and termination's of all employees without discrimination. We define discrimination as basing judgement on race, ancestry, place of origin, colour, ethnic origin, citizenship, creed, sex, sexual orientation, age, marital status, family status, or physical challenges.

- In all cases, individual performance and demonstrated ability will be the foundation of opportunity.

- We are committed to maintaining a workplace where the terms and conditions of employment are equitable and non-discriminatory, and we will provide each person with equal access to the benefits of employment.

- We believe it is the right of every employee to be treated with dignity and respect, within a work environment conducive to productivity, self development, and career advancement based on demonstrated performance and individual ability.

- At the Bank of Bermuda we consider the equal treatment of all human beings to be a company commitment as well as a legal obligation.

- The Bank strives to be progressive and committed to meeting the needs of our employees.

- We expect our employees to treat each other with dignity, courtesy and respect and, in co-operation with each other, to help the company realise its employment equality objectives, and its full potential."

The policy of the Bermuda Government for many years has been that of equality of opportunity for all Bermudians, black or white, male or female. However, many statistics show that the equality of opportunity as measured, for example, in incomes is still elusive. Critics assert, often without providing any substantial evidence, that there is still pervasive racial and gender discrimination in Bermuda and that black male Bermudians, in particular, are not benefitting from this policy to the extent they should.

There is also a widespread belief that employers tend to think in stereotypes of uneducated blacks, efficient whites and so on. Stereotyping is a shorthand way of thinking, a way for unthinking people who are unable or unwilling to cope with the complexity of human nature. However, economic success for the individual, like any other success, depends crucially on a vibrant economy, respect for the rule of law and a fully functioning effective educational system. That in turn requires a commitment to hard work, individual responsibility and stable families.

It is rare to come across anyone in Bermuda who is not in favour of equality of opportunity but the problems begin when the policy is implemented in practice. Equality of opportunity, provides an opportunity not only to succeed but to fail, a point few people wish to discuss. The pitfalls are legion. Being involved with a failed project, missing an important deadline or being a member of a department which is closed because of market changes are just three examples of matters beyond the control of an individual which can go wrong. In fact being successful implies that some (or indeed most) will be unsuccessful - as unlike the race in "Alice in Wonderland" not everyone can be a winner.

I know of no large organisation in Bermuda which does not honestly try to provide equal opportunities and the few racists and misogynists I am aware of are not respected and do not exercise any power in the financial world.

Whilst there is a considerable way to go, it would be wrong not to acknowledge the progress which has been made. There is common consent that from around 1965 (when overt racial discrimination was no longer acceptable as public or private behaviour - it had obviously never been acceptable to the majority black population) - there has been increased equality of opportunity even if there has been many lapses along the way. There are several examples to illustrate this point:-

- Many senior civil servants such as the Cabinet Secretary are black Bermudians.

- There are many more black and female professionals such as lawyers, doctors and chartered accountants.

- The number of professionals, black and white, male and female in white collar jobs in banks, law firms and international companies has increased substantially in recent years.

- Many scholarships are available from organisations like the International Companies Division of the Chamber of Commerce, private endowments, Government and the Banks.

- Many Bermudians from poor backgrounds are engaged in occupations and enjoy opportunities which were never available to their parents or grandparents.

The true measure of a society which is just and which respects the rights of individuals, is not whether a demographically proportional sharing of the good things in life takes place on a group basis, but whether any talented individual of whatever sex, race or religion is able through his (or her) own efforts to make a success of life. Much has been achieved but much remains to be done as we shall see when issues of institutional racism and the glass ceiling are explored.

10. WHY DO BLACK BERMUDIANS EARN LESS THAN WHITE BERMUDIANS?

"It is significant also that black households' median incomes in Bermuda increased far more than white households' over the 1982 to 1991 period, and women's more than men's. The gap between the races remained, but narrowed. Black households' median income increased from 74 percent of the white median in 1982 to about 80 percent of the white median in 1988 and 1991."

DOROTHY K. NEWMAN.[1]

This is a question which is difficult to answer. It should be noted from the outset that, obviously, not all black Bermudians earn less than whites and that there are, by Bermudian standards, many white people who are poor and many in the black population who are wealthy and enjoy high incomes. The picture often painted is that whites are wealthy and politically powerful, and that blacks are poor and disenfranchised from the levers of power. This is a caricature which can be disproved time and time again but allegations of racism tend to play on politically correct feelings of white guilt and black anger whilst, unfortunately, doing little to resolve underlying problems.

There is little objective evidence to prove that black economic deprivation arises from white racism and that reversing residual racism (although that is desirable in itself) will result in blacks enjoying economic prosperity.[2] For many years Bermuda both legally and socially has sought to rid itself of racism but apart from the United States there is no country so obsessed by the subject. It poisons almost every rational debate about the economy.[3]

Whatever measure is used, the evidence is clearly that the black population in Bermuda earns less than whites even after factors like education, experience and age are taken into account. Moreover the black population is believed to own fewer financial assets although it has a higher level of home ownership (45%) than whites (41%).[4]

To determine how badly black Bermudians compare with white Bermudians depends very much on the quality of statistics available and appropriate data was not available until the 1991 Census of Population and Housing. The following table shows the various incomes for different levels of education from which will be seen that the black working population fares worse than the white population in most categories.

[1] "Bermuda's Stride Toward the Twenty-First Century," by Dorothy K. Newman - published by the Ministry of Finance 1994, page 17.
[2] An excellent article on this subject is contained in "Economist Year Book, 1992," page 15 to 17.
[3] See Part IV 8.
[4] Ibid, page 71.

Table 1

Working Population's Monthly Median Income by Occupation Group, Race, and Educational Attainment, 1991

Occupation Group And Race	All Workers	No Formal Certificate	High School	Technical/ Vocational	College Degree	Post Graduate
All Workers	$2,321	$1,898	$2,232	$2,504	$3,219	$4,297
Black	2,156	1,873	2,117	2,359	2,884	4,227
White and other	2,670	1,963	2,474	2,766	3,249	4,450
Professional, technical, related	3,190	2,250	2,711	2,917	3,426	4,140
Black	2,921	2,357	2,563	2,724	3,243	4,156
White and other	3,412	1,833	2,859	3,130	3,531	4,111
Administrative, management	3,431	2,656	3,203	3,476	3,976	5,500
Black	2,731	2,333	2,463	2,958	2,964	4,583
White and other	3,919	3,147	4,000	4,000	4,111	6,000
Clerical	2,120	1,870	2,086	2,260	2,300	5,500
Black	2,071	1,868	2,035	2,219	2,250	0
White and other	2,229	1,875	2,216	2,369	2,327	5,500
Sales	1,851	1,719	1,790	2,000	2,500	5,167
Black	1,743	1,731	1,667	1,813	2,750	5,500
White and other	2,010	1,705	1,975	2,300	2,438	3,750
Service	1,733	1,394	1,977	2,213	2,179	1,750
Black	1,683	1,396	1,936	2,130	2,375	2,750
White and other	1,898	1,382	2,094	2,319	2,100	1,500
Product, transport, labour	2,309	2,250	2,312	2,480	2,200	2,667
Black	2,270	2,224	2,279	2,423	2,083	2,750
White and Other	2,468	2,388	2,462	2,656	2,375	2,500

Source: Bermuda Statistical Department, Ministry of Finance

Many Bermudians would answer the question posed quite simply by stating that blacks earns less than whites because there is economic racial discrimination in Bermuda as evidenced by the existence of insitutional racism. This issue is explored in the next essay. Another reason given is that white households tend to have both husband and wife (or both partners) working whilst this does not occur to the same extent in black households because larger numbers in the black population live alone or with children only. Hence there is a tendency for white households to have two paycheques whilst black households are likely to have only one.

Further it is believed that black single mothers are more likely to be engaged in low wage jobs, like maids, rather than in higher paid white collar employment. It is argued that if black households had the same combination of people living together as white then black household incomes would come closer to that of white households although still not equalling them as black males at all levels tend to earn less than white males.

Black employees in the administrative and management group, for example, earn BD$2,731 per month whilst whites earn BD$3,919 or 43 percent more. A complicating factor in this is that the white population includes a higher proportion of those who work in the highly paid international business sector.

Bermuda is similar to other countries in that having a higher level of education provides a higher pay cheque. There is a greater number of whites whose educational qualifications exceed that of only a high (or secondary) school education although it is reasonably clear from the data that even when blacks have a post-graduate qualification they still earn less than whites. The data listed under administrative, management shows that whites earn BD$6,000 whilst blacks earn only BD$4,583 per month. Ms Sharol Simmons, the executive officer of the Commission for Unity and Racial Equality (CURE), drew attention to this fact by stating that, "Dr Newman's report clearly showed that the largest percentage of individuals achieving masters and doctorate degrees are black, but they are disproportionately under-represented in management and executive positions."[5] The problem with this statement is that executive positions in business rarely require masters, far less doctorate degrees, but tend to place more emphasis on professional qualifications in such relevant subjects as accounting, engineering, insurance, economics (often not that relevant) or law. Masters and doctorate qualifications are sought after by government and academia, two classes of occupation where whites are under represented.

The black population (22%) tends to find itself in the poor category (incomes less than $24,144 per annum) and near poor (12%) (incomes between $24,144 and $30,168 per annum) as the following table shows:-

Table 2

Households' Relative Economic Position by Race, Status, Age and Household Type, 1991

Characteristics	All Households	Poor (less than $24,144/yr)	Near Poor ($24,144 - 40,168/yr)	Middle ($30,168 - $72,420/yr)	Well-To-Do (more than $72,420/yr
All Households	100	19	11	46	24
Black	100	22	12	47	18
White and other	100	15	10	43	32
Bermudian	100	21	11	45	23
Black	100	23	12	47	18
White and other	100	18	9	41	32
Non-Bermudian	100	12	10	48	30
Black	100	19	9	54	18
White and other	100	11	10	47	32

Source: 'Bermuda's Stride Towards the Twenty-First Century.' page 61

---

5 'Mid-Ocean News,' October 11, 1996 page 4.

Although the reported unemployment rate of 6% in Bermuda[6] is modest by international standards, the black population bears a disproportionate burden. 84% of those unemployed are black - more than 4 times that of the white population. The corresponding ratio for the United States is that twice as many blacks are unemployed as whites.

More work has to be done to discover the reasons why blacks in Bermuda consistently underperform whites in the pay leagues. Until this work is done locally we are dependent on research done in the United States. My personal observation is that the black population in Bermuda earns less than the white population for the following reasons :

- Blacks suffer disproportionately from an educational system which fails to provide a sound education for those who are poor and disadvantaged. Education is probably the single most important determinant of the level of income from employment.

- Contrary to what is believed by the public, union membership tends to destroy jobs and lower incomes. Membership of the BIU is predominantly black.

- Crime and drugs are another problem and the black population suffers disproportionately from these scourges which is one reason why improving the climate of safety is essential for the well-being of Bermuda.

- Institutional racism is undoubtedly a factor although data on this is notoriously difficult to acquire and more objective research on the subject is required.

- Over the past 10 years more high paying jobs have been created by international business and black males in particularly have been slow to move into those newly created jobs - largely because of an inadequate education. Morever, many of those jobs require a working knowledge of large countries like the United States and UK and this can only be acquired by working there. Many Bermudians have not had that opportunity.

One of the major lessons of economics is that it is impossible to escape the fact of life that the individual is responsible for his own destiny and that group activism has a terrible record of success elsewhere in the world. It is up to the individual to get an education, do homework, be punctual, save and plan for the future, defer having children until they can be afforded and most important of all understand that no one else is responsible for his lack of success. This was the message which Louis Farrakhan sought to bring to black males in the United States when he organised the one million men march in October, 1995.[7] Blaming someone else for your failure is a Marxist fallacy and cop-out, and resolves nothing. The above qualities have lifted countless poor and disadvantaged out of povery for generations - there is every reason to believe they will do the same for all Bermudians. To have faith in theories of victimisation has been shown as a short-cut to nowhere.

Ending whatever remains of white racism is highly desirable and would do everyone a favour but it would not necessarily do a great deal for those who are

---

[6] I believe this to be high - a figure of about 3 percent would be more accurate.

[7] Even people at the opposite ends of the political spectrum can agree on something.

the poorest and the most disadvantaged in Bermudian society.

In virtually every country in the world income inequality is a subject of major concern. Even in the former communist countries where this was not supposed to happen skilled employees like engineers earned much more than the unskilled. Differences in wages invariably reflects differences in skills, talent, education and personal qualifications. To a great extent the differences in incomes between the white and black populations have more to do with economic class than with race - a situation which tends to be reflected in the United States. However, this view can only be confirmed (or refuted) by having better data.

11. WHAT IS MEANT BY INSITUTIONAL RACISM IN BERMUDA?

"Within a self ascribed economic and social democracy, many personal acts of discriminatory behaviour mount up inside its institutions : the legislature, labour market, education, finance, environmental and land policy, the criminal justice system and health and human services, to name a few. People act out the feelings they have, so that preferential treatment takes place or specific provisions in a law or regulation subtly (sic) impact differentially upon the races. For this reason, institutional racism can be documented only with the use of a carefully designed system of statistical inquiry and analysis."

DR DOROTHY NEWMAN.[1]

Many reports, official and otherwise, underline the fact that the majority Bermudian black working population is under-represented in many socially desirable high paying positions and do not occupy many senior managerial jobs. Even a cursory examination of the management structure of large organisations in Bermuda in 1996 would show that few blacks and women are chief executives. There are a number of notable exceptions, for example, Mr Irving Pearman was managing director of Holmes Williams and Purvey Limited having risen from being a mechanic in that firm's garage.

In most organisations, local and international, the Board of Directors is predominantly white, the chief executive is usually a white male and other senior executives (with rare exceptions) tend to be white males. This means that for the foreseeable future top jobs will be dominated by the minority white population.

By the same token, jobs which pay low wages and are of a low social standing are dominated by the majority black population. The prison population is 94 percent black,[2] there are frequent allegations of discrimination in the criminal justice system and many of the so called 'underclass' are also black. The Shadow Minister for Health, Social Services and Housing Ms Renee Webb was quoted as stating that, "Historically incarceration has been based on race. If you were black, you were more likely to go to prison. This is a clear example of institutionalised racism at work."[3] In short, the black population does less well in the Bermuda economic system than the white population.

---

[1] "Bermuda's Stride Toward the twenty-first Century," page 23

[2] 'The Bermuda Times,' April 4, 1996 page 1.

[3] Ibid.

Many people have questioned the present state of affairs. The main question being this: if the population of Bermuda is roughly 60 percent black, why are the majority of senior managerial or high status jobs not held by blacks? This is an increasingly difficult question and responses referring to qualifications and experience do not satisfy an increasingly vocal number of critics.

One answer given - largely influenced by events in the United States - is that 'institutional racism' is prevalent in Bermuda and that large organisations should examine their hiring, promotional and succession policies to ensure that the black population is fairly treated when competing for prestigious jobs.

> *Institutional racism is a system of procedures/patterns in all walks of life i.e. education, housing, businesses, employment, professional associations, religion, media, etc., whose effect is to perpetuate and maintain the power, influence and well-being of one group over another. It originates in the operation of established and respected forces in the society, and thus receives far less public condemnation than does individual racism. Although more subtle than individual racism, it is more destructive of humanity.*
> The Commission for Unity and Racial Equality.

In the past, "institutional racism" was not an issue for the public or government agenda. Prior to the mid-1960s racial discrimination of an objectionable and open character was the normal practice in Bermuda in much the same way as it was in the United States. The black population was simply not hired to work in large organisations like banks, hospitals or in other large companies. Even in government, it was rare to see blacks occupy senior positions of responsibility, except perhaps in the Police Force or the teaching profession. The practice and official policy prior to 1965 was quite simple - blacks need not apply. If they did the applications were either ignored or lost. This was "institutional racism" with a vengeance.

The denial of equal opportunity to black Bermudians in this period was both morally wrong and economically irrational. The position improved after 1965. In the 1970s and 1980s many in the black population were appointed to senior positions in several organisations but particularly in the Bermuda Government. There was some resistance from reactionaries (and there still is) but in the main there was progress. The original intentions were good and the expectation was that the black population would be brought into the mainstream of commercial employment and that, within a short period of time, the bitterness and injustice of the old discriminatory system would be forgotten and forgiven. Contentment would reign in the work place, and black and white Bermudians would be brothers and sisters in their day-to-day working lives. However, things have turned out quite different from the optimistic and naive days of the 1970s.

This is a puzzling and frustrating position which has exercised the minds of those in authority and Government. Gross offensive racial discrimination no longer exists but a large sections of the black population believe that they have not participated equally with whites in the economic prosperity of the past 30 years and the opportunities this presented for personal fulfillment. The main culprit for thwarting the legitimate aspirations of the black population is believed to be 'institutional racism'. What then is "institutional racism"?

It is the suspicion, or the belief, or even the certainty (which of the three nouns you prefer depends on your view of current Bermudian race relations) that the main insitutions in society fail to give black Bermudians the equal opportunity rights which they struggled to achieve in the 1960s and which they now legally possess. It is a secret insidious process which many believe it to be akin to some mysterious virus, like ebola, which infects and poisons the relationships between black and white Bermudians and with established institutions.

However, despite repeated allegations of its existence there is a paucity of hard evidence to prove its existence. Most chief executives would be horrified if an accusation of institutional racism was made against their organisations. Almost without exception, large established insitutions have in place equal opportunity policies[4] and many take active steps to recruit, train and promote black Bermudian employees.

Insitutional racism is therefore a practice which is notoriously difficult to define and even harder to detect although many are convinced it exists and thrives in Bermuda. For example, Mr Kenneth Dill, the Executive Director of the Human Rights Commission believes it to be a major problem in Bermuda. At a forum at the Bermuda College at the end of February, 1996 Mr Dill was reported in The Bermuda Times of March 1, 1996 as highlighting "rampant institutionalised racism as being a leading cause of the problems that young black men face. He mentioned the discrepancies bewean educational background versus career advancement, stating blacks hold more masters degrees than whites, and more doctorates, yet hold only 34 percent of all administrative and managerial jobs compared to the 61 percent held by whites in this community." These are indeed strong words.

Institutional racism is also thought to refer to the unintended processes and procedures within society's insitutions, like schools, banks, all types of commercial enterprises, the public service, hospitals or any other significant employer which do not produce racially proportionate results from their recruitment, employment and promotion policies. It is not necessarily an act which causes injury, loss or the denial of rights to a specific individual but is the total sum of the unequal effects of business practices upon a given racial group like black Bermudians. Many say that organisations practice institutional racism if a large insitution has 30 managers and less than 20 of them are black Bermudians. Similarly, if the inmate population of the Westgate Correctional Facility (the prison) is more than 60 percent black, it means that the Bermuda system of justice practises institutional racism.

---

4 See for example the Bank of Bermuda Limited's equal opportunity policy set out in Part IV 9.

Thus any practice or policy which results in a disproportionate racial mix is 'prima facie' evidence of insitutional racism. For example, if an organisation has a labour force which differs racially from the general population, or which fails to represent roughly the main racial groups in society, it opens itself to accusations that it is practising institutionalised racism. The critical assumption of institutional racism is that different racial or ethnic groups would be evenly or randomly represented in situations, occupations or social organisations in the absence of racial discrimination. The fact is that notwithstanding years of repetition, this assumption remains wholly unsupported by any objective evidence and this is what makes the case against insitutional racism so weak in the eyes of many in the white population.

The principle of "insitutional racism" rests largely on the 1971 U.S. Supreme Court case 'Griggs v Duke Power' which enunciated the disparate impact standard which defined as discriminatory any practice (in this case promotions based on examinations) , policy or job requirement which fails to produce race and gender proportionality of the surrounding community. The result of this case was that racial imbalance became proof of discrimination whether or not there was any objective evidence to support it. This was a case which caused major offence to minority groups like Asians and Jews who see the proportional argument as a basis for discriminating against them. In the United States , the Jewish population is 6 million, less than 3 percent of the population yet over the past 30 years Jews have composed about 20 percent of senior civil servants and 40 percent of senior partners in major law firms. Almost 90% of Jews enter and graduate from university, and their per capita income is about twice that of the non - Jewish population.

Major institutions such as banks and large insurance companies sincerely believe they do not consciously practice racial discrimination in their hiring and promotions policy. The key word is "consciously" because the concept of institutional racism rests very heavily on the belief that whilst current practices are no longer crudely and overtly discriminatory there is subtle, even unintentional, racial discrimination which results in favouritism for the benefit of white males. It is very difficult, even impossible, to square the sincere beliefs of major institutions that they do not practice discrimination with the conspicuous failure of many black males to reach the pinnacles of commercial success. This is an immensely difficult public relations obstacle to overcome and there has been much soul searching to find a remedy to the problem.

The failure to produce racially proportionate results can obviously arise from real or conscious policies to block or prevent members of an unwanted racial group from participating in the economic benefits of the insitution, or increasingly it may arise from disguised, unconscious or surreptitious practices which adversely affect the unwanted group. Overt racist policies are unlikely to exist in today's society in large organisations because they are illegal, the penalties involved are high or because of adverse publicity; it would be inconceivable (as well as illegal) , for example, to put a crude sign which states "no blacks need apply." Unwritten policies are similarly inconceivable and illegal. Insitutional racism increasingly is seen to be a hidden impersonal force which unconsciously and secretly operates within an institution, or the various institutions of society, for the purpose of preventing social and economic progress of members of the black race.

There are several definitions of institutional racism quoted in the 1995 book "The End of Racism" by Dinesh D'Souza many of which are vague and are difficult to understand by many in the white population[5]:-

"Insitutional racism refers to the complex of institutional arrangement and choices that restrict the life chances and choices of a socially defined racial group in comparison with those of the dominant group."

THOMAS PETTIGREW

"Institutional racism can be defined as those established laws, customs and practices which systematically reflect and produce racial inequalities in American society. If racist consequences accrue to institutional laws, customs or practices, the institution is racist whether or not the individuals maintaining those practices have racist intentions."

JAMES JONES.

"Racism can mean culturally sanctioned beliefs which, regardless of the intentions involved ...justify policies and institutional priorities that perpetuate racial inequality."

DAVID WELLMAN.

In the 1992 book "Paved with good intentions," the author Jared Taylor sarcastically defined insitutional racism as "the villain believers in white racism are left with when they cannot find people who are actually racist".

Professor Swain in her report made the assumption that there was a degree of institutional racism in Bermuda, and if the above definitions are accepted as reasonable by the reader it is difficult to argue against the prevalence of institutional racism. The key determinant is, to what extent should there be proportional representation of the two main racial groups in Bermuda in socially desirable positions of employment or authority? If one accepts without reservation the proportional representation argument, then it is difficult not to conclude there is insitutional racism in Bermuda. If one does not accept that argument, the case for stating that insitutional racism exists is not nearly as strong and it becomes a highly elusive concept.

As Professor Swain made clear in her report the perception by a significant majority, two-thirds in her view, of the male black population that they believe that most insitutions in Bermuda, particularly business organisations, fail to provide equal opportunities for black Bermudians means that corporate Bermuda has a problem and has a mammoth task of convincing the majority of the black population that institutional racism does not exist.

---

5 The chief executive of the Bank of Butterfield was taken to task for stating in a speech in March, 1996 that he was "puzzled by the whole concept of institutional racism."

12. WHAT IS THE GLASS CEILING?

"The male sex still constitutes in many ways the most obstinate vested interest one can find."

LORD LONGFORD.

"Most hierarchies were established by men who now monopolise the upper levels, thus depriving women of their rightful share of opportunities to achieve incompetence."

PROFESSOR LAURENCE PETER.

"Men and women must receive equal pay for equal work in production. Genuine equality between the sexes can only be realised in the process of the socialist transformation of society as a whole."

MAO TSE-TUNG.

There can be little argument about the fact that the life of the modern female in the rich Western countries has improved radically. Modern health care, birth control which frees women from the burden of having a dozen children, and the relatively modern inventions of the washing machine, micro-wave ovens and drip dry materials have been a boon. Women now represent between one-third to one-half of the rich world's working population and their pay in recent years has risen faster than that of men.

There can also be little argument that the life of the modern male has also improved in the twentieth century. Long hours of drudgery on the farm or in factories is now, for most men, a thing of the past although longer hours at the office are taking their place.[1] What has changed is that women, like many other groups in society who believe their rewards and roles are not appreciated, have rightly challenged the inherited assumptions and prejudices which have existed since time began. In addition, there is the basic, almost elementary point that organisations or countries will never reach their full potential if half the brainpower and talent in the economy is neglected or is not used to its fullest extent.

Women in Bermuda are legislators, judges and high status professionals like lawyers and accountants, jobs most of their grandmothers could never have contemplated. Yet from the perspective of the ambitious woman, the world of jobs, wealth and influence is still depressingly closed to much of their talents. Management in particular has eluded too many women although there are several examples of those who have succeeded[2] but for many, sooner rather than later, they bang their head against what is known as the the glass ceiling. In the United States for example, of the 2,500 highest earning executives only 50 were female.[3] Big Bosses who are females are almost as rare as nail polish on the fingers of longshoremen.

---

[1] See "The Overworked American," by Juliet B. Schor.

[2] Miss Jeni Graham is the head of Cable and Wireless, Bermuda: Mrs Susan Wilson heads up Masters Limited; and Jennifer Cartmell head up Texaco's operation in Bermuda.

[3] 'Business Week' - October 28, 1996 page 55.

Nevertheless, women now own about eight million firms in the United States and in Britain women now start up one in four new businesses.[4] But the sad fact still remains that women's progress is hampered by such long standing barriers to social progress as family pressures, prejudice, ignorance, and the failure of current business leaders and others (including many women) to appreciate female talents. Even in Sweden, where women's progress has been greatest and where women serve in top combat positions in the airforce, at the sharp end of building Volvos and make up half of the Swedish cabinet female chief executives are rare. Swedish women tend to do no better than their opposite numbers in the United States and Europe.

Women have entered the labour force in large numbers for many years now and have altered its character in many ways as about half of the participants in the work force are now female. One factor driving this social phenonemon is that the talents and skills required in the past for many occupations consisted to a large extent of brute physical ability, and a degree of competitiveness and agression found mainly in males. In the modern world many so-called "manly" talents are obsolete. Work increasingly depends on what is above the neck not on a strong back and muscular arms.

The new engines of economic change - information technology and globalisation tend to bring greater benefits to women than to men. Jobs abroad in mining, shipyards and factories are disappearing by the millions. Adaptable, flexible, well-trained and well educated service work is from where the new economic growth comes. The same process is at work in Bermuda as the importance of tourism and retailing declines. The brain and the knowledge contained therein is what distinguishes the modern employee from his (or her) ancestors and one of the obvious facts in Bermuda today is that females tend to be more conscientous at school and adapt more easily to the service economy. For example, the majority of scholarships granted in Bermuda are awarded to females, the majority of under-graduate and graduate degrees are earned by women and the skill and experience of women, particularly in the international business sector, is generally acknowledged to be superior to that of Bermuda's males.

There are many questions which arise. Are Bermuda's business organisations taking the appropriate action to create a workplace in which employees of both sexes are assessed, paid and valued for their achievements, productivity and contribution towards business success? Is there equality of opportunity for females and are women's specific needs, like care of young children, accommodated in the business organisation of the 1990s? Are men and women judged by the same criteria? If the responses of women elsewhere are anything to go by, the answers to these questions are that many women are dissatisfied by the current situation.

The "glass ceiling" issue has much in common with the subject of insitutional racism discussed in the previous essay. The "glass ceiling" is so called because it is believed by many women that there is a solid barrier to their recruitment, promotion or advancement in many organisations in Bermuda, but this barrier is invisible and solid like glass so that women only become aware of it when they unexpectedly bump up against it.

---

4 'The Economist,' August 10, 1996.

Evidence of this glass ceiling comes from the fact that:

- Women tend to be clustered in occupations or activities which are low paying, such as teaching or nursing. In large organisations female workers will be mainly secretaries, cooks or cleaners.

- If women are in similar jobs to men, their pay is often less than that of men.

- Women can reach a certain level in an organisation, but when they get reasonably near the top of the hierarchy they hit the glass ceiling and do not succeed men into the jobs of real power, responsbility and high pay.

- Occupations which tend to be dominated by women fail to attract men in any significant numbers or men move out of it and as a result that occupation loses its value, attraction and status in society.[5]

As with insitutionalised racism, most organisations deny, or fail to acknowledge, the existence of gender discrimination and it is often difficult to obtain objective independent evidence that it is widespread. The following are examples of barriers which allegedly exist in the business world and which must be overcome by women if they hope to succeed in achieving equality of opportunity :

- Male managers harbour stereotypes about women believing for example that their career commitment is not as great as that of men, and that they are not as decisive as men if they are in top positions.

- Women are excluded from male networking organisations like golf outings and other sports clubs, and informal meetings which take place in bars, restaurants or clubs.

- Men do not take women seriously believing them to have various mental or character flaws of an undefined nature, for example being more emotional, or lacking confidence when addressing a business meeting.

- Senior managers believe that women tend to be less ambitious, less forceful and less focussed than men.

- Men tend to promote individuals in their own image - the old-boy network.

- Women lack mentors or sponsors in the highly competitive corporate atmosphere.

- The business culture is designed by men, with men in mind and for the benefit of men.

- Women are damned if they are aggressive like men, but if they are not aggressive they are damned because they lack confidence.

- Staff jobs or backroom jobs like human resources, advertising or public affairs which lack real clout in the decision making organisation tend to be staffed by women.

- Women with young children are at a severe disadvantage in that they have to take care of children when they are sick or very young making it difficult to work overtime at short notice or in the highly competitive atmosphere of business stay late at the office for the purpose of showing how committed they are. Few organisations provide child care at reasonable cost or within a reasonable distance of the place of work.

5 Teaching is a good example of this.

According to the U.S. Census Bureau, only 1.1 percent of the female population earned $75,000 or more in 1994, while 6 percent of men did.

Women in Bermuda , it is said are facing the same problems their counterparts are experiencing in the United States and elsewhere but increasingly find it difficult to compete effectively in the male culture which dominates Bermuda business. It was not long ago, say 30 or 40 years ago, when women who married had to resign from their jobs, had lower pay scales than men and were rarely found in the so-called "male" occupations such as accountancy, law, civil service or the police except as clerks, cooks or receptionists. In addition, intelligent and well-educated women dominated two professions, nursing and teaching which were considered to not quite equal to medicine, the military, law and the civil service.

In most organisations the opportunities for both men and women to advance are limited. Senior management is unlikely to pay much attention to employees who are under the age of 30, simply because they lack the experience and confidence necessary to succeed. Potential senior managers are likely to attract attention and be groomed for advancement between the ages of 30 and 45. After the age of 45, most employess tend to be written off as too old (ageism) or are believed to lack the necessary qualities for success.

There is therefore only a short window of opportunity of 15 years for individuals to make their move in organisations, but the ages of 30 and 45 tend to be the years when females have the greatest responsibilities for their children. If women are out of the mainstream, or are unable to work long hours or travel extensively they are unlikely to be in a position to be considered for senior appointments. These are the hard facts of life for both men and women. The age criteria is also a stereotype which can also be as false as some of the ridiculous notions of women noted above. The fact is we do not live in a perfect world, opportunities are limited, competition is intense for senior jobs and luck plays a bigger part in success than many people think.

One of the more obvious facts about Bermuda business life, is that black females tend to possess or demonstrate the qualities required for success in international business to a much greater degree than black men. However, within white collar organisations white males tend to be senior managers and women, whether white or black, occupy clerical, personnel, administrative or support jobs rather than high powered and highly paid management decision occupations. As the corporate game has been for years a man's game, it is not surprising that they are better at it and the old-boy net work is remarkably resilient to change.

> The soundest advice I would give to anybody is to deal with facts and don't be hesitant to voice your opinion if the facts support that opinion. One of the things that women perhaps do better than men is to work cooperatively in a team environment, which I think is the way business is going. And don't assume anything.
>
> Jennifer Cartmell, Head of Texaco, Bermuda.

In the 1990s men in many countries, Bermuda included, are suffering from sluggish real wage growth, insecurity of employment, and the less skilled are being paid less. For working women the economic picture is considerably brighter and they are earning more than was the case in the past. The number of men in the active labour force has fallen whilst the number of women in work has increased.

There is also another trend which until recently has not received as much attention as it should. Well-educated women who are in highly paid jobs tend to marry well educated men, so that family incomes of the middle class are significantly above those who are poorly educated. Time and time again, in the 1990s the question of who does well in the economy is determined by how well (or how badly) an individual has been educated.

The glass ceiling is an issue which will not go away, and neither should it, and in very much the same way as the Swain report indicated that black males believe the system to be rigged against them, corporate Bermuda has also to overcome the female suspicion that they do not receive a fair crack at equal opportunity. In addition, firms may be acting against their own best interests by failing to recruit top managers from such a large pool of female talent. Nevertheless, there is a considerable body of evidence that women are catching up to men and that many Bermudian females are making the most of the opportunities on offer in the international company sector and that many black males are becoming increasingly isolated in dead-end jobs in tourism and construction.

The great challenge for Bermuda business is to change the glass ceiling - which impedes progress - into a glass ladder which leads to success and achievement. The Swain Report is a step in this direction.

13. WHAT IS THE SWAIN REPORT?

"The key question which must be asked within the present context, however, is why segregationist and discriminatory practices, which now seem so idious, were ever instituted in the first place, and why they remained in place for so long? What was the driving force behind segregation? Such questions must be asked here for it is one of the major contentions of this study that in Bermuda as in other post-segregationist societies, some of the same constellation of attitudes, beliefs, and mental associations which originally helped to sustain the system of racial segregation and caste subordination, are still very much present today, though, of course, in a much attenuated form."

THE SWAIN REPORT, PAGE 8.

In 1994 several influential people had raised the point that many Bermudians saw the existing economic structure as being stacked against them. The majority black population, in particular, believed that institutionalised racism was preventing them from being able to benefit from, or to rise in, the flourishing offshore company, banking and other industries involved with financial services. This concern also came at a time when tourism was in the doldrums.

Sir David Gibbons, a former Premier and Finance Minister, and Chairman of the Bank of N.T. Butterfield & Son Limited took it upon himself to raise this senstive issue with Dr. Kenneth Clarke who had done considerable work for the Bermuda Government in the 1970s. He had recommended the services of the consulting firm of Carol M. Swain and Associates in New York. Professor Swain prepared a report for the Bank of Butterfield and the Bank of Bermuda which was made available in the early part of 1995 although not published.

The report involved, firstly, studying previously published material such as the Wooding Report of 1969 and the Pitt Commission Report of 1978 ; secondly, reviewing data gathered by the research organisation of Penn and Schoen also based in New York ; and thirdly, conducting a series of interviews and discussions with various Bermudian individuals from all walks of life including senior civil servants, leading business and professional firms, members of the legislature, trade unions, black intellectuals and religious leaders. In addition, Dr Kenneth Clarke provided guidance and advice from his earlier work in Bermuda.

The report was 82 pages long, and contained several recommendations to deal with the issues of institutionalised racism and glass ceilings (both of which are dealt with elsewhere in this book) but before commenting on the recommendations Professor Swain made several perceptive comments on the social and economic structure of Bermuda as seen from the black perspective.

Firstly, she reviewed the recent history, post 1945, noting that it was rare for black Bermudians to be employed in such areas as the civil service, the two major banks and other privately owned organisations except in the capacity of porters, messengers or janitors. For example, as late as 1965 only 15 blacks were employed at the Bank of Butterfield out of a total staff of 185.

Secondly, she noted the incompatibility of these injustices with the principle of democratic equality, morality and simple justice. She also noted the way in which the employment situation improved dramatically in the 1960s without significant violence (the BELCO riots of 1965 was very much the exception to the rule of non-violent change) and records that this was a "remarkable achievement" by comparison with the more militant experiences of the United States and South Africa.

Thirdly, she reported that "some of the same constellation of attitudes, beliefs and mental associations which originally helped to sustain the system of racial segregation and caste subordination, are still very much present today." These centre around the fact that segregation arose from the white belief that blacks were inferior. She also goes on the say that whites were not the only racial group to exercise such belief as the Japanese did so (and still do) against Koreans, Chinese against Mongols, Greeks against Persians and so on.

Fourthly, whilst such extremist views have changed drastically over the past thirty years, the white population is still prone to use their historic, social and economic advantage to the detriment of the local black population by, for example, subconsciously giving preference to their own kind (both racially and sexually) in both recruitment and promotions for the better paying and more prestigous jobs in the economy of the 1990s.

Fifthly, she sought to explain why, although the situation is immeasurably better in the 1990s than it was in the 1950s, the majority black population is still unhappy with progress made to date. The white population on the other hand are prone to say that things have improved beyond recognition since the 1950s and the 1960s and that therefore black discontent with the status quo is unreasonable. The key to this conundrum is that history has shown on several occasions that when conditions are improved the remaining perceived injustices rankle even more. She used the analogy of the French Revolution of 1789 of which Alexis de Tocqueville (who was the author of one of the best books on the United States entitled "Democracy in America") wrote "the most perilous moment for a bad government is one when it seeks to mend its ways. A grievance comes to appear intolerable once the possibility of removing it crosses men's minds." This is not the place to go into history but similar discontents arose in Russia when Alexander II ended serfdom, or closer to our own time when President Lyndon Johnson was hounded from office after proposing and implementing the most radical social reforms in the United States this century.

Sixthly, she underlined the problems arising from the combination of the remarkable prosperity Bermuda enjoyed in the 1970s and 1980s which took place at the same time as desegregation in society generally, but particularly in the workplace. Black Bermudians had high expectations that much of this prosperity would rub off on them and this was encouraged by political leaders. Much of it did for a few blacks, but much of it did not when, amongst other things, the economy slowed down in the early 1990s because of recessionary problems in the United States. This resulted in diminished opportunities and promotion prospects but at the same time many blacks perceived that the belief in white superiority still existed although in a much attenuated form than before, that the old boy network of white males still exercised considerable informal power and that subtle racial discrimination still existed in the workplace as well as in society generally.

This accounts, in the view of Professor Swain, for the fact that some of the most frustrated, angry and resentful blacks in the community today are those who are the better educated and who have better jobs than the average black Bermudian.

The report identifies black opinion about the future of Bermuda as falling into one of three categories.

(1) **Despairing pessimists**

This is the group which believes that whites will never change, that they will only look after themselves, make token changes and keep blacks locked out of influence, power and financial independence. International companies are just as racist, perhaps even more so, than local organisations and they bring to Bermuda many white expatriates who treat local blacks as inferiors.

(2) **Wait and see skeptics**

This group has much in common with the first, but is prepared to believe that things have improved over the past thirty years and may continue to improve in the future. They are also angry and aggrieved but hope that the future will be better.

(3) **Hopeful optimists**

This group of blacks sees matters differently from the first two. They believe that there has been a fundamental change in society and that racism and discrimination has been consigned to the trash can of history. These "Sunny Jims" recognise that major changes take time, and that if the black population gains the right experience and qualifications when the present generation of senior managers retire they will benefit from the social changes of the past thirty years. Honest, capable, hardworking, reliable people of any race will be able to rise to the level that their talents allow.

Professor Swain believes that each group represents roughly one-third of the present black population. Or put in another way, approximately two-thirds of the black population honestly believe that they will not get a fair crack at opportunity from the existing business community. Whether this is a true reflection of reality or not, it is argued that there is a wide-spread perception in the the black community that equality of opportunity does not exist in Bermuda.[1] It is for this reason that it is necessary for the business community, with the two main banks taking the lead, to implement several reforms to prove that all Bermudians whatever their racial, ethnic or gender background, can participate in the economy and that their opportunities to succeed is limited only their ability and performance on the job.

---

1 See Part IV 9 for a discussion of this

> "In Bermuda, racial divisions appear at all junctures of our day-to-day lives. There is a perception of inequitable practices related to race in our schools; our courts; our political party structure; our sporting events; our cultural events; our churches; our club memberships and our workplaces."

The Swain report made a total of 15 recommendations, most of which were eminently sensible and under the auspices of the Bermuda Chamber of Commerce a committee was established for the purpose of reviewing and analysing the recommendations[2] followed by a discussion of various initiatives which are currently underway. How effective the implementation of the 15 recommendations is, remains to be seen but the fact that major institutions are supporting the recommendations is a hopeful and welcome sign.

The 15 recommendations may be summarised as follows:

1. Employers insitute "diversity awareness" seminars for their employees.

2. Managers be evaluated on their ability to deal with employees from differing racial, ethnic and gender backgrounds in their performance appraisal.

3. The creation of assessment centres to enhance existing career development programmes.

4. Bermuda companies adopt well-defined career development planning programmes.

5. Senior managers take an active role in identifying blacks and women who are capable to promotion and guide and mentor them in the ways of corporate advancement.

6. Companies be more flexible in their job-recruitment standards taking into account such things as prior educational disadvantages and social background.

7. Businesses adopt a school for the purpose of showing the careers and opportunities available to Bermudians.

8. Scholarships and financial assistance be based not only on merit but also on need.

9. Improve the awareness of the variety and quality of further educational insitutions abroad.[3]

10. Make available corporate day care centres for parents with children who are aged four and under.

11. Corporate boards of directors be diversified by seeking qualified blacks and women members representing all segments of the community.

12. Create social outreach programmes to avoid giving offence to employees by, for example, organising social events which include all employees.

---

[2] These were published in 1996 by the Chamber of Commerce in a booklet entitled "A Common Destiny."

[3] The Bank of Bermuda publishes an annual booklet entitled "College Search" which assists parents and students in their college selection.

13. The creation of an outstanding employer award for those organisations which had done the most over the previous year to hire and promote Bermudians.

14. Create a national registry of overseas Bermudians in order to encourage Bermudians to return to Bermuda.

15. Diversify the expatriate pool of labour to encompass countries in the Caribbean and Africa.

Clearly many of the above recommendations can be criticised for being naive or for being impractical. To do this at length would be a tedious exercise but I would recommend that all Bermudians obtain a copy of the Chamber's publication and put forward their ideas as to how the objectives so clearly enunciated by Professor Swain can be put into practice.

One of the most interesting parts of the report was to recommend that Affirmative Action Policies not be implemented in Bermuda because of their failure in the United States. It is to this subject that we next turn.

14. DO WE NEED AFFIRMATIVE ACTION IN BERMUDA?

"What must be understood first about history is that it is irrevocable. Attempts to redress the wrongs of history face the intractable fact that whatever may be done will apply on to the future, not to the past. Most of history's victims or villains are beyond the reach of human power. History is a bottomless pit of wrongs."

THOMAS SOWELL.

"Race should not be a source of power or advantage or disadvantage for anyone in a free society. This was one of the most important lessons of the original civil rights movement."

SHELBY STEELE.

The issue of race, like that in USA is a major dilemma for Bermuda and Bermudians. It has always been thus, and will probably remain that way for the forseeable future. Race is central to the economic issues of the day and it affects such things as employment, promotions, housing, education and a host of other matters. If it is not central it can certainly be found fermenting in the background providing combustible material to those who wish to make political capital out of the most trivial of issues. If the two main races in Bermuda were statistically alike in such things as income and employment race would be nothing more than biological curiosity. Unfortunately, that is not the case which is why it looms over almost every problem Bermuda has to face.[1]

It is also very clear that there is widespread discontent with black economic progress and corresponding failure to participate to the full in the good life which Bermuda enjoys. At the root of the problem is the popular belief that white racism results in the failure of blacks to enjoy the economic benefits of their country.

---

[1] This is explored further in Part IV 8.

This failure (and it is by no means certain that this is the case but it is a widely held belief) has mainly arisen from historical slavery of blacks which has instilled an extraordinary degree of race consciousness which is a curse on modern day Bermuda. The overt racial discrimination continued for at least 130 years following slavery's abolition. If this was not enough there was blatant and unfair treatment of the black population after 1945 which prevented many from moving into white collar well-paid jobs which were being created at that time.

Affirmative action is a policy whose purpose is to give preferential treatment to groups (in the case of Bermuda this would be mainly the black population) in order to correct economic and social inequities of the past and for the victims to compete more effectively in the modern economy. The policy was adopted in order to counteract the effect of custom, tradition, unfair stereotypes, bad schools, poverty, old-boy networks and other factors preventing black Americans from participating in the modern American economy. Such policies are a central feature of racial policy in the United States and elsewhere. Many Bermudians believe these policies should also be adopted in Bermuda in order to spread the benefits of the successful Bermudian economy to all Bermudians not, as it is widely believed, to a small group of largely white males. The market and the Bermuda Constitution are colour-blind in that rights are given to individuals not groups. Affirmative action violates that principle in the name of what many think is an equally noble idea - that of compensating those who suffer as a result of past injustices. It is a difficult issue to resolve because it brings into high-relief fundamental and controversial questions of human and economic rights. The argument comes down, in the final analysis, to making a judgement on the actual benefits and costs.

At the outset it is important to recognise that there is usually statistical disparities between different groups in society whether these differences are racial, religious, of national origin or for any other reason. Jews are prominent in the clothing business, Germans in making beer and pianos, Belgians in diamond polishing, the Scots in engineering, accounting and medicine, Chinese in retailing and restaurants, Christians in the Muslim Ottoman Empire - the list is endless and varied. Few societies, if any, have ever had in their commercial activities a statistical balance which satisfies criteria that each and every group is equally represented. One of the great unexamined assumptions of our time is the one which states that different social, racial and national groups are identical in background and motivation and that any disparity of achievement must be as a result of inequitable treatment by society. Whether Bermuda should follow other countries is a vexed question to which the short answer has to be no.

Firstly, such policies are imposed by governments because the results of competitive forces in the market place have produced results which are not politically acceptable or are politically embarassing. Somehow, the successful are held responsible and accountable for those who do not succeed. These policies have a wretched record of success not only in the United States from where arises most influence over our economic and social policies but also in such diverse places as Malayasia where Malays are given preference over Chinese and Indians, Sri Lanka where Singhalese are favoured over Tamils, and New Zealand where

Maoris are given preferential treatment over the white population. What is not generally known is that the antecedents of affirmative action policies have a long and troubled history usually having been imposed to prevent uppity minorities like Jews and Chinese from highlighting the incompetence of Russians and Malays in business. Jews and Chinese were resented in these two countries because they were different and they had the bad-judgement and the temerity to be excellent at what they did. The equivalent of affirmative action policies were originally used as instruments of repression not for the purpose of creating opportunity.

In India, preferential policies were implemented to protect the hereditary class of untouchables from discrimination by other castes. The policies once implemented could not be contained and group after group came to government seeking protection until the ridiculous situation arose whereby half of the Indian population were protected and the other half became incensed about their treatment. If affirmative action policies don't work in other parts of the world there is no reason why they should work in Bermuda.

Secondly, we should think very carefully before violating the policy of equality before and under the law. It is individuals who have rights not specially protected groups. The idea of judging individuals on their own merits (or demerits) and not on their class or status of their ancestors is more than a fundamental assumption of democratic policy. It is at the centre of the egalitarian revolutions in the eighteenth century in the United States and France and which have influenced democratic governments ever since. Indeed, treating individuals as individuals and ending the privileges of the aristocracy and clergy was what was revolutionary about the founding of the United States and the growth of democracy in the Western world.

Affirmative action has proved to be a denial of the fact that we are all different, the right of an individual to progress in society through merit, of the right to live apart from the conditions under which we are born, and not least the right to say what we think. The case against affirmative action rests squarely on the argument that it is both unfair and unjust for the courts and government to distinguish the legal rights of its citizens on the questionable basis of immutable characteristics like skin colour which are irrelevant to job or academic performance.

In November 1996 in California there was a political intitative[2] to end affirmative action the text of the resolution reading, "The State shall not discriminate against, or grant preferential treatment to any individual or group on the basis of race, sex, color (sic), ethnicity, or national origin in the operation of public employment, public education, or public contracting." The initiative was approved by a large majority and is the first formal rejection of the policy of affirmative action.

Affirmative action touches every sensitive nerve in American politics - race, class, gender and opportunity for advancement as expressed through the educational and economic system. The issue has emphasised colour consciousness in what theoretically should be a colour-blind society. Unfortunately, affirmative action partakes of the thing (racism) it is meant to cure. The logical flaw is that it

---

[2] This is equivalent to a referendum.

is not possible to cancel out one kind of unfairness by introducing an equal and opposite unfairness.

Thirdly, race (or ethnic) relations do not improve, they become worse. Mixing race and politics almost without exception leads to inflamed relationships , a lack of tolerance and increasing hostility between the protected group and other citizens. In other parts of the world, particularly the United States, affirmative action has become a programme for giving statistical representation to race, gender and class. This has proved to be an impossible task in the United States and in a small community like Bermuda commonsense says that it just would not work effectively. It generates a vast bureaucracy which depends on affirmative action for the income and jobs it produces as well as its political influence.

> "In America whites once set themselves apart from blacks and claimed privileges for themselves while denying them to others. Now, on the basis of race, blacks are claiming special status and reserving for themselves privileges they deny to others. Isn't one as bad as the other?"
>
> Stanley Fish

Fourthly, Bermudians are very much a mixed race of people - of long term residents there are not many who are purely black or purely white. Indeed, Mr Sanders Frith-Brown who looks white argues that he is 1/32 black and therefore classifies himself at census time as black. The nineteenth century was notorious for its half-baked sociological theories of race and ability. The fact is the belief that races and groups are discrete and different groups with inherently different aptitudes is false. There is only gradual genetic differences between different races and all merge seamlessly one into the other. Physical differences, like skin colour, are merely adaptations over centuries to different climatic and other conditions. Affirmative action distorts the vision of a colour blind society and tends to be replaced by the reality of a colour conscious society and it subverts the principle of equality. It does not seem much like progress to use half-baked 19th century biological theories of eugenics as a basis to determine 21st century social policies. Rights belong to individuals not organised interest groups and probably least of all to members of a particular race.

Fifthly, preferential policies tend to create corrosive doubt in the eyes of both blacks and whites about the real accomplishments of blacks. Many whites in the United States often view black doctors as having only qualified because of some academic quota at medical school. Black success is often viewed as a kind of commodity which whites control and dole out to blacks by lowering objective standards. This is a dead form of economic progress or reform.

Sixthly the costs can be astromonical, "Forbes Magazine"[3] reporting that the financial impact of affirmative action may be as high as four percent of GNP - about as much as the US government spends on education. The fact is any policy which provides jobs on the basis of race rather than competence will result in economic inefficiency.

---

[3] See the edition of February 15, 1993 in the article entitled "When quotas replace merit, everybody suffers."

Thomas Sowell, an American economist, examined[4] affirmative action polices all over the world and concluded that:

1. Affirmative action commences as being a temporary arrangement but goes on forever.

2. Within the so called disadvantaged group, those who are least disadvantaged end up as the major beneficiaries. Put bluntly, why should the son or daughter of a wealthy Bermudian black doctor, banker or lawyer receive government assistance to obtain a job over a poor underpriviledged white whose father is a truck driver. Not all whites are wealthy and privileged and not all blacks are poor and underprivileged. There is also the fact that there is great disparity between the incomes within the black population in Bermuda.

3. The policy encourages group polarisation and increases conflict between the races

4. Although not entirely relevant to Bermuda, people fraudulently claim to be members of the protected group as when one native American contractor in Tulsa, Oklahoma who had blue eyes and an Irish name claimed membership in the Cherokee Indian tribe on the basis of an alleged great-great-great-great-grandfather.

5. Preferential policies generate tons of literature about their noble objectives and good intentions but few words about their failure (or successes if they can be found) to reduce inequalities.

Sowell concluded that affirmative action is in practice the legal granting of economic privileges to officially sanctioned groups but is disguised by the mask of equality of opportunity.

The United States has experienced what is known as insitutional racism[5] and the glass ceiling[6] which prevents women from realising their full potential and has chosen affirmative action as the main mechanism for combatting both of the evils. This is a legal and administrative means of making amends for past racial and sex discrimination by requiring employers to take an applicant's race or sex into consideration when appointing, or promoting an employee. It has the distinct disadvantage of offending the principle that merit and individual talent should be the only criteria for such appointments.

Over a period of 30 years or so the desire to assist those burdened by a racist or misogynist past has degenerated into a vast numbers game or a quota system which results in opportunity being defined not on the basis of merit and other objective criteria but membership of a racially disadvantaged group. Affirmative action is based on the false assumption that what keeps American blacks, women and other minorities from achieving equality of opportunity is white racism and sexism, and that the way to eliminate these evils is through the adoption of affirmative action which sets goals or targets (but not quotas) to be achieved by important insitutions like business firms and universities. Affirmative action calls attention to, and makes important race and sex - qualities which the various Civil

---

[4] See "Preferential Policies," page 15 and 16 and for a wider discussion of the issue. See "Race and Culture," both written by Thomas Sowell.

[5] See Part IV II for a discussion of this issue.

[6] See Part IV 12 for a discussion of this issue.

Rights Acts had stated should not matter at all. Paradoxically, they make race and sex decisive matters in determining whether an individual gets a job or gets promoted.

Affirmative action was originally meant to be for defined historical racial discrimination against black Americans and it was supposed to be temporary. As organised interest groups grasped its importance in the way Government money and privileges could be dispensed, other organised groups representing Hispanics, native Americans and women were added as other groups too recognised that a distinct advantage could be gained by being officially classified as disadvantaged or victimised.

So great has been the wish to gain the lucrative status of victim that many writers have claimed that more than 100 percent of Americans can at one stage or another claim to be protected by affirmative action programmes. A female black Muslim could conceivably claim victim status on the grounds of race, sex and religion. Combining the experiences of American blacks, Latinos, Asians, women, homosexuals, Native Americans, Aleuts, Pacific Islanders and others is both false and demeaning. The doctrine which once said that individuals were all equal before the law and that wealth, parents, background, pedigree, race, religion, sex or national origin were irrelevant, had somehow been converted into a doctrine which said that certain immutable characteristics like race, sex and national origin were matters which were important in determining what rights could be enforced by the American justice system.

Equality before the law and equal treatment by the state as guiding principles for public administration were no longer thought to be important. The individual is not important, what is important was the group of which he was a member. Unfortunately, equality before the law is being superseded by a new principle - a statute based legality comparable to feudalism whereby legal rights depend on such things as race and gender. If that group is favoured by the state it can enjoy certain privileges ; if the individual is not a member of the group he could no longer expect equality of treatment under the law. Ironically, it is the practice of racial discrimination in the name of equality with legal protection masquerading as justice. In his *"I have a dream" speech in 1963 Dr Martin Luther King Jr said "I have a dream that my four little children will one day live in a nation where they will not be judged by the colour of their skin, but by the content of their character."* Implementing affirmative action in Bermuda, at least in the way it is practised in the United States, will mean that that day is further away than ever.

There is a final compelling argument against affirmative action and it is this. The guts of the debate is something of a paradox. Black Bermudians who understandably seek equality of economic status with white Bermudians must emphasise their limited achievements in commerce in order to justify the establishment of preferential policies. At the same time, establishment whites must also underline that the achievment of black financial equality cannot be attained without their influence and support. The paradox is that the establishment of affirmative action implies that the alliance between Bermudian blacks and Bermudian whites is not an alliance between equals. Blacks who stress that they need some special treatment to succeed in Bermudian society are flattering the white power structure and underlining their own weaknesses. Whites who exercise power and who believe blacks have been economically penalised because society has wrongly discriminated against them are showing condescension towards blacks and promoting the idea of their own superiority because they are exercising their power for the benefit of those weaker than themselves. Affirmative action gives credibility to the lie that blacks can only succeed if whites condescend to help them. The fact of the matter is that black aspirations can only be realised by the efforts and initiatives of the black population of Bermuda. Black Bermudians need the help of anyone except themselves.

The unspoken assumption is that blacks are not responsible for their own lives, and that progress is dependent on the goodwill of the white population. This is an illusion, and a prison worse than anything that the Westgage Correctional Facility can offer. Black leaders by insisting that the only problem Bermudian blacks face is white racism are condemning many young blacks to an enslavement similar to that which existed in the early 19th century. The debate about affirmative action illustrates the way in which most white and black Bermudians view the world. Blacks don't believe whites care enough about racial discrimination. Whites don't think that blacks care enough about pulling themselves up by their own bootstraps. In a sense both are correct.

Most Bermudians, black and white have understood quite clearly that, like all people anywhere else in the world, they are responsible for their own lives and that there are enough obstacles to economic success without inventing them.[7] Affirmative action invariably turns into affirmative confusion.

15. SHOULD BERMUDA FOLLOW THE REST OF THE WORLD AND ESTALISH A WELFARE STATE?

"The American economy is set up for failure. The welfare state once looked like a good idea, but after six decades, a formerly self-reliant population has been transformed into an entitlement dependent one. Many inner-city families have been destroyed, and government has assumed responsbility for the medical care and income of retirees."

PAUL CRAIG ROBERTS.

The Old Testament taught that governments should act in the capacity of a shepherd and look after those poor who were unable to look after themselves, after all of it was Jesus who said, "The poor you always have with you." Modern western governments have had a long tradition going back over 400 years of making provision for those are hungry, homeless or are otherwise destitute although the widespread availability of benefits is a relatively modern innovation.

---

[7] Many people may regard me, a white middle-class middle-aged man, as arrogant by expressing views about the effectiveness, or otherwise, of affirmative action because I am unable to understand what it is like to be black and poor. This can be a valid point but the way to demonstrate this is to refute the arguments.

In 1816, an eccentric English pamphleteer called Thomas Bunn warned of an "accumulation of distress among the lower orders" and he called for a series of benefits for the poor other than a rudimentary and arbitrary Poor Law then in existence. If his advice was ignored he argued England risked the sort of revolution which had taken in place in France at the end of the eighteenth century where the aristocracy had been decimated for failing to take care of the poor. It was not for another century that Bunn's ideas gained widespread acceptance in Western democracies. Excluding philanthropists like Rowntree (of the candy bar family) the conventionial wisdom was that either poverty did not exist or that the undeserving poor had only themselves to blame for their plight. Any proposal to implement a series of government sponsored hand-outs was frowned on because it was unlikely to encourage reckless procreation. However, social reformers and politicians increasingly became aware of the social distress and by the 1880s unemployment was regarded as being a major cause of social ills ranging from illegitimacy to crime.

The intellectual battle was won in both Britain and the United States by the early twentieth century and piecemeal social programmes were introduced for the purpose of correcting the social inequalities created by a market economy. Following the hardships and deprivations which arose from the widespread unemployment during the Great Depression in the 1930s, governments in Europe and the United States implemented in the 1930s and 1940s a whole range of social welfare benefits for their population which fell under the umbrella title of the New Deal in the United States or the "welfare state" in the United Kingdom. The variety of programmes implemented were viewed as a guardian angel or a safety net against the chronic insecurity, fear and poverty which was so prevalent in both countries during the 1930s.

In Bermuda we have been fortunate in that the numbers of poor have been relatively small compared to the levels in the United States and countries in Europe, and the provision of welfare services has been mainly left to private charities like the Salvation Army and the LCCA all of whom have worked hard on behalf of those left behind in the economic race. Unemployment for example has always been relatively modest by comparison with other countries.

The range of benefits which arise in the modern welfare state are huge. Here are some examples from the United States and Europe:-

- child allowances;
- old age pensions, with mandated cost of living adjustments;
- free medical and health coverage;
- mandated and subsidised vacations often as long as 8 weeks per annum;
- public housing at subsidised cost;
- payment from the public purse whilst on strike;
- job security provisions;
- unemployment benefits which can last forever.

These are wonderful benefits to enjoy and get for free and the workers in Europe and United States should be having a wonderful time - the only problem is that they are not. The guts of the problem is that such benefits are not really free, they only appear to the financially naive to be free at the point of use but at the end of the day someone has to pay for them. They are paid for through the tax system by imposing a crushing level of taxes on the workers at a level which would make the Bermudian labour force do a double take. Social security costs, including the portion paid for the employer, can reach as much as much as 70 percent of the employee's paycheque which has the result of driving up labour costs which in turn makes the country less competitive in the world economy. As governments increase the tax burden to pay for the smorgasborg of benefits, it simultaneously generates incentives to move production and jobs out of the country to cheaper locations elewhere in the world.

> "Experience should teach us to be most on our guard to protect liberty when the government's purposes are beneficial. Men born to freedom are naturally alert to repel invasion of their liberty by evil-minded rulers. The greater dangers to liberty lurk in insidious encroachment by men of zeal, well-meaning but without understanding."
>
> Justice Louis Brandeis of the United States
> Supreme Court.

Sweden is probably the best (or the worst) example depending on your point of view, of how matters can get out of hand. Social expenditures are 40 percent of GDP, the national debt is about 90% of the annual GDP, and labour costs are increased by almost 50 percent in order to finance the benefits provided by the state. These costs become so high that unemployment soars because labour is so expensive.

The unemployment rate also increases because generous unemployment benefits mean that working is not a very smart way to make money if you don't have a great affection for work, which is the position of most people. Why go out in the cold and snow to labour in a factory when you can get 70 percent of your current income by staying in bed? The labour shirkers also have a bad influence on those who wish to work but are not all that enthusiastic about it in the first place. When a number of people get paid to do nothing there is a tendency to encourage others to behave in the same way. The welfare state tends to disconnect the relationship between reward and effort - one of the fundamental assumptions of the capitalist system - by creating disincentives to work, to save and to show intitiative and entrepreneurship. Unemployed people who insist only on the ideal job will stay unemployed for a long time if they are either independently wealthy (which is highly unlikely) or if the government subsides them to stay unemployed. The higher the subsidy the higher the degree of unemployment. Another severe disadvantage is that individuals who were never intended to be beneficiaries when the the system was established adjust their behaviour to take advantage of the benefits created.

So pervasive and ingrained has the system become that workers view their long vacations and job security as basic human rights which cannot be taken away. Politicians having promised all the benefits without imposing the necessary taxation are almost powerless to deal with the economic problems they have created. The system is also paralysed by self-serving interest groups, and a bloated bureaucracy dedicated to preserving their own privileges and existence. The concept of acquired rights of employment and benefits is so deeply ingrained in the workers' consciousness that many would find life very different, even intolerable, without them.

In Belgium, expenditure on welfare policies has made the national debt so huge, almost 150 percent of annual GDP, that it is sinking the country. At the current level of debt about 40 percent of the Belgian Government budget is used to pay interest on the national debt and is crowding out other useful Government expenditure which has to be deferred like repairing roads or improving the educational system. Taxes are at a penal level and there is widespread tax evasion with funds flowing into the tax-haven competitors of Bermuda like nearby Luxembourg. When the costs of welfare state benefits are met by penal taxation and deficit financing the transfer of incomes is reversed. The wealthy tend to own large parts of the National debt and when 40 percent of the budget goes from the poor taxpayer to the wealthy debt holder there is clearly a transfer of wealth from the poor to rich, not from the rich to the poor as is commonly thought.

The question of whether Bermuda should implement a welfare state is really answered by what has happened elsewhere in the world. It is wonderful to promise all the benefits listed above but when it comes to paying for them it is a very different story. Huge administrative costs are imposed collecting taxes from a group of workers to pay the benefits to another group (sometimes the same people). When the true costs are assessed as to who pays for what, it is hard to escape the conclusion that selling the welfare state as a major benefit to the working population violates the principle of truth in advertising .

Two of the worst examples of government programmes which have gone seriously wrong are in the United States. Firstly, low income housing is characterised by crime, drug-dealing, and vandalism and despite huge government investments many housing projects have been abandoned as unworkable. Anyone who has driven around the Bronx in New York sees buildings which are a disgrace to a modern state. The second example, is that the poor in the United States, particularly the black population, have become poorer and more demoralised as more welfare money is spent to improve their condition. The welfare state despite all the good intentions unfortunately encourages dependency, erodes initative and in the end destroys the human spirit. Do we want that to happen to Bermudians? I rather think not. However, we who are reasonably comfortable need to remind ourselves of what Herman Melville (the author of Moby Dick) said many years ago, "Of all the preposterous assumptions of humanity over humanity, nothing exceeds most of the criticisms made on the habits of the poor by the well-housed, well-warmed, and well-fed."

16. ARE UNIONS THE FRIEND OR FOE OF THE BERMUDA LABOUR FORCE?

"The organised trade unionist have not only outstripped the well-to-do middle class, they have become the principal exploiters of the poor and the humble. Like all aristrocrats they cling to their privileges at the expense of everyone else."

A.J.P. TAYLOR.

The headline in 'The Royal Gazette' of December 14, 1993 was inflamatory, *"Gov't against the workers - Simmons."* It continued, *"Quite frankly, I think that the workers of Bermuda are going to have to rise up against the Government."* Mr. Ottiwell Simmons is reported to have said this in the context of the dispute between the BIU and Pink Beach Cottage Colony.

Like most other workers in Bermuda at the time, I had no intention of rising up against the Government even if I understood what was meant by that exhortation to revolution. Indeed the story probably created another long yawn from the public who were fed up with the antics of labour and management battling it out on the front page. However, the headline and the story illustrated three major myths about the union movement in Bermuda.

Firstly, unions wish to give the impression that they represent all employees. This is not the case as they represent a minority of the labour force; about 24% in Bermuda and about 15% in USA. A call to action therefore applies to less than one quarter of the labour force, and in fact strikes a sympathetic chord in only about 2%. Most employees, though by no means all, identify quite closely with their employer recognising an important fact of life, namely that when the company for whom they work is prospering they also do quite well as the interests of capital and labour are increasingly difficult to disentangle. There is only one thing worse than working for a company that is doing well, and that is working for a company which has gone broke; ask any former employee of the Bermudiana Hotel, PanAm or Eastern Airlines what it means to lose a job, salary and career.

The financial distress of the hotel industry (since 1988 Bermuda's major hotels have lost a staggering $47.5 million)[1] is due in large part (but not wholly) to the short-sighted policies and powers of the BIU. Job security and high wages can only be guaranteed by the customer coming back, healthy, steady profits and an adequate return on capital. It cannot be guaranteed by unions bargaining with employers.

Unions love to foster the legend that there always has to be some sort of battle going on between employers and employees. That is wrong. Today's union leaders have a vested interest in keeping employers and employees at each others throats in order to maintain their power base and in doing so they jeopardise the welfare of their members. In point of fact the interests of employers and employees are broadly similar and most employees in Bermuda understand that simple fact. As the 'Mid-Ocean News' reported on 23rd December 1992 *"The 18 month*

---

[1] As reported by the Bermuda Hotel Association in December, 1996.

standoff between the BIU and HEB has marked a shameful new low in obstinacy, intransigence and bullheadedness, one that has impacted directly on every single local resident in one way or another."

The second myth constantly bandied around by unions is that if it was not for them, their members would, at best, be working for next to nothing and at worst be at the mercy of unscrupulous employers. Again wrong, wrong, wrong. The wage or salary of any employee is based largely on conditions of supply and demand, like the cost of any other product. Unions are able to affect the price paid for their labour largely because of the legal privileges and immunities granted by law and custom. The most important of these are that unions cannot be sued in tort for the harm caused to innocent parties because of their actions. Add to this things like compulsory membership, employers collecting union dues, the absence of any vote before a strike can be called (teachers are a notable exception to the mob rule philosophy) and one can see the ways in which free market rules are subverted. As Nobel Laureate Friedrich von Hayek said *"We have now received a state where (unions) have become uniquely privileged institutions to which the general rules of law do not apply."*

Incomes of everyone in the labour force can only be increased if the quantity of goods and services supplied is also increased. If the labour force is fixed in size, as it is to a great extent in Bermuda, incomes can only rise if productivity rises.[2] Productivity rises in the main because of new and better ways of doing things so that the goods produced increases as employees become more efficient at their jobs, or move into jobs where higher value is added. However, in most parts of the world, Bermuda included, the organisation most resistant to new methods and improved productivity is trade unions and the BIU is at the forefront of resisting change.

- Substitute sufficient trolleys at the airport for porters - not a chance the BIU may go on strike.

- Work on the docks when it is raining - are you kidding union members may get wet.

- Allow a bartender to act as a bellboy at a hotel when things are quiet - are you mad. One man will be doing the job of two.

This resistance may make sense if you are the union member involved but only for the very short term. In the long term resistance to change is slow motion job destruction and we have seen this in Bermuda in the hotel and construction industries where union representation is at its highest. Between 1988 and 1995 employment has fallen by about 10% in the hotel and restaurant industry. Very few of those in Bermuda without a job are likely to fix the blame on union policies largely because of the concentration on the short term and the inability to see clearly the long term effects of shortsighted policies. Clearly, the BIU cannot claim all of the credit for this job decimation but given their neanderthal approach to employment they can claim the lion's share of success. "Credit for job decimation," should be the newspaper headline. Unfortunately, many members of

---

[2] See Part I 18 on the subject of productivity.

unions are not able to make the connection between unions resisting change and the job destruction that ultimately takes place. They are not alone in this; in the US and UK industry after industry from steel to shipyards to coalmining has seen jobs destroyed whilst unions refuse to face the facts of life.

This brings me to the third myth of unionism - that it represents "a revolution" as evidenced by the words of Mr. Simmons reported in the 'Royal Gazette.' The fact of the matter is that unions favour the status quo, they resist change because change makes them feel uncomfortable. They have never grasped that change and progress are really one and the same thing. On the other hand capitalism[3] which is supposed to be conservative, is by its very nature creating change and never is, and can never be, stationary. Capitalism is therefore a form of revolution because its path and consequences can never be predicted with accuracy. Some industries, such as computers and computer software, now swing through technological change so rapidly that they are basically unstable. No one quite knows which companies, much less which employees, will be around next year.

Our massive off-shore financial industry was not created by the small minds that reside in the BIU but in several foresighted entrepreneurs who saw an opportunity and grasped it. Compare this with the organisation of the BIU whose officers are not always elected (it was alleged that Mr. Simmons was President for life before he retired in 1996), where strikes are called without a secret ballot, where dissent is not tolerated and whose financial records are not readily available to members. Unions revolutionary? They are the most conservative, reactionary and backward institutions in Bermuda. Without the dynamism of the free enterprise system we would live in a stagnant economic world, trapped in spiders' webs like those communism created so effectively in Cuba and Russia, where original thought and new ideas were considered immoral and declared illegal.

The central drama of the Bermuda economy is NOT the struggle between rich and poor or between black and white - their interests are not all that divergent - but the struggle between the future and the past, between the desire to invest in new ventures and the union's impulse to preserve existing jobs and privileges. This opinion is in sharp contrast to the politically correct propaganda we hear and read so frequently. The fact is that the BIU and other unions are the reactionaries and it is Front Street and international business which is revolutionary.

Let us end by giving due credit to the BIU. In several areas they provide services which many members value. The Credit Union, the Co-op, sponsorship of retirement benefit funds, or even comradeship in times of need are examples of the way the BIU has served the interests of its members well.

Many employers are not paragons of virtue. Important matters like wrongful dismissal, racism, or safety are important matters to which unions have given their attention and the membership has benefited as a result. Unions clearly have an important role as their members' representative against management stupidity, abuse of power or big headedness. But in matters of the redistribution of wealth, job protection and even obtaining higher wages unions are largely incapable of meeting their objectives and often work against the best interest of their members.

---

3 See Part I 8 and 9 for a discussion of capitalism.

In believing that they can influence the big picture the only power unions have is to keep their members poor. The real opponent of unions is the employer whose business thrives and whose employees benefit from its efficiency and fair distribution of the wealth created. That is why unions so frequently attack companies who meet these standards.

Unions may move in several ways. If they take the first choice and stay as they are they will, in Bermuda, follow the path of their brothers in U.K. and U.S. That is become largely irrelevant to the wishes or aspirations of most working people. Dinosaurs in a cyber-space world. A second choice is to try and dominate the political process by, for example, being a major partner in the political process. The BIU, the ABUT and The Bermuda Public Services Association are taking this option, pretty much as unions have done with the Labour Party in U.K. and the Democratic Party in the U.S. In taking this tack, much could be achieved.

The third course is working with management to improve productivity, competitveness and the quality of the Bermuda product, especially in tourism. Unfortunately, that idea does not seem to have penetrated union thinking in Bermuda, as it has done, for example, in Japan and is increasingly being done in U.S.A. Even in Britain, for years the place where union stupidity ruled, the leadership is beginning to understand the importance of reform. "The union agenda should be competitiveness, and making things smarter and more efficiently." [4] At the end of the day, in order to meet the aspirations of their membership unions have to take this option. To do otherwise is to sell their Bermudian membership and the rest of Bermuda down the river.

17. IS THERE AN ECONOMIC ARGUMENT TO BAN TRADE UNIONS?

"It is one of the characteristics of a free and democratic modern nation that it have free and independent labour unions."

PRESIDENT FRANKLIN D. ROOSEVELT, 1940.

Banning trade unions could not be accomplished even if someone was foolish enough seriously to propose it. When totalitarian dictatorships arise such as the world has witnessed in countries like the former USSR and Hitler's Germany, one of their first acts is to ban unions. Why? Because unions are able to represent and organise large groups of people whose interests, by definition, are not always identical to those of the state or employers.

Any proposal to ban unions is very different from stating that unions should not have special privileges under the law which is one of the disadvantages of our present arrangements in Bermuda. Unions were established in the first place to represent groups of workers who were suffering from injustices such as unsafe working practices, unscrupulous employers who ignored the law and other abuses which can easily arise when the parties are not of equal standing. The most

---

4 John Monks the head of the Trades Union Congress, reported in 'Business Week,' December 16, 1996.

powerful ally of trade unions are unscrupulous and rapacious employers. Some unions have abused their power and they are able to do this because they are not held accountable at law in the same manner as everyone else. What should be banned is not unions, but their privileges under the law.

The rule of law, one of whose main principles, is that each person (which includes corporate bodies like unions and limited companies) is equal under the law. For unions this is a dangerous concept because it holds every individual accountable for his or her own actions. The radical idea about Western democracies was the principle established following the French and American revolutions, namely that the individual is placed at the centre of things and is responsible and accountable for his own actions and for his own well being. The concept of immunity under the law breaks that responsibility and accountability which is why trade unions often act against the best interests of their members.

One of our most cherished and fundamental freedoms is that nothing can prevent people organising to look after their own interests. Trade unions are said to be one of the great estates of the realm and provided they have no special privileges and state dispensations, they should be just as free as boy scouts, chambers of commerce and the Roman Catholic Church to act in their own and members' interests, be listened to and have their views respected by those in authority.

Banning unions, even if it was possible, would be a major blow against the rule of law, against our best economic interests and against the workers whom they represent. Anyone who proposes that course of action is against personal liberty.

18. DOES POLITCIAL INDEPENDENCE REALLY MATTER TO THE ECONOMY?

"Then there were the islands, fortresses and coaling stations, strung out along the shipping lanes. Gibraltar, Malta, Aden, Singapore and Hong Kong stood along the orient route. St Lucia guarded the West Indies, Bermuda lay in mid-Atlantic, Halifax in Nova Scotia was the home of one British squadron, Esquimalt in British Columbia the base of another. In every sea a ragbag of islands announced the imperial presence."
    "PAX BRITANNICA - THE CLIMAX OF AN EMPIRE" BY JAN MORRIS.

Bermuda has been a British Colony for all of its inhabited existence, since 1609 and is the oldest British Colony. It is unusual in that the push and rush for independence which overwhelmed the old colonial world after the Second World War and earlier, created little or no interest for the people of Bermuda. Such movements as there were for Bermuda to gain independence were received by the people with a distinct lack of enthusiam and they attracted only minority and sporadic support.

The Progressive Labour Party (PLP) has always advocated independence for Bermuda since its formation in the early 1960s but it always downplayed the issue at election times because it was certain to lose votes from the undecided voter. It was not until 1995 that a major effort to gain support for independence gained momentum from a major part of the governing United Bermuda Party (UBP).

Not too long ago the words British Empire or British Commonweath aroused the pride of most of the British population and Bermudians ; today it arouses feelings of nostalgia in some, ambivalence in others, and in a small sensitive minority feelings of inferiority coupled with a sense of outrage. Bermuda was a very small part of a huge enterprise called the British Empire which for a period of over 400 years ruled about a quarter of the world's population and the same percentage of the world's land mass. Its engineers surveyed and built railways and roads, its missionaries converted native peoples to Christianity, its merchants opened up new markets, its people settled empty continents, and its civil servants administered places as different as Tonga and Hudson's Bay. It was a colossal adventure carried out in the main by young men who wanted adventure and wealth, and like most large human enterprises the good and the bad interacted. It is not difficult to find many examples of both in this immense undertaking.

In Bermuda's case the British Government has rarely interfered in recent times in local issues except to prevent the execution of a condemned murderer or to restore order after a period of rioting which it did in 1968 and again in 1977. The British Government is seen, if it is thought about at all, as a benevolent uncle who provides a steadying influence in a turbulent world and who rarely, if ever, acts in a capricious or unfriendly way to the locals. To the outsider it is a curious situation when the local population has little interest in the creation of a Bermudian nationality, a Bermudian flag or membership in the United Nations. At the same time, to the British Government, Bermuda is considered something of an embarrassment when it wishes to hold on to a status which most of the world rejected decades ago.

The theoretical arguments for independence are very strong. Nobody wishes to be bossed around by someone from a foreign country. Self determination seems to be synonomous with self-respect. It appeals not only to the concept of national freedom, but to personal liberties and to Thomas Jefferson's inalienable rights to life, liberty and the pursuit of happiness. Just as a cantankerous George III stood in the way of the saintly George Washington so colonialism as a abstract political system appears to stand in the way of Bermudian aspirations of self-rule and taking an adult role in the conduct of Bermudian affairs.

Being a British colony does not bring any direct financial benefit to Bermuda. Firstly, there is no automatic development aid; the local population neither enjoys the social security nor other benefits available to the British public in UK. Bermuda does not receive any subsidy, stipend or subvention from the British Government. There is no automatic right of Bermudians to settle or work in the U.K. There are some minor, indirect, benefits such as having an economic adviser seconded from the Bank of England, the Governor is usually some well-connected and reasonably capable former civil servant, politician or military man, and the British Government pays for Bermuda's defence and foreign affairs. However, these responsibilities are not onerous - no one wishes to invade

Bermuda - and with a population of 60,000 Bermuda has only a very limited direct interest in foreign affairs.

Secondly, the absence of having to support diplomats in the United Nations, or in the hardship posts of Washington and London, or a modern defence force means that the cost of government is reduced somewhat when one considers that the costs of such dubious benefits can only be spread over a small population. Bermudians are inveterate travellers, many work for international companies and may require the assistance of a consulate in the event of unexpected mishaps and they are able to call on the British Embassy wherever they may happen to be. To pay for that benefit on a world scale would be beyond the capability of any small country.

Thirdly, the most compelling argument of all for colonial status, is that international companies are attracted to Bermuda because it has an honest, impartial and efficient legal system. A major part of this is that there is the right of appeal from the Bermuda courts to the English[1] legal system and ultimately to the Judicial Committee of the Privy Council. Many of the international companies are in the long-term insurance business where there is a strong possiblity that they could be taken to court over a dispute worth several million dollars. Cases like this could take up to ten or fifteen years to come before the courts and could have such a major impact on a company's financial position, even put it out of business or deplete significantlly the value of the shareholders' investment. It is therefore critical to have an efficient, respected and capable legal process under which major cases can be impartially decided. The English legal system is one of the most respected in the world (the American is one of the least respected) and it is therefore crucial to avoid having the English system displaced by one which theoretically would be worse.

To have a company's future wholly dependent on a legal system in a small island community is a risk which few international companies would wish to take. Their asurance is that in the event of corruption, incompetence or mistake, international companies can appeal to courts in a jurisdiction which has the confidence of the business world.

Many independent nations also have the right of appeal to the Judicial Committee of the Privy Council and the argument is made that if Bermuda was an independent Commonweath country, that right of appeal would still be available to international companies, especially if such a right was enshrined in the Bermuda Consitution. What that argument neglects to say is that as an independent nation Bermuda would be able to abolish such right of appeal at any time by amending the Consitution, admittedly a long drawn out process, but one over which the international companies have little influence. So long as Bermuda remains a British Colony that right of appeal cannot be taken away.

In 1994 to the astonishment of the electorate the issue of independence was raised by the Premier who having narrowly won a general election in October 1993 saw an issue which he thought would galvanise the electorate, unite Bermudians and retain the black vote for the UBP. On 4th February, 1994 Sir

---

[1] It is English not British as the Scottish legal system is different.

John Swan advised the House of Assembly of the Government's intention to request the Governor to establish a Commission of Enquiry to examine the issue of whether Bermuda ought to remain a Dependent Territory (a colony in old fashioned language) of Great Britain, or become an independent nation within the British Commonwealth. His statement to the House contained a vague statement that there was a "very strong belief that the forces at work in the world are profound in nature, and that Bermuda will not escape the effects of these changes." What these mysterious forces were and how profound they would be was never explained but in subsequent debates it was implied that if Bermudians did not vote for independence under the guidance of Sir John Swan these malign forces would somehow subvert the future of a prosperous independent Bermuda.

In principle, the task of the Commission of Enquiry was quite clear and straightforward. Its job was to examine the advantages and disadvantages of the two options but would not recommend a particular course of action. On completion of its work, a referendum would be held so that the people of Bermuda could make the decision based on the information contained in the report of the Commission of Enquiry. The Commission was composed of five members of the legislature, all of whom were senior members of the majority UBP. They duly reported to the people of Bermuda in a Green Paper presented to the House of Assembly on 3rd February, 1995.

When the Green Paper was published as "a factual objective position paper...intended to serve as a basis for discussion rather than as a commitment by the Government to a particular course of action" it was greeted by the public with a variety of reactions. A few found it of interest; others were increduluous that it treated the voters like idiots; many were sceptical; a number found it misleading and biased; and even more were scathing. It did not earn high marks from commentators for its objectivity, factual accuracy, or its credibility. Like Kermit the Frog on the Muppet show it was clearly not easy being green. Most voters believed they had been given an ultimatum; either go independent with the UBP or go independent with the PLP. It read like a sales pitch for a second hand car avoiding solid useful information but making up for it with vague hazy generalisations and feel-good pop psychology.

The main stumbling block was the economy. Bermudians had never been impressed with arguments about the flag, national identity and pride, membership in the United Nations, or its influence in the rest of the world. The main question voters wanted answered were; what were the economic benefits to Bermudians and what was the cost? There were four options with regard to costs. The least expensive was estimated at BD$798,557 and the most expensive (which included ambassadors in New York and London) came to BD$2,329,505. No one really believed the estimates. The financial questions were studiously avoided for the simple reason that there were almost no economic benefits (at least none that anyone who understood finance could find) and the costs if determined accurately could have led to a tax revolt.

The section of the report which was entitled "Economy and Finance" amounted to three pages containing a collection of the most meaningless cliches to be found outside a soap opera. Due mention was made that Bermuda did not receive any aid from UK, or contribute anything to UK. Public debt was noted as being only 15% of GDP, and that Bermuda had double AA credit rating. The only statement worthy of note related to international company business and was an unsubstantiated assertion that "there is little evidence that would lead one to believe that those characteristics which have made Bermuda attractive to international company business in the past would disappear simply because the country chose to be independent." There was however quite a bit of evidence. The International Companies Division of the Chamber of Commerce had conducted a survey ot its membership and found that 88% of its membership believed that independence would have a negative impact on future business and the economy in general. The Bank of N.T. Butterfield in a written submission stated "This bank is aware of arrangements already in place whereby business would be moved automatically from Bermuda should independence be sought."

The comments on tourism echoed the complacent views expressed about international business. With no evidence it was reported that, "There is no reason to believe that, should Bermuda choose to be independent, there would be much, if any, diminution of our British atmosphere" which a paragraph earlier were acknowledged to be contributory factors in tourism success.

Public criticism of the Green Paper became increasingly shrill as time went on and the cohesion of the governing United Bermuda Party looked increasingly precarious. Senior ministers then openly took positions in favour of independence which was spearheaded by the Premier who for reasons which baffled most people, took it upon himself to urge the population to vote for independence in a referendum and saying that if there was a no vote he would resign. "The factual objective position paper" began to look anything but factual and objective.

As referendum day, 15th August 1995 approached the debate became more and more heated and shed less and less light on the subject. The public however remained strangely passive, many refusing to believe the pantomime unfolding before their eyes, many bored by the endless talk, even more were alarmed by the potential loss of international business, the drop in consumer spending and the fall in real estate prices.

Even those who supported independence were split such as the opposition PLP, which favoured independence, called on their supporters to boycott the referendum on the even odder grounds that it was not democratic and that the way to decide the independence issue was a general election - presumably on the grounds that the question of independence would get loss in the maze of more substantive issues. The whole question was becoming increasingly bizarre and unhinged from reality. But more was yet to come.

The referendum which should have been held on the 15 August, 1995 was delayed by one day because Hurricane Felix struck on referendum day. The Emergency Measures Organisation through the Cabinet Secretary, a civil servant, announced that the referendum would be postponed to an unidentified later date. Some government MPs commenced an action in Supreme Court to seek a ruling that no one had the power to postpone the vote. The President of the Senate, Albert Jackson, appeared on television condemning the action, and His

Excellency the Governor worked behind the scenes to bring order to the mess. Government recognising a potential fiasco then reversed itself saying there had been a misunderstanding and announced that the vote would take place the next day. The electorate by a margin of three to one (see box for the actual result) voted to maintain the colonial status quo , one of the consequences of which was that Sir John resigned.

Total number of eligible voters	37,841	All Bermudians 18 years and older*
Number who voted	22,236	58% of total electorate
"Yes" to independence	5,714	25% of those who voted
"No" to independence	16,369	73% of those who voted

(*and about 350 non-Bermudians who were registered to vote on 1 May 1976)
There were 153 void ballots.

The net result was that the people of Bermuda voted against political independence from the United Kingdom because;

1. There was a fear that international business would suffer.
2. There was a lack of confidence in the politicians supporting independence.
3. The estimated costs of independence were believed to be unrealistic.
4. Nobody understood what benefits Bermuda would achieve by being independent.

The business community breathed a collective sigh of relief that the fiasco was over and that some semblance of credibility could be restored to the battered markets of housing and the stock exchange and that confidence in the economic and political system could be restored. Bermudians could return to being just Bermuda Inc.

19. ARE BERMUDA'S ECONOMIC POLICIES APPROPRIATE FOR THE 21ST CENTURY?

"The political problem of mankind is to combine three things: economic efficiency, social justice and individual liberty."

JOHN MAYNARD KEYNES.

It is the height of arrogance for someone like me to suggest that there should be major policy changes to an economy which has achieved so much over the past 50 years. One can justify this arrogance by stating that no economy is perfect and that policies should always be reviewed from time to time, in order to improve matters and to take into account circumstances unforseen when policies were established. There is also the danger of wishing that Bermuda and the world could be as it ought to be rather than recognising that there can be no perfection anywhere. The main five changes I would recommend have been stated elsewhere but at the conclusion of this series of essays it may be worthwhile to re-emphasise them.

Firstly, there needs to be concerted action to reverse the slide in major hotel profits over the past 10 years.[1] When an industry is unprofitable it means essentially, that employees are not adding value to the product in a way which allows for expansion in the future or which will enhance the standard of living for everyone. The tourist industry is the biggest employer in Bermuda, is able to absorb relatively unskilled labour and transform it into a force which generates jobs, provides opportunities for advancement, and foreign exchange for Bermuda. This is a major achievement for the industry and is a neat fit with the international company business. Given the size of Bermuda which constrains our ability to generate new industries there is no real alternative opportunity for most of the labour force.

The tourist industry is subjected to intense competitive pressures as more and more countries turn to tourism to earn foreign exchange. Places which hitherto had never featured as major tourist destinations such as the Czech Republic, Costa Rica and Thailand are increasingly becoming competitors to Bermuda. As the lack of foreign exchange limits a country's ability to raise its standard of living, more and more countries see tourism as an easy mechanism by which to earn foreign currency. Hence there are more and more new entrants to the industry and as a result it is extremely difficult to balance consumer demand with supply and establish price stability and as a result there can be sub-optimum returns to investors. Tourism is now something of an empty core business which is characterised by:

- Capital costs which are high and often fixed when compared to variable costs such as the cost of supplies.
- international capacity can be increased without reference to demand, and demand can move easily and quickly from one country to another.
- Demand can be difficult to predict. Unlike purchases of staples like motor gasoline, shoes and housing the demand for vacations vary with the state of the economy, consumer tastes or airline schedules.
- The demand in a commodity business like tourism is highly dependent on price.

The second policy change I would recommend is to make a bonfire of many of the restrictive protectionism policies which may have served Bermuda well in the past but could now strangle our ability to adapt to the new era of globalisation. There are two main candidates for the axe:

1. The 60/40 rule which restricts foreign investment to 40 percent of any enterprise. This, it is believed, protects local firms from being taken over by foreign interests and preserves the Bermudian identity. In fact, the major employers in Bermuda, apart from the Bermuda Government, are non-Bermudian. Major hotels and large international companies are all foreign owned. The only employers of any size who are Bermudian are retailers, construction firms and banks. Foreign corporations should be viewed as helping Bermudians to become more efficient and hence raise standards of performance rather than as being a threat to the taking over of Bermuda by

---

[1] Many proposals were made by the Commission on Competitiveness.

foreign interests. Capitalism is a form of economic organisation which pays attention to profits, not patriotism or jingoism. Government policies have been more concerned with who owns what in Bermuda rather than what the Bermudian labour force learns to do and what skills it can acquire for the future.

2. The restrictions whereby Exempt Companies cannot own Bermuda property or office accommodation. Once a firm establishes a presence in Bermuda and employs Bermudians it does not make sense to prevent it from putting down roots.

A more subtle argument is that if local companies are not exposed to competitive pressures they become less efficient and sooner or later are unable to compete effectively for the consumer dollar. The consumer can easily modify his behaviour to get around such protectionism measures which is exactly what Bermudian consumers do when they go on shopping expeditions to the United States. Sheltered from competitive pressures local firms are not forced to innovate or pay attention to changing consumer tastes and the result is that they go into slow motion decline. The hard fact of life is that protectionist policies do not protect Bermudian businesses. They tend to disguise inefficiencies and prevent necessary changes until too late.

The third policy change is to reduce Government involvement in the economy. Bermuda is very fortunate that government intervention by comparison with other countries is very limited and in my opinion is a major reason for Bermuda's past record of success. However, increasing regulation - immigration is a good example - blunts the efficiency process, as does an increasing share of GDP being spent by government. The performance of certain government departments could be improved by doses of privatisation, candidates for this being the Post Office, Departments of Tourism and Education.[2]

Government debt is not considered to be a problem area for Bermuda. However, notwithstanding the AA credit rating government debt now stands at approximately BD$180 million or about 10 percent of GDP[3] a level which I believe to be unacceptably high for a small island community which is so dependent on only two major industries.

Fourthly, Bermuda has to resolve the issue of race relations.[4] It bedevils and complicates any discussion about the economy. Preferential policies have not worked elsewhere and are unlikely to work in Bermuda. This is an unbelievably difficult problem to resolve. Race has had a significant impact on human relationships for centuries and is increasingly a source of friction in the work place as is gender discrimination, its close relative. In country after country racial tensions poison the social atmosphere and sink the economy. Guyana has tensions between the black population and East Indians, Malaysia between Malays and Chinese, Uganda between Africans and Indians and Fiji between indigenous Fijis and people of Indian descent.

---

2 See Part II 16 and 17.

3 This figure excludes unfunded pension liabilities which are not recorded on the budget statement. See Part III 20 for more details.

4 See Part IV 8.

Contemporary Bermuda is a long way from these racial disasters and there is considerable friendship, cooperation and dare I say it affection between the two races but at the end of the day blacks have not participated in the prosperity, or the job market to the extent impartial and reasonable observers would have expected them to have done. Politics expresses beliefs, whilst economics is concerned with costs incurred if policies are wrong, and the benefits which arise if the policy is correct. To get the policies wrong will incur costs at a time when costs need to be controlled in order to combat competitive pressures as well as generating additional frustration in the black community whose patience is not inexhaustible. To get it right, means that Bermuda can put racial animosities behind and get on with the job of raising living standards for all.

Finally, drastic steps need to be taken to improve the climate of safety.[5] Crime has increased dramatically, albeit from a very low level, in recent years and there has been a welcome reduction during 1996 because of a police reorganisation and new senior officers. Traffic continues to plague Bermuda - still a minor problem by comparison with other countries - and the standards of driving and safety are deplorable. Many years ago Bermuda advertised itself as the 'Isles of Rest' but increasing prosperity and traffic ended that. A relatively simple solution to the problem of speeding from which much of our problems arise would be to install a "governor" on all motor vehicles to prevent them from going above 40 kilometres per hour - still five kph above the maximum legal speed limit. Bermuda's main selling point is its relatively unspoiled environment and it seems the height of folly to spoil it by unchecked traffic growth.

Each of these five policy changes are difficult to achieve but would improve what has been a tremendous economic record of success. May it long continue.

Epilogue: WHAT ARE THE STRENGTHS, WEAKNESSES, OPPORTUNITIES AND THREATS TO THE BERMUDA ECONOMY?

"Bermuda is in the service business; we don't create the next new industry (sic). These new industries won't be created by Bermuda, they will be created by individuals in other parts of the world seeking solutions to problems. Bermuda must be prepared to work with those people, to be partners with those people in developing and implementing the solutions to those problems."

THE COMMISSION OF COMPETITIVENESS, 1994 PAGE 362,

In most business organisations it is common practice when establishing business plans to devote a chapter to the company's business strengths, its business weaknesses, the opportunities for expansion and improved profitability and the threats to its future and core business. The shorthand way of referring to this process is known as a SWOT analysis. For a country the equivalent to an annual business plan is the budget process in which the government's spending and taxing policies are reviewed although only rarely is a formal SWOT analysis done although I have always believed this to be an excellent way of concentrating the mind.

---

5 See Part III 10 for a discussion of this issue.

The main strategic goals for Bermuda are relatively straight forward (this does not mean that they are easy to attain) and are as follows :-

- Balanced growth consistent with care for the environment.

- Opportunities to create jobs for Bermudians and full participation in the economy for everyone.

- The ability to earn foreign exchange - on which everything else depends.

- The maintenance of social stability particularly the relationship between the two main races.

What then is the appropriate SWOT analysis for Bermuda?

1 <u>STRENGTHS</u>

- Location close to the United States - one of the world's wealthiest concentrations of people, coupled with access to New York - the world's major financial and commercial centre.

- The absence of debilitating income, capital gains and corporate taxes which have a tendency to sap commercial initiative.

- A corresponding absence of detailed and expensive environmental and financial regulation which increases costs to unacceptable levels.

- No parasitical legal system comparable to the United States where legal costs are estimated to be about 2 percent of GDP.

- A legal framework which inspires business confidence and which is governed by the British legal principles and British legal appelate system. Critical to this legal framework is the continuation of Bermuda being a British colony as this ensures that the legal framework cannot be broken by governments hostile to international business.[1]

- A history of political and financial stability. Bermuda is one of the most politically stable countries in the world where political violence and corruption is rare. The Bermuda dollar is effectively tied to the U.S. dollar and to paraphrase Calvin Coolidge the business of Bermuda is business.

- Bermuda's two main industries complement each other. Tourism is labour intensive, capital intensive and land intensive - three factors of production which are in short supply. International business on the other hand is knowledge intensive which allows Bermuda's physical and intellectual infrastructure to be used in a highly efficient manner consistent with the preservation of Bermuda's physical environment.

- Bermuda enjoys one of best physical environments in the world. Its beauty, cleanliness, architecture, sporting facilities and weather makes it an excellent place in which to work, to visit and to do business.

- A well developed economic infrastructure of good communications by telephone, air transportation links to the Eastern United States, Canada and UK, hotel accommodation (although that is ageing and by comparison with other countries is sub-standard), and internally excellent roads, power and energy supply and harbours.

---

[1] This issue is discussed further in question IV 19.

This is an impressive list of economic strengths and is an excellent platform on which to base future prosperity. There are few countries in the world which are able to put together such a battery of strengths.

2 WEAKNESSES

As so frequently happens, strengths can change into weaknesses when economic conditions and circumstances are subject to change:

- In an earlier essay I drew attention to the importance of the United States economy to that of Bermuda.[2] The majority of tourists to Bermuda come from the Northeastern area of the United States so that when economic conditions sour Bermuda suffers a corresponding drop in business. In addition, Bermuda is vulnerable to changes in the tax laws of the United States as many international companies are American owned. A change in emphasis in an American tax bill could have severe repercussions on our insurance industry.

- Bermuda is one of the most densely populated countries in the world. Maintaining the level of business at the appropriate level without destroying the very qualities which attract people to Bermuda in the first place is a difficult process but one which has been very effectively managed in the past. However, as international business and to a lesser extent tourism becomes more complex the additional highly-skilled people necessary to run business cannot as a matter of logic be filled from the local population to the same extent as in the past. This creates social as well as economic pressures. Maintaining the balance between the physical and social environment becomes an even more difficult balancing act.

- This is closely tied in with the fact that with a small population being able to compete in highly sophisticated international markets imposes limits on the ability of Bermuda to continue to grow - or even maintain the status-quo. Bermuda has been spectacularly successful in blending the needs of business with that of the local skill pool. Globalisation, intensified competition and increasing specialisation may make that objective increasingly difficult in the future. In knowledge intensive industries the skills and talents required to be successful belong to people who cannot be dictated to, cannot be driven and can just as easily pull up stakes and leave Bermuda. In the modern world in which the rules change daily, and markets are unstable and in which the customer is central, only organisations with a flexible, innovative and skilled workforce will be able to succeed.

- As competitive forces become even more ferocious in tourism and international business the issue of costs becomes highly critical. Customers in a highly competitive environment are not concerned about the costs of the producer - they are concerned about their own costs. Moreover, they are no longer loyal (our repeat visitor) if costs are too high relative to the quality of the product. They demand continuously increasing value and quality of product in what they buy. Quality service and price are the key elements of new economic equation - elements which Bermuda has not been good at

---

2 See Part II 1.

providing. Bermuda is an expensive place to visit and in which to do business because of high costs of land, housing, telecommunications and most of all labour. To continue to enjoy the fruits of international business Bermudian labour will have to meet international standards of productivity which is not an easy thing to accomplish. In the modern world, being competitive is highly dependent on the professional skills and quality of people, who are increasingly seen as the main invisible asset of organisations. Creativity, intelligence, skills in key areas such as technology and marketing and the ability to think laterally and strategically are important qualities to be engendered. If Bermuda costs and productivity are not in line with the rest of the world - and much of the evidence suggests that they are not - this becomes a major weakness and customers will tend to go elsewhere, as we have seen in tourism.

- Bermuda's protectionist policies are a weakness.[3] Immigration restraints, restrictions on the ownership of property are only two examples of policies which hobble our ability to compete effectively. Such policies may have made sense when the world was a very different place. Now ideas, skills, money, people and even markets can move with an ease which was unheard of 20 years ago.

Discussing weaknesses in economy can have a depressing effect - hence the nickname of economics being the dismal science - but in a period of rapid change future opportunities will only arise if we have the ability to jettison policies which are no longer relevant or appropriate. Let us turn now to the opportunities available to Bermuda and Bermudians.

3 OPPORTUNITIES

Opportunities can be distinguished between those which qualify Bermuda to be a participant in the modern world and those which give it a sustainable competitive edge. For example, Bermuda's close historical and geographical links to the United States and Britain have been of critical importance but as the world becomes smaller because of advances in information technology and improvements in transportation these advantages assume less importance.

The major opportunities for Bermuda are:

- Services rather than manufacturing are one of the major growth areas in the world economy. As the world becomes wealthier quality time becomes increasingly important. Vacations, participation in sports, healthy living and opportunities to relax are examples of how Bermuda can capitalise on what people wish to spend their money. As the western world ages, protection of capital from taxation and from confiscatory regimes assumes critical importance. Bermuda is a safe refuge for funds seeking to escape from hostile governments.

- Major financial service providers and financial institutions wish to come to Bermuda but are often discouraged by the lack of sympathetic immigration authorities or restrictions on ownership with business partners. To benefit

---

[3] This is discussed in Part I 15.

from opportunities in the 21st century market place it is desirable to terminate 19th century economic practices. This was done when the insurance market was established for captive insurance companies in the 1960s and 1970s and a whole new industry was spawned.

- In 1995 Bermuda's foreign military bases were closed. Almost at the stroke of a pen Bermuda's land area increased by ten percent and a factor of production which had been in short supply for years was suddenly available for development. A commission has been established to determine how best this land can be utilised and it is much too early to assess what their success is likely to be. However, there are exciting possibilities.

- The future belongs to those who possess knowledge and how to apply it.[4] For bright able Bermudians opportunities are unlimited because the possession of knowledge can be used anywhere. Opportunity is the opposite side of the coin from threats - those who are unable to function in the modern economy will be of little value to Bermuda or to themselves.

4 THREATS

Threats to Bermuda's economic well-being can be either external where Bermuda has limited power to influence decisions made elsewhere which affect its economy (the closure of the US, British and Canadian military bases is a good example) or internal where Bermuda through active and enlightened policy can have significant control over the threats. A good reputation and an established name associated with quality service can help insulate a country from sudden shocks. But new rivals or new technologies can rapidly shift the ground beneath the feet of the best known and most respected of names. To a great extent that is what happened to the Bermuda tourist industry in the 1980s.

It is important to understand that Bermuda can never be a master of its own economic destiny - although that statement can also be made about even the largest economies. Bermuda is simply too small and too insignificant.

(a) External

- Other countries which are major competitors are rapidly improving their economic infrastructure and catching up with Bermuda. New hotels, improved telecommunications and friendly fiscal environments are only a few of the improvements made by Bermuda's competitors in the last few years. Even in the less developed parts of the world it is easy to make immediate and inexpensive international telephone calls. What was a major strategic advantage 10 years ago is now commonplace throughout the word in light of the privatisation of most domestic telecommunications companies.

- The flat tax proposals proposed by Malcolm Forbes in the 1996 Presidential primaries is an example of a threat to Bermuda's low tax environment. This has been endorsed by the House Major Leader, Representative Dick Armey[5]. Western governments have now been convinced of the merits of low taxation as an essential ingredient for sustained long-term economic growth. If these governments enacted tax reforms to make income and cor-

---

[4] This is explored in Part III 9.
[5] See "The Freedom Revolution," by Dick Armey.

porate taxes less penal Bermuda would be a less attractive location for international business. The tax loopholes which exist in foreign tax systems, particularly in the United States and Britain, are oxygen to the financial services industries in Bermuda. Take them away and the industry could wither on the vine which is why one of the biggest threats to our future is sensible taxation reform in those countries.

- Other major competitors to Bermuda such as the Channel Islands, Grand Cayman and the Isle of Man also have a UK based legal system.

- Other jurisdictions have been envious of Bermuda's success in tourism and international business. Grand Cayman, in particular, has copied almost word for word Bermuda statutes and has implemented many of Bermuda's policies for attracting international business. The services Bermuda provides to tourists and business can be, and is being, replicated by competitors so that competition threatens the careful building-up over the years of the Bermuda brand. One of the concerns constantly voiced by Bermuda's business leaders for several years now is that Bermuda is pricing itself out of the market, some of which is driven by increased government spending. Increasingly in this competitive world Bermuda's customers are price conscious and concern for price tends to eliminate any emotional attachment. One of the major issues of protectionism is that businesses are not forced to become competitive when they and the Bermudian employee are protected from the rigours of market competition. The economic nationalists have a simple solution for economic problems - protectionism. Impose barriers to new thinking and efficiency, make immigration more difficult, create new controls and prosperity will be locked in to Bermuda. This is pure nonsense but there are many people who swallow this baloney. Nations all over the world have discovered the enormous benefits which arise because of competition over monopoly in the production of such diverse goods as air travel, telecommunications and financial services. There can be a short-term advantage but in the long-term policies have to be judged not by their short -term effects but their impact on the economy in the long-term.

(b) <u>Internal.</u>

I would include the following as major internal threats to Bermuda's economy:

- The increase in crime and the deterioration in motor vehicle driving standards. Bermuda has repeatedly and successfully sold itself as a peaceful, safe and environmentally friendly location and visitors regard personal safety as a major attraction of Bermuda. Assaults with deadly weapons, random murders and attacks upon teachers are a daily fare in 1996 when 10 or 20 years ago such things were unheard of. In July, 1996 a young Canadian girl was brutally murdered; in August, a Canadian Senator was robbed and assaulted. The headlines in the 'Royal Gazette' gave some details of the robbery and the next lead story was about potential job losses in the hotel industry. The two headlines are closely connected. Crime discourages tourists which reduces jobs and incomes. If criminals (and reckless and dangerous drivers) were also viewed as economic saboteurs the threat to the well-being